NUN

NUN

A Memoir

MARY GILLIGAN WONG

HARCOURT BRACE JOVANOVICH, PUBLISHERS

SAN DIEGO   NEW YORK   LONDON

The author and publisher are grateful for permission to quote the following material: The lines from *Becket* in the epigraph are reprinted by permission of Coward, McCann and Geoghegan, Inc., from *Becket* by Jean Anouilh, trans. by Lucienne Hill. Copyright ©1960 by Jean Anouilh & Lucienne Hill and are also credited as ©1960 by Jean Anouilh and Lucienne Hill by permission of Dr. Jan Van Loewen Ltd., International Copyright Agency, 21 Kingly Street, London W1R 5LB. The excerpts on the part title pages of Parts I and IV are from *The Last Catholic in America* by John R. Powers. Reprinted by permission of the publisher, E.P. Dutton, Inc. The lines on the title page of Part II are copyright 1946, 1974 by Mary McCarthy. Reprinted from "The Blackguard" in her volume *Memories of a Catholic Girlhood* by permission of Harcourt Brace Jovanovich, Publishers. First published in *The New Yorker*. On the part title pages of Parts III and V are excerpts from *Final Payments*, by Mary Gordon. Reprinted by permission of Random House, Inc. Finally, on the Part VII title page, we quote from "Little Gidding" in *Four Quartets;* copyright, 1943, by T.S. Eliot, renewed, 1971, by Esme Valerie Eliot. Reprinted by permission of Harcourt Brace Jovanovich, Publishers.

Library of Congress Cataloging in Publication Data
Wong, Mary Gilligan.
Nun.
1. Wong, Mary Gilligan. 2. Ex-nuns—United States—
Biography.   I. Title.
BX4668.3.W66A35   1982   271'.9'024 [B]   82-47656
ISBN 0-15-167739-5

Printed in the United States of America

B   C   D   E

CONTENTS

Yet it *would be simple enough.*

Too simple perhaps.

Saintliness is a temptation too . . .

Their hair shirts, their fastings,

their bells in the small hours summoning one to meet You,

on the icy paving stones, in the sick misery of the poor ill-treated human animal

I cannot believe that all these are anything but safeguards for the weak.

In power and in luxury and even in the pleasure of the flesh, I shall not cease to speak to You, I feel this now.

You are the God of the rich man and the happy man too, Lord, and therein lies Your profound justice . . .

Lord I am certain now

that you meant to tempt me with this hair shirt, object of so much vapid self-congratulation!, this bare cell, this solitude, this absurdly endured winter cold and the conveniences of prayer.

It would be too easy to buy You like this, at so low a price.

I shall leave this convent, where so many precautions hew You round . . .

I shall go back to my place, humbly, and let the world accuse me of pride, so that I may do what I believe is my life's work.

For the rest, Your will be done!

—Becket *by Jean Anouilh*

PREFACE

In 1961 I became a nun. After a year of postulancy I took the habit of the order: my head was covered with bands of tight linen and my body was buried in yards of French serge. I wore black to symbolize that I was dead to the world and its ways. I wore layers of figure-disguising clothes to help me die to my sexuality. I covered my head with a veil to show that I was a virgin consecrated to Christ.

As an active, participating member of my family I was dead. A family photograph taken at the time shows the family gathered for the camera: in the center the oldest son holds a picture of the sister who had left all things to follow Christ.

I would never again share a family meal, never talk to my family on the phone. The only time I would be allowed to visit my home again would be for the funeral of a parent. Mail would be censored, visits limited. I signed legal documents relinquishing all rights of ownership: for as long as I remained a nun, everything I earned or inherited would go to the order.

I remained a nun (also called a sister or a religious) until the end of 1968. The following summer, had I stayed a member of the order (also called a community or a congregation) I would have taken perpetual vows which would bind me to the order for the rest of my life.

Many years, many lifetimes, have passed. Today I am a wife, a mother, and a clinical psychologist; my life, both inner and outer, bears little resemblance to that of the young girl who once gave her psyche to be "spiritually formed" as a Ro-

man Catholic nun. Not too long ago I was being introduced as
a speaker at a National Organization for Women (NOW) con-
vocation, and I was suddenly struck by the irony of it all. I was
to speak on "The Liberated Woman and Sexuality," and as I
thought back on my not-so-distant past I couldn't help chuckling to myself as I took the microphone: "You really *have* come
a long way, baby!"

For years I tried to hide my past. For one thing I didn't
want to be stereotyped. The most welcome compliment you
can pay a former nun is to tell her that you never would have
suspected, that she just doesn't seem the type. For another I
was weary of providing grist for the mills of a thousand lay
psychologists. It seemed that when I *did* talk openly about my
years in the convent, I was always barraged with the same
predictable round of questions: Did you really have to shave
your head like in all those nun movies? Is it true that there are
secret tunnels connecting convents and the priests' rectories?
Did you *really* go all those years without any sex?

Not all the questions were so crude and intrusive, of
course, and not all the questioners had difficulty understanding why someone would enter the convent in the first place.
Some—the more pious—were puzzled not by the phenomenon
of someone's entrance into the convent but by her departure.
A nun's life was full of prayer and peaceful serenity; how
could anyone leave all that for the few tawdry baubles the
world had to offer? Too polite to ask such a question, many of
the pious churned it over within themselves and arrived at the
only plausible answer: *sex.* Why else would one leave such an
idyllic life? Though they'd try to hide their distaste and scurry
quickly away after exchanging a few polite words in the back
of church, we former nuns could always read their faces.

But there were others who asked polite, thoughtful questions about my entrance, my departure, and all the years between. These were the questions that troubled me the most
and motivated me perhaps more than all the others to take

refuge in anonymity. There was too much that I myself still didn't understand—how could I begin to explain it to others?

Eventually, however, as I began to come to terms with my past (psychotherapy and human potential training such as *est* were immensely helpful in this process) I found myself *wanting* to talk about it to anybody who would listen. As the memories started to flood back I began to write, and friends were soon encouraging me to write a full-length book.

I read through the extensive journals I had kept during my convent years. Introspection and reflection had played a major role in our lives, and most of us had kept "spiritual notebooks" in which we recorded the daily ups and downs of our progress along the spiritual path. I had kept all of these journals, and they were extremely helpful now.

Next I did research to find out what had been written on the topic in recent years. Both *The Nun's Story* and *I Leap over the Wall* had been published before I even entered the convent and described a world very different from that experienced by American girls who entered convents in the early 1960s. There had been a sprinkling of more-recent articles and books, for example, Mary Griffin's insightful *The Courage to Choose*, but for the most part I discovered as I began to have more contact with former nuns that many were reluctant to even reveal their past *identities*, much less tell their stories in print.

Eventually I interviewed over forty former nuns who, like myself, had been members of active orders during the 1960s (*active* meaning orders dedicated to teaching, nursing, or other good works, as contrasted with *contemplative* orders where the focus was on contemplation, solitude, cloister). They shared numerous experiences and stories; one even allowed me to read a memory journal she wrote as a part of her postconvent therapy. I interwove their stories with mine, fictionalizing names of places and characters and blurring certain details that might have revealed identities of persons or groups. Everything reported here actually happened either to myself or to one of the women whom I interviewed. In some cases the stories were so dramatic that I hesitated to include them for fear that I would be accused of exaggerating or sensationalizing. I finally decided to include them, not because they were typical of convent life at the time but because they were not as atypical as some might think.

Mainly, however, the book is *my* story, an intimate account of my years in the convent, as well as an attempt to share, with as much self-knowledge as possible, the inner workings that propelled me into the convent in the first place, those that kept me there for seven years, and those that motivated my eventual decision to leave.

From my present perspective the good of my years in the convent far outweighed the bad. Friends in the world married parish sweethearts, often right after high school, and parented the large families expected of them as good Catholics; entering the convent prevented me from weaving similar webs of commitment and entanglement until I would have the opportunity to grow to know myself and my options. As a young Catholic growing up in a small midwestern parish, my options seemed few. By the time I left the convent in 1968, the breadth of my options had expanded considerably.

Those of us who entered the convent in the late 1950s and early 1960s were the last groups to be trained by the old method. The minutiae of our lives were prescribed by canon law drawn up in a nineteenth-century male-dominated Church. We were to strive for humility, self-abnegation, and childlike dependence on the will of superiors.

But even as we were being trained, change was in the air. In October 1962 Pope John XXIII presided at the opening of Vatican II in Rome, the ecumenical council that was to change the entire course of Roman Catholic Church history. He called the Church to *aggiornamento*, renewal. Soon Cardinal Suenen's book *The Nun in the World* was being read in refectories (convent dining rooms) and the whole shape of convent life began to change. Eventually, as convent walls began to crumble, there was a huge exodus of nuns from their orders. Whirlwind change continued to revolutionize convent life during the late 1970s, and by the time the 1980s arrived nuns' lives in no way resembled what we had known in the days before Vatican II.

Nuns today are free to live in apartments and other non-traditional living situations, to wear lay clothes, and to choose their own preferred paths of service to the world, called apostolates or ministries. My aunt, for example, an energetic, forward-looking member of the order to which I formerly belonged coordinates a home for retarded adults.

To most contemporary nuns the 1970s brought a series of uphill battles as they struggled to reassess and reformulate their lives and to free themselves of the negative effects of conditioning that had now been officially abandoned by most orders as "psychologically unsound, a tragic mistake." As Mary Griffin states in *The Courage to Choose*, "What we were reacting against were the elements of totalitarianism which effectively nullified our efforts to be persons." Extensive community resources were expended as communities sent troubled sisters to psychotherapists and brought in consultants and experts of every type in a sincere effort to reverse the effects of much of the earlier novitiate training. Sisters taught to constantly search their souls for faults and failings now learned to be gentle with themselves and to forgive themselves. Sisters taught to dress under their nightgowns in order to be clothed even when alone were now encouraged to accept and to give expression to all aspects of their personalities, including their sexuality. Sisters taught in the novitiate to ask permission before taking a drink of water at the drinking fountain were now encouraged to be independent and decisive. It was a radical about-face, and those who stayed long enough felt its benign effects.

But what of those who left *before* such changes? Sociologist Erving Goffman, in *Asylums*, described old-style convents (along with sanitariums, orphanages, mental hospitals, penitentiaries, army barracks, and monasteries) as "total institutions . . . forcing houses for changing persons . . . a natural experiment on what can be done to the self." As I interviewed former nuns, I discovered a whole group of women who had taken part in the "experiment" and were still suffering the effects. Without the benefit of the "deprogramming" that those who stayed received, they had been left to grope their *own* way back to health and happiness—and some were still groping. There had been no warm supportive community to understand their conflicts or to support them emotionally and financially while they worked through their conflicts. Friends, husbands, and even psychotherapists found it hard even to *believe* what they were told; how could they be expected to really *understand?*

Until I started this book, I, like many former nuns, had prided myself on the fact that I wasn't bitter: bitterness, like "nunniness," was considered the mark of immaturity in our former-nun world, and the bitter, like the nunny, were studiously avoided. Most of us, in fact, vied with each other to show that we had emerged from the convent with shining mental health. As I interviewed former nuns, however, I came to realize that a whole group of women had left with the old antiself training still intact in their psyches. Some of them had gone through painful convent experiences that the more fortunate of us knew nothing about, since they had been forbidden to talk about such experiences, even with close friends. Who was I to criticize them for being angry and bitter?

Not all former nuns are as at peace with their pasts as they would have you believe. This fact had been brought home to me quite vividly in 1978 when a former-nun friend and I put a notice in our college alumnae newsletter. The notice simply stated that we were interested in locating and communicating with fellow band members (the group of women you entered the convent with were called a band) who had entered with us in 1961 and had in subsequent years returned to the world. Though we weren't sure how many received the newsletter, we thought it would at least be a start.

The results were startling: only a few responded, and of these most made it clear that they had spent years trying to conceal their backgrounds and were not interested in having that information made public now. The newsletter staff had offered ongoing space for names, addresses, and news updates, but those we talked to were adamant: "Whatever you do, don't print *my* name there. . . ."

A few years later we decided to try again: the twentieth anniversary of our group's entrance into the order was coming up; sixty-six of us had entered together that September day in 1961, and only eleven remained in the convent. Surely some of the old gang would come back for a twenty-year reunion!

The congregation itself was currently involved in a similar effort to reestablish contact with ex-members. With the help of the congregation's current superior general who provided names, addresses, and encouragement, we were able to locate all but fourteen of our former band members. This time the response was more heartening: almost one-third wrote to express their enthusiasm and to reserve a place at the reunion.

Yet there were others who refused to respond to letters and calls; still others voiced fierce trepidation and even anger. One wrote: "Why would I want to go back and relive a whole chapter of my life that I've tried to forget?" Another put it this way: "My daughter is six now and has nuns in school. I live in fear of her finding out someday! No, I've put all that behind me now; I'd rather just forget it ever happened." More than one admitted to claustrophobia every time they set foot on motherhouse grounds (a motherhouse is an order's home and administrative center, as well as the residence of the mother general). One decided to come but only on the condition that she be able to obtain hotel reservations in town. Another would come but would keep her car nearby at all times in case she felt the sudden need to leave quickly.

Despite fears and reservations, the reunion was a huge success and a time of healing and reconciliation.

During the course of the reunion I had an opportunity to

share finished portions of my book with some of the people who were there. One declined to read it: "I don't think I'm ready to face all that. . . ." Another liked it but warned: "A lot of ex-nuns are going to see your book in the bookstore; they'll buy it, put a brown wrapper on it, and then read it when nobody's looking. Then what are they going to do with all the feelings that are stirred up after twenty years of keeping it all inside? I almost think you should put a list of phone numbers of crisis centers in the back, just in case things start coming up and people aren't able to deal with them!" Another warned that many Catholics would accuse me of making it all up: "You know how some of them still want to put nuns on such a pedestal!" One thought that I had painted a much-too-rosy picture: "Are you sure we were in the same order?" Most simply assured me, "Yes, that's it; you've got it all down."

I also had an opportunity during the reunion to leave my manuscript with two women whom I had always admired. Both hold positions of considerable influence within the community. One said: *"Nun* tells your story with amazing accuracy. . . . I hope the book will reach an audience that appreciates its sensitivity and candor." The other said, "It seems as if all of us, in many ways, are truly at the same place—searching—wanting to relish the present and the experiences of the past that brought us to where we are now. I can understand how writing your book helped you heal a lot of your disassociation with your past because in reading it, it also helped some of us to do the same thing."

In the process of healing my own disassociation with my past, I had been instrumental in helping to heal that of some of my sisters; no acknowledgment could have thrilled me more. I knew at that moment that I wanted to finish and publish my book as soon as possible—for my sisters both in and out of the convent, for me, for all of us who would be sifting through and sorting out the pre-Vatican II convent experience for the rest of our lives.

ACKNOWLEDGMENTS

My special thanks go first of all to my parents, Herb and Amy Gilligan. Good Catholic girl that I am, I had been concerned that this book might cause them pain and embarrassment, but they freed me by encouraging me to tell the truth no matter what. I am also grateful to my aunt, Sister Agnes, who was the inspiration for my becoming a nun in the first place; she wholeheartedly supported me in writing and attempting to publish this book. My brothers and sisters, Andrea, Patrick, Daniel, Cathy, and Beth (Dan's wife), have remained my closest friends through it all, giving love and support; my children, Aran, Raam, and Atria (Pat's daughter, but our closeness runs so deep that I claim her as my own), have been admirably patient with me when I holed up in my room and typed for hours at a time. (Aran in particular freed me from a mother's guilt by blossoming into an extremely likable, self-sufficient young man of 7, despite my many hours "away.") Luisa, Raam's nanny and our family housekeeper, by being there for Raam when I couldn't be and keeping household chaos to a minimum, freed me to write in peace. And at the hub of it all, Elwyn, my lover and friend and husband of ten years, encouraged me every step of the way; without his love and support this book may have never blossomed forth.

And there have been others. My agent, Peter Ginsberg, of Curtis Brown Associates, Ltd., stuck by me through thick and through thin (much of it thin), and my typists Margaret Mendoza and Sandy Anderson, in addition to typing the manuscript, provided all sorts of encouragement and assistance. The Frank and June Mayo family helped with various logistics, and clients and friends offered support in a variety of ways.

Lastly, I'd like to thank my sisters—both those who are currently members of religious communities and those who have left. By sharing with me their experiences and insights, they helped me weave a tapestry that tells not only my story but theirs as well. I am grateful to them all.

I ⸱
GOOD CATHOLIC GIRL (1943–1957)

Then, there were two major religions in the world, Catholic and "Public." Catholics went to St. Bastion Grammar School, had long summer vacations, had to get off the sidewalks when a Public kid told them to since the sidewalks belonged to the Publics, and were constantly yelled at by adults who would say, "I expected better behavior from you Catholic kids, with all those nuns watching over you."

Publics went to Seven Holy Tombs Public School, had shorter summer vacations, were often subjected to "What can you expect from Public school kids" glares from adults, and went to a number of different churches in the neighborhood, which, according to the Catholics, were all the same anyway.

—The Last Catholic in America *by*
John Powers

1
THE SEX TALK

Carefully locking the door, Sister Perpetua, with just a touch of color in her usually pallid face, addresses us.

"Girls, it is my grave duty to warn you about certain dangers that threaten your soul and body."

No one shifts; no one breathes. Just ten minutes ago, Father O'Meara had suddenly appeared at the door of our eighth-grade classroom and led the boys away in single file. No explanation had been given, but then no one had expected one: as pastor, Father O'Meara owes an explanation to no one.

It is October 14, 1956, and the eighth-grade boys and girls of Precious Blood Grammar School, Peoria, Illinois, are about to receive their first sex talk.

Without moving my head I let my eyes wander over the girls' side of the room. Everyone sits ramrod straight, their hands folded stiffly on top of the desks. Trying to distract myself, I study Ann's new pageboy and Mary Alice's new skirt. I mentally calculate that Mary Alice must have starched her crinolines three times: I admire the way her skirt forms a fashionable arc around the desk. Without taking my eyes off Sister Perpetua, I reach down and adjust each of my bobby socks carefully; just yesterday I invested a good part of my allowance in foam-rubber rings designed to plump my socks to appropriate proportions and to turn them into fat white sausages ringing my saddle shoes. I am glad I won't have to stuff them full of toilet tissue anymore.

Eventually Sister Perpetua's words slither through the

cracks in my distractions. "Girls, you must beware of any feelings of attraction that you may have toward the boys. What worldlings call 'sex appeal' was created by God to lead to marriage and to the procreation of children. Arousing such feelings too early can only lead to proximate occasions of sin."

One or two girls begin to breathe again, and one giggles into her hankie, pretending to blow her nose. Sister Perpetua stares her quiet.

She goes on. "If the boys like your company, you really shouldn't be flattered; in fact, you should wonder if they see you as an easy mark. Maybe your skirt's too short or your sweater's too tight; maybe you're leading them on by being too friendly. You're not little girls anymore, you know; you have to learn to keep your distance."

I glance over at Ann, the first girl in the class to wear a bra. Ann always wears a baggy cardigan over her blouse even on warm days, and I notice that she hurriedly buttons it across her bosom as Sister Perpetua talks.

Behind Ann sits Francie, who is at the other end of the spectrum. Though I can't see her face, I presume it's covered with a sneer—it usually *is* whenever nuns talk about something that she doesn't think they have any business discussing. Sister Perpetua, in particular, inspires her scathing remarks: "Why should I listen to Perp-the-Twerp? What does she know about the world? She's the type that was probably born in the habit." Less well-endowed than Ann both in mammary tissue and in maidenly modesty, Francie was recently sent home for having facial tissues stuffed in her bra. Though bra checks are not a regularly scheduled part of the curriculum, Sister Perpetua now and then keeps the girls in the classroom during recess so that, one by one in the cloakroom, each can prove that she isn't supplementing what God has given her.

Warming up to the subject, Sister Perpetua now reminds us that most Americans are very pagan and don't share the Church's viewpoint regarding purity. "My dear girls, if you want to preserve your morals, stick to your own kind. Non-

Catholics just don't have the same high moral standards that we do."

Thinking it over, I realize that she's right. The lack of discipline in the public schools is just one more example of non-Catholic moral depravity: all of us have heard stories about how kids get by with talking in class and mouthing off to the teachers. One friend of mine transferred to the public school and never adjusted to it: the first day, she stood for the teacher's entrance and was almost laughed out of the room. There's just no doubt about it: because of the habit they wear and the vows they take, nuns command a respect that no ordinary teacher can command.

I also think about the girl from the public school who became pregnant the year before and had to drop out of school; the whole neighborhood had buzzed with the scandal. Of course it was also true that one of the Catholic high school girls had suddenly disappeared in the middle of her senior year. Her parents said that she had gone to Maine to live with an aunt for a while, but my fourteen-year-old Catholic schoolgirl's brain does not make the connection.

Dropping her voice to underscore the seriousness of what she is now about to say, Sister Perpetua points out that God gave man a nature far more sexual than that of woman. "The normal married woman does not find as much satisfaction in sexual intercourse as her husband does: she finds her greatest joy in the bearing and raising of her children."

Francie lets out a little exasperated whistle through her teeth, as if to say she doesn't exactly think that Perp-the-Twerp is in much of a position to compare the two experiences, but Sister Perpetua goes right on.

"Never forget the intensity of the male sex drive. Too many girls have forgotten, and that's how rapes have occurred. The sex drive in a man is so strong that it's asking a lot to expect him to control himself once he's aroused. Most rapes occur because a girl has dressed or acted seductively, has led a man on."

Sister Perpetua continues to describe the land-mined terrain of Catholic puberty, but I am no longer listening.

Other girls might be doomed to an adolescence of conflict about how far to let a boy go and how much to confess in confession once she lets him go somewhere. Other girls might have to keep a careful watch both on the male of the species and on their own baser impulses.

I, on the other hand, will be spared all that. I will be free to devote my energy to important matters and noble deeds. Even as I sit there in my crinolined skirt and saddle shoes, a perfect replica of every other girl in the room, an elevated destiny surrounds me like a cloak, setting me apart and above.

I, Mary Agnes Gilligan—named for the Virgin Mary and a nun aunt and born of an Irish family that is proud of its ancient faith—am going to be a nun.

2

GROWING UP CATHOLIC

It hadn't always been this way, of course. As a young child I had always taken it for granted that I would one day grow up, be married, and settle down in the neighborhood with a houseful of children. My husband would be Catholic and, I hoped, Irish, and if he happened to have played for Notre Dame, so much the better. We would have a picture of the Sacred Heart in the living room and holy-water fonts by each doorway, we would say the family rosary together every night, and every Thursday night we would watch Bishop Fulton J. Sheen on television.

Like most girls of my generation and upbringing, I left the what-will-I-be-when-I-grow-up questions to the boys, confident that my future choices would be pretty much limited to what kind of wedding dress I would wear, what kind of china I would select, and how I would decorate the nursery.

Even though I had an aunt and a cousin who both were nuns, the thought of my eventually following in their footsteps was a possibility that never occurred to me. I would never want to leave home like that: I even became homesick when I went to camp for a week! Besides, who would want to live with a bunch of women when you could marry Prince Charming and have him charm your life forever? To top it off, nuns didn't have babies, and I wanted more than anything to have a houseful of babies.

But if it never occurred to me to be a nun, it also never occurred to me to be anything other than the most devout little girl in the parish, the shining star of proud parents. Old snapshots show me leaving the house my first day of school, the beaming firstborn, loved by all. The love of my parents surrounded me like a shield; I knew that the whole world would love me.

And at first it did indeed seem that way: I felt secure in the friendship of school and neighborhood chums and basked in the attention of my teachers. Much of the nuns' attention stemmed from the fact that my father remembered all too well the way some of the nuns had snubbed the poor kids when he had been a child, lavishing their attention instead on the children whose wealthy parents were always bestowing the nuns with gifts. I would later learn that many teaching sisters at the time of the Great Depression were paid as little for their services as maybe a couple of chickens or a few dozen eggs. Such a meager existence undoubtedly had a lot to do with their attitude toward an occasional wealthy benefactor. At any rate, determined to offset any similar neglect of *his* children, my father made it a point to cater to the nuns in any way possible. He frequently sent us off to school with big stacks of scrap paper, culled from back rooms of the *Peoria Sentinel* where he worked as circulation manager, and on Saturdays he was usually available to provide transportation if a nun had some errand to perform.

Unlike the nuns in some orders, the nuns in our parish didn't drive since the massive starched caps surrounding their faces prevented adequate peripheral vision. (Parish school children down through the years had, needless to say, taken full advantage of this handicap.) My father therefore spent numerous Saturday mornings driving nuns to their various appointments. Because they were forbidden ever to be alone with a man, a nun who had an errand that called her "abroad" (convent terminology for "outside the cloister") took another nun along as a sister companion. Like royalty, the two would sit primly and properly in the back seat, which my mother had gotten up early to clean meticulously, while my father chauffeured them around town. Thanks to my father's earnest efforts—and those of my mother, who also sent flowers from the yard for classroom May shrines—the nuns' favor beamed down on me, and I walked in a state of grace.

But then in second grade an incident occurred that made me realize that all the scrap paper and chauffeuring and flowers in the world would not be enough. There were other parish gods who needed to be propitiated—more-powerful ones.

It all started when Sister Maria Lucy chose me to be the angel in the school's annual religious pageant. Only one second grader each year was so honored, and my parents were overwhelmed with pride. Money that had been allotted for more-urgent domestic needs was immediately reallocated to new patent-leather shoes.

The next day the sky fell in. Apologizing profusely, Sister Maria Lucy broke the news to my startled parents: Father O'Meara had unexpectedly informed her that *he* had selected as angel the daughter of one of the parish's more-prominent families. My mother promptly went to confession and confessed that for the first time in her life she had hated a priest. My father fumed. And I, at the age of seven, received my first lesson in how the parish authority structure worked.

In later years it became even more obvious to me: the nun might be the heavy in the classroom and she might do an excellent job of drawing up lesson plans and designing bulletin boards, but more-important parish or school decisions called for a man's cool, levelheaded competence. Despite her elevated spiritual state, no one forgot that a nun was, ultimately, just a woman.

Priests, on the other hand, were men and therefore superior: Jesus had chosen only men for His Apostles, and Saint Paul had warned women to be subject to their husbands. By virtue of their priesthood, priests reached dizzying heights that we couldn't even imagine, just a notch below the cardinals, bishops, and archangels. Only a priest had the power to turn bread and wine into Jesus' Body and Blood, and only *his* hands touched Jesus' flesh: that was why housewives laid out a special set of hand-embroidered towels by the bathroom sink when a priest came to visit, threatening family members with their lives if they dared to touch them.

The nuns were always the first to emphasize a priest's exalted status. If a complicated theological question came up in religion class—for example, whether you could, in an emergency, baptize a baby with coffee—a nun would always say: "Let's have Father come in and tackle that one!" Nuns held doors for priests; they laughed at priests' corny jokes; when a priest showed up at the classroom unexpectedly, nuns stopped midsentence and gestured for everyone to rise to their feet, the whole class as one. "G'morning, Father; g'morning, Father," the nun bowed demurely, awed by the visit of this great dignitary and then humbly tiptoed to the back of the room as he took center stage. When the priest was ready to leave, the nun always requested sweetly, "Could we have your blessing, Father?"—a signal for us to slip to our knees, *fast*. A booming voice would intone "*In nomine patris et filii* . . . ," a consecrated hand would raise in blessing, and the Spirit of God would descend on the children of Precious Blood Grammar School.

So I soon learned to stay on the priests' good side too, intuitively sniffing out the kind-father types and staying far away from the ones at the other end of the spectrum. Of course, few of us had much real contact with the priests: at Mass they always had their backs to us as they mumbled Latin at a faraway altar; in the confessional they forgave our sins from the other side of a screen that blocked out everything but the scent of their shaving lotion and the hiss of their three-Hail-Marys prescriptions. Our spiritual fathers, like our physical fathers, were usually off doing their important work, and just as with our physical fathers, the distance only contributed to the mystique and the reverence we felt for them.

It was not so easy to revere and fantacize as superhuman the women who, like our mothers, were down there with us in all the not-so-glamorous details of everyday life, cleaning up the vomit of the child who was ill, yelling at us to clean out our desks, mopping up the puddles from our wet galoshes in the cloakrooms. Like our mothers who threatened "Wait till your father gets home!" the nuns always sent the *really* naughty children to the rectory for the priest to handle; though they never would have admitted it, I'm sure both mothers and nuns savored these moments when *Father* got to be the bad guy.

To be sent to the rectory you had to do something *really* bad. Ordinary things such as whispering to your friend behind a desk top or passing a note across an aisle were usually handled by a swift crack on the knuckles with a ruler or a jab with the pointer. (The pointer was supposed to be used for the geography map, but few nuns seemed to know that.) If it happened too many times, you were assigned to write "I should not talk in school" 500 times. It was really unusual when a nun became carried away and assigned a lengthier penance, but it *did* happen occasionally—such as the time Thomas Schultz was caught with a *Playboy* magazine in his speller. He was told not to come back to school until he had written the Ten Commandments 5000 times. He eventually returned a month later, after he had used all his allowance money to hire the neighborhood kids to help him. His parents had questioned the severity of the sentence at first, but when they found out what he had done they thought the sentence rather mild.

Most infractions involving obscenity—violations against the Sixth Commandment—were sent to the priest. Typical infractions might be the drawing of a dirty picture and having a nun find it, or the throwing of a boy/girl party at your house. Boy/girl parties, where everyone drank cokes and ate pretzels and danced to the latest 45s, were strictly forbidden since they brought boys and girls together in situations that prematurely aroused their passions.

You could also be sent to the rectory if you were reported for attending a condemned movie or reading a condemned book. Each month the Legion of Decency published movie ratings which were posted on the bulletin board in the back of church. Condemned books were listed in the church's *Index of Forbidden Books.* (Before I had even heard of Emmanuel Kant, I heard the dictum that Catholics can't read Kant.) Before reading *any* book that discussed matters of faith or doctrine, we were to check the pages in the front for a *nihil obstat* and *imprimatur,* official certification that the book was free of doctrinal errors and would not endanger Faith or morals.

Staying on the priests' good side wasn't, ultimately, too difficult for me since it primarily involved staying out of trouble, a skill I had well mastered over the years. Others might boast talent in sports and hobbies, but goodness was my thing: I honed my goodness carefully, keeping it razor sharp and shiny.

I may have been rejected as angel in second grade, but I would have my revenge: by virtue of my goodness, I would be the parish's angel in the end.

A similar fall from grace took place within my family circle as the years passed, and with it came a similar fierce determination to climb back into angeldom, come hell or high water.

I liked to look at the big photo albums containing my baby pictures. My parents looked so fresh and young, so totally enraptured with this new little being for whom they had prayed so hard during the early, barren years of their marriage. I liked to remember how my mother would spread a blanket for the two of us under the lilacs in the backyard and sit for hours with me, sewing clothes for my dolls. I liked to remember how Dad would give me long, leisurely piggyback rides before I went to bed at night and then read me to sleep or tickle me until I begged him to stop.

Even a new baby sister, just two years younger, didn't change things all that much. There was still plenty of lilac time, plenty of Mom, and plenty of Dad. Less than a year later, a brother followed and then, before my mother could catch her breath, another brother. Again in a little over a year there was another arrival, a third girl—five children, a year or two apart.

Each birth was celebrated as a blessed event, a time of rejoicing; yet somewhere in the midst of it all I noticed that my mother was beginning to show the strain and that my father looked tired and drawn. The diapers and the bills were piling up, and it was demanding an almost superhuman effort to keep up with them.

I would have worried consciously about having to share mother and father with so many siblings had it not been for the fact that a new overriding worry had begun to weigh on me and to drive less-noble concerns underground. I was ten years old and my life had a new nexus: I was consumed with worry about Mother.

I was never sure exactly what was wrong with her, though I'd hear her talking to her friends on the phone, whispering darkly about something called "female trouble." I knew that she had never completely recovered from her last two babies and that from time to time when she gave up and went to bed, she was hemorrhaging again. I knew very little about anatomy, but I *did* know that all this bleeding and fatigue from day to day had to do with being a woman, with those secret mysterious parts of a woman's body that could cause so much trouble. The joys of being female were beginning to look rather dubious.

I also began to question my girlish dreams of domestic bliss as I watched Mother. Sometimes it seemed that she simply dragged her body from one day to the next, fighting a war that could never be won. She would iron mountains of clothes, then just when she reached the bottom of the basket, there'd be another load from the clothesline. The baby would be sick, and as soon as she was well again, one of the other children would come down with the flu. Cooking dinner for seven took much of the afternoon; then within a few minutes all signs of the accomplishment would be erased, leaving only a stack of dishes to be washed. It went on and on with no relief in sight. Sometimes at night I would lie awake, listening through the vent that went from my bedroom to the kitchen: I would hear my parents talking and arguing late into the night, their voices fraught with tension and desperation. Where was this all going to end?

So I began to climb my way back to angeldom by becoming not just the good girl but the rescuer, the one who would eventually save my mother from her pain. I did everything possible to try to ease her load: I refereed my brothers and sisters when they bickered, I rushed in to solve potential conflicts so that Mother wouldn't have to deal with them, I took over many of the domestic duties. I lived in fear of Mother ending up like one of the parish women I had heard about: one had had a nervous breakdown and now lived on tranquilizers and shock treatments; the other had hanged herself with clothesline rope one gray winter morning as she hung out clothes in the basement. I was determined to never let such a fate befall Mother: I would save her. I bit my tongue when she was cross with me, and I held back the angry words that wanted to come tumbling out. I sheltered her, as much as was in my power, from unpleasantness. I forgave her her moodiness and her angry outbursts. Most of all I never let her know my own pain.

It was only in the neighborhood that I didn't have to bear such a burden of goodness. Most of my neighborhood friends were non-Catholic, and I found their company worldly and exciting.

Parochial school separated boys and girls (girls on this side of the classroom/playground/issue; boys on that) with every intention that the schism be a deep one, but after-school play in the neighborhood healed the schism. Here boys and girls played together, climbing trees, riding bikes, and playing hide-and-go-seek on warm summer nights. Something stirred in me when boys were around, and I liked the feeling.

As we grew older, I became as giggly and boy crazy as the rest, cultivating a string of neighborhood boyfriends, exchanging secret kisses, and learning a few of the things that they didn't teach us at Precious Blood. It was to my more sophisticated neighborhood mentors that I turned when I had questions. Once, for example, our sixth-grade nun was intent on our keeping our rosaries under our pillows at night: "If your fingers start to wander to forbidden places of your body, tempting you to indulge in self-abuse, you can distract yourself by saying a decade (ten Hail Marys) of the rosary." At the time I was preoccupied with a strange and disturbing phenomenon called acne; my mom was always nagging at me to keep my hands away from my face. Preoccupied with pimples, I presumed that the nun was simply joining forces with my mother. It was only when I looked around and saw that the girls had all turned red and that the boys were snickering behind their desk tops that I realized the nun wasn't referring to our faces.

But "self abuse"? Surely the nun wasn't referring to what I thought she was: nuns weren't even supposed to *know* about such matters. But my neighborhood sources, when I talked to them later that day, assured me that the nun had indeed said something dirty.

Nuns were *always* saying something dirty, and I hated them for it! It was OK out there on the street—my girlfriends and I all told dirty jokes, passed around the latest issues of *True Confessions*, and listened intently to the girls who knew the most—but when nuns stood there in front of the room and made their dumb comments right in front of the boys, we hated it.

There was also the time the nun was encouraging us to say frequent aspirations, short little prayers whispered to Jesus; for example, "My Jesus, mercy!" or "All for Thee most Sacred Heart of Jesus!" She explained that aspirations could shorten the sentence of some poor soul burning in purgatory; depending on the aspiration, you could win him a reprieve of fifty or even three hundred days. I was delighted and began to collect reprieves, or indulgences, like pieces of real estate in a board game in the hope that the various suffering souls to whom they were applied would someday return the favor.

My delight at learning this new game of acquisition soon turned to ashes, however, when the nun became carried away and started using the term more commonly used in the convent: "Ejaculate frequently!" she enthused. There was a giggle or two from the girls' side of the room, but mainly a pained, blushing silence. The boys' side rocked with half-muffled laughter. I didn't know what the word meant, but my neighborhood instructors came to my rescue later that day, and I laughed with the rest. But the anger remained: I sure wished nuns wouldn't say things like that!

I felt the same distaste whenever Mother wanted to talk to me about the facts of life. So when she would quietly close the door to the bedroom and perch on the edge of my bed, small-talking her way into a heart-to-heart, I would politely but stoically listen, showing no interest, volunteering no questions. We would both go away satisfied—she that she had done her maternal duty, and I that I had convinced her of my total lack of interest in such matters. It was a lie that worked well on both sides, and it would be only a matter of time before I, too, would believe it.

As I increasingly concerned myself with goodness, religiosity began to flower. Soon I was fretting over the fate of non-Catholic friends' immortal souls. Church teaching was clear: "Outside the Church there is no salvation," and the thought of neighborhood pals burning in hell for all eternity was just too much for me. So I did my best to convert them, and those I couldn't convert I taught the Act of Contrition, just in case. I knew that an Act of Contrition spoken at the moment of death could wipe the slate clean even for a non-Catholic.

Two of my Catholic friends, Ann and Rosemary, were also a worry to me. Ann's father wasn't a Catholic, and she and her mother spent a lot of time lighting vigil lights in church and praying that the poor man would come to his senses. The nuns also prayed, which made Ann feel better since everyone knew that nuns' prayers were more powerful than ours were.

Rosemary's dad had run off with his secretary, leaving her mother with four kids to raise. She had remarried but had gone against church law in doing so; as long as her first husband was alive, he was her rightful spouse and she was therefore living in adultery. Rosemary didn't know which way to pray: she feared for her mother's salvation, but she didn't want to lose her stepfather. Eventually I came up with the idea of praying that her real father would die. It made me feel rather strange and witchlike to try to pray somebody into his grave, but I didn't see that we had any other choice. We had started a novena, a series of nine prayers or devotions, with his death as our special intention when Rosemary came to me with the good news: the pastor had petitioned the bishop for a special dispensation, and it had been decided that Rosemary's mother could live with her new husband—cook his meals, wash his socks, and raise his children—anything but have sexual intercourse with him. Rosemary and I were ecstatic, and we presumed that her mother was too; after all, the nuns were always telling us that sex for a woman wasn't a big deal. Rosemary and I sent prayers to heaven, thanking God for sending us such an understanding, humane, progressive bishop.

Though my acceptance of Catholicism was total and unquestioning, it hadn't always been so with my ancestors. An old family Bible contains the hand-scrawled account of how my mother's family first arrived in this country. According to the story, in the early 1700s an Irishman seduced a nun, persuading her to leave the convent and to run away with him to America where they could escape the wrath of pious relatives. Equally pious descendants had little interest in preserving unsavory stories for posterity, so no further details are known. The family boasted many priests and nuns, and preferred to pass on to their children devout, uplifting stories of family members who had clung to the Faith through thick and thin. There was the ancestor, for example, whose baby died at sea during her trip to America: determined that her little one have a Catholic burial once they set foot on land, she hid its body in a pillowcase so that authorities wouldn't find it and toss it overboard.

My father's family similarly prided themselves on being "old Catholic" in the same way that some people pride themselves on being "old rich," but the Catholicism that had run in the family veins for generations had not always been so docile. Union-organizer Grandpa Gilligan, for example, was as feisty and stubborn in dealing with the clergy as he was in dealing with management. In fact, Grandpa boycotted Sunday Mass for twenty years while relatives wrung their hands in despair. Grandpa was living in sin; what if he died in his sleep? There would be no funeral mass and no proper Catholic burial in a proper Catholic cemetery; his unfortunate remains would be deposited unceremoniously in the public graveyard like those of a common Protestant. What greater shame could befall a family?

Indifferent to their warnings and pleas, Grandpa George smoked his pipe by the fire each Sunday as the family trudged off to church. Some said it was because the pastor had sent a lowly assistant to officiate at George's wedding. Others said it had to do with the fact that Grandpa had been excommunicated because of his membership in the Knights of Pithias, a Mason-like organization suspected of worldwide anti-Catholic maneuverings and sinister plots against the pope. Most, however, felt that George simply shared the ambivalence of many Irishmen toward the clergy.

When the terrible potato famine had swept over Ireland in the mid-1800s, many priests had supported payment of the landlord's tax, even though paying it had often meant leaving one's starving children to rot in the fields with the potatoes. George's father, John, had been one of the lucky children: a relative had put him on a boat bound for the United States. Irishmen never forgot the betrayal: beneath their sometimes saccharine deference to the clergy often boiled an ancient rage.

As the family became less shanty Irish and more respectable, it also became more conservative and more conventional in its Catholicism. The anti-Catholic sentiment so characteristic of small midwestern towns of the time only served to draw Catholics together and to cement their loyalty. Dad recalled being taunted as "cat lickers" as they walked to school each day; Mother remembered the night she sat on her front porch watching the Ku Klux Klan parade past the house, fiery crosses and all. She remembered her terror when a clothespin was thrown onto the porch, a warning that her family's home, being Catholic, had been selected by the KKK for burning. Initially, Catholics had clustered into parishes along strict ethnic lines, hanging onto the religious culture and customs of the old country. But ethnic lines began to blur in the 1920s and 1930s as Catholics felt the need to stick together.

Then too, many parish pastors were Irish immigrants: in my day young priests would sometimes refer to this particular breed of pastor as "the FBI" (the foreign-born Irish), and sociologists would point out the role that such pastors played in shaping United States Catholicism. Italian, German, and Lithuanian parishioners often had no choice but to set aside ethnic loyalties and accept the effusive Irishness of their pastors. Sometimes they fought back, however: for example, the parish where my Irish grandfather and his German wife raised their children was predominantly German, and one Sunday the pastor referred to the Irish as "God's chosen people" just one time too many. The entire congregation stood up and walked out as one.

By the time George's son Herbert met pretty young Amelia at a Catholic Young People's meeting in the late 1930s and proceeded to marry her and sire five children, ethnic identity was no longer much of an issue. The times were by now more tolerant; it only mattered that one was Catholic and fiercely loyal to the one true Church.

I loved being Catholic, loved the security of knowing that I was a member of the only church that could trace its bloodline all the way back to Christ. Each Sunday as high mass ended, the organ would begin "Holy God, We Praise Thy Name" or "Long Live the Pope," and everyone would rise. It was always an ecstatic moment for me: I would stand there between my mother and father and unite my voice with the other voices resounding throughout the Church. I especially liked hearing the men's voices, deep and strong, reminding me that ours was not a religion for sissies. The world might mock us for our faith, but together we stood firm. Shoulder to shoulder we raised our voices to heaven, confident that all the world's truth was contained within Roman Catholic doctrine, that the pope was our unerring interpreter of God's design for humanity. It was a wonderful, all-embracing world view, safe and secure, and under its umbrella I felt protected from the capricious pagan world just beyond its rim. As long as I hugged the center, resisting any impulse to leap ahead or skip off to the side to smell the flowers, my salvation was assured.

I knew, of course, that there were other religions: Baptist, Lutheran, Greek Orthodox, and so on. Since they were really all the same, based as they were on various distortions of Roman Catholic Truth, we lumped them all together into an amorphous non-Catholicism, sometimes called Protestantism. Though we had never met any, we had heard of Jews; we knew for sure that theirs couldn't be called a religion since they didn't even believe in Christ.

Although the Church forbade us to take part in heretical worship services, I was always curious about what went on inside a non-Catholic church. One day I received permission to attend a neighbor's wedding in a nearby Protestant church. The only stipulation was that I not participate in worship or prayer.

As soon as I entered the church, I felt the difference: just as I'd suspected, the church felt empty and cold, devoid as it was of Jesus's presence. I knew that Protestants believed that Jesus was present at communion time in some vague way, but only we Catholics dared to believe in Transubstantiation, the doctrine teaching that the literal *substance* of the bread and wine was changed into the Body and Blood of Jesus. Catholics kept consecrated hosts (Jesus's Body) in tabernacles, or golden receptacles, on church altars at all times, so our churches were always filled with what we called "the Real Presence."

As I looked around, I realized with a shock that I was the only girl in the church wearing a hat. No red tabernacle light flickered a reminder that Jesus was on the altar; no incense or bells created a feeling of reverence. Even the cross in front of the chapel was empty, as though the bloody reality of the Crucifixion was an embarrassment to Protestants. We Catholics prided ourselves on the fact that we hung crucifixes, not bare crosses, in our churches and homes.

The service itself seemed empty and strange. At the end

of the Our Father they tacked on an unfamiliar, obviously inauthentic ending, "For thine is the kingdom . . . ," and during the service they read from the Bible a lot, interpreting it, of course, in their own way. Folding and refolding my white gloves, I remembered something from a Sunday sermon: "Even the devil can quote Scripture to suit himself!" Thank God we Catholics had the Church to guide us in interpreting Scripture and didn't need to depend upon our own unreliable minds, the way the Protestants did.

I now knew for sure that my own thoughts and feelings could not be trusted and that the Church was the source of all truth.

Despite my growing uneasiness with my own body and its urges, my ever-increasing cynicism about the bliss inherent in the matrimonial state, my intense piety, and my desire to save the world, it took a radical turn of events in seventh grade to force me, once and for all, to abandon childhood dreams and to open myself to other options.

For in seventh grade something terrible and freakish began to happen: I grew taller and taller while the boys seemed to stop growing altogether. Boys who had been eager to dance with me at neighborhood dance parties now left me sitting by the record player; girls who had loved swapping details of puppy love with me stopped inviting me to their slumber parties. I suddenly felt gangly and awkward, irreparably odd, and out of place.

To make matters worse, kickball was fast becoming popular among the girls. We played every day at recess and after school. I was no good at all, a fact that did little to reverse my declining popularity. We chose teams each day, and I always stood there like some mute farm animal being auctioned. One of the last ones chosen, I would take my place in the outfield and pray that the team that had mercifully chosen me would not be too dreadfully disappointed by my performance. But the more nervous I became, the more I dropped the ball, and the more popular kickball became, the more rapid was my slide down the social scale. It no longer seemed to matter that I kept my bobby socks plumped, my crinolines starched, and my pageboy combed under just so; I stood on the sidelines at kickball games and dances—if I was invited at all—and increasingly wondered if this was what had happened to Laura Appleby.

Laura Appleby lived down the street and worked in town as a secretary; although twenty-five, she still wasn't married. I'd see her walking past the house each morning, accompanying her parents to Mass. Everyone in the parish whispered about what a shame it was—"and such a nice girl, at that!" It was said that her mother made constant novenas to Saint Ann, the patron of spinsters—"Ann, Ann, send me a man!" was the unofficial invocation—but no eligible suitor had come along. More than anything, I didn't want to end up an old maid like Laura, fussed over by parents and prayed for by parishioners, but I was increasingly afraid that I might. An old maid in the family: that was all my parents needed!

3 &.

VOCATION TALKS
(SEVENTH AND EIGHTH GRADES)

The stage was now set. I had mastered my role as good girl at school, at home, and in the neighborhood. I now began to look for a place where I could bring my holiness to fruition.

Just at this point, the long-robed Vocations recruiters began to appear on the scene, bringing their invitation to "Come follow Christ" to seventh and eighth graders in parish schools throughout the city. High school was near; it was time we considered the possibility that God might be calling us to spend four years in a minor seminary for boys or a convent prep school for girls. If a boy felt himself called to be a priest or a brother, or a girl "heard the call" to be a nun, such sheltered high school environments could protect the fledgling Vocation. Vocation talks were a standard part of seventh- and eighth-grade routine.

First came the recruiters for the priesthood and the brotherhood: handsome, fresh-scrubbed young men who sat on the edge of the teacher's desk and cracked jokes. We were all really impressed with their casualness: "I didn't know priests and brothers were so human!" we'd marvel to each other at recess, "and so handsome!" we'd sigh.

Recruiters spent a lot of time talking about how seminarians weren't weirdos and how they got to do normal things like play basketball and chew gum. Sometimes they'd show slides of the seminary, and 90 percent of the slides showed seminarians picnicking, playing baseball, or drinking cokes. They stressed to the boys that a Vocation was a call from God and that it was important to listen carefully in case He might be calling. "If you think He might be calling you but you're not sure, the best way to test it out is to sign up for a high school seminary. There you'll get a taste of what the priesthood is like, and then you can decide for yourself."

Nuns were similarly represented. A pretty young thing (on both scores a sharp contrast to the nuns who taught us every day) would come to talk about how she had been a red-blooded American girl too and about how she had loved nice clothes and going out on dates. "But then I began to discover that worldly pleasures left me empty and unsatisfied," she would testify with a faraway look in her eyes. "Saint Augustine exclaimed: 'Our hearts are restless till they rest in Thee, oh Lord.' Only giving myself completely to God has brought me peace and happiness." Then she would distribute brochures showing young girls, all of them radiantly beautiful and blissfully happy, strolling arm in arm across a picture-postcard campus. The brochure made it obvious that Christ wanted brides who were normal, red-blooded American girls.

After a few of these talks, no one had any confusion about what the word *Vocation* meant. Nobody came to talk to us about what it would be like to be a chemist, a social worker, or a stewardess; a *Vocation* (with a capital V) meant one thing: you were called by God to leave all things and to follow Christ as a nun, a priest or a brother. (I would later learn that priests and brothers hold theologically distinct places within the Church; for now I only knew that priests could celebrate Mass and hear confessions and that brothers could not.)

To have a vocation was to have a special calling. Your mom and dad would be very proud of you; *everyone* would be very proud of you. There was nothing really wrong with the way your parents lived: if they sent their kids to Catholic school, didn't use birth control, and were active in the Knights of Columbus and the Altar Society, there was a good chance they would make it to heaven too. It's just that there were higher callings, and if you *really* wanted to do something special for God and for humanity, the way to do it was to become a priest or a nun.

It was the idea of specialness that fired my imagination. Images of visiting my aunt and cousin rose up before my eyes: everyone always treated them with such respect and reverence. We'd dress up in our Sunday best and sit all prim and proper in their convent parlors, presenting them with homemade cookies and boxes of chocolates. When we went to visit other aunts and uncles, we'd wear our old clothes and play out in the backyard with their kids. The thought of *my* brothers and sisters one day bringing their children to visit the aunt who was doing something *special* with her life suddenly became very intriguing.

My parents had never suggested that I might want to be a nun someday; in fact, they always took great pains to not express career expectations to any of their children. But I knew deep down that becoming a nun was one sure way of making them proud of me. In the non-Catholic world, boys became doctors or lawyers and girls became the wives of doctors or lawyers as a way of fulfilling their parents' fondest dreams. In our Catholic world, the families that were most esteemed were those that were blessed with a priest or a nun. If I decided to become a nun, I would win for my parents the special heavenly crown reserved for those who give a daughter to the Lord.

But I still had my doubts. The thought of never having children of my own troubled me deeply. I talked to one of the recruiters about it and she assured me that nuns had children, lots of them, and that the spiritual motherhood they experienced in the classroom was every bit as satisfying as physical motherhood. I doubted that she was in a position to compare the two experiences or that she knew how sweet a newborn smells when you hold it to your heart, but I reminded myself that God doesn't give a cross without also giving the strength to carry it.

I asked the same recruiter why priests had more privileges than nuns, why they could smoke and drink and drive big cars. She seemed startled by my question, as though it had never occurred to her to ask it herself, and then she said that it was probably to make up for the fact that priests gave up more. I pondered that for a while and then realized she was again reminding me that sex wasn't really a big deal for a woman. But I knew *that* by now: knew that the word I had sometimes seen in *True Confessions, nympho*-something, referred to a woman who liked sex. I told myself that if the recruiter was right, as I now suspected she might be—if spiritual motherhood *could* eventually make up for the sacrifice of physical motherhood, if giving up sex wasn't *that* much of a sacrifice for a woman—then maybe I should give this vocation thing another look.

I entered eighth grade in 1956, and a month later a representative from the order to which my aunt and cousin belonged came to talk to our eighth-grade class. I already knew a little bit about their community, the Sisters of Blessing. I knew that their apostolate was primarily teaching and that they numbered about 1800 nuns, most of them teaching somewhere in the midwest and the south. I also knew that the order ran a prep school at their motherhouse about 100 miles away. I had often visited my aunt and cousin there at Saint Raphael's in Avington and was always moved by the simple, wooded beauty of the 150-acre campus.

Before the talk began, I introduced myself to the representative, Sister Roseanne, S.B. (Sister of Blessing), and told her that I had an aunt and a cousin in her order. She said that she knew them both and that both were "fine community women." She asked me if I had ever considered the possibility that I might have a Vocation. I told her that the thought had crossed my mind, and, smiling, she advised me to listen carefully to her talk: "You might hear Jesus calling you loud and clear."

I didn't hear Jesus, but I *did* hear Sister Roseanne and I was mesmerized by her message. She talked about the glories of serving God and His people, of helping to change the world. I was stunned: no one had ever told me that I, a mere girl, might actually be able to make a contribution to the world. Most of the women saints to whom we girls had been told to pray could boast of only one thing: they had kept their virginity intact. We read gory stories about how Saint Lucy, Saint Agnes, Maria Goretti, and the rest had been tortured, had been branded with irons, or had had their breasts cut off because they refused to surrender their virginity. As far as I could see, that was the extent of their contribution to humanity.

The men saints were the ones who inspired me: Saint Francis, who gave up everything in order to live simply; Saint Martin de Porres, the black man who worked unstintingly among the poor; Saint Vincent de Paul, who said that the poor will forgive you the good that you do them but only if you love them enough. Now here was someone saying that I, a female, could make a contribution to the world. The thought was breathtaking!

Sister Roseanne stressed that if a girl even *thought* she might have a Vocation to be a Sister of Blessing, it would probably be a good idea to test it out by attending the order's prep school. (I learned later that some nuns in this order and in others disagreed with this theory, feeling that a girl should attend a "normal" high school before making such a decision. Some orders didn't even *have* prep schools for this reason.) "Look at it this way," Sister Roseanne said. "You might go and discover that God isn't really calling you. At least you'd *know*, then; it would be a lot better than living your whole life, always wondering if you had turned your back on a Vocation."

My heart pounding, I looked at the pamphlet Sister Roseanne had given me. On the front was a picture of a church full of brides of Christ in nuptial finery; inside was information about the important work that Sisters of Blessing were doing in their various schools. As I contrasted a nun's life with the lives of the other women I saw around me, convent life began to look increasingly attractive. A teaching nun traveled all around, meeting all kinds of interesting people. But the important thing was that she was helping the world.

Sister Roseanne said that a feeling of being drawn to be a nun was a pretty clear sign of God's will and that you didn't have to hear a little voice. The feeling of being drawn was definitely there: the more I thought about it, the more I realized that this must be *it*!

And so it was decided as so many decisions are, not in one conscious moment of clear vision and choice but in many semiconscious moments that lead one into the other: I would be a nun. It was my destiny, my fate. God was calling and I would answer.

Sister Roseanne ended her talk by asking us to pray for Vocations: "The modern urge for riches, comfort, and pleasure is preventing many young men and women from following Vocations. Pray with me that more young people will find within themselves the generosity and the idealism to join Christ in His important work."

She then taught us a rousing song about Catholic Action, reminding us that we were the hope of the future. I sang with a heart bursting with excitement, with confidence that I had at last found my niche. I would commit myself to a great cause, a great mission: I would leave all things to follow Christ, to join His army of youth, to fly standards of truth, to fight for Christ the Lord.

4 §✑
GOD'S CHOSEN ONE

It took me a few days to get up nerve to break the news to Mother. She was peeling potatoes in the kitchen one day after school and I small-talked with her for awhile, trying to summon the courage. Taking a deep breath, I finally plunged: "Mom, I want to go to the Prep School next year. I think I have a Vocation."

It was a dark, wintry day, and some shadow that had

lurked outside now entered the kitchen. It was as if the very pronouncing of the words had allowed something new and ominous into my life—a destiny, perhaps. I found myself shivering uncontrollably.

Mother looked up and gave me a thin smile, the smile of one bowing to a proud yet somehow tragedy-touched fate. "Dad and I had a feeling you might be telling us that one of these days."

For a moment I felt a sharp pang of disappointment, almost of anger. I had agonized over this decision, sharing it with no one; yet she had apparently known all along what I would eventually do. She wasn't even surprised. It was almost as if she knew me better than I knew myself, and I didn't like that one bit!

I asked her how she had known, but she just smiled and reminded me that mothers have ways of knowing. "After all, when I was your age I too wanted to be a nun, but I never followed through. I have a feeling you'll follow through. I think you've got what it takes."

It was a compliment, a validation, and it dulled the anger. She gave me a little hug and told me that Daddy would be home late; I could talk to him later that evening.

That was it. It was exactly the reaction I had expected: pride, but pride riddled with sadness. I knew that she was happy for me and proud to be doing a great and noble thing in giving a child to God, but I also knew that her heart grieved at the thought of the good-byes to come.

Later that evening I talked to Dad and he had much the same reaction. I seemed a little young to be leaving home and he would miss me terribly, but if I was sure that this was what I wanted, I should follow my heart. In his eyes I saw a bittersweet blend of pride and pain that I would only see again a few years later when he put his oldest son on a plane bound for Vietnam. Then, as now, he would be simply doing his duty as a parent, fulfilling his obligation to Church and country. If there was pride, it sprang from the conviction that his off-spring were being sacrificed for causes of such cosmic proportion that they dwarfed the human suffering of the individual. If God or duty calls and you have to sacrifice your firstborn, so be it!

Once the decision was made, my life had a new focus. Everything seemed to revolve around the new life that was waiting for me just around the corner.

Word soon traveled around school that one of the eighth graders had a Vocation. I suddenly had more friends than I had ever had in my life: they were all considerably older than I and were dressed from head to toe in black, but I was in no position to be choosy. Nuns who had never even seemed to know I existed now came out of the woodwork to ask me how I was doing and if I were excited, and they offered to answer any questions that I might have. They admitted disappointment that I wasn't joining *their* order but they professed to be happy for me just the same. (I would later learn that nuns who were successful in bringing new Vocations to the order go in the unwritten *Who's Who* of that order.)

Both my aunt and my cousin began to write me long, inspiring letters, and they encouraged me to write to them and to let them help me in any way they could. Being a superior in the order, my aunt had something of an inside track and so was able to send me a wardrobe-and-supply list long before the other girls received them. She suggested that I ask for tons of men's linen handkerchiefs for Christmas and that I start watching for sales on white, drip-dry nylon blouses. She also suggested that I wait to buy shoes and stockings: she had gotten wind of some changes in regulations that might be coming down soon, and it looked as if candidates, or girls attending the Prep School, might be wearing ordinary black hush puppies and sheer stockings in the future. Until now they had worn the same high-heeled "granny" shoes and heavy black stockings that the nuns wore. I thought my aunt was awfully smart to make such practical suggestions, and it gave me a good feeling to know that I had someone in there looking out for me and getting the scoop on changes before they even occurred.

Most of the kids in the class now viewed me with a mixture of reverence and curiosity: What was it like to hear God calling you? Did you hear a little voice in the back of your head or something? Are you really going to go to school 100 miles away? The year before, a sister of one of the kids had gotten married and had moved to a parish on the other side of town. That was unusual enough, but 100 *miles!*

I wrote an essay entitled "My Vocation" for a diocesan-wide contest and won first place, a check for fifty dollars. I was suddenly the darling not only of the nuns but also of the entire parish. When the time came to select an angel for the school pageant, I was the unanimous choice, a poignant reversal of the slight my family had suffered six years ago when I had been suddenly expelled from angeldom.

In my family too, my rightful place had now been restored. The much-loved first child, I had fallen from grace to become just one of many, but by virtue of my Vocation my specialness was again secured. I reveled in the pleasure of being the special daughter, the extraordinary daughter, the daughter who had made good.

The days passed quickly now. Candidates were to check in at the Prep School on September 15, the feast of Our Lady of Sorrows, and there was much to do before then. Mother and I shopped for drip-dry white blouses, shoes, underwear, nightwear, handkerchiefs, supplies: I would be fitted for the blue jumper uniform when I arrived at school. I was also to take a cotton smock to wear over my uniform when doing housework, aprons to be worn at mealtime, and a cotton skirt to be worn over my gym suit when picnicking, hiking, or otherwise engaging in rough activities. Jeans, Bermuda shorts, slacks, and other worldly clothes were to be left at home: we would wear our blue serge uniforms seven days a week. The only jewelry allowed would be cufflinks. Sweaters should be blue or black.

When we weren't shopping, Mother and I sat at the kitchen table sewing on name tags and trying not to talk about the good-byes to come. Now and then our hands would brush and I would feel the sadness that filled my mother's body, weighing down her every vein and artery with sodden heaviness. She felt the same thing in me, and we both would blink back tears, saying nothing. If we just could make it through the summer and the first few days of separateness, we knew we'd be OK.

Throughout the summer, I took the bus downtown once a week to meet with other girls who would be attending the Prep School in the fall. Upperclass members arranged these little get-togethers, and I was always impressed by how friendly and solicitous they were. Usually we'd start by attending noon Mass at the cathedral; then we'd go to a nearby drugstore for malts or cherry colas. I liked the girls I was meeting—they didn't seem weird or nunny at all—and I looked forward to getting to know them better in the fall. What a joy it would be to hang around with people who shared my goals and aspirations!

My aunt wrote and commended me for my regular attendance at these little gatherings. She stressed the importance of surrounding myself with people who would support me in my Vocation: the devil would be on the lookout for any way to sway me away from my chosen course, especially during these last few months, so I should be especially careful in choosing the company I would keep.

And so the year sped by, faster than I ever could have imagined. Decisions and choices, many of them barely conscious, had led one into the other and culminated in a life-script that would govern the next fifteen years of my life. There was nothing to do now but to put one foot in front of the other and to play the thing out.

On a gray day in September 1957, we loaded the family Chevy with all my Prep School gear and began the two-hour trip to Saint Raphael's, my new home.

II

BOARDING SCHOOL (1957-1961)

In order to understand my happiness, which might otherwise seem perverse, the reader must yield himself to the spiritual atmosphere of the convent. If he imagines that the life we led behind those walls was bare, thin, cold, austere, sectarian, he will have to revise his views; our days were a tumult of emotion. In the first place, we ate, studied, and slept in that atmosphere of intrigue, rivalry, scandal, favoritism, tyranny, and revolt that is common to all girls' boarding schools and that makes "real" life afterward seem a long and improbable armistice, a cessation of the true anguish of activity. But above the tinkling of this girlish operetta, with its clink-clink of changing friendships, its plot of smuggled letters, notes passed from desk to desk, secrets, there sounded in the Sacred Heart convent heavier, more solemn strains, notes of a great religious drama. . . .

—Memories of a Catholic Girlhood *by*
Mary McCarthy

LEAVING HOME (1957)

"Saint Christopher, patron saint of travelers," Dad intones; "Guard and protect us on our journey," we answer. Checking the rearview mirror to be sure there are no bicycles behind him, Dad turns the key in the ignition and slowly pulls out of the driveway. A plastic Saint Christopher suctioned to the dashboard bobs up and down, promising protection.

Mother takes her beads, dainty and silvery, from her purse and begins the rosary. Whenever we say the family rosary at home or have other Catholics from the neighborhood over for a neighborhood rosary, Dad leads on big black beads. But when he's driving, Mother takes over, intoning each Hail Mary in a firm, peppy voice intended to dispel drowsiness and to keep everyone's mind on the business at hand. And it *is* business, vitally important business, for as the nuns are always reminding us, "The family that prays together stays together." To forget or neglect this important truth is to lead to a breakdown of the whole family unit.

I pray seriously on pearly white beads that I've used ever since my first Holy Communion back in second grade. Next to me in the back seat, Andrea, twelve, blows silent bubble-gum bubbles: their pink sweetness invades my prayer and I give her a pained look. Immediately she picks up the refrain loudly and out of time: "Holy Mary, Mother of God, pray for us sinners now and at the hour of our death. . . ." The boys, Pat, ten, and Dan, eight, sitting next to her, join in for a loud "Amen."

When the rosary is over, we put our beads back in their

cases, confident that though other families may suffer divorce and similar calamities, ours never will as long as we're faithful in saying Our Lady's rosary. In the same way, we feel confident that our journey today will be safe, since we have entrusted it to Saint Christopher: if we hear the wail of an ambulance or see a fire truck go whizzing by, we will make a sign of the cross for the poor victims, realizing that if it weren't for the protection of Saint Christopher, we too might be sprawled out all bloody at the edge of the two-lane highway. So far the trip looks like any other family trip we've ever taken: Mom and Dad in the front seat with one child between them—today it's Cathy, seven—the other four of us squashed together in the back seat.

I think for a moment of other family trips. Sometimes we'd even take Grandma: either Mom would hold one child on her lap, or we'd double up in the back seat, scooting over as much as possible so as to not kick Grandma, who always rode in stoic silence by the left window. In the process of scooting over, of course, we had to be careful not to kick over the covered potty jar that rode on the floor by the right window. Yet, despite our crowdedness, it never would have occurred to us to see these trips as anything but the greatest fun. Other kids' parents might save their money for a cruise to the Caribbean or a new bedroom set, but our parents spent their time and money on us, and we loved them for it, bragging that we went somewhere different every summer. "I wish *I* had parents like yours," we'd always hear, and we'd be proud. Two parents, five kids, a grandmother, and a full potty all piled together in the same car didn't bother us at all; we knew that this was what family togetherness was all about.

But today is different—radically different. This trip is not like other trips, for sadness lurks right around the corner just waiting for an opportunity to attack.

Trouble is brewing in the back seat now: Dan, his head covered with golden stubble from one of Dad's famous burr haircuts, claims that it's his turn to look at the map. Pat, similarly stubbled, counters that his ten minutes aren't up yet. Bickering turns to blows and when Mother's threats don't achieve results, Dad, who rarely hits, aims two good swats in the general direction of the problem. The car swerves, and Mother, who rarely hisses, hisses: "Watch the road, Herb! You just missed that big semi!" To which Dad then hisses "I know what I'm doing! Don't nag me!" Startled by the unexpected voltage of the exchange, both draw back immediately and retreat into silence.

The car is quiet now, and the sadness we have all been trying to hold at arm's length moves in. As long as there were details to handle, squabbles to settle, and the usual chaos of a family traveling by car, we were safe. It is the silence that betrays us, opening the door for thoughts about the purpose of today's trip.

For a moment everyone sits in frozen silence, staring straight ahead. Eventually Andrea scoots over and without a word squeezes in between the boys, making it clear that she will personally see to it that there will be no further fights in the back seat. I watch her in amazement: for the past few weeks she increasingly has played the role that I have always played—that of organizer, referee, Mother's little helper. A familiar struggle goes on inside me. Part of me is relieved that she'll be able to fill my shoes so well and that Mother will have the help she needs. Another part (the part I do my best to keep squashed down) hopes that my shoes will be just a bit too big to fill. After all, I *am* still the oldest, and I hope that no one will forget that during my absence!

Immediately I'm remorseful. How could I have such feelings toward my own sister, especially when she's been so nice to me lately? Like today: usually we'd fight over who would sit by the window, but today she insisted that *I* take the coveted seat. And it's not just today: she's been really different for the past few weeks as if she realizes, as I do, how much we're going to miss each other.

Somewhere beneath the fierce rivalry there has always

been an equally fierce, if unacknowledged, closeness; it has taken the imminence of separation to bring it to the surface.

Suddenly Dad pulls himself together, remembering his responsibility as head of the family to pull everyone else together. He dissolves the silence by the most effective means possible: he asks if anyone's hungry yet.

A deafening cheer goes up, and everyone begins to look for a place to eat. An orange-and-black fast-food sign appears on the horizon with its promise of frosty mugs of root beer and sizzling hotdogs, and soon Dad pulls in. A waitress in a short skirt runs out to take our order.

Pat deliberates over mustard or catsup until the gum-chewing waitress shifts her weight impatiently. Two or three times she turns her head in the direction of the other cars, reminding us that she is a *very* busy woman. I am mortified and everyone else is too; we all yell at Pat to make up his mind and that the poor woman doesn't have all day. Pat, flustered, decides to go with mayonnaise. With an apologetic smile that says "Please forgive me; you know how children are," Dad sums up the order politely and thanks her for her patience. He tells her that she's got a rough job and that it's amazing that she can keep her cool so well. Her whole face brightens. My handsome father charms one more woman, and I am again impressed. As she walks away, Dad catches a look on Mother's face and confides, "I really don't see why they have to wear their skirts as short as that, especially with kids around and all. It's disgusting." Mother nods in agreement, and Dad intones our Grace before Meals.

Once all the traces of lunch have been napkinned away, Dad steers the car back onto Highway 93 and begins the last leg of our journey. Still no one talks about where we're headed; no one asks the familiar "Are we almost there, Dad?"

A familiar sign announces AVINGTON 15 MILES. Saint Raphael's is located just a few miles outside of Avington, so usually at this point on trips to visit our aunt and cousin, someone starts a happy chant of "Fifteen miles to go, fifteen miles to go! You walk a mile, you ride a mile, fifteen miles to go." Today there is silence. Is it my imagination that Dad is driving more slowly than he's ever driven before? On my part, it's all I can do to keep from praying for a flat tire.

Dad turns on the radio, dialing a station that plays only happy, light music, the kind they play in dentists' offices. Usually Andi would protest, begging him to get the station that plays the top ten, but today she wants to keep the peace. I, too, would rather hear the top ten—dreamy teenage love songs and sexy rock 'n' roll—but I'm careful not to let anyone know. Now that I have evolved from good girl to future nun, it's all the more important that my reputation remain beyond reproach.

Maple trees drop leaves on golden cornfields as we pass, and I think about this matter of my reputation.

Through my years as good girl I had always been entrusted with special little responsibilities around the school. I had run errands for the nuns, carried notes from one to the other, and frequently been given the special privilege of being excused from history class in order to clean the chalkboard erasers by beating them against the school's brick wall. Once I became a future nun, I was even allowed to carry things into the convent, where worldlings never ventured: "After all," the nun had twinkled as, trembling, I entered the holy of holies, "you're almost one of us now!"

But there had come a breaking point: Perp had asked me to write down the names of everyone who talked while she was out of the room, and I had refused. I thought about what Sister Roseanne had said about Jesus wanting normal, red-blooded American girls, not holy-holy types who prayed all day, and I set out to sow a few mildly wild oats of my own.

During the last six months of eighth grade, I "talked to my neighbor" (nun talk for whispering across the aisle) so many times that my conduct grades dipped as low as my academic grades soared high. Far from being upset, my parents seemed to greet each checkmark in deportment with half-disguised amusement, almost approval. It suddenly occurred to me that they had worried about my goody-goody reputation even as they took a certain pride in my goodness and that they shared with me a certain ambivalence on this issue of goodness.

But it didn't take me long to discover how futile was my one last stab at normalcy, at acceptance by my peers. When I bragged about my low conduct grades in the presence of a group of school hotshots, they stared at me in silence. Eventually one of them took me aside and set me straight: "Look, don't try to be cool. We know you by now: we've gone to school together for a long time, and being cool just doesn't fit. It's phony. We like you better when you don't try to pretend you're one of us."

The rebuke was devastating, making it only too clear that no matter how much I tried I would never be accepted among the red-blooded American girls of the world. A failure at worldliness, I would now turn my attention to making it in a whole different world, the world of the convent. If I liked rock 'n' roll and jitterbugging and sometimes even boys, no one would ever know.

Dad is now back to work, staving off the sadness with all his might. His defense is witty, constant conversation until I want to scream at him: *Stop! I can't stand it!* Mother is no better: Dad stops to take a breath and she fills the silence with nonstop chatter: Did I remember to stop and say good-bye to old Mrs. Roberts? She is such a sweet old soul, and she always appreciates it so much whenever I stop in to see her on my way home from school. And did I pack my Benadryl? We'll probably be taking lots of walks in the woods, and I'll need it if my weed allergies start to flare up.

The questions, the chatter, go on and on and on until I think I can't stand it any longer. *"Everything's not fine!"* I want to scream. "I am fourteen and I am leaving my mom and dad, my brothers and sisters, my house, my dog, my rock collection, and my vanity table with the fancy ruffled skirt. Why doesn't anyone let me crawl into my corner of the back seat and cry?"

But then the guilt comes with huge heavy feet, stomping down the anger, driving back tears, preventing sweet release. I remind myself that they're only trying to make the day easier for me, for all of us. What's the matter with me? Why am I so irritable? Why don't I appreciate what they're trying to do for me? "Sweet Jesus, help me to be less selfish, to think of others, not self, and never *ever* let me hurt them, no matter what."

We are nearing the campus now: a familiar lake and a familiar sign—JOE'S CATFISH SANDWICHES—tells us we are almost there. Mother asks if I sewed my name tags on that last batch of handkerchiefs, and I assure her that I did. My voice is steady, matter-of-fact, and for a moment I'm not sure it's my voice. Not the slightest trace of what I am feeling seeps through, which makes me happy.

Knowing that the minutes are now few, I crawl into the secret world inside me and think back on yesterday, my last day at home. It had been a gorgeous fall day, a perfect day for climbing apple trees, and I had climbed to the top of my special tree and sat there for a long time. In a secret, silent ritual designed to mark the day as important and memorable, I had looked around at everything that made up my little life—my house, my neighborhood, my secret hideouts—and tried to burn the memory deep in my brain. I had ended my private little ceremony by patting my tree and assuring it that though I would be gone for a while, I would be home for Christmas and that the minute I got home, no matter how cold or snowy it might be, I would climb back up to my special place and things would once more be as they had always been. I lied a little bit in that last part, however, since the truth was that something deep inside told me that I was at some major turning point in my life and that things would *never* again be the same.

6 ᵍ◈
SAINT RAPHAEL'S

The big Saint Raphael's sign now appears specterlike out of nowhere, and Dad turns onto a small road that leads up a wooded hill. Memories of past visits now rise to greet me.

For as long as I can remember, we have been coming to Saint Raphael's each summer to visit my aunt, Sister Agnes Anita, and my cousin, Sister Donald. Sister Agnes Anita teaches seventh and eighth grades at a parish school in Indiana and is superior of her convent. (A superior is administrator of a local house; she answers to the superior general, who is the head of the entire community.) Sister Donald teaches first grade at a parish school in Dayton, Ohio. The two only see each other when they are home at Saint Raphael's each summer. Because of my aunt and my cousin, I know a lot more about nuns in general and the Sisters of Blessing in particular than most youngsters my age.

I know that a nun is someone who wants to give herself totally to God by professing the vows of poverty, chastity, and obedience and by joining a religious community. If a girl wants a life of seclusion and prayer, she goes to one of the contemplative orders, for example the Carmelites; if she prefers a life of active service in the world, she joins an active order. Some orders, such as Maryknoll, specialize in missionary work; some specialize in nursing; most orders in this country specialize in teaching. Each order has a unique Holy Rule dating back to the order's foundress but governed, to a large degree, by Church law; a unique habit, or mode of dress; and special customs and traditions.

I have learned quite a bit about the history of the Sisters

of Blessing from my aunt and cousin. I know that in the early 1800s a small group of pious women came together in their little French town, Chantille-sûr-Longe, to devote themselves to teaching children whose religious education had been neglected during the French Revolution and the Napoleonic era. A whole generation had been exposed to nonbelief and cynicism; it was time to bring the children back to the faith. Teaching the children and caring for the sick in their homes, these women eventually formed themselves into a religious congregation officially recognized by the Roman Catholic Church.

In the mid-1800s the congregation sent missionary sisters to America, led by a young sister named Sister Matthew. The missionary sisters lived in a log cabin in the woods of Illinois and eventually formed their own distinct order, acknowledging Mother Matthew as their foundress. Today the order numbers almost 1800 nuns and runs a number of schools throughout the country, including a rather prestigious girls' college on motherhouse grounds, St. Raphael's College.

I remember our family trips to visit Sister Agnes Anita and Sister Donald in midsummer. We'd all dress up in our Sunday best and sit on park benches under the trees as we waited for the bells that announced the start of visiting hours. As the big doors finally opened and my aunt and cousin came bustling out, everyone laughed and cried and hugged and kissed. They'd always have presents for us—holy cards and religious medals—and they'd ooh and aah over how much we'd grown. We'd sit and talk politely for awhile, as was expected of us, and then we'd be off to explore the campus while the grown-ups sat and talked.

The best part of the day always came when the nuns went inside for lunch and we spread a picnic under the big old trees. It never occurred to us to question why the nuns couldn't have lunch with us. They were separate, apart, almost ethereal in their sacredness: to observe them doing something as mundane as eating would have seemed an irreverence bordering on blasphemy. So we never thought it strange that when lunch-time came we'd go our separate ways, or that if we brought them a box of chocolates they'd have to wait until we left before sampling them.

In the same way when my father took out his camera and started photographing everything in sight, we never questioned it when they turned their backs to the camera. There were strict rules prohibiting nuns from posing for pictures, and any photographs had to be taken on the sly. My father was inordinately proud of his collection of snapshots showing blushing, protesting nuns, caught off guard. Again, we took it for granted that this rule, too, was appropriate: after all, to us, nuns hardly had bodies. The only skin we saw floated on an ocean of wool and starched linen and beads. We saw their faces and their hands, but these appeared to be white islands of flesh, seemingly unattached to anything else. So it was right and fitting that these bodiless creatures should decline to do anything so worldly and vain as to pose for a picture.

But today we are not coming to visit—the reality hits me again. Today I will not picnic, play, and then go home with my parents when the sun goes down. Today my parents will go home and I will stay. It is a desperately lonely feeling, so huge and overwhelming that it crushes any girlish excitement that wants to sprout. Every time I feel a rush of eager anticipation at the thought of starting a new life, I again realize the circle that is being broken today.

A young girl en route to a more-typical boarding school for the first time might experience a certain homesickness at first, but she never forgets that the going away is only temporary. There will be phone calls home and visits, and at the end of it all she'll marry some nice boy and bring grandchildren home to Mom and Dad. The circle will be unbroken.

I on the other hand will not be allowed to call home, and both in-coming and out-going mail will be limited and monitored. My family will be allowed to visit me three times each year from 10 A.M. to 4 P.M. on scheduled visiting days, and I will go home for Christmas and for summer vacation. But at the end of four short years, convent doors will close behind me and I will never come home again.

By entering the Prep School I am taking a first step toward a total breaking of the circle: I will die to myself and my worldly past, to my personal history and my private identity. A new being, more holy and pure than the old, will rise up from the ashes, but for now there must first be the death of the old.

7 &

GOOD-BYES

With the speed of a hearse approaching a cemetery, our Chevy approaches the big iron campus gates. James, the old watchman, waves us inside and we begin our descent down a majestic, tree-lined drive called simply "the boulevard."

Suddenly the amazing beauty of the place catches me off guard: I have never been here in the autumn, so I am completely unprepared for such splendor. The trees that always greened the boulevard's path in summer now blaze with red and orange, dropping fat leaves that dally past the car window. Behind more trees, stately old college buildings, Le Baron, Royce, and Grailey, observe the autumn grandeur like pince-nez'd Viennese dames.

Just past Grailey, Dad turns right onto a smaller road and pulls up in front of Lafayette Hall. One of the older buildings on campus, Lafayette Hall contains the elegant college ballroom, the dining room, and a number of classrooms. St.

Raphael's Preparatory School for Girls is also housed here, tucking itself into various sections of the building not needed for college functions: candidates' schedules are carefully synchronized to prevent their ever "being in the college girls' way."

We climb out of the car in front of Lafayette Hall, and blue-uniformed girls wave from a windowsill three flights above. I remember meeting them at one of our weekly gatherings. They look so happy to see me: how wonderful that I'll have so many friends here, friends who want the same thing out of life that I do! For a moment or two my heart sings with the glory of it all, the grandness, the nobility.

Then Cathy clutches desperately at one hand, and Dan the other: they've been doing this for the past few weeks, wanting to be with me wherever I go. I am gripped by the feeling that I am leaving my own babies, flesh of my flesh. How can I do this to them? To me? Jesus, give me strength!

A smiling candidate comes up to the car and greets us. She points Mother and me in the direction of the principal's office and offers to help Dad carry my trunk to the dorm.

It is my first opportunity to view the uniform that I will wear for four years: a navy-blue wool jumper and a long-sleeved white blouse. The jumper's a little too long but not really too bad. I'm sure glad they got rid of the black stockings and granny shoes: most of the girls now wear sheer nylons and fashionable black shoes.

Mother and I find our way to the second-floor office of Sister Bernard Clare, the principal. A tall, stern-looking woman, Sister Bernard Clare looks to be in her early sixties, though you can never be sure with a nun. She greets us with a holy smile, a tiny, thin kind of smile that twists the lips a perfunctory bit making it obvious that the wearer finds it hard to pull herself away from ecstatic prayer in order to handle the trivia of everyday life. I know immediately that I am in the company of a saint.

"Welcome to St. Raphael's Preparatory School, Mary

Agnes," she says. I start to explain that the *Agnes* is just a middle name and that I never use it, but she interrupts me, explaining: "There are many girls here who have Mary as a first name, so we often use middle names so that we can keep everyone straight. Besides, your dear aunt is such a holy woman, an exemplary religious; I'm sure you'll be proud to bear her name." I nod humbly, and she turns to Mother: "We all think so highly of your sister, Sister Agnes Anita. I'm sure she'll be a wonderful role model for Mary Agnes to follow."

Mother draws a checkbook from her purse and writes a check for half the annual tuition, $125. Summoning her courage, she tells Sister Bernard Clare that I'm allergic to wool: is there any way she could arrange to have a nonwool uniform made for me? Sister Bernard Clare smiles her holy smile again and gently takes Mother's arm, as she walks her to the door. I now note that Sister Bernard Clare is not only a saint, she's also warm and compassionate: she didn't have to take Mother's arm that way!

"She'll do just fine, don't you worry," Sister smiles as she turns to greet another parent.

"What a saintly woman!" Mother exclaims, "and so motherly. It makes me feel good to be leaving you in such good hands. She's probably right about the uniform, too: I probably worry unnecessarily. And besides, when you're running a school you can't start making exceptions or else *everyone* will want special privileges. It would have been nice if we could have gotten a special uniform made, but I can sure see it from Sister's side. Besides, one can't always expect to get what one wants in life. . . ."

Leaving the office, Mother and I stand in the middle of the hallway looking at a little card Sister Bernard Clare has just handed me. "Welcome to the Prep School!" it says and then states that my dorm number is 23, my storage compartment number is 4, my study hall place is row 2/seat 3, my chapel place is row 3/seat 2 (Saint Joseph's side), and my refectory table is 6. The last line, oraclelike, reports "Your guardian angel's name is Jenny." For a moment I am startled: our grade school nuns never even told us our guardian angels *had* names! Is this some kind of esoteric information to which one becomes privy only when she joins the convent?

Just at that moment, a short, bouncy blond with a gorgeous smile comes up to me and reaches out her hand. "Mary Agnes, my name is Jenny. I've been assigned to be your guardian angel for a few days: that's what we call the older girl who kind of helps you find your way around." Jenny takes my information sheet and begins to translate.

"This simply means that you have the twenty-third alcove in the dorm, that you store your Sunday uniform in storage compartment nineteen. In the study hall, you first count rows. . . ." Jenny's voice goes on but I am no longer listening: an increasingly familiar feeling has once more gripped me. Where are Dad and the kids? Some magnet tugs at me to take Mom and run and find them. Time is short. I won't have much more time with them; better to spend every minute with them now, before it's too late. It's a panicky feeling with which I've become increasingly familiar over the past summer.

I tell Jenny that maybe we can handle all that later and that I'm eager to unpack. I glance at the hall clock: 2:30—an hour-and-a-half to go before visiting hours will be over and my family will be required to leave.

We climb a wide flight of wooden stairs to the dorm, and here we find Dad and the kids. The kids are restless, and Dad says he thinks he'd better take them outside. Mother says she'll help me to unpack, and then we'll be down.

I look around at the dorm, a huge room with about thirty beds. By each bed there is a dresser with two drawers and a plain wooden rocker. I can see that there is just enough space by each bed in which one person can stand and dress. Four white curtains hang on rods around each alcove, and Jenny points out that these curtains are always to be left open, except after night prayers or when we are ill. In the morning after we have dressed and made our beds, the curtains are again to be pulled back so that our alcoves will be ready for inspection.

Mother and I with Jenny's help begin to unpack my trunk. Gowns and underwear go in the bottom drawer, toilet articles in the top. Jenny gives me a painted cigar box for the toilet articles I will carry to the lav: plastic cup, toothbrush, toothpaste, soap dish, talcum powder. Other necessities—hand cream, feminine napkins, deodorant, curlers, shampoo—will stay in the drawer; towel and washcloth will be hung on big racks in the lav.

I take out a little music box I had always kept on my dresser at home: seeing it on my new dresser somehow comforts me. Somehow it makes me feel less disconnected from everything that has gone before.

Jenny breaks the news as kindly as she can. "I'm sorry; you'll have to send that home with your mom. It's kind of a dumb rule, but we're only allowed to have a picture of the Sacred Heart and two other religious articles on our dresser. Did you bring any statues or religious pictures that are special to you?"

The words are hardly out of her mouth before Mother takes the music box and stuffs it in her purse, apologizing for not having known. "I have a sister who's a nun, I should have known. . . ." Like a child who has been reprimanded, she hastens to apologize, to make amends.

I now take out a small statue of Our Lady and a plastic crucifix that glows in the dark. The plastic crucifix is special to me: my brothers and sisters gave it to me last night at a little bedtime going-away party. They had served soft drinks and cookies and, as usual, everyone had dragged their mattresses off their beds and onto the floor of my room, where we had talked until Mom and Dad thumped on the ceiling and told us to go to sleep. For years my parents would talk about these strange children of theirs: they had scrimped and saved so that each child could have a room of his or her own, but when it came time to do homework each evening, everyone still congregated around the same old kitchen table; when it came time to go to bed, everyone still pulled their mattresses off their beds and into Mary's room for a giant family pajama party. About the only time everyone didn't huddle together in my room was when there was a thunderstorm and we'd all pile in with Mom and Dad while the thunder cracked around us. If the lightning was very bad, Mom would sometimes get up and light holy candles, placing them in the bathtub so that if they were knocked over they wouldn't hurt anything. It was eerie to get up to go to the bathroom in the middle of the night and see those candles flickering there as the lightning flashed at the window, but it was a comfort to know that they had the power to ward off evil spirits and to keep the house from being struck by lightning. It was even more comforting to climb into a warm bed between Mom and Dad. Needless to say, I don't exactly look forward to sleeping by myself in a narrow white bed with narrow white sheets. I hope there won't be too many storms.

Jenny sets the statue on my dresser next to the Sacred Heart picture that's already there and shows me how to position the crucifix on my pillow. We are to keep our crucifixes on our pillows during the day, she tells me, and to kiss Jesus's body right before falling asleep.

Jenny now points out the room where robes and slippers are to be kept, where Sunday shoes and uniforms are to be stored. No shoes or slippers are to be left under the bed; no robes are to be left hanging on the rod. "The dress you wore today won't be needed until it's time to go home for Christmas, so it will be stored until then. We wear our uniforms seven days a week."

Jenny pulls the curtains around my alcove and brings me a size 14 uniform. She and Mother step out of the alcove and within minutes I emerge fully dressed as a candidate. We open the curtains and prepare to go downstairs. The dorm clock says 3:42.

Downstairs we find Dad sitting on a stone bench near the car. Dan and Pat are listlessly throwing a baseball back and forth as Andi watches, just as listlessly. Cathy sits, unusually quiet, on Dad's lap.

Dad doesn't see us approaching, and I stop short.

I'm not used to seeing him with tears in his eyes. And there's a strange, haunted look on his face that I'm sure I've never seen before. It suddenly dawns on me that he is wavering here at the last minute, on the brink of saying "To hell with this crazy thing." Some mad impulse in me shoots up, just for a flash, wanting him to say it; wanting him to stand up to God, to destiny, to Jenny, to Sister Bernard Clare, to all of them; wanting him to grab me by the hair, shove me in the car and take me home.

But the moment passes, both for him and for me. Just another temptation the devil has put in our path. Now is the time when we need to be strong. My watch says 3:46.

Seeing us coming, Dad smiles and tells me how nice I look in my new uniform. He reminds me always to keep in mind that I can come home whenever I want. He goes on to say that Sister Agnes Anita is probably right: I should probably stick with it at least until Christmas and then make my decision. "That's the only way you'll know that you've really given it a fair try."

My watch says 3:54. Mother is weeping silently now, and soon we are all crying, clinging to each other one last time. The 4:00 P.M. bell rings and Mother and Dad pull away, saying that it's time to go. They pile their four youngest, still crying, into the car.

I don't watch them go, I don't wave. Numbly I turn away and join the group of desolate youngsters being herded into chapel for afternoon prayers.

I kneel in my pew and let the tears run down my face. We have Benediction and then some priest drones on and on about how appropriate it is that this is the feast of Our Lady of Sorrows, that we should unite our suffering to hers. His elocution goes largely unnoticed, however, for practically everyone is crying uncontrollably.

8⧽.

CANDIDATE

Jenny looks for me after prayers and leads me to a small room off the refectory where prayer books and veils are stored. There's a large wooden cupboard and in it a pigeonhole for each girl. Before prayers Jenny helped me to bobby pin a white lace veil to my hair, and she now shows me how to fold it and store it in my pigeonhole until next Sunday. During the week I will wear the black lace veil that waits in my box.

I follow her into the refectory, a white boxy room with faded religious prints on three walls and two small windows on the other, and she shows me my place at one of the tables. Though the room is filling quickly, there is a tomblike silence. I stand quietly in front of my chair as Jenny goes off to find her own place. I fold my hands in front of me as the others are doing and let my eyes wander around the room.

There are maybe ten square tables, set with white linen tablecloths and heavy white dishes; seven or eight uniformed girls stand around each table. At the front of the room Sister Bernard Clare and her assistant, Sister Joan Ann, preside at one of the tables. Both nuns have their eyes cast down, as do most of the girls in the room. The handful who are looking around have a certain shell-shocked expression on their faces, and I know that they must be newcomers like myself.

Sister Bernard Clare says grace; then a loud, happy roar fills the room. Girls chat and hug and wave to each other across the room, until Sister rings a little dinner bell. "Take your seats, girls; there'll be plenty of time later for getting together with your friends." The clamor diminishes somewhat as each girl puts on the apron that's folded on her chair: Jenny had brought mine down before prayers. Seventy wooden chairs scrape along the hardwood floor as each girl takes her seat.

I take a linen napkin from a plastic napkin ring that reads *Mary Agnes Gilligan* in clear blue letters. Plastic napkin rings, ordered from a mail-order house that specializes in conventual items, are a recent concession to modernity and efficiency: those of many of the older girls are engraved silver. Following the lead of four other girls at the table—their self-assurance indicates that they are upperclass members—I extract my napkin and tuck it into the top of my uniform.

Excited conversation flies around the table as friends who haven't seen each other for three months now reconnect.

"You've got a great tan: what'd you do—spend your summer at the pool?"

"My folks have a place at Lake Hodges, and I hung around there a lot. You look pretty good yourself. What's the latest around here? I got back too late to see anyone before prayers. Looks like ol' Bernie's got a new assistant: do you know anything about her?"

"Only that her name's Joan Ann and that she taught at All Hollows in Dayton last year. Seemed pretty nice when I met her. We *need* somebody nice around here instead of the old hags they always send us. I swear they sent Bernie here because nobody on mission could stand her!"

Three girls giggle and one stares disapprovingly. "Sorry, Sister Mary Holywater," says the offender, making the sign of the cross in mock repentance, and the conversation shifts abruptly.

"So how about the mortality rate—where do we stand? Did Babs make it back?"

"Babs is back, and so is Charley, but *Lillah* left—can you imagine? Nobody had any idea. I guess she's been going out with this guy for a couple of summers and he asked her to marry him. Jan says she knew about it for a while. I guess Lillah even showed her his ring last spring when she was struggling over what to do, but the rest of us were shocked."

"She would have made such a wonderful nun," says Sister Mary Holywater, shaking her head sadly.

"Now she'll make wonderful babies," says her counterpart brightly, and everyone laughs.

Two upperclass members in bibbed aprons push a large metal cart through the refectory door, and there's a temporary lull in conversation as everyone surveys the cart's contents. Soon more girls in bibbed aprons emerge from a small room off the refectory and begin to carry heavy white platters to each table. There are cold cuts, fresh bread from the campus bakery, coleslaw, and big bowls of creamed peas.

The girl at the head of the table, marked as a senior by a small white cross at her left shoulder, pours herself a glass of water from a metal pitcher that has icy evaporation running down the side and then passes the pitcher to the girl at her right. Surveying the serving silverware laid out in front of her plate, she selects a fork and stops for a moment to calculate: she counts the cold cuts and then the number of girls at the table; she takes a piece-and-a-half of minced ham. When the bread is passed to her she delicately cuts a slice in half, taking care that her fingers only touch the half she selects. After all the dishes have been passed around the table and everyone has begun to eat, another freshman and I start to make a sandwich, but seeing the upperclass members daintily eating their cold cuts with a fork, we decide against it. One of the freshmen asks timidly if there will be any butter for the bread, and the senior replies that it's a community practice of penance not to eat meat and butter at the same meal.

The feeling that I have stumbled into some strange and foreign world solidifies within me. I think wistfully of hearty German/Irish suppers at home, and I long for Mom's smoked sausage and fried apples, for corned beef, cabbage, and mashed potatoes.

Conversation swirls on around me: upperclass members reach out in friendly conversation, but I am numb to it all. Servers come around with pots of coffee and milk, and one of the girls shows me how to hold my cup over my right shoulder, indicating my preference. If my cup is turned down when the server comes around, it means I don't want anything to drink.

The freshman next to me holds her cup up for coffee, and seeing her shocked expression when her cup is filled, the senior quickly apologizes. "I'm sorry; I forgot to tell you: they only serve *café au lait* here, coffee with milk. It's a French custom going back to the days of Mother Matthew. I found it really hard to get used to at first, but now I actually like it better this way." The freshman nods and continues to pick at her food. The freshman seated at her other side isn't eating at all. I feel somehow united to both of them in a sisterhood of pain.

Outside our silent sisterhood, everything whirs on: there is excited chatter and conviviality; the refectory door opens and a cheer goes up as the metal cart is once more wheeled into the room: ice cream and a lavishly decorated cake are to be tonight's dessert in celebration of everyone's safe return. Tables are quickly cleared of other serving dishes, most of them completely empty, and dessert is served.

When dessert is over, I watch in amazement an intricate cleanup ritual. The big metal cart delivers to each table a pan full of hot soapy water and a small mop for washing dishes, a smaller pan for collecting scraps, one linen towel for drying glasses, and another for drying the rest of the dishes. One girl does all the washing, moving the pan from place to place. Each girl dries her own dishes; once they are dry, she positions her pieces of silverware just so, moving them together then turning them under and covering them with her plate, which is also turned over to protect all from dust. Each girl's napkin ring with folded napkin goes on top of the plate; at the upper right, next to it, go her glass and cup and saucer, all turned over. Everything is now ready for the next meal.

While all this has been taking place, other girls have been tidying up the linen tablecloth: crumbs are brushed into the refuse pan and the dish mop is used to rub out any minor stains. One of the older girls has spilled a few drops of coffee on the tablecloth, so a bowl is placed under the stain and boiling water is poured through the cloth until the stain disappears. Tablecloths and napkins are changed on Saturday; napkins are also changed on Wednesday, but only very bad stains warrant changing the tablecloth before that. There is much milling around during the whole cleanup procedure, and many take the opportunity to visit friends at other tables.

Eventually Sister Bernard Clare rings the bell and again there is instant silence: Grace after Meals is said and then conversations pick up once more. Aprons are folded and left on refectory chairs, black veils are picked up from pigeonholes, and everyone heads for the recreation room down the hall, laughing and jostling and seeking out old friends as they go.

The four stories of Lafayette Hall circle around a large courtyard with sidewalks, leftover patches of browning summer grass, and concrete urns that probably once contained beautiful flowers but now sit cold and barren. Windows line the hall that leads to the recreation room, and I stare out at the courtyard as night begins to fall.

My parents are probably reaching home right about now. I picture them carrying the two youngest, sound asleep, in from the car; I see a warm, welcoming light shining in the kitchen. Sadness encapsulates me like a see-through glass shell.

Beyond it, I can see what is going on around me, but I can't touch it, and nothing can touch me.

The Prep School recreation room is at the end of the hall, just past the entrance to the college dining room. It is a large, rather dark room, furnished with a number of comfortable old couches and chairs pushed together into circles. Flowered drapes hang at the long windows, and there is a piano in one corner.

Someone tugs at me to come sit with her group: it is Elaine, a fat girl with greasy unkempt hair and terminal acne. I met her at our weekly Prep School get-togethers in Peoria. She hugs me and tells me how glad she is to see me and, lying, I tell her how glad I am to see her.

But Elaine is familiar, a link to the past, and so I sink down into the big overstuffed chair beside her. Besides, I tell myself as she rattles on nonstop about Peoria news and gossip, Elaine like every girl here is part of Christ's Mystical Body: would I be uncharitable to Christ?

Jenny comes up and asks me how I'm doing—am I going to be OK? She squeezes in between Elaine and me and puts her hand on my knee. It's obvious that she doesn't think that being stuck with Elaine will be the best thing for my spirits. "You're my angel child, you know, and I'm going to take care of you. Come on over here a minute. I want you to meet a couple of my friends."

She proceeds to lead me over to another circle where she introduces me to everybody. Everyone is kind and friendly. A silver tray laden with chocolates and other goodies comes to the circle and Jenny encourages me to sample them: "We use the French term for *snack* here, *collation*. There's usually a col-lation tray at each recreation, except during Advent and Lent: parents send candy and bring it on Visiting Sundays. We also have collation each day after school. Sometimes there's a des-sert from the night before—you usually have to be the first one there if you want to get in on the dessert! Arlene Likowski's father owns a cookie company, so there's always tons of

Likowski cookies around. And there's always all the milk you can drink. Anyway, eat up; don't be shy." She takes two more chocolate-covered cherries off the tray and puts them in my hand.

"You know what they say," adds another girl, smiling: "A good appetite is a sign of a Vocation."

"Then I *sure* must have a Vocation!" says her friend, patting the bulge in her uniform right below her belt. Everyone laughs.

Though grateful for the attention and impressed with everyone's friendliness to newcomers, I long for recreation to be over. I just want to be by myself, to pull my alcove curtains around me, and to let my capsule burst. Sadness is, to me, a very private thing to be shared with no one.

Recreation doesn't last long: Sister Bernard Clare rings her little bell and says it's been a long day; she knows we're all tired. Besides, many of us still have unpacking to do.

She goes on to say that total silence, called profound silence or grand silence, is to be observed each evening from the end of recreation until the end of breakfast. "Profound silence should be taken extremely seriously. It should not be broken except in cases of dire emergency. You should use the time to reflect on your sins and shortcomings of the day and to formulate resolutions for the next day so as to not repeat those faults. Most important, you should spend time preparing a place inside for the Divine Guest who will come to you in Holy Communion tomorrow morning."

"Our Lady will be watching to see how serious you are about the vocation her Son has so graciously given you. If you are meticulous in keeping the rules, she will know that you are sincere. She will teach you all the virtues that you will someday need if you are to work in Christ's vineyard." Her homily over, she says solemnly, "Goodnight, girls," and seventy voices answer "Goodnight, Sister." She lowers her eyes and everyone follows her out of the room, pinning on their veils as they go. No one speaks.

Savoring the quiet, I follow the rest to a small chapel where we say night prayers and then up three flights of stairs. Upperclass members disappear down dimly lit halls on their way to their rooms, and we freshmen find our places in the dorm. Jenny is there beside me, bringing my robe and slippers from the closet, pulling the curtains around my alcove and demonstrating how to turn back my spread according to regulation—all without a word. She now gives me a little kiss on the cheek, then turns and disappears down one of the corridors.

Too desolate to feel the balm of Jenny's concern, I set about making it through the next forty-five minutes. Jenny has warned me that there will be a warning bell at 9:25 and that at 9:30 all dorm lights will go out: if I'm one of the unlucky ones who's still in the tub after lights-out, I'll have to grope my way back to bed in the dark, my precarious navigation dependent upon a careful count of rows and curtains. I undress hurriedly and put on my robe and slippers. Underwear goes into my laundry bag; it will be sent to the laundry on Saturday. Blouse and nylons are to be washed out by hand. Taking the blouse and nylons, a towel and washcloth, and my toilet article box, I set out for the lavatory.

The bathroom area consists of three tiled rooms. The center section contains tubs, each in a little room of its own; on either side is a section containing sinks and toilet stalls. Connecting the three rooms is a large open room filled with racks for drying clothes, as well as long tables with pans to be used for washing hair.

I use the bathroom and then wash out my blouse and stockings and hang them to dry. I check to see how long the tub lines are: only two or three are waiting for each. I decide to brush my teeth later. The line moves remarkably fast: a few take time to cover themselves with talcum powder, leaving a fine fragrant dust on the floor next to the tub, but most, well-trained not to indulge the body, forgo even this feminine luxury. A hedonistic few—defying warnings against giving the body, the prison of the soul, too much attention and pampering—will fill the tub from time to time and loll around in contraband bath oils and bubbles, while everyone else giggles appreciatively or fumes righteously, depending on their point of view. Eventually, however, these rebels will be reported for their indulgence and indolence by one of the school "saints" who is, of course, entirely motivated by concern for their spiritual good. There are no hedonists afoot tonight, however, so the line moves rapidly.

The lines also move pretty quickly because we're not allowed to wash our hair in the tubs: hair is to be washed only in the big porcelain pans out in the hall. You fill your pan at the janitor's sink, carry it to the table, scrub with shampoo, carry the pan back to dump the old water and get new (your wet head dripping the whole time) for as long as the whole procedure takes. Only the speediest—and those with the shortest, thinnest hair—can fit hair washing into a typical evening: most shampooing has to wait for Saturday, when there is more time.

Seven-and-a-half minutes after I take my place in line, I am filling the tub. Even had I been more hedonistically inclined, I wouldn't find the situation all that inviting: the hottest water is barely lukewarm, and it's gray, almost black, in color and slightly sulphurish in odor. The tub itself is riddled with deep rust stains under each faucet.

I bathe as quickly as possible, taking care to be as unaware of and uninterested in my body as possible; then I dry and put on my robe. A can of cleanser by the tub and a cloth over the side cue my next step, so I give the tub a good scrubbing.

Eventually I count my way back to my alcove: two aisles over and five curtains down. The warning bell rings: five minutes to go. I twirl a few fast pin curls into my hair and then reach into my bottom drawer for a package I've been waiting to open. Sister Agnes Anita had sent it to the house but had specified that it not be opened until my first day at Saint

Raphael's. Finally having a moment to myself, I tear open the wrapping and discover a small black looseleaf notebook filled with typed pages. Inside is a note explaining that it's a community custom to have a spiritual notebook, a little book where you write your thoughts or passages from spiritual reading books, passages that have particular meaning in your life. The note goes on to say that during the past year she had been copying out things that she thought I might find inspiring, and this little notebook is her gift to me.

Turning to the first page I see a picture of Mom and Dad and the kids standing in the backyard. It is the first family picture I've ever seen where I'm not standing right there in the midst of them, and my first reaction is one of shock, almost as if I've died and am now looking back on those I've left behind. The feeling of apartness, of isolation, is precisely that drastic.

Beneath the picture my aunt has typed a little prayer: "Keep these loved ones, dearest Lord; keep them in Thy care. I left them for You. Take care of them for me!"

I put the notebook back in my drawer and climb into bed just as the final bell is ringing.

A few more curtain rings scrape metal as the late stumble in: something is dropped, something falls and breaks. There's general shuffling and blind rooting around and finally silence.

Someone swears softly in the anonymous darkness: "Oh shit!" There are giggles and then again the silence.

As silence settles, soft, stifled crying is heard here and there throughout the dorm. One girl sobs desperately, right out loud. My protective capsule shatters into a thousand fragments as I sob into my pillow. I fall asleep on a sea of muffled and not-so-muffled sobs, knowing that I am not alone.

It will be years before I hear the story of my family's grief that day: grief, like illness, problems, and worries, will be carefully shielded from my view. Only many years later will I learn that no one spoke to each other the whole way home that gray day in 1957; that, arriving home, Pat proceeded to beat his drums so hard that they broke, and that Dan huddled despondently in a dark corner of the garage where no one could find him. Andi and Cathy cried all night and could not be comforted. And in the still of the night, my parents held each other and reminded each other that God's love was a balm that could heal any wound, even heartbreak.

9 &

FIRST DAY

A sharp, cold bell awakens me, and I know immediately that the day will hold little time for homesickness. I look at my watch: 5:45. Sister Bernard Clare's voice cuts through the morning cold, "Benedicamus Domino!" (Let us bless the Lord!) and muffled sleepy voices throughout the dorm answer "Deo Gratias!" (Thanks be to God!).

Jenny has told me how little time there is for getting ready in the morning, so I resist the urge to crawl under my warm blanket for just one more minute. She has also told me that getting out of bed promptly is our first opportunity to practice penance each morning: "There is a saying in the community that you should rise from bed as if your bed were on fire." I can't seem to muster *that* kind of enthusiasm, but I do force myself to put my feet on the floor and stand up. I sit back on the bed immediately—the wood floor is icy cold!—and grope frantically under the bed for my slippers.

By now metal rings screech across metal rods as curtains are pulled back throughout the dorm, and hurried steps outside my alcove warn me that I too must hurry. I pull my robe around me and grab my box of toilet articles. My pace picks up as more and more girls come flying out of their alcoves, practically knocking me over in their haste.

When I get to the lav, morning smells of toothpaste, overly sweet, fill the air. I see now why everyone has rushed so: lines of three or four are already waiting by each sink. I use one of the toilets and then grab my towel and washcloth from a rack. Thank God nobody's towel has the same color stripes as mine! I take my place in line and as soon as my turn comes, I splash some cold water on my face, since there is no hot water this morning. I brush my teeth with a few rapid squishes.

Next I hurry to the rack where I hung my stockings and blouse the night before: in dismay, I find that the rack is weighed down with other stockings and blouses looking exactly like mine. I search blouse collars frantically until I find my name tag and I grab a pair of stockings that look like they might be mine.

Once back in my alcove I dress as quickly as I can. The stockings I have grabbed have runs in them, so I frantically dig in my bottom drawer for another pair. Oh, no! I must have left them in my storage cupboard: no time to run to get another pair. I pull on the stockings with runs and offer the humiliation to Jesus: "All for Thee most Sacred Heart of Jesus." I remind myself that my suffering, united with His, has the power to save some poor unfortunate soul from purgatory this very day. I give my hair a few quick brushes: there is no time to primp or to idle in front of the mirror, but that is no hardship for me. My mother long ago taught me that giving excessive attention to one's appearance is vanity and a waste of good time.

I pull my sheets tight, tucking the corners just so the way Jenny taught me, and pull up the white chenille spread, making sure the bottom hangs evenly all along, exactly 2 inches from the floor. I clear the top of my dresser, leaving only the regulation picture of the Sacred Heart and a ceramic statue of Our Lady, and put my crucifix on my pillow.

Metal scrapes metal again, as curtains are opened throughout the dorm and blue uniformed girls put robes and slippers away. Two by two we line up near the door of the dorm and wait in silence.

The wind rattles the big old windows; I look outside, seeing nothing but black. It is a harsh and sobering experience for a youngster newly stripped from the family nest. Forbidden to reach out to other human beings for comfort or solace, I have no choice but to face the unavoidable, primitive realities of the dark and the cold. For a moment I shiver uncontrollably.

And yet there is something in the stripped-down starkness of it all that appeals to me, for I want to put worldly comforts and distractions aside for a while and get down to some basic substratum of life where I can find out what life beneath the deceptive fluff is really all about. If there are monsters in the darkness, I want to face them instead of running from them forever. It is a Shaker-like life that I seek, unfettered by worldly concerns and accumulations, simple, pure, and uncluttered. I will find out what matters, *really* matters; simplicity and even hardship will be my allies in the quest.

Another bell jangles the morning cold; following Sister Bernard Clare, we file down one dark corridor after another, two by two. We pass the rooms where the upperclass members sleep and descend a wide flight of stairs that take us to the second floor. Here in the midst of offices and classrooms and study halls, our silent procession pauses at the shrine of the Little King.

The tiny statue is clothed in a festive green cloak in keeping with the liturgical color of the day, and as we line up in front of the shrine the older girls begin to sing. The song has a lilting melody, and I am moved by the sound of clear, bright girlish voices singing together, the first crack in the morning's total silence. The hall's windows look out onto the courtyard, and I can see that the dawn is just beginning to break.

The procession winds down the stairs and past the refectory and into the long silent hallway that connects Lafayette Hall to the main Church. Though I have never been inside, I know that the central motherhouse building connects to the Church on the other side.

Here our procession pauses, and we now line up in twos according to where we sit in chapel, seniors first, juniors next, and so on. As I pin my veil on I can hear the nuns chanting their morning office, an ecclesiastically approved set of Latin chants for nuns; their voices sound like morning bells as they waft the morning chant, Lauds, heavenward.

When Lauds is finished, we file into Church a few minutes before Mass is ready to begin. I take out my new *Saint Joseph Missal* and mark the "Ordinary of the Mass" with one ribbon, the "Proper" (the prayers unique to today's particular feast) with another. Daily missals such as the *Saint Joseph Missal* and the *Saint Andrew Missal* have come out only recently: they have the Latin Mass translation on one side and the English on the other, enabling the daily churchgoer to follow what is being said and done at the altar. I am proud of my dexterity in finding my way through my new missal.

Mass begins, and I follow along for a while. As usual, however, I begin to grow groggy and lightheaded as Mass wears on, and as usual I rebuke myself for my lack of devotion. I picture Jesus in Gethsamane rebuking his sleeping disciples, "Could you not watch one hour with me?" and I realize sadly that I have let Him down again. Jesus was willing to go through so much suffering for me, and I can't even keep myself awake and alert for Him!

When I was a younger child we weren't even allowed to drink water for twelve hours before receiving Communion, much less *eat* anything. Our grade-school's drinking fountains all wore little cloth covers before Mass each morning, and when we brushed our teeth in the morning we were careful not to swallow any water. I frequently became so ill in Church that I had to go outside for air. It's not so bad now that we're allowed to drink water before receiving Communion, but lightheadedness and grogginess are still a problem. It never occurs to me, as I struggle each morning to bring my unruly body into control, that maybe bodies are to be listened to, that maybe they have something important to tell us when they rebel. To my way of thinking, only lazy weaklings use such excuses. Jesus didn't use any excuses, did He: "Don't crucify me today, I've got a headache"? No. If the body rebels, it is simply a matter of willpower once more taking control.

Mass continues past the Consecration where the miracle of Transubstantiation occurs, and on to Communion. Throughout the Church there is a rhythmic thumping as each person beats her breast and affirms "Domine non sum dignus!" ("Lord, I am not worthy!") three times as if to physically drive deep inside this sense of personal worthlessness. Only when we hang our heads in hopelessness and self-disgust, only then are we capable of being rescued: "Say but the word and my soul shall be healed!" Peace of mind is available to us but only after we have abandoned all hope of being the source of our own peace. Salvation is from the outside, to be waited for and hoped for—and never deserved.

Preparations for Communion now begin in earnest: my fast has prepared my body for Jesus's coming, and it is now time to prepare my soul. I take out the little prayer book that I received on my First Communion Day and begin to read the before-Communion prayers. I look at the holy picture marking the place on the front cover: all satiny and white is a radiant young girl being guided through life by her guardian angel. Her hands are pointed in front of her like steeples, and she looks so sweet and angelic. On the back cover is my second-grade nun's message, in perfect nunly script, reminding me that she hoped my soul will always stay as pure and white as it was that day. Every time I read her words I become more determined to never let her down.

Communion time comes, and one by one we file out of our pews and up to the communion rail. I point my fingers together in front of me, doing my best to look like the girl on the holy card.

I kneel at the communion rail and wait for the priest. First comes an altar boy who holds a gold plate, called a *paten* against my neck: the paten is there to catch any microscopic particles of host that might tumble to the carpet or to catch the host itself in case it is accidentally dropped. I stick out my tongue, and the priest presses Jesus's Body onto it. Rising, I return to my seat as the host dissolves. I am careful not to let any particles touch my teeth as we have often heard frightening stories of children who have forgotten and chewed up a host and been struck dead immediately. The Body of Jesus is not to be chewed.

Back in my pew, I am full of reverence for my Divine Guest. I hide my face in my hands as we have been taught and talk heart-to-heart with the God Who now dwells within me. I tell Him I love Him, that I am here on a quest to find out what really matters, that I want to help Him to make the world a happier place for everyone. I ask Him to smile on Mom and Dad and the kids, to help me not to miss them too much, to be patient with me if I do miss them. I listen for anything He might have to say to me, but there is only silence: peaceful, smiling, loving silence.

When Mass is over, we eat a silent breakfast while an older girl reads aloud from the Life of Christ. I do my best to listen, but I am somewhat distracted: I'm not used to eating bananas with a fork or oranges with a spoon.

After breakfast Jenny is right there to guide me through the next steps. "Well, angel child, how'd you do?" she smiles.

I smile back and startle myself with the sound of my own voice. "Not too bad. I've never gone that long without talking in my whole life, but I kind of liked it. It was great not having to be all cheery at breakfast—my family always tells me I'm a real grouch in the morning!"

"I know what you mean," Jenny laughs, tossing her blonde curls. "I'm no good for anything in the morning 'til I've had my coffee!"

Jenny now leads me out of the refectory to a little room where she hung my smock the day before. As I put on my smock, she gives me directions about the next part of the day's routine.

"Every morning after breakfast, we all do our employments for about a half-hour. An employment is a small house-cleaning job that you're assigned for a month: every day you're responsible for keeping that part of the building spick-and-span. Then at the end of the month you get a new employment. Doing your employment well is considered as important in the eyes of God as saying your prayers. Your employment for the month is to clean the winding stairs. I'll show you where to get the cleaning supplies." I am struck by the fact that Jenny is obviously one of the all-American girls Sister Roseanne had talked about. Though bouncy and pretty and not at all holy-holy, she is not embarrassed to speak of God, or to advocate doing one's job well for His sake. I like her even more.

I follow Jenny to another small room where she opens a cupboard and takes out a broom, a dustpan, a dust mop, dust rags, and a large piece of flannel. She then leads me to the winding stairs and tells me how to proceed. "You start at the third floor and sweep all the way down with the broom, making sure you get into each corner. Then you go back up, dusting the banister as you go, and this time come down with the dust mop, picking up any dust left by the broom. The piece of flannel is to be folded under the dust mop. Then afterward you sweep the flannel off outside and put it away until tomorrow. Any questions?"

Assuring Jenny that her directions are clear, I set off for the top of the winding stairs, marveling at how they twist and coil their way to the top. I have never seen stairs quite like this. Soon I am engrossed in my job: it feels good to be doing something physical, something simple and monotonous and concrete. Each time I lean my weight into the broom—into the left corner, across, then down—I feel that I am somehow pulling the various fragments of my life into some simple, solid focus. It's a warm, satisfying feeling.

When I finish cleaning the winding stairs, I take my piece of flannel and my dust mop and follow a group of laughing, chattering girls who seem to be headed outside on a similar mission. The door opens, and I walk into an autumn paradise: a clear sun warms the morning's chill and the sidewalks are covered with still-damp leaves, crimson and golden brown. Somewhere in the distance, leaves are being burned.

When we are finished, I follow the girls back inside. We put our cleaning materials and smocks away and head for the second-floor study hall, where instructions are about to begin. It is 8:30 A.M.

The study hall is large and sunny. I pull my little card out of a pocket and search for my desk: row 3/seat 11. I lift the top and find my notebooks and school supplies already inside: that Jenny really *is* an angel!

Sitting down, I take out my box of treasures: a cigar box full of holy pictures, medals, and relics accumulated through eight years of going to Catholic school and having nuns as relatives. Holy pictures are small cards with pictures of Jesus, angels, or saints on them. Medals of silver or gold can be worn on chains around one's neck, dangled from one's watch, pinned to one's underclothes. Relics are pieces of a saint's bone or pieces of cloth that have touched a saint's body: usually they are pressed between two plastic disks that are then stitched together to form a little badge. While my brothers collected baseball cards, I collected marbles, then bubble-gum comics, then washcloths from soap-powder boxes for my hope chest: now I collect religious articles, a more practical choice since nuns, and therefore future nuns, use them for all gift giving.

I rifle through the box, seeking a perfect gift for Jenny. This picture of the Good Shepherd in pink and blue robes is lovely—or what about a Maria Goretti badge? Though Maria Goretti hasn't been declared a saint yet by the Church, everyone knows that eventually she will be since she preferred to be murdered rather than submit to the desires of a sex-crazed man.

Eventually I find a picture of a radiant angel with shiny gold hair, just the thing for Jenny, *my* gold-haired angel! I flip it over to the back and, filling my fountain pen, write a little note thanking her for all that she has done for me. I am just signing my name when everyone rises around me: "Good morning, Sister!" I, too, jump to my feet as Sister Bernard Clare strides into the room, intoning the sign of the cross out loud as she enters. Everyone joins her for another round of prayers.

There is some rustling and shuffling as everyone clears her desk; then there is silence. Standing in front of the teacher's desk at the front of the room, Sister Bernard Clare folds her hands piously in front of her and begins to speak.

"Our instructions this morning will be short, girls, as classes start today and there are many details to be handled. Those of you who are in the upper classes, let me start by congratulating you. The world, undoubtedly, presented many enticements during the summer; yet you had the maturity to remain firm in your Vocation. Maturity: that's what it's about. And I congratulate you. As you have already noticed, I am sure, a number of girls didn't make it back. Apparently they didn't have what it took to persevere in this kind of life. It's not an easy life: Christ asks nothing short of *total* commitment, and it takes a certain caliber of girl to persevere, to withstand temptation. Not everyone has what it takes, so let's not judge too harshly those who have fallen by the wayside. Instead, let's keep them in our prayers. I'm sure they'll need all the prayers they can get.

"I would also like to welcome those of you who are freshmen and to congratulate you, too, on overcoming all the obstacles the devil can place in a girl's path once Jesus calls her to be His own.

"Now that you are here the devil will be quite active in trying to get you to veer from your chosen course, and the most powerful tool he will use will be homesickness. Nothing will make him happier than to have you give in to homesickness: every year at least ten freshmen leave the first week because they can't take the homesickness. Will you be one? Will you be so easily persuaded to turn your back on Christ's call?"

Sister Bernard Clare goes on to recount story after story of girls who spurned Vocations and later birthed stillborn children, died in car accidents, or developed cancer. "But always remember, the choice is yours," she says after scaring the hell out of us. The choice is yours: a Vocation or stillborn children.

Schedules are handed out according to class: all the seniors take the same classes, all the juniors, and so on. Stacks of books are to be picked up from the tables in the back of the room. I look at my schedule: as a freshman I will take English, math, religion, history, Latin, French, and chorus. I take the books I will need for my morning classes and leave the others in my desk. I follow the upperclass members down the hall.

First there is a stop at a statue of the Sacred Heart, where we sing a song asking Jesus's blessing on our day, that we might be diligent, industrious students, a credit to the order. The senior in charge of bell duty for the week now rings the bell, and the seniors head off to math, the juniors to English, the sophomores to religion, and the freshmen to Latin.

There are five Prep School classrooms, including a chemistry lab, and our teachers are either college students who are doing their practice teaching or nuns. Each class lasts fifty minutes with a five-minute break in between classes.

Noon comes quickly: Angelus bells ring over the campus as we join Catholics throughout the world in this traditional prayer to Our Lady. "The angel of the Lord appeared unto Mary. . . ."

At lunch there's some sophisticated analysis of the new teachers ("Miss Crandall's really pretty; it's a shame she wears such drab colors!") and a few lingering references to summer good times. Conversation turns to food.

"I wish they'd stop serving us the college girls' leftovers: this Jell-O is like rubber. Look at it; I could bounce it across the room!" Laughter.

"I know. I wonder why we can't have normal things like pizza and hamburgers and potato chips sometimes."

"Potato chips! We'd probably have to eat them with a fork if we did!" More laughter.

The conversation swirls on, becoming rowdier and rowdier. Every now and then, the pale, bespectacled girl they call "Sister Mary Holywater" (her real name is Louise) tries to protest: "You shouldn't be setting such bad example for these freshmen." Nobody pays much attention to her.

One of the older girls, bright-eyed and friendly (the others call her Marnie), now turns to us freshmen and asks if we got enough to eat. "You're in starvation corner, Mary Agnes—that's what we call the last place at the table—but hopefully you won't be there forever. We sit at the table according to class, but every week we get new seat assignments, so next week you might end up ahead of the other freshmen at your table. Start praying to Saint Teresa: she won't let you down!"

"Don't brainwash her with that Saint Teresa stuff," complains another girl. "She may be the patron of the junior class, but she didn't win you the basketball tournament last year, did she? I'd place my bets on Saint Michael."

"Here, here," says the senior, taking another forkful of meat loaf. "On Saint Michael and on the senior forwards—right, little sisters?"

"Right!" agree two younger girls in unison. Seeing the bewilderment of the table's three freshmen, one of them explains: "You see, we have big-sister and little-sister classes here. Since we're sophomores, the seniors are our big sisters. You're freshmen, so your big sisters are the juniors. There's a really special relationship between sister classes. It's kind of hard to explain, but you'll soon see what I mean. Like the big basketball tournament at Thanksgiving: juniors play the seniors and freshmen play the sophomores, and the sister classes do everything they can to support each other, making pom-poms and practicing cheers and storming heaven with novenas to their sister-class's patron saint. As soon as you guys get settled in, one of the first things you'll do is have a meeting so that you can choose a patron saint, class colors, and a class motto."

"And the next thing you'll have to do is bone up on your shots!" winks Marnie, who I now realize is a junior and therefore our big sister. The thought of having a whole class of big sisters sounds appealing after a lifetime of always having been *myself* the big sister. "I think we're going to have a *great* little-sister class," she adds as she beams at us three freshmen.

Venturing a glance at the two freshmen next to me, their faces still as blank and dazed as my own, I marvel at her confidence, and yet I am touched by her friendliness, by the friendliness of all of them. For the past few years I have hung out at the edges of cliquey little packs of gum-chewing girls and have been forced to be content with the occasional crumbs they would throw me. Now all of a sudden I find myself in a strange wonderland where I can start from scratch, where no one knows my past social status (at Precious Blood if you were once on the bottom, you were *always* on the bottom), where, if

I admit to liking rock 'n' roll, no one will take me aside and tell me that I shouldn't try to act cool. Seniors even talk to freshmen in this wonderland.

After lunch there are more classes. At 3 P.M. everyone once more descends the winding stairs, this time to collation.

Collation is laid out in a little room off the refectory. There's leftover cake, fresh bread from the bakery, big sticky tins full of peanut butter and jelly, big gray cans of milk from the dairy. By the time I reach the front of the line the cake is gone, so I make myself two peanut butter and jelly sandwiches and down them quickly with two cups of milk. I am eager to go outside.

Once outside, I am submerged in a crowd of laughing, chatting girls waiting for the afternoon walk to begin. Soon Sister Joan Ann appears and a little group gathers around her, obviously trying to persuade her about something. A cheer goes up and the word goes around: "We're going to the orchard!"

Every day, no matter the weather, we will take a walk at 3:00 P.M. Sometimes we'll walk around campus, and sometimes we'll take a longer walk out past the cowbarns to Saint Pat's Lake. On Saturdays, when there's more time, we'll often walk out the back campus gates and through the small village that rims the campus. Most of the time our superiors will take care to keep us on the back part of the campus, away from the college girls. Like poor cousins in the home of wealthy relatives, we are always to know our place and that we are never too conspicuous.

Sister Joan Ann waits for everyone to gather to go over the rules about walks. We are to always keep an arm's length from the girl in front of us; no one is ever to walk in front of the presiding sister. We should stay always with the group, and if anyone needs to go back to the building for any reason, she should first obtain permission from the presiding sister.

Everyone listens in silence; then there is boisterous talking and laughing again as we set off. I fall in with a group of freshmen. It's my first opportunity to talk to some of my class-mates, aside from a few quick words between classes.

I spot the girl who sat next to me in math class, Mary Ellen I think she said her name was. The extraordinary friend-liness of everyone boosts my confidence and I strike up a conversation.

"I heard somebody say you're from Los Angeles: that's a long way! You sure have a lot of guts to come so far."

She smiles. "I know. I still can't believe I'm so far from home. This is the first time I've ever been outside California. I really had a hard time persuading my parents to let me come since we don't have enough money for me to fly home for Christmas or anything, but I really felt sure that this was what God wanted me to do. I could have studied to be another kind of nun and stayed closer to home, but I didn't want to. I had the S.B.s in grade school and I think they're the best."

A tall, lanky girl from Boston, Bonnie, now joins the conversation. "I know what you mean. I used to be taught by the Pauline nuns and I didn't like them at all: they were too strict. The S.B.s are really neat, at least the young ones. Our eighth-grade teacher, Sister Mary Louise, was a real doll. Sometimes she'd even stand around the playground after school and talk to us. That's when I first decided I wanted to be a nun. Sister Mary Louise always seemed so happy and peaceful: you could tell she really liked being a nun."

"That sounds like Sister Clare," adds another girl ex-citedly. "She taught our seventh grade and everyone loved her. She really knew how to control the boys. Nobody walked over Sister Clare! But she was really human, too. She had pretty brown eyes and the most gorgeous skin you've ever seen. I'm sure she broke the heart of more than one man when she announced that she was going to enter the convent!"

"Mary Louise, too," says Bonnie. "We were always trying to find out something about her background, but you know how nuns are about letting you know their past: they won't even tell you where they went to school! Finally somebody found out where she went to high school and we got an old yearbook and looked up her picture: she had been prom queen the year before she entered the convent!"

"You guys were sure lucky!" I exclaim. "I've never gone to school to an S.B. I only know about the community through an aunt and a cousin who are nuns."

The offhand remark produces the desired result: all four now give me their full attention. "You have both an aunt and a cousin who are S.B.s?"

"Yeah," I say casually. "It's pretty neat: they're both really cool nuns. My aunt, in fact, went to the Prep School with Sister Joan Ann. Don't tell anyone else I told you this but Sister Joan Ann told me the other day that she and my aunt used to slide down the winding-stairs banister together all the way from the fourth floor to the first floor when they were freshmen!"

We all giggle at the thought of rotund Sister Joan Ann whizzing down the banister, and Bonnie suggests that the four of us try it some time. By the time we arrive at the orchard, we are old friends. "Boston Bonnie, what was it you called a rubber band today: an elastic?"

"Sure, what do *you* call it? I think you guys are the ones who talk funny. Who ever heard of calling tonics soda pops?"

"Tonics!!!" Everyone howls.

"And how about Annie here! Annie, where're you from?"

"Low-v'l, what's the matter with y'all?" says Annie with a grin.

I am astounded by the strange accents, the unusual vocabulary: everyone in our parish had sounded the same, except Mary Lou Lanning who had a lisp. It's beginning to dawn on me that there's a big fascinating world beyond Precious Blood Grammar School and even beyond Peoria.

When we arrive at the orchard, I pull my sweater tight against the crisp bite in the autumn air and listen to a song sung by the older girls as they pick apples.

I help everyone pick apples for future collations. As the sun begins to sink, we head back to Lafayette Hall, past the cannery, where domestic sisters (those who perform various domestic chores instead of teaching) put up apple sauce and apple butter for the long cold winter; past the bakery where fresh loaves of bread are being taken out of ovens and delivered to the various campus buildings in time for supper. Soon the 4:00 bells ring out across the campus calling nuns to Vespers, the afternoon office.

We arrive back at Lafayette Hall with fifteen minutes in which to climb three flights to the dorm, put sweaters away, use the bathroom, wash our faces, and maybe get a fresh handkerchief. When the bell rings, we are once more veiled and lined up outside chapel as we wait for Vespers to end.

When Vespers is over, we say the rosary with the nuns. Mother Mary Rosalie, the order's superior general, leads and since it's Monday, the day for the joyful mysteries, after each decade she announces a specific joyful incident in Mary's life, an incident on which we should meditate during the coming decade.

Once the rosary is said, Benediction follows, a solemn ceremony full of incense and candles and Latin chants. During Benediction, Jesus's Body is removed from the tabernacle for a few moments and placed on the altar in a golden vessel called a *monstrance*. Ancient chants of adoration, "Tantum Ergo" and "O Salutaris," are sung and everyone kneels erect, breathless at the realization that the small host encased in gold is actually the Body of the Lord Himself. If anyone happens into chapel while the Lord's Body is so exposed, instead of performing the usual one-kneed genuflection, she quickly drops to both knees and bows deeply before entering the pew.

At 5:30 there is supper, followed by an hour of study before recreation. I work on a Latin translation and do a page of math problems. I barely finish diagramming ten sentences for English when the recreation bell rings. I had thought I might have time to write to my family, telling them about my first day, but there is barely time to finish my homework! Bonnie and Mary Ellen are waiting for me at the study-hall door, and we head off to recreation together.

One of the older girls is playing the piano when we arrive, and a small group around her is singing. She is picking out the melody the best she can from some popular sheet music she has brought back from vacation.

I edge my way up to the singing group, and sitting down beside the piano player, begin to turn pages for her as we sing. When she is tired of playing, I move to the center of the bench. Tentatively at first, I finger the keys, playing various popular songs; before I know it, there's a crowd around the piano, asking me if I know this song or that song. Being able to play by ear, I manage to accommodate most of the requests. Exhilarated by the experience of being "discovered," I play until I think my fingers will drop off.

It is only after I am in bed that I realize that we have been kept so busy all day long that there has been little time for looking back, for homesickness. Now that it is night, homesickness begins to creep back like some nocturnal thief who stealthily bides his times all day and then tiptoes in when the house is quiet at last. And yet I can tell that the ache in my heart is already beginning to heal itself. I think about Mom and Dad, but I also think about Mary Ellen and Bonnie and wonder if they are sad tonight too: they are so much farther from home than I am.

Sleep is beginning to come now. For a while I nurse my sadness like a warm, comfortable breast, somehow realizing that it won't be long now before I will be weaning myself naturally, effortlessly. I am tired, so tired. It has been a long, long day.

10 ᗌ
SETTLING IN

Following days are much the same: the unvarying routine of my new life settles in around me like a well-worn, trusty blanket. Classes and homework take up much of the day during the week; on Saturdays we clean and press and confess our sins, readying our home, our wardrobe, and our souls for a new week.

Saturday mornings we spend longer at our employments, scrubbing, waxing, buffing, and polishing silver, until all is in readiness for Sunday, the Lord's day. Like housewives buzzing around preparing the house for the husband's arrival, we clean until our knuckles and knees are raw and then hurry upstairs to wash our hair and iron our uniforms. The altar on Sunday will be covered with fresh clean linen and dewy flowers: how insulting it would be to Jesus were we, His future brides, to appear before Him on His special day with dirty hair or mustard spots on our uniforms!

I like Saturdays: compared with the lockstep schedule of the week, they seem freewheeling and easy. Nuns like to keep their floors polished to a high gloss, so each Saturday the school's large industrial buffer makes the rounds from one employment to another. While we are awaiting its arrival or waiting for a coat of wax to dry, there's usually time to wander around to other employments and visit friends. Sometimes we saunter into the kitchen and talk the cook into giving us pecan rolls and coffee left over from breakfast. *Café-au-lait* is the symbol of being grown up in this tiny school where alcohol or cigarettes bring immediate expulsion; eager to prove my coming of age, I quickly acquire a taste, even a craving, for coffee.

Before heading upstairs to wash our hair, we all gather in the rec room for an hour of chorus. A college music major teaches us, pondering seriously as she makes decisions about who are altos and who are sopranos. She does her best to induce us to take "I Dream of Jeanie with the Light Brown Hair" seriously and to breathe from our diaphragms, but suddenly removed from Sister Bernard Clare's ever-watchful eyes, we giggle and cut up and give this brilliant young musical genius (it is whispered that she has already been awarded a scholarship to Juilliard) a generally hard time.

A rough, unadorned room with chipping green paint on the walls and a yellowing crucifix hung between the two windows, Lingerie is so called because it is here that laundry bags are dumped into big laundry carts twice a week, and it is here that we pick up our clean underwear two days later. Each Tuesday and Saturday morning before morning prayers, the silent little nun who works in the campus laundry wheels the cart of dirty laundry onto the rickety old elevator and over to the laundry. Two days later the cart is back, and a small task force of girls is assigned to put the clean clothes into the appropriate boxes. Each girl has a laundry box with her name on it.

I usually go to Lingerie first, before washing my hair, in hopes of using one of the two steam irons. The other irons are the old type without steam.

Before doing anything else, I give my uniform a good brushing with a wire clothes brush, as I do each night. There's a little bowl of water and a black rag, obviously a piece of an old habit, by each iron: wetting the rag I rub each spot until it disappears. For worse spots there's a bottle of ammonia. When I've finished brushing and despotting, I turn my uniform inside out and press it: I cover each pleat with a damp pressing cloth, leaning into it with the iron with all my weight until it surrenders and promises to stay pleated until the next Saturday.

While pressing our uniforms and washing our hair, we

continue the lighthearted bantering and joking. Given the many rules about silence—silence in the dorm, in all halls and on all stairs, in study hall, and en route to chapel—*any* time when conversation is allowed is cherished and celebrated.

Saturday afternoon there is a long walk, followed by time for spiritual house cleaning. For this we gather in the crypt chapel under the main campus church.

The chapel under the larger church is called the crypt chapel because the remains of Mother Matthew and her five cofoundresses are entombed here. Visitors to the crypt take turns kneeling on the wooden kneeler in front of Mother Matthew's tomb; they write special intentions on little slips of paper and touch them to the tomb, praying that through Mother Matthew's intercession they will be granted some favor. Candidates are frequently exhorted to pin a relic of the foundress onto their clothing and to pray for miracles. A lengthy, tedious procedure, *canonization* means official Church recognition that a holy person has attained eternal bliss and can now be called a saint; and Rome usually demands verified miracles as proof of sainthood. Every now and then, the rumor spreads that another miracle has been attributed to Mother Matthew, and we whisper prayers of thanksgiving, confident that our beloved foundress will soon be honored as she deserves.

The crypt chapel is the site of candidates' confessions every Saturday afternoon. We work on our homework in the study hall until the freshmen are called to go to confession. Then we descend the dark, cramped stairs at the back of Church and line up in the wooden pews outside the confessional. Kneeling on the hard wooden kneelers in the crypt's death-smelling semidarkness, we categorize and tabulate our sins in preparation for confession.

I have a gilt-edged devotional book that helps me in my computations: the section entitled "Examination of Conscience for Young Women" provides a number of questions that correspond to each Commandment.

The first Commandment: Have I entertained any doubts against the faith, read any anti-Catholic books, or let myself have feelings of repugnance toward religious practices? Have I consulted fortune tellers or given way to pusillanimity? I mentally check no to all of the above including the pusillanimity: I assure myself that if I can't even pronounce it or define it, I surely couldn't have given way to it.

To some questions I have to answer yes, and I search my actions and attitudes of the past week in order to compute how many times I committed sins in each category. Have I shown annoyance at the advice of priests, parents, or superiors? Have I not tried hard enough to suppress feelings of hostility? Have I yielded to dejection and sadness? Have I eaten or drunk immoderately or studied my palate too carefully? Have I hurt my neighbor's reputation by detraction?

Given my present cloistered life-style, other questions bring chuckles. Have I dressed immodestly or with excessive finery, simply to attract admiration? Have I been to dances and plays of a dangerous nature? Have I sinned through undue familiarity with persons of the other sex or allowed improper liberties to be taken with me? Have I listened to the addresses of a non-Catholic with a view to marriage?

When I have confessed my simple failings to the priest who waits there in the darkness, I join my classmates who are making the stations of the cross, kneeling to pray at each depiction of some point along Christ's way of the cross: Jesus falls the first time, Jesus falls the second time, Jesus is crowned with thorns. Kneeling at each station, I read a little meditation book that helps me see the connection of Jesus's suffering to my life: *my* sins crown Jesus with thorns, *my* faults make him stumble and fall. "My sweet Jesus, I will try this week to do better, to remember that it is You that I hurt every time I fall, every time I sin. Help me to be more mindful!"

When I am through making the stations, I sometimes kneel, feeling a mixture of curiosity and terror, in front of the picture of Christ's bloody face that is the object of so many whispered rumors. Some say the likeness, framed in a semi-dark corner of the crypt, is so gory and realistic that people have been known to faint when they gaze upon it for any length of time. Others say that the picture has been known to ooze real blood when certain particularly holy nuns have knelt before it.

Study time follows, its length dependent on how long I pray in the crypt, and then afternoon prayers. After supper, we leave our black veils in our boxes and take our white ones with us to recreation: now that our home, bodies, clothes, and souls have all been scrubbed fresh and clean, we are ready for the Lord's day, for the start of a new week.

When Sunday finally arrives, we start the day with the incredible pleasure of sleeping late. On rising, we dress in Sunday uniforms and freshly polished Sunday shoes and head off for Maria Chapel, the main campus church.

Maria Chapel is well known for its architectural grandeur, its soaring ceilings, and its imported marble altars, as well as for the pomp and splendor of its liturgical celebrations. Each Sunday, a few moments before 10:00 A.M., the college students dressed in caps and gowns line up in the back of the Church waiting for the processional music to begin. Soon the rich tones of the organ announce the start of the procession, and the students solemnly file in. Once they have taken their places, we slip quietly into side seats behind the marble pillars and crane our necks to see.

Campus chimes announce the hour, the altar is radiant with candles and flowers, and the choir, a carefully selected and trained group of young nuns, stands ready. All the lights go on, everyone stands, and the organ beams again: High Mass begins.

After Mass, we file out unobtrusively so that we are out of the way before the college students solemnly process out of Church two by two; soon they fill the halls with their happy Sunday chatter and the scent of their perfume. By the time they pass our refectory en route to their dining room, pulling off black gowns and mortarboards as they go, we are already having brunch. Though Sister Bernard Clare is always admonishing us to stay away from the college students—"They're of the world, and you're not"—I soon discover that she needn't bother for in their eyes we're just lowly high-schoolers—and pretty weird ones at that! About the only time they even acknowledge our existence on their campus is during these little forays past our refectory on Sunday morning: they peek in our windows and giggle as they point out to their boyfriends the sanctimonious little creeps who clutter up their classy campus.

Sunday afternoon is relaxed and leisurely: we catch up on homework, write long chatty letters to our families, and work on various class projects. On Sunday night we go to bed and the week starts all over again.

With each passing week I am increasingly certain that this simple, orderly life is for me.

What is it about Prep School life that I find so appealing? There are so many things: the simplicity, the orderliness, the sleek singleness of purpose. I give myself totally to God for Him to do with as He wills. All details of my life now fall within that one smooth context: all thoughts that I should be somewhere else, should be doing something else, fade away. God will make His Will known to me if I but listen, if I but keep my heart open. There is no struggle, no adolescent crisis of identity: God has called and I have answered. It's as simple and secure as that.

There are other reasons too why I find the life appealing. For one thing, I am suddenly free to be all that I can be intellectually. I am not restricted by unwritten codes that remind me that boys don't like girls who are too smart, that *no one* likes girls who are DCRs—damned curve raisers: the classrooms of Precious Blood were full of such unwritten codes.

At Precious Blood the nuns always put me along with all the other "good" kids in the back row since they knew they could trust me. "Bad" kids sat up in front so the nuns could keep an eye on them. In these days before the principles of positive reinforcement made teachers aware that attention to negative behavior breeds more negative behavior, Catholic schoolchildren were well aware that one attracts the nun's attention by causing classroom problems. Before I learned what the game was, I was always enthusiastic about my classes, raising my hand whenever I knew an answer. In seventh grade such enthusiasm and participation came to a drastic halt, for whenever I raised my hand the nun would purr benignly, "I know that *you* know it, Mary." Then with the satisfied grin of a cat who has found a fat mouse, she'd call on some ill-fated soul who was napping. At that point I stopped raising my hand altogether.

Being a brain at Precious Blood won no brownie points from peers, and brownie points of questionable practical value from the nuns. At the Prep School, on the other hand, clowns and troublemakers win their share of the laurels, but high grades also boost one's status. There are no handsome quarterbacks for whom to compete, and if there are fashion shows to win, they are of decidedly limited scope. We vie to have the most up-to-date, least-nunny shoes, the shortest skirts (who can hem hers the shortest without being caught?), the most tailored, chic-looking blouses (Ivy League, button-down collars are "in"), and cufflinks that hint of family wealth. Details that no one outside our little world would notice, such as pleats that stay pleated and smocks sewn from a fashionable print, are all noticed by us, full proof that no amount of anti-vanity conditioning can squelch a young girl's desire to look attractive.

Yet it is in the classroom that most of the competing takes place and, an achieving Capricorn by nature, I throw myself into my studies with surprising vengeance. Martha MacIntyre wins plaudits today for an accurate Latin translation; tomorrow I will make sure mine is even more accurate. Anna Fogarty is chosen to read her essay in front of English class as the teacher beams; I will use a flashlight after lights-out to start jotting down notes for an even more-brilliant essay. Teachers in the Prep School spend long hours correcting homework, and a carefully thought-out report is rewarded with carefully thought-out comments and praise, written in red in the margin. Receiving papers with these little ego-boosting comments scrawled in the margin is like receiving a daily fix of heroin. When I occasionally slack off and turn in a mediocre paper, I am deprived of my heroin and become distraught: I quickly pour all my energy into the next day's assignment, and soon my place in the sun is again assured.

It is likewise in the area of peer respect that I find confirmation that I am indeed in the right place.

During the first month, many girls leave: eleven of our original thirty-two are gone by the end of September. There is no official mention of the departures, either before or after, and those who plan to leave are sternly warned to say nothing to their friends. Fearing that one bad apple will spoil the whole batch, superiors take care to remove the bad apple quickly before the effects have a chance to spread. We simply come to breakfast one morning and find an empty chair. Napkin ring and apron are gone. A name is carefully removed from all lists. After the shock and grief and anger at not being told have worn off, the face of one more classmate fades from memory.

Far from being an inhibiting factor, the riskiness and the impermanence of friendship under such conditions only adds to the excitement of burgeoning friendship among the survivors. As buddies begin to find each other and little groups begin to form, I find, to my amazement, that instead of clinging to the edges of some tight-knit, crinolined little clique, I have somehow wound up right at the hub of things. The most popular, influential girls in the class are my best friends: they ask my opinion, laugh at my jokes, and beg me to come sit by them at recreation. Can this really be happening? In an all-girl world I do all right: it is in a world that includes boys that I am an abysmal failure. An old decision accumulates mass far beneath the surface of consciousness.

Despite my new social status, however, the memory of grade-school rejection is still raw, prompting compassion for less-popular classmates. Sniffing out my bleeding heart, a whole coterie of social rejects begins to follow me around. There's Irma, a disheveled mess: a grungy gray slip shows beneath her uneven hem, dandruff covers the shoulders of her uniform, and the cuffs and collars of her blouse are always soiled. The second day we were there, Sister Bernard Clare at evening recreation had reminded us to wash out our blouses that night. After years of experience, she apparently realized that many of the girls in her charge had never had to do anything for themselves at home and needed to be reminded of some of the more basic principles of hygiene. Apparently she underestimated the extent of the ignorance in such matters, however: a month after we were there, Irma practically raised the roof—and cleared the room!—by asking when Sister Bernard Clare was going to tell us to wash our blouses again.

Poor Irma. Nobody told me that the most loving thing I could do for her would be to tell her the truth. Unwilling to hurt her feelings, I lecture myself as I have so often been lectured, reminding myself that Irma, like every other member of the Mystical Body of Christ, the church, is an *alter Christus,* another Christ, and that I should accept her exactly the way she is. With clenched teeth I dole out all the tolerance I can muster in the name of Christian charity.

There are others, too, buck-toothed girls with glasses as thick as cola-bottle bottoms who try to atone for their ugliness by nonstop wittiness that isn't witty, and girls who whine about their various illnesses or about how homesick they are: all of them gravitate to Mother Mary Agnes and she always has time for them. My friends ask why I let such losers hang around me. I too begin to feel that I am eaten alive by parasites, but I don't know how to cut them off without hurting their feelings.

This commitment to never, ever hurt anyone's feelings places a definite burden on me; yet nothing detracts from my overall sense of having found my niche in life. Peace of mind, intellectual satisfaction, peer acceptance: the hundredfold of heavenly happiness that Christ promises to those who leave all things to follow Him seems already to have arrived.

Were I to have any lingering doubts that I have found my niche, the wide range of opportunities that the Prep School offers by reason of its smallness and its location on a college campus are enough to put an end to the doubts once and for all. Because of the school's tiny size, there is ample opportunity for each girl to experiment with different talents and interests, to be a big fish in some section of the tiny pond. Within two months I am holding my own as a guard on our freshman basketball team, I who could hardly catch a kickball. I practice my lines for a leading role in the freshman play, take lifeguard training, play the piano in the school orchestra, and provide much of the accompaniment for school musical productions.

Because of our location on a college campus there are opportunities that never would have been available to me had I attended Saint Malachy's High School in Peoria. Practically every week there is some cultural offering in the college auditorium: a lecture on modern art, a Shakespearean play presented by a touring company, a ballet performance, a group of madrigal singers. Frequently, Prep School students provide the entire audience, aside from a handful of relatives and friends, for senior music recitals. These expose us to a wide range of piano, organ, harp, flute, and vocal music. There are movies, plays, and concerts, and—as long as we sit quietly in the auditorium balcony, laughing and clapping only when the college students laugh and clap—we are welcome to attend all of them.

When we're not praying, studying, recreating, or "getting cultured" as we put it, any remaining cracks in our schedules are filled with class projects and celebrations. One of the first things I learn as part of my overall Prep School training is the fact that nuns love celebrations and they will find any excuse—be it a saint's feast or the end of exams or a first snowfall—to hang crepe paper and balloons, prepare skits and songs, request cake and ice cream from the kitchen, and generally whoop it up, nun's style.

As freshmen we will be responsible for our share of the celebrations, but first we need to come together as a class and to make some decisions. We need to vote on class patron, colors, and motto. So in a noisy, rambunctious meeting in late September we choose red and white for our colors, red for fortitude and white for purity. With an eye to the coming basketball tournament when we will play the extraordinarily athletic sophomores, we choose Saint Jude, patron of hopeless cases, as our patron; instead of the J.M.J. (Jesus, Mary, Joseph) we are required to write at the top of our school papers, we now resolve to write J.M.J.J., the extra J, of course, representing our beloved patron Jude and proudly proclaiming our sisterhood under his auspices.

As if to leave Saint Jude an out, however, we choose as our class motto "Not my will but Thine be done." In the sad eventuality that we *lose* the tournament, we'll be able to attribute our defeat to the Will of God rather than to any lack on the part of our patron.

Once we have handled these matters of class identity, we begin preparations for the Foundation Day party, a traditional freshman responsibility. Celebrated in early October, Foundation Day honors Mother Matthew's original arrival in America and her foundation of the American Sisters of Blessing. We decorate the refectory with fancy centerpieces and table favors, drawing on the creative skills of freshmen who are artistically inclined; those more creative in other areas write funny songs and skits for evening recreation. Each girl's talents are utilized in some way.

Halloween nears, another freshman responsibility. A

classmate's father sends money for decorations and refreshments, and she is appointed chairman of the event. She selects me as her assistant—I feel so important!—and she and I, along with Bernie Clare, take a cab into town to buy supplies. It is the first time we have been off-campus since coming to the Prep School, and we have a marvelous time: we buy cider and doughnuts and candy corn and every kind of prop for the haunted house that we will set up in the rec room. Yet when the day is over and we return to Saint Raphael's, I realize that "the world" out there is beginning to look less and less attractive to me. Everyone in town had seemed so strained, and harried, rushing here and there; returning to Saint Raphael's is like returning to peace.

Once Halloween is over, we begin plans for the November birthday party which will honor all those born in September, October, and November. There will be four of these parties through the school year so that everyone's birthday is eventually honored. As in so many things, we are being introduced to conventual customs, but in a gradual way. In the convent the celebration of birthdays—reminders of one's earthly roots—will be strictly forbidden. Here, birthdays are played down, celebrated only by these group parties. Feast days, on the other hand, will be celebrated with much hoopla: each canonized saint has an assigned feast day, a day when that saint and all namesakes are honored by Catholics throughout the world. For example, when my birthday arrives, I will receive packages and greetings from home, but the day will be pretty much ignored by school friends. A few days later, however, on the feast of Saint Agnes, I will be showered with feast-day gifts and cards.

11 🙰.
VISITING SUNDAY

The minute I wake up, I know there is something different in the air. I long to get up, to put on my robe and slippers, and to go to see what it is. But I remember the rule about not getting up before the bell rings in the morning. I turn over and try to sleep again, to take advantage of Sunday morning's luxuriously late rising, but I find I am too excited. We will rise as usual, attend Mass, then have brunch. We will gather in the study hall to try to study. One by one our names will be called and we will descend the front marble stairs: the day for which we all have been waiting so long will begin. It is November 8, 1957, our first Visiting Sunday.

For two weeks now we have talked of nothing else. Yesterday, Lingerie was a hive of activity as everyone brushed her Sunday uniform, then brushed it again and ironed it until the pleats were shiny. Shoes were shined until we could see our faces in them, and brand-new blouses and handkerchiefs were taken from our trunks for the occasion. Lying in bed I mentally go over each detail for the twentieth time and finger each pin curl to be sure it has remained bobby-pinned in place through the night. There are sounds throughout the dorm as other nonsleepers shuffle around in their alcoves, handling last-minute details: I hear the scrape of metal brushes as suede shoes are brushed once again, the sound of bobby pins dropping into fruitcake boxes. Rule or no rule, I decide that nobody's going to get the jump on me on this day of all days: I rise from bed and begin to make my bed as I wait for the bell to ring.

Still the air has that peculiar stillness, a hush and softness that mutes the edges of the bitter-cold monastic morning. Living now closer to nature in the midst of the woods, I have developed a new sensitivity to all of nature's subtle little shifts, and I again ask myself what is so different about this morning. The bell rings, and as soon as I emerge from my alcove I have my answer.

Small groups of silent, breathless girls are clustered around the big old windows. I edge my way to the front so that I too can see: *snow!* The campus has become a fairyland scene too pristine for words. My eyes fill with tears as I realize what a beautiful gift Jesus has given me, just one of many constant little gifts He has bestowed on me now that I am His own. Our first visiting Sunday, our first snowfall: the joy of it all caresses my heart, reminding me that I am loved eternally and unconditionally, that I do indeed walk a path that is blessed. "Thank you, Jesus, thank you," I whisper, convinced again that such peace and contentment is worth any sacrifice that is asked of me.

Mass and brunch seem to go ever so slowly: I pick at a sausage and take a few bites of a pancake. I try to imagine how close to the campus they are by now. Are they as excited as I am? Will they be one of the first families to arrive? The reader drones on; will brunch never end?

When brunch is over at last, I receive permission to go to the dorm. I again comb my hair and brush my uniform and check the mirror to be sure that my pleats are hanging straight. Though not usually so compulsive about my appearance—more usually, in fact, eschewing such a preoccupation as worldly and vain—I am nevertheless by now fully addicted to ritual, and my only way of ritualizing such a special day is to surround it with little combing, brushing, and pressing ceremonies.

The snow is still coming down as I enter study hall, and for a moment I stand at a window and watch as it lines the branches of the tall pines outside the windows. The thought that Dad might be even now swearing at this early snow and at the consequently bad roads never occurs to me. Snow, for me, has no negative qualities.

As a child I would wake on a snowy morning and listen to the radio news as Mother stirred the oatmeal: "There will be no school today for public schools on the south side of Peoria. These Catholic schools will also be closed today: "Saint Bernadette, Little Flower, Precious Blood. . . ." A whoop would go up throughout the house, except by Mother who would have us under her feet all day: "No school! Hooray!" Noses would press against the windows as we would try to calculate if the snow was sticking and if there would be enough to build a fort in the backyard.

Carless, carefree life at Saint Raphael's will prolong my childlike love for snow through nine winters. While others dig their cars out of the snow and struggle to start them, or cancel airplane trips because cities are snowbound, snow to me will simply mean idyllic winter scenes and snowball fights and tobogganing adventures followed by steaming-hot cocoa. In this as in so many things, convent life, by removing responsibilities and worldly concerns, will prolong a state of wide-eyed, stargazing childlikeness, and for this I will one day be ever so grateful.

Sitting down at my desk, I take out a book and try to study. Two aisles away, Bonnie and Mary Ellen are both crying silently as they write long letters to their families: I know that today will be hard on both of them since neither family can afford the long trip to see their daughter. I take out two of my favorite holy cards and write little messages assuring them that I'll be thinking of them today and that I'll save some of Mom's chocolate-chip cookies for them. (Mom had written to ask what kind of special goodies I wanted her to bake for the big day, and chocolate-chip cookies had been at the top of the list.)

I have just delivered both notes when Sister Joan Ann enters the front of the room and reads a list of names of girls whose families have arrived. "Deborah Heitner, Alice

O'Toole, Laura Schmidt, Barbara Jones, Mary Agnes Gilligan. . . ."

My heart pounds and my knees begin to tremble: the moment has arrived at last. I walk back to my desk and, trying to act calm, put my book away. My friends are not deceived. "Calm down!" they giggle as I stumble past their desks, kicking over stacks of books along the way. I hurry down the front marble stairs and into the lobby, and sure enough, there they are, all six of them as excited as I am. We kiss and hug and kiss again. The kids tug at my arms, tug at my clothes, fighting over who's going to hold my hand, and I long for arms long enough to hold them all at once.

"You look great, Toots, but have you lost a little weight?" Dad beams, hugging me. Mom squeezes me tight, crying: "I cry when I'm happy too, you know!" she grins through her tears. The kids vie with each other to be the first to tell me all the latest news from home.

"Did you hear that Spunagles' house got robbed?"

"No fair! I wanted to tell her that!"

"Why don't you tell her about the puppies?"

"Oh yeah—the O'Tooles' dog had puppies!"

I *ooh* and *aah* at all the news. Pat joined the Future Priests' Club, Andi's room was painted, Dan got an A in arithmetic, and Cathy started piano lessons.

Eventually I laugh and tell them we've got all day: they don't have to fill me in on everything all at once! I get my coat from my locker and ride with them in the car around to the back of the campus.

"Did you know Mom made chocolate-chip cookies for you?" A subtle hint.

"Well, where are they? Let's dig in!" The box is quickly produced, and, queen for a day, I pass the cookies around for the hungry beggars to sample. Remembering Bonnie and Mary Ellen, I somehow manage to get the lid back on while there are still a few left.

In a little wooden lodge, a popular gathering place for

college-girl picnics and outings, Dad builds a fire and we all huddle around it, mellow with the joy of once more being together. Mom brings out hotdogs for roasting; there's also baked beans and my favorite kind of potato salad and, afterward, Mom's cottage-cheese pie, another favorite. Two other prep school families also spread their lunches in the lodge: from time to time we exchange a few words, but for the most part each family keeps to itself, savoring these precious moments of having the family back together again.

When lunch is finished the kids go out to play in the snow, and Mom and Dad and I head into the recreation room where the other candidates have gathered with their families. I parade my parents around to meet all my friends: I want them to see how well liked I am and to assure them that they'll never again have to worry about my social status. We sit around and talk for a while and decide to drive around campus to check out some of the little shrines we always visited when we came here to see my aunt and my cousin.

The day passes quickly, and when the 3:00 P.M. bell rings out over the campus I stop talking immediately, right in the middle of a sentence. My parents have often seen my aunt and cousin stop midsentence like this to unite with Sisters of Blessing throughout the world at the sound of the 3:00 P.M. bell. I've been here less than two months and already I know the prayer by heart, showing that I am a real part of this community. I can tell they're impressed.

There isn't much time left now, and it is starting to become cold outside, so we make a fire in the lodge and roast marshmallows. I feel a chill *inside* when I realize that this glorious day is almost over. I feel again as I did when I left them the first time: in a kind of a panic to make the last minutes as beautiful as possible, to stockpile all the loving and hugging and tender touching, to roll it all up into a ball that I can unwind in lonely moments. It is probably the physical closeness that I have missed more than anything: the cuddling, the snuggling, the tiny hands placed so trustingly in mine.

Time is beginning to hang now, heavy and ponderous. We grope for things to say, something to make these last few minutes more bearable. Finally Dad says they have had a great day, but he wants to get an early start before it gets too dark. The kids have school tomorrow and they shouldn't go to bed too late. Besides, Christmas isn't that far off now.

One part of me wants to protest, to persuade him to stay right to the last minute. Another part of me knows that he's right, that he is in effect letting us all off the hook of lengthy, torturous good-byes.

I help them pack the car as I blink back tears. Saying good-bye is still hard, but I notice to my amazement that it is not nearly as hard as it had been the first day. Is this the way it will be: will it keep becoming easier and easier, until good-byes no longer open wounds that otherwise are healing nicely?

This time I wave bravely as they pull away. My thoughts turn to Bonnie: I wonder how she is doing, how she has weathered the day of meeting everyone else's families, moving from one to another like an orphan.

It suddenly dawns on me that something has shifted. The last time, leaving had meant saying good-bye to my family and walking into a whole new situation, a world of strangers. This time I am leaving people I love in order to be with people I am growing to love, and that makes all the difference in the world.

I no longer feel chilly inside as I walk back into Lafayette Hall. In fact, as I see the lights going on in the windows, I feel the same way I always felt when I came back to the house at the end of a day of playing in the neighborhood. The kitchen light would be on, and as I came in the back door I could smell supper on the stove. I felt content and loved, completely at home.

That is the way I feel now, although it surprises me a little bit to think how quickly this has happened: Saint Raphael's is starting to feel like home.

THANKSGIVING

Thanksgiving arrives, and college and commercial students leave to spend the weekend with their families. Since we won't be going home (a first transitional step toward the day when we won't spend *any* holidays with our families) our superiors keep our minds off the Thanksgiving dinners that we are missing by making sure that every minute of the weekend is filled. Excitement surrounding the Thanksgiving basketball tournament, where seniors play juniors and sophomores play freshmen, is whipped to a high peak. For days ahead of time, those who will play in the tournament spend every spare moment in the gym, practicing shots and plotting strategies, while those who won't be playing elect cheerleaders, make pompoms, and decorate the gym with streamers representing the various class colors.

Only when the excitement of the day is past does the reality hit me that it's Thanksgiving and I'm not home with my family. Only then do silent, bitter tears come.

I think back to last year's Thanksgiving when the house was packed with so many relatives that some of them had to eat on TV trays in my room: they had all come to celebrate my last Thanksgiving at home. After the last piece of mince pie was devoured, the women gathered in the living room and the men retired to a back room to drink beer and play poker. We kids went outside to ride bikes. I was still just Mary, then: now I am Mary Agnes, future nun, and I will never go home for Thanksgiving again. I cry until there are no tears left to cry.

Soon after Thanksgiving, we mark the first Sunday of Advent, the season of preparation for Christmas, by lighting a purple candle on the traditional advent wreath in study hall. Like the advent wreath we had always lit at home, it is fashioned of pine branches and sits festooned with purple ribbons in a place of honor. Each of the four candles is lit on a different Sunday leading up to Christmas: there are three purple candles denoting the darkness of the world without Christ (these are lit on the first three Sundays of Advent, and a fourth pink candle is lit on Gaudete [Rejoice] Sunday, the Sunday right before Christmas). My heart dances when I realize that I'll be home in time to light the last candle: Christmas vacation will begin the week before.

December days crackle with excitement: not only is Christmas almost here, but we're actually going home! Rec room, refectory, and study hall are all gaily decorated (though a jolly Santa candle on Bonnie's dresser is quickly confiscated), and practically every evening is spent in final rehearsals for the freshman Christmas play.

13 §

CHRISTMAS VACATION

Christmas vacation arrives at last, and, breathless with excitement, I put on worldly clothes and lipstick and join the fashion parade of girls strutting through the halls, modeling their stylish wardrobes, proving to each other that they really *do* know there is life out there beyond bells and schedules and blue-serge uniforms.

Irma, smelling as bad as usual in her civvies and looking

even worse, rushes up and hugs me: "All for Thee most Sacred Heart of Jesus," I pray silently as the odor overwhelms me. "You *are* going to write me, aren't you, Aggie?" she asks petulantly. Again remembering Christ's injunction to love the unlovable—after all, Irma meets the job description perfectly—I catch my breath and assure her, with as much Christ-like love as I can muster, "Of course, you mean a lot to me."

Jenny comes racing up, stunning in a straight wool skirt and matching sweater, her blonde hair clean and shiny. Once in the odor zone, she gives Irma a long contemptuous look, starts to say something, but changes her mind. Holding me at arm's length she surveys my going-home outfit: "You look gorgeous, angel child!" she marvels, and then hugs me. Picking up her suitcase, she gives me one last bit of sisterly advice: "You be good, but not *too* good, y'hear?" Thinking ahead to the predictable round of holiday shopping, cooking, decorating, and quiet visits with friends that will fill my days, I return her wink and knowing smile, saying nothing.

Jenny heads off down the hall, her spike heels and sexy, sparkling aliveness an affront to sterile convent corridors. For a moment I want to run after her, to beg her as my angel to help me one last time. Maybe she can tell me: is there some cure for terminal goodness that I don't know about? Some safe proven way "out," where I don't have to hurt anyone or disappoint my parents or rock any boats? But Jenny is gone now— the winter sun catches the gold of her charm bracelet as she turns and waves one last time.

Left to answer my own question, I remind myself that exciting holidays, like so many other things in life, are undoubtedly the sole prerogative of tiny blonde cheerleader types like Jenny, that such golden girls undoubtedly have problems of their own: who would want to be liked just for her looks?

Finally, I decide that staying around the house baking chocolate-chip cookies isn't really so bad.

As the familiar Chevy pulls up in front of the fountain, I kiss and hug the rest of my friends. Bonnie is flying home to Boston, and Mary Ellen is spending the holidays with a classmate's family in Chicago. Dad carries my suitcase to the trunk (the entire family has come to get me), and soon we are on our way, singing Christmas carols the whole way home.

Arriving home, I am struck by how small the house feels: almost like a dollhouse. Having gotten used to ceilings that soar high, I now feel constricted, almost claustrophobic in this house of my growing up. Or is it that there are now parts of me that don't seem to fit here, parts that have budded in the few short months that I have been away?

The pin-neat order of the house also strikes me, and I again remember that I am no longer plain old Mary; I am Mary Agnes, future nun. Everyone has worked for days to get the house ready for my coming, as I used to help to ready it for the coming of special guests. It will be this way throughout the three-week vacation: I will be treated like visiting royalty. Mom will cook all my favorite meals; Dad will bring home special treats from the bakery.

Dad carries my suitcase up to my room, and I follow close behind him. I am relieved when I find that everything has been left exactly the way I left it. When Dad leaves, I put on a pair of jeans and an old sweater and hurry off to honor my vow. Once there, perched high in the apple tree—*my* apple tree—I again connect with all that I was before I became Mary Agnes. I sit there for a long time, wondering if Mary and Mary Agnes will ever meet and meld instead of fighting all the time. Eventually Mom calls from the back door, announcing supper.

Mom has fixed smoked sausages and fried apples. Mary kisses her and thanks her for cooking her very favorite supper; Mary Agnes is mortified when Dad and Pat put their elbows on the table.

During the first few days at home, Mary Agnes holds sway as I seek to share my new cultural enlightenment with the not-so-enlightened back at home. I do my best to teach my hopelessly boorish brothers and sisters some manners—that you don't cut up pancakes all at once, but cut a row at a time with your knife and then cut off little pieces with your fork; that when you take a piece of bread off the bread plate, you should be careful not to let your fingers brush the other pieces; and that your knife should always be turned *toward* you when you lay it across your plate.

For a while, eager to please and grateful to have me back, everyone is most cooperative. Dad watches in amusement and Mother sighs: "I did my best to teach them. Maybe they'll listen to you." Mother herself had studied with the Sisters of Blessing and had done her best to carry a sense of refinement and good breeding into family life. But white linen tablecloths had become stained with baby food, silver spoons had been sneaked outside for backyard digging, a potential formal dining room had been preempted as a nursery for yet another baby, and the lawn of her dreams had become a neighborhood baseball diamond. "The kids will only be young once," Dad had reminded her when she protested, and as usual she had given in, knowing he was right.

Eventually, as days pass and the boarding-school conditioning begins to wear off a bit (Mother knew it would), I settle into old ways and everyone breathes a sigh of relief. Mary is home at last.

Days pass quickly as Christmas nears: there is much to be done. The *crèche* scene that Dad gave to Mom on their first anniversary is set up under the tree, and all the little statues, except that of the Babe of Bethlehem, are arranged inside. Like Santa Claus, the Babe will come in the dark of night on Christmas Eve. The younger children ask many questions: Where did the three kings come from? What's myrrh? How did the shepherds know to follow the star?

Eventually, however, they are in over their theological heads, and I do my best to elucidate Church doctrine.

"What do you mean Joseph isn't Mary's husband?"

"God is Mary's husband, and she can't have two husbands, can she?"

"Well, no, but . . ."

"Because she was so holy, God chose her to marry Him and to be the mother of His Son Jesus."

"But . . ."

"Joseph was more like a protector. He never touched Mary or did anything vulgar: he just took care of Mary and the Christ Child."

"But (the objection is finally blurted out) I thought it took a man and a woman together to make a baby, not just a woman. I don't get how . . ."

At this point Mother jumps in and saves the day. "But, you see, God can perform miracles whenever He wants, like the time Jesus walked on water and the time He changed water into wine. Sometimes we just have to take things on faith without asking too many questions. Nonbelievers ask questions."

Abruptly changing the subject, she now asks, "Does anyone know who else is going to get married to God?" Pat throws another handful of tinsel on the tree and says, "Yeah, Mary." "That's right," she beams. "That's why we're all so proud of her, right?" Everyone says, "Right."

The reality of what this convent thing is all about is starting to hit Cathy, the youngest, bit by bit, and she now asks incredulously: "You mean you won't have babies when you grow up?"

I swallow hard, but again Mom comes to the rescue: "Oh, she'll have children, lots and lots of children," she says cheerfully, "but they won't come out of her tummy: she'll be a teacher and all the kids in her classes will be like her children."

Not overly impressed with the explanation, Cathy nevertheless decides to drop the discussion and climb up on my lap. "Don't worry," she whispers as she nestles close, "I'll always

be your baby. Just don't go away to school again, *please!!*"
Blinking back tears, I assure her that the vacation's going to be
very, very long, which doesn't really comfort her much, but
too tired to protest, she drifts off to sleep. I hold her tight and
dread the day when someone breaks the news to her that I
have just three more Christmases left at home, that there will
come a day when I will leave and not return.

Sensing the gloom that has fallen over the room, Dad
says, "Hey, why such long faces? It's Christmas!" I pick up
Cathy and carry her up to bed. I sit on the edge of her bed and
cry for a while, then I splash some water on my face, come
downstairs, and join in "Deck the Halls."

One of the hardest things about being at home is the
pressure I feel to be happy all the time. In the Prep School
where superiors seem to lurk in all the corners of our lives,
there is little time or place for private grief. If we seek privacy
in the dorm, for example, closed alcove curtains during the
day quickly bring the sound of approaching beads, a probing
interrogation.

At least in the Prep School, however, I can always escape
to the chapel: it's a great place to hide if you feel blue or just
want to be by yourself for awhile. You can cry your eyes out as
you read and reread a letter from home: it's hard to distinguish
you from the pious types who are crying in repentence for
their sins. You can read a forbidden book that you brought
from home. (*Forbidden* doesn't necessarily mean pornography.
The only books allowed have either a spiritual theme or are
required for some class.) As long as you take care to cover the
jacket with a plain brown cover, everyone will think that you
are pursuing spiritual growth by reading some holy work. Like
outlaws in the churches of old, we find sanctuary in the
chapel.

At home there is no chapel refuge; there is only my bedroom. This is an adequate hideout for a while, but only until
Dad notices that I am missing from whatever the rest of the

family is doing at the moment. There must be something wrong: did someone upset me? Soon there is a familiar knock at my door and Dad stands on the threshold, waiting to be invited in. He small-talks at first: he'll have to show me the nice robe he bought for Mom; the weather forecaster says we may have snow for Christmas; he thinks that Cathy may suspect about Santa Claus. Eventually, when he realizes that he's doing all of the conversing, he suggests that I call up some of my old friends and invite them over for caroling tomorrow night ("Thanks, Dad, but I think I'd rather just kind of stay around here. . . ."), that the Jackie Gleason show will be on in ten minutes ("Maybe I'll be down later. Right now I just want to sit here and watch the snow fall for a while. I promise, Dad, I'm OK. Don't worry about me!").

But Dad *does* worry, of course, and later that night after the house is quiet, when Mom and Dad at last have a few moments together in the quiet of their bedroom, they talk, as usual, about their children, and Dad brings up his concerns.

"I don't know, Amy; she seemed kind of sad tonight. Are you sure everything's OK with her?"

"I think maybe she's just missing her friends a little bit."

"Missing her friends?" The thought has never occurred to Dad. Of course, that's it: she misses her friends! She's probably bored at home and can't wait to get back to school! He falls asleep much relieved.

Meanwhile, up in my room, I watch the sleeping faces of my brothers and sisters and miserlike count my gold: remaining days at home are precious nuggets. I want to be careful to spend them wisely.

Only a few days remain before Christmas now. We light our fourth Advent candle and sing "O Come, O Come Emmanuel." Since the beginning of Advent I have been saying the Christmas miracle prayer every day. Mother says that if you say it fifteen times every day without missing a word right up until Christmas Day, Our Lady will reward you by answering all your Christmas wishes. Sometimes I fall asleep on my knees by the bed before the fifteen are finished, but always I rouse myself, start at the beginning of the prayer again, and keep plugging away until I am absolutely sure I have completed fifteen.

Each day the number of incoming Christmas cards grows, and we hang them on a ribbon along the wall. Protestants send cards with holly wreaths or candy canes on the front, which shows their lack of awareness of Christmas's deeper meaning. Catholics send nativity scenes. Dad is especially furious when people sign their cards *Merry Xmas*, leaving Christ out altogether: "It's becoming a pagan feast," he says sadly, resolving to do all he can to put Christ back into Christmas.

When Christmas Eve arrives, the family as usual spurns the big, showy Christmas Eve midnight Mass, opting instead to fulfill their Sunday obligation at a simple quiet Mass on Christmas morning. This way sleepy children won't have to be dragged out into the midnight cold; besides, who needs such ostentation?

After Christmas I continue to accompany my parents to Mass each morning. Pious women coo all over me after Mass as Mom and Dad beam.

"I think it's so wonderful what you're doing. Lord knows we need more young people like you! God bless you, Mary. We're proud of you."

The parish nuns hover over me, too, asking me how I'm doing and reminding me not to neglect my prayers during the vacation. "We should never take a vacation from God!"

There is only one other teenager at Mass, Michael Kilty, a thin, solemn youngster who attends the minor seminary. He and I exchange nods and perfunctory smiles each morning as we leave Church, but we never talk. In his third year at the seminary, Michael has already been taught the dangers of too much contact with the female of the species and has heard story after story of seminarians and priests who have been led astray by the wiles of a woman. The rector's prevacation speech always compares women with bees: "Never forget, boys, that women are like bees: they'll make honey for you, but they'll sting you if you get too close." Michael never gets too close.

A few times over the holidays, I get together with old girlfriends from Precious Blood: they are eager to hear all about the Prep School and we sit around drinking cola and eating pretzels while I tell them funny stories. They especially like the story about our math teacher who always spits when she talks and about how Katie, who sits in the front row, solved the problem by one day putting up an umbrella when the spit started flying. Katie came close to being expelled, but the nun curtailed her spitting considerably. My friends like this story and other stories of similar boarding-school antics.

Toward the end of the vacation, the mother of a Peoria candidate, Margaret Andrews, throws a party for all the Peoria candidates. Everything is formal and proper: a lace tablecloth covers a mahogany table, and the table is set with fine china and crystal. There are name cards and little ceramic swans at each place, and everyone uses her best convent-school manners.

Feigning a headache, I call Dad and ask him to pick me up early. As I wait for his knock at the door, I daintily pick at a hard, perfectly rectangular block of Neopolitan ice cream. Unlike ice cream cones at home which sometimes melt and run down your chin, observing no firm, prissy boundaries, even the ice cream in this ladylike world is tightly, coldly corseted. I can't wait for Dad's knock at the door.

Mary Agnes's silly longings for refinement and elegance clamor no more: Mary is back in charge. It is Mary who wants to get out of here as fast as she can, feeling that her very presence here among the "riddie-biddies" (my family's word for the rich) is a betrayal of her simple, nonmaterialistic roots. It is Mary who looks forward to the ride home when she and Dad will laugh and cut up and crack jokes about people who live in big houses and drive big cars and think they're better than other people.

If Mary Agnes has any lingering opinions of her own, any high-brow aspirations, she doesn't breathe a word of them to anyone—even to Mary. Her day will come soon enough. For now she watches in silence as Mary takes her last stand.

14 ❧

SECOND SEMESTER

When we return to Saint Raphael's the seniors move on to the next step of their training, the novitiate. We sometimes pass them on walks and wave to them; no other contact is allowed.

Our big sisters, the juniors, are now in charge: they handle all senior duties such as ringing bells and locking up the building at night, and they wear the little white crosses that indicate that they are next in line for the novitiate.

I am homesick for a few days—vacation has opened an old wound—but soon I am involved in my comfortable little routine again, happy to be back with my friends.

"Hey Maggie, we've been looking for you. Come play the piano so we can sing."

A familiar nickname, a familiar welcome: I sit at the piano and soon all thought of home is once more forgotten, washed away in an ocean of friendship and song.

The months after Christmas bring more parties and feasts, more convent counterparts to worldly feasts. On Saint Valentine's Day, for example, while girls in the world send lacy valentines to special male friends, Prep School celebration revolves around Jesus, our future Spouse. A junior is selected to represent each of us as Jesus's valentine sweetheart: she dresses in a long white gown and, announced by trumpets and surrounded by attendants, processes into the refectory to take her place of honor next to a red-robed Little King statue.

Sister Bernard Clare, at instructions, continues the Jesus-as-Sweetheart theme:

Just as in the world a boy asks a girl for a date, in the same way Jesus, the Divine Lover, beckons you from His lonely tabernacle to come be His date. How He longs for you to come visit Him there, to whisper little words of love and offer little caresses of mortification. . . .

My girlish heart is moved: Jesus is courting me. Old day-dreams of wedding bells and orange blossoms now return, and I begin to look forward to the day when I will join myself forever to this Divine Bridegroom.

There are parties and feast days, movies and plays. There are silver trays of candy at recreation each night and hot cobbler for dessert each Tuesday and Thursday. We walk and sing and laugh until our sides hurt. We study and swim and play basketball and then drop into bed and fall immediately to sleep.

And through it all, I am spurred on to greater and greater academic achievement by the red-inked comments: "Good job, Mary Agnes." "Original insight, Mary Agnes." The praise tastes even better than the silver-trayed candy and the Thursday hot cobbler, and I do everything in my power to keep it coming. I carry around French vocabulary in a little notebook, practicing it over and over as I sweep a floor or wait in line for chapel; I ponder a report for religion class, thrashing it out in my mind as I make my bed. No moment is wasted: Mary Agnes will *not* be outdone.

Before we know it, Easter nears and Bernie surprises us with the news that Reverend Mother has decided to let us go home for Easter. Home for Easter: it is a reprieve beyond our wildest dreams. Our minds awhir at the thought of brightly colored eggs and juicy Easter ham and the frilly Easter clothes we thought we had put behind us once and for all, we write our parents and tell them the good news.

By the time I arrive home, thirty days of Lent are already behind me with only ten left to go. Protestant kids are already scarfing down jelly beans and chocolate eggs. I watch them sadly, knowing that they are missing Easter's true meaning.

For us Catholics, preparation for Easter began back on Ash Wednesday when the priest pressed ashes onto our foreheads, reminding us not to put too much stock in earthly life since we started as dust and would one day return to dust. In grade school, the vain and worldly among us always washed off the ashes as soon as possible, but those of us who were more devout always left them on all day. Protestant kids would tease "Your face is dirty!" but we knew that that was what being a Christian was: being willing to stand up for your convictions. Unlike Peter who three times denied knowing Christ on that fateful night in the Garden of Olives, we professed our allegiance loud and clear.

On the first Sunday of Holy Week, Palm Sunday, I attend Mass with my family. In remembrance of the palms that the people carried when they welcomed Jesus into Jerusalem, palms are blessed by the priest and passed out to the congregation. Each person carries a palm in a procession around the Church and then takes it home, braids it into fancy strands, and tucks it behind a picture of the Sacred Heart of the Blessed Mother. Through the year our palms will remind us not to be like the people of Jerusalem who greeted Jesus with enthusiastic hosannahs and then turned their backs on Him before the week was ended. Carrying my palm, I ask Jesus to help me persevere in my vocation so that I will never, ever turn my back on Him.

On Holy Thursday, the day of Christ's last supper, the

sacred Host, Jesus's Body, is removed from the tabernacle and exposed on the altar in the same golden monstrance used at Benediction. Since it would be unthinkable to leave Jesus exposed on the altar with no one to visit Him, parishioners sign up to take the "watch" at all hours of the day and night.

Mother and I sign up for the 1:00 A.M. watch, and as I kneel there trying to keep my eyes open, she prays devoutly, ramrod straight. How does she do it: take care of a house and five kids, and still have so much fervor? I feel hopelessly inadequate next to her. I again hear Christ's rebuke to His sleeping disciples: "Could you not watch one hour with me?" Defeated again by my own laziness and my lack of self-discipline, I spend most walking moments in self-disgust. Only the realization that self-disgust can be a prayer in itself consoles me. *"Mea culpa, mea culpa, mea maxima culpa"* we pray at Mass, beating our breasts in self-loathing. "Through my fault, through my fault, through my most grievous fault": in such self-loathing is the Lord pleased.

At 2:00 A.M. other watchers come to take our place, and we go home and crawl back into bed. A few short hours later we wake to one of the most solemn days of the year, Good Friday.

The whole family attends church services between 12:00 P.M. and 3:00 P.M., the hours when Jesus hung on the cross. The Litany of the Saints is chanted, *"Santa Francesca, ora pro nobis, Santa Lucia, ora pro nobis . . . "*; then the priest in solemn purple vestments puts a large crucifix in the center of the Communion rail, and one by one we come to kiss it. The Church is silent, tomblike: all the statues have been covered with purple shrouds since the beginning of Lent, clappers are used instead of bells, and the organ is turned off. Everyone stands during the account of Christ's suffering, His "passion" . . . my legs tremble from standing in one place so long, but I remind myself that this is nothing compared with what Jesus suffered. Eventually the priest reads, "And then Jesus expired," at which time we kneel and bow our heads.

When the service is over, Christ's Body is removed from the tabernacle and the tabernacle light is extinguished. The tabernacle door is left ajar, a further reminder that Christ is no longer present in the Church. For two days we will experience what we know the Protestants must feel when they pray in their empty churches, devoid as they are of the Real Presence.

Good Friday afternoon is gray and bleak, and as usual there is rain. We return home and watch the blackening sky in awe, reminding each other that all of nature cries on this sad day. Protestant friends, blind to all of this, call and ask if we want to come over, if we want to go to a movie or something, and we assure them that we wouldn't think of pursuing our own pleasure on such a mournful day. If we keep doing our best to set a good example, maybe someday they'll see the light.

Good Friday passes ev . . . er . . . so . . . slow . . . ly. . . .

Eventually, however, it's Easter Saturday, and preparations for Easter now begin in earnest. There are eggs to be dyed, houses to be cleaned, and corsages to be made from fresh spring flowers. At last the day is almost here: how happy I am that I have stuck it out these forty days, praying and sacrificing and carrying my cross so valiantly. And now it is time for the glory!

Easter morning dawns. Baskets are stuffed with goodies we have denied ourselves for forty days: we taste a chocolate bunny and a maple egg, and then we put them back in our baskets until after Mass. Mom, my sisters, and I have new Easter dresses and bonnets: Dad proudly pins a corsage, fashioned from flowers from the yard, onto each of his girls. The boys in ties and navy suits dig into their Easter baskets again, and we nag at them, reminding them not to smear chocolate all over their new clothes. Eventually we're off to church, where an exuberant Easter Mass bursts with full organ and alleluias, lilies and candlelight. Our beautiful statues, having emerged from their purple shrouds at the Easter Vigil service the night before, now seem to join in prayer, while mothers in new lavender hats count their fresh-scrubbed chicks as they file into Church.

Easter, spring daffodils bursting through hard-frozen winter in parish yards: Christ's Resurrection gives meaning to it all. Yet it wouldn't be the same ecstatic high had it not been for the Crucifixion, Christ's and ours, as backdrop. It is a lesson that is indelibly etching itself in my psyche: "You can't have the glory without the cross." In future years it will still be there preaching at me from across the years, shaping my life in many subtle ways, pressing me without my even knowing it to always take the road that leads to glory—the long road, the high road, the hard road—the way of the cross.

Saint Raphael's is lovely in the spring, all balmy and blossomy. The magnolias drop big blossoms along the boulevard, and the ravines are full of jonquils. We take many walks to the apple orchard just to see the blossoms.

Spring fever makes silly freshmen even sillier. We laugh and giggle over the various pranks: a short-sheeted bed, ink in the holy-water founts, salt in the sugar bowls. Laughter in chapel is especially delicious: the tiniest thing can start us giggling, and we soon discover that there's nothing quite as delicious as wildfire laughter spreading through a solemn chapel. We do our best to stifle it—pews rock like geysers ready to erupt—and we can feel our superiors' disapproving stares boring into our backs. But it is no use: the more we try to hold it back, the more it bursts through in little red-faced spurts that make us laugh all the harder. Eventually we give in to it, and the relief is like nothing we've ever known. There is so much pent up in our adolescent hearts, our adolescent bodies: only in laughter does some of it have a chance to come crashing through.

SUMMER

Summer comes quickly, and our parents come to take us home for summer vacation.

I sit around the house for a few days but soon become uncomfortable: conditioned by bells and schedules and activity-packed days, I am no longer able to sit around and do nothing.

Since the Prep School curriculum offers no typing classes, I decide to teach myself to type. Someday I will be busy in the Lord's service from morning to night; while I still have the time I should seize the opportunity to prepare myself by developing as many skills as possible. There is no room for boredom or goalless, directionless drifting in my scheme of things. My future life work will be important and significant, so every moment that prepares me for that work is likewise fraught with importance and significance.

I carefully schedule my days, inventing inner bells and schedules. In the morning I assiduously practice my typing; in the afternoon I take my recreation. I know that recreation is as important as prayer and work in the development of a well-rounded, happy nun.

Sometimes Mother drives us to Hanford Pool, the municipal public pool, and sometimes we splurge and pay the dollar that lets us use the nearby private pool for the day. Usually, however, I spend the afternoon playing tennis with Karen, my friend from Precious Blood.

Father Ted, the parish's new assistant pastor, is our tennis teacher: twice a week he tutors us and a handful of others at the portable net setup in the school playground. Karen and I are soon addicted, playing every afternoon, all afternoon. Father Ted watches us, beaming: "You'll be so good by next summer that you'll be able to represent the parish in the CYO (Catholic Youth Organization) citywide tournament."

In July the family packs up everything and sets off on another family trip, this time to Yellowstone by way of the Rockies. Realizing that nuns don't take pleasure trips and that their summer vacations are usually spent at the motherhouse, my parents know that if I'm going to see this glorious country of ours, I'd better see it now before it's too late.

When we return, I spend a week in Chicago with my Prep School friend Liz. We go clothes shopping and play golf with her father and stay up half the night laughing and talking about some of our adventures as freshmen. It feels good to think of how far we have come since those first days when we feared Bernie Clare the way we feared the bats in the night.

Like the bats, Bernie seemed to have a secret, silent radar system that guided her. We'd be whispering at a drinking fountain, and she'd all of a sudden swoop around a corner and remind us that there was to be no talking in the halls. We'd be giggling in some shadowy bend of the winding stairs, and she'd appear out of nowhere to rebuke us for laughing and talking on the stairway. Even standing and gazing out a window could bring a secret attack: Liz loves to remind us of the time I was staring idly out a third-floor window, and Bernie Clare from a second-floor window let out a yell that reverberated throughout the courtyard: "*Agnes Gilligan!*" she shrieked, blasting me out of my daydream. Even the silent dust in the courtyard had jumped in terror.

Because of Bernie Clare's crepe-shoed swooping and snooping, I had developed what would be a lifelong habit of living with a half-formulated explanation always ready on the tip of my tongue: "I needed to speak a moment to Alice because . . . ," "I was staring out the window because. . . ." Eventually, however, our fear of "Old Crepe Shoes" had waned somewhat, and we had become bolder. Though still too fearful to make many waves myself, I had nevertheless become the cheering squad for bolder classmates who did their best to frustrate and infuriate her. Trying to provoke a nervous breakdown was the only way we knew to fight back.

Night after night Liz and I savor the stories. We recount the exploits of Bet who finally got kicked out for smoking in the lav, of Tina who was caught smuggling out secret love letters to a boyfriend. We are quite confident that no other class in the whole history of the school has ever caused so much excitement.

16 §≈

SOPHOMORE YEAR (1958-1959)

When we return to school in the fall, we spend the first recreation listening to the 45s that some of the girls have brought from home. The wilder among us share exciting details of hot summer romances, and I listen in silence, convinced that there really *is* something wrong with me. Doesn't anyone else spend Saturday nights watching Jackie Gleason?

For the next few days, everyone continues to play records and to swap stories, and it is fashionable to walk around red-eyed and sad, mourning summer's lost delights. I watch and wait in silence, angered at the intrusion of that other world into the world I have created for myself here. I know enough of that other world to know that its rules are confusing, its games deadly. I know enough to realize that I was a dismal failure there almost before I had started.

Eventually, that other world is forgotten once again as old friends rediscover each other and settle back into the comfortable routine of Prep School life. I am much relieved.

Now that we are sophomores, the game plan is clear: we want to create as much mischief as possible in order to maintain our reputation as the *bad* class, the rebels. It is therefore with great delight that I discover that because of the school's increased enrollment—there are now almost ninety of us—another bedroom suite has been preempted as Prep School quarters, and I will share it with five of my craziest friends. The new suite is at the top of the winding stairs, far from other Prep School quarters. Our superiors lament the distance as the six of us smile benignly: won't it be a shame to be so far away?

Since other upper-class areas all have names—Saint Ann's Hall, Saint Matilda's Hall, and so on—we think long and hard, trying to come up with a name for our new suite. Eventually we decide on Holy Innocents Hall, priding ourselves on our sophisticated sense of irony.

We settle into Holy Innocents, and soon profound silence becomes a thing of the past. Amazingly, the new superior who has replaced Sister Bernard Clare, Sister Mary Rose, never comes to check on us. We soon find that she is a motherly type, not much given to Bernard Clare-type sneak attacks. Night after night we lie awake, plotting new pranks and giggling over old ones.

During the day, too, we sneak away to Holy Innocents whenever we can. Sometimes we take cookies from the collation room and stash them in our drawers; sometimes cigarettes are smuggled in and we sit on the bathroom floor and smoke them, throwing the butts down the toilet.

When spring comes, we put on contraband Bermudas and sleeveless blouses and sunbathe out on the tiny, hidden balcony outside our room. And sometimes Holy Innocents is a perfect hideaway for secret little chats with PFs.

A PF is a particular friend: when we're not being lectured on the impropriety of behavior such as swinging our arms as we enter chapel, chances are we're being lectured on the dangers of particular friendship. If one is to live a communal life, one must keep one's friendships general and must resist the temptation to become too close to any one girl: special friendships, particular friendships are a cancer that eat at the heart of community.

No one says anything about a certain fear that eats at the hearts of our superiors as they watch our friendships with so much vigilance: the word *homosexuality* is never mentioned. We are simply told to follow rules that seem to have no meaning: never sit on the edge of the bed, never pull your dorm curtains closed during the day, keep your bedroom door open at night, and don't spend too much time with any one person. Having no earthly idea what the big fuss is, we know only that particular friendships are bad, that they have to be carried on underground, and that makes them ever so exciting and enticing!

Jenny is my PF: we exchange friendship rings and write each other little notes in chapel. Each night before the lights go out, she comes to Holy Innocents to give me a little hug and to kiss me on the cheek, reminding me again that our friendship is very special to her. Our friendship is so special to *me* that when she occasionally doesn't make it to Holy Innocents before the last bell, I am distraught: is she mad at me? Has she found another friend more special than me?

But Jenny sticks to me, giggling with me when I'm high and leaving inspiring little notes under my pillow when I'm low.

Because of Jenny, I find this year's Saint Catherine's Day particularly hard.

Saint Catherine's Day, so named because it had formerly been celebrated on the feast of the great Catherine of Siena, is the traditional day of feasting and celebrating in honor of the soon-departing seniors. Until this year, the seniors always entered the novitiate in January, but starting this year they will first complete high school and then enter the novitiate the following September. The Saint Catherine's Day celebration is also different now since it is no longer celebrated on Saint Catherine's Day.

The juniors, who are in charge of planning the day, do their utmost to keep all their preparations a secret. Not only do they not reveal the date of the coming celebration, they totally deny any knowledge of the feast. Since September the seniors have been warning them that they'd better begin their preparations, and the juniors have been assuring them that they have no idea what the seniors are talking about. There are even traditional songs that the seniors sing at recreation to remind the juniors that Saint Catherine's Day is near, and there are traditional songs with which the juniors answer with blank faces. "Saint Catherine's Day? What's that?"

Back and forth it has gone until this morning. Now the priest surprises us all by turning to the congregation just before Mass and announcing: "This Mass is being offered for the senior class by the junior class." The juniors had taken up a collection among themselves and presented the priest with a Mass donation.

There are gasps of surprise among the seniors: their big going-away party has begun at last. The refectory is gaily decorated, and each senior pins on her uniform the green and gold class ribbons that are waiting by her place. There is no school for seniors today: the juniors have planned a whole round of special activities. First there is a visit with the Mistress of Postulants and the Mistress of Novices, the women who will guide their spiritual journey during the coming three years: they will be postulants for the first year and novices for the next two years. Next comes an hour visit with their future Spouse in the tiny perpetual-watch chapel where Christ's Body is exposed on the altar night and day.

There is a special lunch and afterward a scavenger hunt. Between classes, we hang out the windows and watch our big sisters enjoying their special day. There is free time in the afternoon and then a special audience with Reverend Mother. Afterward comes dinner, the high point of the day.

The seniors are served a special feast by candlelight in the recreation room; flowers and decorations are everywhere. Favors and gifts, all lovingly provided by the juniors, wait at each place. There is also the traditional postulant doll and the traditional scissors for the future postulant's sewing box.

After dinner, the rest of us join them in the recreation room for cake, cola, and class songs. At the appointed time, the sophomores line up in front of the room—as usual I am at the piano—and sing an individual tribute in honor of each big sister.

For Joan, for example, we've prepared a parody of "Devoted to You":

> Joanie dear, you'll soon be there,
> Spending each day in His care.
> Guess by now we know that you're
> Devoted to Him.

There are more songs about walking hand-in-hand with Jesus down the road of life. Each song is punctuated by open sobs and noisy nose blowing, also traditional. At Jenny's song I am crying so hard that I can't even play; they go on without me, as I blow my nose and struggle to pull myself together.

> Jenny, dear, we'll miss you when across campus
>   you go.
> We'll miss your cheery smile and the sparkle
>   that you show.
> We know you've always waited just to be His
>   lovin' bride—
> Please pray for us dear Jenny when you're
>   on the other side.

When the song is over, friends who know how special Jenny is to me rush up and hug me, murmuring sympathetic words: I glance over at Jenny and see that she is crying, too, but smiling at me with brave eyes.

Bravery is what Saint Catherine's Day is all about, what the convent is all about: young lives offered on the altar of religious devotion; brave, heroic smiles as all that might have been is burned away.

When each class comes forth to sing its song, we sing our brave, swaggering songs about sophomore pep and then a touching parody of "They Try to Tell Us We're Too Young": "They try to tell us we're too young," we sing, "too young to want to be a nun. . . ." Even our superiors now have misty eyes.

Eventually the seniors sing. First comes a rowdy song to remind the juniors about the responsibilities that will soon be theirs.

Next comes a reminder to the younger girls to enjoy their freedom because soon they *too* will be asked to sacrifice their lives.

> Enjoy yourselves; it's later than you think,
> Enjoy yourselves, while you're still in the pink.
> The years go by, as quickly as a wink.
> Enjoy yourselves; enjoy yourselves;
> it's later than you think!

Martyr-heroines in some great religious drama, the seniors pause just for a moment to look wistfully at those of us whose time has not yet come; then, putting such unworthy thoughts aside, they bow to destiny and to duty and sing movingly of the nuptials to come when they will be married to their suffering Lord.

It is a grand and glorious immolation, and we admire them so, admire their courage, their selflessness, their noble, shining martyrdom. If anyone has been so cold as to resist crying up to this point, tears come now.

Saint Catherine's Day 1958 is now over. Sister Mary Rose

rings her little bell and says, "Goodnight, girls!" and we file out of the room in silence.

Jenny is waiting for me when I return to Holy Innocents. We go out on the balcony—it's a moonlit April night—and she stuns me with an unexpected confession.

"I've been wanting to tell you this for a while, angel child," she begins, "but I didn't want to upset you. The thing is: over Christmas I met this guy at a party. I went out with him a few times and we started getting serious really fast. We've been smuggling letters back and forth, and I'm afraid I'm really falling for him."

The hard part is over now; so she continues: "I didn't want to be a bad influence on you, so I didn't say anything. I had to talk to somebody, so I ended up telling Sister Mary Rose. I didn't tell her too much and definitely *not* about the smuggled letters. She was really neat: she just kind of listened quietly and didn't give me all that perseverance shit." It is the first time I have heard Jenny use such language, but I am so startled by what she is telling me that I don't even react.

"In fact," Jenny goes on, "she told me that sometimes such strong feelings for a man are a sign that God is calling one to be a wife and mother, instead of a nun. You can't believe the weight she took off my shoulders when she told me that!"

"I'm still not sure, though," Jenny says thoughtfully. "I'll be letting so many people down if I leave. There's Mom and Dad—they're king and queen of the parish because of me!—and there's my eighth-grade nun: she had such high hopes for me! Then there are all my friends here, especially you, angel child. . . ."

I mumble something to the effect that Jenny shouldn't think about me or any of us in making her decision, and I try to assure her that I know she'll make the right decision. I pray that my voice doesn't betray my confusion: Sister Mary Rose's more liberal perspective is attractive to me, but old warnings about ex-nuns birthing stillborn babies and agonizing in fiery car accidents die hard. A flash of jealousy, of wanting to protect her also come up when I try to picture Joe: what boy could be good enough for Jenny?

Relieved that she no longer needs to keep Joe a secret from me, Jenny hugs me. "I still haven't made any decisions," she assures me, "in fact I'm still not sure Joe isn't just the biggest temptation old Satan ever sent my way. Since I've come this far, I'll probably go on and enter the novitiate and give it a whirl for a while. Maybe God will give me the grace to forget Joe and I'll end up the best little nun you've ever seen." Jenny flashes one of her old superconfident smiles, and wanders off to struggle alone with Satan and his temptations.

Feeling that the earth has begun to tremble beneath me, I fall to my knees and try to steady myself. Again that frightening, chaotic world out there has reached a menacing hand into my secure little world. Is there no escape?

17
SUMMER

Summer arrives and I award myself for my fairly proficient typing skill by spending practically every day on the tennis court. Father Ted follows through on his commitment to enter us in the CYO tournament, and I play mixed doubles with a shy crew-cutted boy named Walt. To the amazement of all three of us, Walt and I, without ever having exchanged more than a word or two on or off the court, walk away with a mixed-double trophy.

In late July the family heads off to the east coast to see Washington, D.C. "If you're going to teach history someday, you should at least know something about the nation's capital!" Dad declares as he drives along the Pennsylvania Turnpike. He lets me drive for a while—he's been teaching me all summer—but when the family becomes too nervous he takes the wheel again.

When we return, Jenny comes through town during a cross-country trip with another girl who is entering the novitiate with her in September. Jenny assures me that she has decided to try to forget Joe, to not let him stand in the way of her lifelong desire to be a nun. Surely, if God wants her, He will help her to erase Joe from her memory.

We drive around town in Jenny's friend's convertible, and we smoke a lot of cigarettes in celebration of their last few days in the world. When they leave, I sit in my room for hours at a time, smoking the cigarettes I now so proudly carry in my purse and playing "Since You've Gone" over and over on the record player. Mom and Dad notice both the melancholy and the cigarettes, but they don't say a thing.

18 ᔐ

JUNIOR YEAR (1959–1960)

When I return to school in the fall (it is now 1959), I am not surprised to hear the rumor that Jenny left after only a few weeks in the novitiate. Eventually I hear from her: she hadn't been allowed to write as a postulate, of course, but she now wants me to be one of the first to know of her departure. It had taken only a week or two to convince her that novitiate life wasn't for her: Joe had never left her mind for one second, and she discovered that what she really wanted to do was to marry him and to have his babies. And so she had left. They had married a week later, and she is happy to announce that it won't be too long before she'll be sending me baby pictures. She hopes I am happy, that I will continue to persevere in my chosen vocation: she will keep me in her prayers and she hopes that I'll do the same for her.

I write back, telling her that I am happy for her and that I will indeed keep her in my prayers. I don't tell her of the stillborn-baby fears or the fiery car-accident fears, though they still dance at the edges of my mind when I pray for her. And I tell neither her nor myself that under all the defenses and all the bloodless philosophizing and theologizing, there sleeps a Mary who, if set free, would envy her, would love to wander off into the sunset with a real, live prince charming of her own.

But Mary doesn't wake much these days, and when she does, Mary Agnes has little patience with her silly, wouldn't-it-be-nice prattle. If Mary will one day rub the sleep from her eyes, stand on two feet, and *insist* on being heard, you would never know it to look at her now. For now she has abdicated almost totally: Mary Agnes's rule goes unchallenged.

Other best buddies have abandoned Vocations over the summer, but instead of giving in to the grief and confusion that wants to erupt in me, I throw myself into my studies with more intensity than ever before.

Junior year in general brings a sobering, a settling down. It's all right to be silly and wild when you're a freshman or sophomore, but by the time you're a junior you should be a little more mature, a little more serious, a good example to the younger girls. Our little Holy Innocents gang disbanded in June: two of the other members fell by the wayside during the summer. I am now assigned a room with a quiet girl who isn't any bother and who leaves me alone to my thoughts, for which I am by now rather grateful.

A new person comes into my life, someone who will have a major influence over my next two years. Her name is Sister Saint Agatha, and she will be my English and civics teacher during the next two years.

It doesn't take us long to discover Sister Saint Agatha's eccentricities. She runs our civics class as if it's Congress: in order to participate in a class discussion, one is required to jump to her feet and ask to be recognized by the chair. "Miss Gilligan speaking." "The chair recognizes Miss Gilligan." Or if someone is still making her point: "Miss Smith still has the floor, Miss Gilligan."

Saint Ag also feels strongly about the importance of clear and distinct speaking. To teach the timid to project their voices, she has them leave the classroom and recite "Thanatopsis" from the end of the hall. "Project!" she bellows as we all giggle hysterically.

At other times in a similar attempt to teach precise enunciation, Saint Ag asks questions on the preceding night's homework and requires us to answer with our lips, without emitting a sound, as if speaking to a deaf person. "Answer with your lips," she barks, and again we are all reduced to giggles.

When Saint Ag isn't lecturing us on the importance of clear enunciation, she's usually warning us about the danger of creeping socialism and atheistic communism and worldwide zionism. Each day we are required to memorize long sections of the Constitution and to stand up and recite them in class; each day we are reminded that the country is fast slipping away from the ideals of its founding fathers. Goldwater and Buckley are required reading for the course, as are various antisemitic tracts that warn us that the Jews are, at this very moment, scheming to wipe out Christianity and take over the entire world.

———

Inundated with Saint Ag's passionate arguments and those of all the right-wing writers we are required to read, I go home at Christmas with a suitcase full of John Birch literature and a head full of ideas about how FDR and the unions have ruined the country.

My Democrat, union-organizing father is ready to throw me out of the house: "That crazy nun's a goddamned reactionary. How can the order let her poison your minds with such crap?"

It's the first time that I've ever heard Dad use such strong language—I didn't even know he knew words like that!—and it's also the first time I've ever heard him criticize a nun. For the first time I realize how passionately he feels about FDR and the unions and the ideals of the Democratic party. We have many long sessions around the kitchen table at night: he tells me how he came close to losing his job because of his union activities and how FDR supported the unions and saved the country when it was on the brink of disaster. With angry eyes he tells me that Hitler was able to exterminate so many Jews precisely because so many people in Germany felt the way Saint Ag does. Brought back to my good democratic senses, I return to school at the end of vacation and proceed to argue my way through a year and a half of civics classes.

But if Saint Ag is a wildly fanatical civics teacher, she is also the best English teacher I have ever had: she loves great literature with as much passion as she hates liberals and communists, and I find her love strangely contagious.

All of a sudden new vistas open to me: I read Chaucer and Dante and Shakespeare; I memorize Donne and Wordsworth and Coleridge. Worlds that I had never known existed now open their gates, and breathless with anticipation I tiptoe into each. My destiny might limit me to a few nunly joys, a narrow nun's bed, but through reading I can transcend all limits and lead a thousand lives, experience a thousand joys. With Wordsworth I can traipse through a field of sunny daffodils; with Shelley I can wander through Europe in wanton debauchery. How fortunate I am to have been given this key to all the joys and pleasures that the world has to offer!

And so it is that through contact with crazy Saint Ag I begin to read and study for the sheer joy of reading and studying, rather than for the red-inked comments penned in my margins.

19 §∞
SUMMER

Summer arrives. I now have only two summers left in which to sample the world and its delights before putting worldliness behind me once and for all. "Live it up before you give it up," we whisper to each fellow conspirator as we leave for summer vacation.

And so I set out to live it up. The only problem is: I'm not too sure *how* I am supposed to live it up.

Smoking is living it up, so I drive around town with my girlfriends, smoking pack after pack of my cigarettes.

Drinking is living it up, so I attend a cousin's wedding and afterward the bride's sister takes me barhopping. I drink so much beer that I can remember little the next day, but one thing is sure: I've lived it up!

Dating is another live-it-up issue, and for two years now I've been secretly praying that I'll have at least one date before the convent doors close behind me. How glorious it would be to take to the convent with me a whole treasure chest of stories like Sister Roseanne had when she first talked to us about Vocations, stories about all the men who were madly in love with her and wanted to marry her, whose hearts were broken when she entered the convent.

But it doesn't look as if my prayers will be answered. The only boys I even come in contact with are Michael Kilty, the seminarian (remembering the story about the bees, he keeps his distance), and shy Walt, my tennis partner. Walt is so shy that it's all he can do to ask me the score in the middle of a game.

Perhaps in my new job . . .

Dad is an old friend of the owner of Lakeland, the south-side country club and, proud of my new lifesaving credentials, he approaches his friend about the possibility of my being hired as a summer lifeguard at the club's pool. Arnie considers for a moment. There would be definite advantages to having a future nun as an employee: she'd sure as hell be more honest than most teenagers, and she'd be more likely to keep her eyes on the pool instead of on the handsome male guards. Besides, hiring a future nun is undoubtedly somewhat akin to hiring the handicapped, a noble civic-minded deed that is sure to bring blessing in this life or the next. Arnie is a devout Catholic, a fourth-degree knight in the Knights of Columbus. Arnie says, "Sure, Herb, why not? Tell the kid to come down and talk to me." Dad slaps him on the back and promises to return the favor someday: "We boys from the old neighborhood have to stick together!"

Dad approaches me about the lifeguard job and I am excited. Seventy-five cents an hour just to sit in the sun and acquire a great tan: how could I refuse? I think of all the great lifeguarding tales I'll be able to tell my students someday: maybe they'll be so impressed that they won't even think to ask me whether I went to my senior prom.

I don't tell Dad any of these thoughts, and he doesn't tell me that the reason he got me the job was so that I'd have some real life experience before entering the convent. It's pretty obvious, now, that I'm going to follow through on this convent thing: he's happy for me that I seem so sure about what I want, and he's rather proud of the choice I'm making. His only concern is that the choice be a free one, that I'm exposed to other viewpoints and other life-styles, and that I'm aware of other options. The pool job will be a great opportunity for me to get out and to be around other teenagers, to make friends: yes, Lakeland seems the answer, the perfect answer.

From my perspective, too, there couldn't be a better job. I walk the 2 miles to work each morning: I'm there before anyone else arrives so that I have the pool to myself for an early morning swim. When the pool opens, I watch my section of pool from a lifeguard chair high above the pool; then at the end of fifteen minutes the head guard blows her whistle and everyone rotates to another chair. At the end of the third shift, it's break time: hot and sweaty from my forty-five minutes in the sun, I dive off the chair into the pool's cool blue water. At the end of the fifteen-minute break, it's back into the chair again. And so the day passes: bake, bake, bake, cool off, bake, bake, bake, cool off.

When I am hungry, I send one of the younger kids (I know most of them by name: their parents drop them off every day on their way to the golf course) to the clubhouse to buy me a cheeseburger and a shake.

Don is one of those golden bronzed lifeguards over whom all the girls swoon, and he has a golden bronzed girlfriend who sometimes comes to have lunch with him on his break. I have become friends with both of them, a fact that has made me begin to question some of my old beliefs. For one, there has been the belief far beneath the layers of consciousness that handsome, successful people with straight teeth and winning smiles cannot be trusted, that they're somehow phony and superficial, and that they're never quite as deep or sincere as people who have really had a rough life. Suffering builds character: golden children can't be expected to have much character.

But here are Don and Stephie, golden children who amazingly enough seem also to have hearts of gold. They listen attentively as I talk about Prep School life and my plans for the future.

"I thought of being a nun once," Stephie says softly, almost wistfully, surprising me to no end.

"Until I came along and corrupted her," Don teases, extending a sun-lotioned arm and pulling her close. I almost have a sense in that instant that he is pulling her close to snatch her out of a wistfulness that might still hold some lingering threat. But Stephie laughs and snuggles close, and the faraway look recedes under dancing eyes.

My contact with Don and Stephie also brings into question another old belief that has rumbled around in my psyche since Precious Blood days: a belief that the male of the species cannot be trusted; that his intentions, as far as women are concerned, are usually less than noble; and that he can't be expected to exhibit womanly traits such as sensitivity, caring, gentleness. As the belief had cemented itself to my soul, I had, of course, made an exception for my father for, like many young girls, I adore my father unreservedly. He is all the things that most men aren't. My heart reeks with secret envy of my mother: how incredibly lucky she was to find him, given all that I now know about the faults of other males! In order to match her good fortune—to surpass it even—I will have to leave the earthy plane to betroth myself to the Son of God. Where else in this earthy wasteland could I expect to find a man better than my almost perfect father?

And yet my contact with Don has made me begin to doubt all that. Though a honey-tongued talker, Don also knows how to listen; though downright sexy, he's never crude or vulgar. I take that back: sometimes he's crude and vulgar, but in such small, harmless doses that I almost find it appealing.

It's one of those stormy evenings that lifeguards love: the rain is falling gently on the pool, and soon the lightning will be close enough so that we can blow our whistles and tell every-one to leave the pool. Then we'll be able to retire to the club-house and listen to the rain fall. We'll eat fried onion rings and drink icy colas while we play poker and marvel at our luck: there's nothing quite as delicious as being paid a decent wage for doing absolutely nothing at all. If the storm lets up, we'll let everyone back in the pool, but if we're lucky, light-ning will flash and thunder will rock the heavens and everyone will go home, leaving us to our well-subsidized poker game.

The other guards have left for the day, and Don and I watch the handful of people who are left in the pool. We check our watches, timing the thunder, trying to determine the proximity of the lightning. We also try to estimate the mood of the remaining swimmers. Wait too late to order them out of the pool and we might have a few electrocutions on our hands if lightning hits the pool; order them out too early and they'll go bitching and moaning to Arnie.

I walk around the pool to the right, stacking up pool chairs as I keep one eye on the heavens. Don walks around the pool to the left, his careful eyes dredging the bottom. He will never forget the horrible moment last summer when his eyes routinely checked the pool and came across the body of a child, lifeless and bloated, pressed against the bottom near the 6-foot line. Right there by that light: Don sees the spot again as he has seen it so many times in his nightmare, and he turns away quickly.

But all is quiet tonight: there's nothing on the bottom but a drain top somebody has pulled out of place and a red plastic ring for which some kids have been diving.

The rain is still coming down, but the lightning doesn't seem to be any closer. The swimmers don't seem to have any intention of leaving. Frustrated at the thought of the poker game we're missing, I blow my whistle more loudly than usual at two kids who are chasing each other along the edge of the pool. *"Walk!"* I shriek. "You guys had better quit messing around or I'm gonna throw you out of the pool. I've had enough of you today." Seeing that I mean business, they quit messing around. Thinking ahead to the days when I might have to control an unruly classroom, I pride myself on the good practice I'm getting and on the fact that I'm one of the guards that the kids take seriously. The other day I even threw out one of the big jocks from the high school when he brought glass beer bottles into the pool area. It did not matter that I felt all weak and trembly when I went to lower the boom: both the jock and I knew that I had Arnie, Lakeland, and a lot of big strong guards behind me. I look forward to the day when I will have the Sisters of Blessing, the big strong Catholic Church, and God Himself behind me: that will *really* be authority!

I wade through the baby pool on my way to stack more chairs, and Don yells at me: "Mar, are you crazy? That thing's a fucking cesspool. I wouldn't walk through there if they paid me: ninety toddlers must have peed and drooled in there today!" Don doesn't usually talk this way around me since I'm a future nun, but I like him so much that I don't mind. Besides, I kind of like it when he lapses into forgetfulness about my noble future and treats me like just one of the gang, the average teenager I'll never be.

We walk back to the big pool and sink into two lounge chairs. The thunder and lightning have backed off now, and only a light drizzle falls on the remaining few swimmers. Out of the blue, Don starts telling me about his disillusionment with the Church, and at first I listen quietly. "I left the Church when I was sixteen. Of course to my mother's way of thinking, one never really leaves the Church: one just falls away. I haven't fallen away; I've graduated!" Don says it calmly, not bragging, as if stating a simple fact.

I am shocked and I want to say so, but I think better of it. I want to let Don know that the reason one can't leave the Church is because baptism leaves an indelible, absolutely unerasable mark on the soul, identifying one as a Catholic forever. He doesn't seem much interested in such theological fine points at the moment, however, so I say nothing, biding my time. I have read some books on winning back the fallen-away, and all the writers stress the importance of first hearing the person out. "You can't fill a full pitcher!" is the warning that stays in my mind. I'll let Don empty his pitcher before I proceed to show him how wrong he is.

"Believe me, I was as Catholic as you are. We had holy-water founts by all the doors in our house, and I always made sure to take some holy water and make the sign of the cross every time I entered a room.

"Touch your forehead, then your chest, then the tip of your left shoulder, then your right," Don says, demonstrating. "Touch your right shoulder first by mistake and you screw it all up and have to start over. I even knew that I had to keep some water on my fingertips the whole time if I wanted to get the whole 600 days indulgence, so I made the sign of the cross real fast so that the water wouldn't dry before I was finished!"

The picture of Don making a fast sign of the cross so that the holy water doesn't dry on his fingers makes me giggle in spite of myself.

Don goes on. "I don't know how it was at your parish, Mar, but at Little Flower there were special days throughout the year when every time you entered Church you could earn a plenary indulgence—not just one of those little temporary things where you freed a holy soul for a hundred days or so, but a plenary indulgence where you set him winging on his way forever. The Church always looked like a hive of bees on those days with everyone coming and going, coming and going: you'd stop inside and say the necessary prayers, step outside and catch your breath, and then back in you'd go to pocket another plenary. I tried to get every indulgence I could: I wanted them for Jimmy."

Don blows his whistle at a boy who is running along the pool and then continues his account. His face darkens as he remembers. "My friend Jimmy died a mysterious death when we were in third grade: the doctors never did figure out what was wrong with him. Every day Sister Robert Marian would light a holy candle and put it on the desk where he used to sit—I guess it was supposed to ward off evil spirits or something. That really spooked me out. At any rate, when Jimmy first died, she told us that Jesus loved him so much that He wanted him to come be with Him. That's why He took him to heaven. I can remember hoping that it would be a long time before Jesus would love me that much!

"So at first I thought Jimmy was safe with Jesus. Then the damn nun started dropping these little hints that we really couldn't be sure *where* Jimmy was; after all he *had* reached the age of reason when he died. He had received First Confession and Holy Communion, so he was old enough to be capable of sinning. Of all the luck: if Jimmy had died the day before he made his first confession, the fact that he was baptized would have sent him straight to heaven. All the unbaptized babies of the world would have watched in envy from nebulous Limbo where they hung, neither here nor there for all eternity because their parents failed to have them baptized or because whoever *did* baptize them forgot a word or two of the magical incantation. Jimmy would have had their envy for all eternity if he had died just a few months earlier. I never quite forgave his guardian angel—wasn't that what our guardian angels were supposed to be for, to protect us from such disasters?"

I open my mouth to answer and to protest Don's irreverence. I have begun to wonder if I am committing a sin of bad example by sitting here and listening to such blasphemy.

But Don doesn't give me a chance to interject: soon he's off and running again, and I again try to bide my time. Does it take so long for all pitchers to empty? Are all so full of poison? New at this converting game, I am still feeling my way. "Holy Ghost, guide me; give me Your wisdom, Your patience, Your sense of timing. And when the time *does* come, help me to know exactly the right words to say."

Don is still talking about Jimmy, and I see now that he's no longer joking around. "From third grade to sixth grade, I spent half my time trying to gain indulgences for Jimmy. Oh, sure, just one good old plenary would have done the trick, but I asked the nun and she said one could never be really positive that God applied the indulgence to the particular soul one had in mind. What a way to keep me on the hook, to keep me scurrying in and out of church, grabbing for all the indulgences I could get!"

He takes a breath, satisfies himself that I'm still sitting in the chair and am still breathing, at least barely, then continues nonstop: "And do you know what that was all about, Mar? It was all about good old Catholic guilt!" Don's eyes are blazing now, and he lowers his voice almost to a whisper, as if going to confession. "Jimmy and I, the week before he died, were off in the woods together 'abusing ourselves.' That's what the nuns called it, wasn't it: 'self-abuse'?" Without waiting for a reply (thank God for that; my face is crimson and I am embarrassed beyond belief!) Don goes on: "I walked around for three years convinced that if Jimmy was burning in purgatory it was because I taught him to abuse himself! Deep down somewhere, I even thought I had killed him: God was punishing him for the terrible thing he had done, which meant of course that God would be out to get me next. For three solid years I lived in fear of the great hitman in the sky, too ashamed and guilty to mention my heinous sin to anyone."

Sensing my embarrassment, Don puts an arm around me, and his tone is now soft and conciliatory. "Mar, I apologize from my heart if I have hurt or offended you. Sometimes I just get carried away. The thing is, if you're going to be a nun, I want you to be a good one, not one of those naive ninnies who taught me in school. As a nun you'll have a lot of influence: the kids you teach will either be carefree fun-loving kids, the way all kids should be, or they'll be full of guilt and scruples the way I was. The kids who will have you as a teacher will be getting someone very special. I just don't want you to be like a lot of nuns who don't know the first thing about the world."

Though I'm still somewhat disappointed at not winning my first convert, Don's words have nevertheless touched me. "Don, I don't agree with all your points, but I have to admit that you've made me stop and think about a lot of things."

That night Dad and I are watching the Jack Benny show on TV, and at the commercial he asks me how the job is going. I tell him about the new mat they got for the 10-foot to make it less slippery, and the new holes that Arnie's adding to the golf course. Though I tell him I'm making lots of friends, I don't say anything about my conversation with Don. Is that what he had in mind when he wanted me to have a little more exposure to the world, a little more contact with kids my age? I doubt it.

Jack Benny comes back on after the commercial, and at one point he makes a quip that's rather off-color. Dad gets up, turns off the TV without a word, and asks me if I'd like to play a game of cards.

It's 9:50 A.M. and we're getting ready to open the pool. Already it's hot and sticky: the place is going to be packed.

Don and I have the first shift, and Stephie is helping us to unstack the chairs and to put up the umbrellas.

Out of the blue Stephie says to me: "Don and I have this friend we've been wanting to introduce you to. He's really cute, and such a nice guy: we know the two of you would hit it off together. How 'bout it, Mar: would you like us to fix you up with him?"

At first I am startled. I see Don watching me out of the corner of my eye, so I take care to keep my face passive while I think. But I can't keep my heart from leaping: this is the moment I've been waiting for, praying for. I flush with excitement.

Suddenly, however, an old fear snakes its way up and seizes me at the throat, forcing words that I know I will regret a thousand times over in days to come.

"Thanks, Stephie; I'm really flattered, but I'm afraid we're not supposed to date."

I can hear the final thud of a coffin lid over some part of me, even as I say the words. I know that there are no school rules forbidding dating and that some nuns consider dating inadvisable for candidates, while others feel just as strongly that such experience is invaluable. I also know that neither opinion really matters to me: what pressed the coffin lid closed was fear.

"But Mar," Don begins to protest, but Stephie cuts him off. "Don't push her, Don; she has to do what she thinks is right, to follow her own conscience."

Encased in an increasingly familiar numbness, I begin a tedious bloodless explanation of the ramifications of the vow of chastity. I soon find I needn't bother, however, for having made one last attempt to draw me into their world, Don and Stephie give up and go on their merry way. "Just because you lured one girl away from the straight and narrow doesn't mean you have to make a habit of it," Stephie teases, and Don grabs her shoulders as if to push her in the pool. They kiss and dive in the pool together, and I am left to my ideals, my fear, and my coffin.

20 &

SENIOR YEAR (1960–1961)

Stephie and I don't see each other much after that; then she enters Saint Raphael's College as a freshman in the fall. I am now a senior in high school. Though she has told me to watch for her on campus, when I do see her the first time I turn away so that she doesn't see me. She is walking by with a group of laughing, chatting college girls: they are dressed like typical coeds, and I can hear them talking about the football game they attended the previous night. I, on the other hand, am dressed in my usual dowdy-looking uniform and am surrounded by the usual herd of ninety or so.

Last summer we were two teenagers, laughing and talking and soaking up sun. For a moment our worlds merged; for the briefest moment there was a chance that they would *keep* merging. Then a further decision was made—a further decision which ratified and made solid many older decisions. And we had gone our separate ways.

Senior year passes quickly. Novitiate is just around the corner now, and I stave off a certain sense of panic by intensifying my pursuit of spiritual perfection.

I now have two role models, my future Spouse Jesus and His virgin mother Mary, and I strive diligently to emulate both of them.

First there is Jesus. As a child I often stared at the picture of the Sacred Heart that hung in our living room. I knew from religion class that Jesus had asked Saint Margaret Mary to carry to the world His message that He wanted us to pray and sacrifice in order to make reparation for all the pain His heart had suffered because of people's sins. It was the sacrifice part that confused me at first: I could imagine how praying would help Jesus feel better—I would tell Him I loved Him and that He should not mind all those creeps who did mean things to Him—but I sure couldn't figure out how my giving up chocolate bars would make Him feel better.

Eventually I learned, however, that suffering and self-sacrifice were valuable currencies, as valuable as prayer, and that by subjecting *myself* to suffering I could somehow make *His* load lighter, could somehow make up for the self-indulgence of selfish worldlings. The value of sacrifice and of self-denial: it was a lesson that, once learned, would seep into countless corners of my psyche until I too would learn to cherish my suffering like so many badges of honor.

As far as the suffering of fellow human beings was concerned, I also learned that their pain obligated me to do my fair share of the suffering—that if they hurt, my first obligation was to hurt too. If my burden of self-torture seemed heavy at first, I eventually found that it ultimately freed me from any real responsibility for my world: it wasn't necessary that I *do* anything about the problems of the world, about hunger and war and poverty, only that I feel guilty. Guilt became, in the end, a comfortable refuge.

Mary is my other role model. One Sunday a month we make a retreat: we spend the day in silence, praying, meditating, and reading holy books. Once a year, usually in January, we make a three-day retreat under the spiritual guidance of a trained retreat master, frequently a priest.

This January, the January of my senior year, the retreat master is an eloquent Jesuit with strong handsome features and gray flecked black hair.

Propping my spiritual notebook on my knee, I take careful notes.

"Look in your spiritual mirror," the Jesuit thunders. "You may not like what you see. Are you proud, vain, giddy? Do you talk too much?"

His voice suddenly softens, becomes gentle. "Now look at Mary when *she* was your age: Modest . . . gentle . . . (he pauses dramatically after each adjective, allowing us time to squirm as we compare ourselves against Mary) neat . . . retiring . . . soft-spoken . . . quiet. . . . Mary walks quietly, speaks softly, never sulks or shouts." Then again the thunder: *"Are you like Mary?"*

The Jesuit's eloquence touches me to the core. I look in my spiritual mirror and realize that I have a long, long way to go.

———————

There are a few Prep School modernizations during my senior year. In the winter we are allowed to wear slacks when we go ice-skating or tobogganing, and in the spring a few of us seniors are permitted to hit tennis balls against the gym wall during noon recreation. College tennis courts remain strictly off limits to us, of course, but as long as we stay out of the college girls' way, we are allowed to practice our shots against the gym to our hearts' content.

I play each day, rolling up my blouse sleeves and pounding all my little frustrations and conflicts into the brick wall of the gym. At the end of each workout, my uniform is dripping with perspiration, especially as the days grow warmer and more humid, but my body and psyche experience a certain sweet release.

21 §≈.

SUMMER

In June, my family arrives for our graduation. Ten of us have persevered to this point, and one more will drop off during the summer, leaving nine of us to enter the novitiate together. Though we wear gowns and mortarboards and process down the aisle of the main Church accompanied by "Pomp and Circumstance," the ceremony is short and simple. Afterward there is a brief punch-and-cookies reception in the rec room, but none of us stays long. Our last summer in the world beckons, and we are eager to make the most of it.

We say our good-byes to the younger girls, knowing that it will be a long, long time before we see them again, if at all.

We say good-bye to our fellow graduates, knowing that the next time we see each other we will be dressed in the long black dresses of postulants.

Though the sensible thing would be to drive home with my family, I opt to live it up in all the ways I know (at least the ways that don't scare me too much), so I decide at the last moment to fly home, though the trip is a scant hundred miles. I have never flown before, and I doubt that I ever will have the opportunity again. Like a terminal-cancer patient with only a few months left to live, I seek out all life's little pleasures.

Mom and Dad have prepared a small graduation party. All the presents are things I will be able to use in the novitiate: men's linen handkerchiefs, scentless hand cream, a black pen-and-pencil set. The big party, an open house in my honor, will come later in the summer, a week or so before I leave.

So here I am at the beginning of summer. I have just graduated from high school and I want to hoard the days ahead as a miser hoards gold. I become obsessed with the problem of how to spend my time. On the one hand I want to spend as much time with my family as possible; on the other hand there's a gnawing feeling that I should be out there doing the things that normal girls my age are doing. I feel the conflict and sense that my parents feel it too. All the unspoken words hang in the air as the days wear on. We fight a lot over little things, especially Mother and I, and we cry a lot each time we make up. But somehow we never quite manage to say the words that are aching to be said.

Most days are again spent lifeguarding at Lakeland. Don and Stephie have moved on to other jobs, but Don stops by occasionally to say hello.

"I still wish I could get you to kick up your heels a bit before you bury yourself in that convent," Don sighs, sinking into the pool chair next to me. "I keep hoping somebody will come along and seduce you before it's too late, but who's gonna have the nerve to mess around with Christ's ol' lady? It's like you've got *Bride of Christ* blazoned across your forehead or something, and who wants to risk angering a jealous Jesus?"

I blush furiously and do my best to protest his irreverence, but Don's genuine fondness shines through and I am charmed in spite of myself.

By the end of summer, everything is in order. My trunk is full of clothes and supplies, enough to last me through the three years of novitiate. At that point I will take a vow of poverty along with vows of obedience and chastity, and the community will begin to provide for all my needs.

A list of conditions for admission has been sent to my parents, and they go over it carefully: applicants should be sound in mind and body without any notable deformity; they should be sincere and earnest and determined to submit to the direction of superiors; they should not be older than twenty-eight; though no dowry is required, they should bring whatever money they can to help defray the cost of their training; they should be perfectly free, having no one depending on them and having no debts; they should not have been members of another religious order; they should present certificates of baptism and confirmation, a letter of recommendation from a pastor or confessor, and a certificate of health from a doctor; they should be of legitimate birth, of irreproachable character, and of a family free from blemish, reproach, or hereditary diseases such as insanity and epilepsy.

There is some family concern over the last condition: a great uncle had been quite senile in his old age, and Grandma wonders if that falls under the insanity part. If anyone worries about the free-from-blemish-or-reproach part, no one admits it.

The necessary papers and documents are sent to Saint Raphael's along with a signed affidavit affirming that I had indeed been of legitimate birth.

There are last-minute parties: a party at a friend's house, an open house at home. At the open house I drink champagne for the first time, convinced that it will also be my last. An article in the daily paper announces my imminent departure and I receive all sorts of letters from misinformed Protestants, begging me to think twice before I throw my life away at such an early age. We pile the letters on the kitchen table and read them over, chuckling. "They'll shave your head, and they won't let you out," we read, and we double up with laughter. Don't Protestants know that modern convent doors swing both ways, that not all orders shave their heads? It was one of the first questions I had asked my aunt, and she had assured me that most Sisters of Blessing just cut their hair very short, that only a few older nuns shaved their heads. The fact had consoled me immensely, convincing me that I was entering a very modern, very enlightened order.

Somehow we make it through the last couple of weeks, and it is almost a relief when the day of departure actually arrives.

This time I don't surround my leaving with little ceremonies—there are no little bedside parties with my younger brothers and sisters, no solemn vows pronounced in the top of apple trees. I just want to complete the leaving as quickly and as painless as possible: this is where it's all been heading, these past four years, so I might as well get on with it. It is almost as if I have at last reached the fourth stage of dying about which the various writers on death and dying speak—that of resignation.

Years later I won't remember much about the final trip to Saint Raphael's, except that my parents drove me there and unloaded my luggage methodically, saying little. Though I will learn that this had been the most unbearable day for my parents, this day of final leaving for me had only been one of numbness.

A smiling novice greets us at the door of the novitiate and shows us to the stiff little parlor where we will say our good-byes. I watch the hands on the clock circle slowly, lethargically, as I search for something comforting to say. Only empty, vacuous sentences come out, and I know it is no use.

Dad keeps humming George M. Cohan's "Always Leave Them Laughing When You Say Goodbye," a tune he often asked me to play for him on the piano these last few weeks, and Mother and I do our best to laugh at his feeble little jokes.

Seemingly out of nowhere, a picture that I saw in a mission magazine comes up to inspire me, a picture of bloated-bellied babies and thin-ribbed old men with desperation in their eyes. Jolted out of my self-pity, I realize again that I have a grand and glorious future ahead of me, a life of total commitment and service. Jesus said that once you put your hand to the plow, you should never look back. Enough looking back: it is time to move on!

I wait for the end of one of Dad's jokes; then I stand up and tell my parents that there's no sense dragging this out, that we're all only too aware of the pain of lengthy good-byes. As I walk them to the door, I remember Christ's injunction that if anyone wants to follow Him he must leave father and mother behind. A good clean break. I whisper in my heart, "I am yours, Lord Jesus; give me strength." I kiss my parents good-bye without crying, and if they cry, I don't notice. A good clean break.

My parents leave, and the big novitiate doors swing closed behind me.

III &.
FORMATION (1961–1966)

Behold the handmaid of the Lord, said Mary to the angel; be it done
unto me according to the word. As a reward for the loss of a normal
life she became the mother of God. As the daughter of my father I
thought my fate as inevitable as hers, as forcefully imposed, as impossible to question. I could no more refuse my father than Mary
could have refused the angel coming upon her, a finger of light. . . .

. . . In the years that I lived as the daughter of my father I had
always been greeted with reverence and delight by shopkeepers, by
people carrying groceries. I was the good daughter. I took care of my
father. I had nothing to fear. Faces were open to me, for mine, they
believed, was the face of a saint. . . . As the daughter of my father I
was above reproach. Can I explain the perfect luxury of that position, so rare in our age?

As the daughter of my father I lived always in sanctuary; think of
the appeal of sanctuary, pure shelter! As a child, when I read about
the Middle Ages I was fascinated by the idea that there was one
automatic safe place, the simple inhabitance of which guaranteed
safety from accusing mobs and ravening bandits. I had won myself a
place there as the daughter of my father.

I had won sanctuary by giving up my portion, by accepting as my
share far less than my share.

I had bought sanctuary by giving up youth and freedom, sex and
life.

—Final Payments by Mary Gordon

22 §🔊

POSTULANT (1961–1962)

At first I don't recognize her. Her slim, athletic body is hidden under yards of black serge, her sun-streaked hair is bound by tight-fitting linen. As if yearning for the touch of summer sun, two blonde curls push their way out from under her *serre-tête* (head binding) and tense fingers hasten to shove them back inside, as if embarrassed by the rebellion.

Aside from those two wild curls, nothing else about my old friend Suzy betrays her old rebelliousness, her old feistiness. Is this *really* the same girl who was almost thrown out of the Prep School three times? The same girl who made Sister Bernard Clare's nervous breakdown a personal cause?

From somewhere within all that serge and linen, a thin hand reaches out, and for a moment the old Suzy dances in her eyes. "Hi, Maggie, it's good to see you. My name is Sister Myriam Rose now, and I've been assigned to be your guardian angel." The dance is over, Suzy recedes.

I take her hand and squeeze it affectionately, trying to feel again the old bond. Her hand is red and rough, and I suddenly remember that as a second-year novice she now divides her day between domestic work and prayer. Suzy always prided herself on her carefully manicured nails; now they're chewed to the bone. It occurs to me that Suzy doesn't seem very happy, but I quickly remind myself that I am observing with the eyes of a worldling. Suzy is undoubtedly much holier now, much closer to God—she surely experiences an inner joy that I will only know once I too have submitted to the necessary spiritual surgery. For the novitiate is a hospital: we enter it with all kinds of cancer of the spirit and all varieties of debilitating, deadly worldliness. In the hospital we smile bravely as we go under the knife, confident that the pain will be well worth the end result. We will leave our petty egos behind and new radiant, smiling, purified beings will emerge: *nuns*. Suzy is undoubtedly right in the throes of the operation now, her pain only temporary. I want to hug her, to tell her how proud I am of her, but a certain stillness in the air makes me think twice before indulging in such exuberance.

We are standing just inside the door of the novitiate, and I have just said good-bye to my parents. For the first time I glance around the building that will be my home for the next three years.

The novitiate could not look more different from the building in which I have lived for four years: an efficient-looking brick building, long and functional instead of tall and ornate, it was built as a result of the current community growth spurt. The enthusiastic community song now brags of a sisterhood eighteen-hundred strong, and rumor has it that there will be over sixty postulants this year. Our entrance into the novitiate was even delayed a week because there were not enough beds for all of us. Christ's proud army is growing by leaps and bounds: how fortunate I am to be a part of its bold forward thrust! What great things I will one day do for the world, swept along by the vision and force of such a strong committed army!

As I survey the novitiate's clean antiseptic lines, its modern red brick, its glass and its chrome, I have a moment's nostalgia for Lafayette Hall's storybook views from each big old window and laughing girls in each creaky hall. Yet another side of me appreciates this clean, no-nonsense building and the singleness of purpose it bespeaks for I am ready to get down to business now. Funny how, now that the commitment has been made and the novitiate doors have swung closed, there is this new peace, this new single-mindedness!

Suzy first leads me into a tiny room called the portress room. Here the religious world meets the secular: no seculars are allowed beyond this point. (*Secular* refers to anyone who is not a priest, brother, or nun, be the person a virulent atheist or the Dalai Lama.) Novices are assigned portress duty on a rotating basis: the portress's duty includes greeting all visitors and answering the novitiate phone (the Mistress of Novice's office has the novitiate's only other phone). The portress smiles politely as I sign in and then goes back to her black-booked prayers.

Next, Suzy and I step quietly into the novitiate chapel directly across from the front door. It is now late afternoon and the autumn sun pours through the stained glass, throwing sharp edges of color through the chapel. There are big bouquets of orange and russet mums on the altar, and everything is clean and bright. My eyes fixed on the tabernacle, I pray silently to the Divine Prisoner hidden there. "Well I made it, Jesus. It wasn't easy but I did it. Now give me the strength to persevere, to die to myself and to let You live in me, to put the past behind me and think only of You." I am filled with peace.

Suzy genuflects devoutly, and I follow suit; we make the sign of the cross with holy water, and soon I am following her down the terrazzoed hall into the cloistered area. We pass the stiff, formal parlors where a few families still weep their good-byes. Remembering my own grief a few short years ago, my heart goes out to them. I never would have believed this day could have been so painless for me! I congratulate myself on how much progress I've made in controlling my emotions, but then I immediately berate myself for my lack of humility, my arrogant self-congratulation. Will I ever learn?

Suzy hurries along, speaking only when necessary. I will soon learn that a good nun breaks silence only for reasons of necessity, charity, or courtesy. For now, silence still feels cold and unfriendly, so I keep up a steady stream of banter. Remembering Suzy's deep, resonating laugh, a laugh that could send sparks through the bone-dry stillness of a chapel and ignite a forest fire of mirth, I think that maybe if I can make her laugh I'll be able to contact the old Suzy again.

"Guess who I saw over the summer, Suz? Charlie! She looks fantastic and seems really happy. We got to laughing about old times and she reminded me about the time . . ."

Suzy has been walking beside me saying nothing, but she now stops and turns to me. Aware of her obligation to initiate my novitiate training, Suzy explains in a voice full of sisterly charity and patience: "My name is Sister Myriam Rose now. When we enter the novitiate we leave the world behind, and with it, old names, old ways of doing things. Everyone here is to be addressed as *Sister*: as soon as you're dressed as a postulant you will be Sister Mary Agnes. In the same way, we try not to talk about our worldly pasts too much: we should make a clean break with all that."

A clean break—again I have forgotten. Though her words sting at first, I know that Suzy is right and I tell her so, thanking her for the reminder. Through the years I will receive rebukes and criticisms with similar bowed-head humility, with similar expressions of gratitude. Sometimes, as now, it will be all I can do to keep from melting into a pool of tears under the assault, but I will save my tears for later private moments. Taught to reply "Thank you, Sister; I deserve much more" when criticized, to see each rebuke, each tongue lashing, as an opportunity to abandon stubborn pride, I will bite my tongue and struggle with an unruly ego that urges me to fight back, to protest. Death and resurrection, the constant theme: only if the seed dies can it be born to a new life. My ego must die if I am to let Christ live in me.

Silenced at last, I follow Suzy as she points out other parts of the novitiate. Here is the priests' dining room where visiting priests and the priest who says Mass each morning are served. Priests, like seculars, never eat with the nuns.

Everything in the priests' dining room is elegant and ornate in keeping with a priest's exalted status. There is a beautiful Chippendale table with one heavy chair; a china cabinet holds Waterford crystal and Limoges china and silverware that is polished once a week. As we pass Father's dining room on the way to the refectory each morning, we see two carefully chosen servers hovering around his table, handing him freshly squeezed juice, making sure that his coffee is hot, and I chuckle to think of old Protestant stories about the tunnels connecting convents and rectories. Little do the Protestants know: nuns and priests aren't even allowed to take their *meals* in the same room!

Suzy now leads through doors marked *No visitors beyond this point*. There is a large modern kitchen, all chrome and tile, and a small dining room, called "second table," where the servers eat. On the other side of the hall is the scullery where dirty dishes are run through a large industrial dishwasher.

At the end of the hall, we come to the refectory: windows on all sides give an expansive view of the back of the campus. Since neither the sleeping area nor the chapel has windows, it is here in the refectory that I will catch my first glimpse of day each morning. The day and I will unfurl together: I will sip my coffee in silence and watch the sun breaking over trees and barns. Month after month I will watch as one season ripens, fulfills itself, and then dies; month after the month the rain and the wind and the soft-spoken snow will teach me gentle lessons. Though I don't know it now, these early-morning reflections, unstructured and unfettered and full of childlike tranquil awe, will ultimately save me from the effects of harsher, distorted lessons that threaten to crush my spirit. It will be a gargantuan struggle, but nature's gentle voice will triumph in the end.

Suzy helps me find my place at one of the long linen-covered tables that run the length of the room. She informs me that as in the Prep School refectory seating will be changed each week, and she shows me how each long table is sectioned into "tables" where six or seven share food and conversation. Conversation with people sitting at adjoining tables is discouraged. Seating assignments represent the will of superiors and thus the will of God, so one should concentrate her attention on the sisters at her table. I look at my napkin ring: a typed label saying "Sister Mary Agnes" is taped to the top. Permanent napkin rings will be ordered six months from now when we receive the religious names by which we will be known for the rest of our religious lives. Mary Gilligan, Mary Agnes Gilligan, Sister Mary Agnes: what further name; what further changes?

We leave the refectory and I follow Suzy to an elevator next to the scullery. She pushes the button and soon we are on the second floor.

Suzy points out that a library divides the second floor into two wings, that each wing is divided by green partitions that form individual cubicles. Counting our way through a maze of windowless metal walls, we find my cubicle. There is a built-in metal closet and a metal bed covered with a plain white spread: again the spread falls exactly 2 inches from the floor. Between the bed and the closet there appears to be just enough room in which one person may stand and dress. Most of the space today is occupied by my trunk which was carried by two novices to my cubicle earlier in the day.

Seeing my trunk sitting there, an oasis of the familiar in this desert of uncharted metal, I experience a moment or two of homesickness.

Suzy continues to tell me all the important things I need to know about my new life, but despite myself and my earnest efforts to put the past behind me, the past summer once again flashes before my as yet undisciplined eyes.

All summer long my trunk had sat by my window as sounds of the neighborhood floated in: children playing hopscotch in the street, ice cream trucks chiming. All summer long I had packed my trunk, a bit at a time, as if letting go all that was familiar a bit at a time.

Mother had sewn four calf-length black cotton petticoats, carefully following the regulation pattern. The petticoats had gone on the bottom of the trunk, and next had come shorts and vests. Shorts (long white cotton drawers) and vests (men's round-neck T-shirts) had been ordered from a mail-order house for nuns, along with heavy black stockings, thick-heeled granny shoes (a pair for Sunday and a pair for every day), black slippers, black tennis shoes, a long black robe, and a black and all-concealing nunly swimming suit. All were neatly folded and piled in the trunk in quantities calculated to last the three years until I would take vows and become a full-fledged member of the community. From that time, all my material needs would be handled by the community.

Next had come white nightgowns. "They should be a size or two too big so that you can dress under them," my aunt had warned, and sensing her embarrassment I had asked no further questions. My aunt remembered her own novitiate days: a stern novice mistress had emphasized that a novice should always be "decent," even when alone. At night she was to put a white muslin "night shawl" around her shoulders as she undressed; in the morning she was to dress under her nightgown.

I packed garter belts and bras, white and plain and devoid of lace or frill. The supply list specified that no article of clothing was to have decoration or ornamentation: shoes with fancy swirls over the toes would be sent home as would frilly nightgowns or underwear. (One girl's grandmother would knit her a gorgeous shawl, and she would be allowed to keep it only on the condition that she cut off the fringe.)

Supplies were to be equally plain, equally neutered: any last stubborn vestige of feminine frivolity would be immediately squelched. A whole room at the novitiate would be filled with supplies that had been confiscated, that would be used for Christmas presents for the "help": gowns touched with tiny pink rosettes, garter belts ornamented with contraband lace, delicately scented hand lotion and soap. Every time we would receive a box of supplies from home, a superior would

go through it carefully, examining and sniffing, careful to censor anything that would remind one of home, of the world, of
one's sex, or of one's femininity.

In the old days even bras had been forbidden. Now allowed, they are still regarded by many of the older nuns as
silly, altogether irrelevant pieces of apparel.

In the same way, mirrors have only recently been allowed:
there is one mirror in the second-floor bathroom and one in
the first-floor bathroom, and each postulant is allowed a small
stand-up mirror in her cubicle. Though it is still considered
vain for a nun to give too much attention to her appearance,
postulants may now use mirrors when combing their hair. My
aunt would one day tell me the story of how, in premirror
days, postulants always liked to have tin sewing boxes so that
they could steal glimpses of themselves by peering in the tin.
One day, however, my aunt had been caught in the act, and
the superior had rung her little bell and addressed her in front
of the group: "You look very lovely, Sister Agnes. Now would
you like to kiss the floor for your vanity?" While everyone
watched, aghast, my aunt had gotten down on her knees and
kissed the floor.

Suzy is continuing to point out regulations about my
cubicle—vests and shorts are to be neatly folded in the top
drawer, gown and robe should be hung on this hook. The
riptide of the past is powerful, but I gradually swim to shore.
Eventually, I am near enough to hear her voice.

"You will keep in your cubicle only what you will need
for the next few months; everything else will be stored in the
trunk room downstairs. In a few moments I will leave, and
you will put on the garb of a postulant."

Suzy then reminds me that just as in the aspirancy we are
never to sit on the edge of the bed. As with so many regulations, no explanation is given, though I presume it is a matter
of practicing poverty: sitting on the edge would wear down the
mattress. Because of the regulation, she explains, we are to
kneel on the floor to put on our stockings: "You put one

stocking on while you kneel on one knee; then you switch. It takes a little balance to keep from falling over at first, but you'll soon get the hang of it.

"Once you have put on underwear, shorts, vest, stockings, and shoes, you will put on this black cotton *waiste,* a French term for 'blouse,' and this serge skirt." Suzy holds both up for my viewing and then holds up an apron that appears to be as long as the skirt and to be fashioned from the same material. "This apron is to be worn over your skirt all day, except on Sundays: after supper each evening, you'll leave it on your chair until breakfast." Suzy explains: "A housewife wears her apron all day as she busies herself around the house; then when her husband comes home she combs her hair and takes off her apron and tries to make herself as lovely as possible. In the same way, we wear our aprons as we go about our daily tasks and take them off to rendezvous with our Divine Spouse each morning at Communion."

Without stopping to catch her breath, Suzy goes on: "This pocket is to be pinned at the waistband of your petticoat: you'll be able to reach it by reaching through the slit in your skirt. Your pocket will come in handy for your handkerchief, rosary, pen, and all sorts of things—postulant pockets are famous for being weighed down with everything from apples to cookies to God-knows-what else." Suzy grins an old familiar grin, and something of the old Suzy comes dancing through. But it is just for the briefest moment; soon she is pious and solemn once more, a model novice.

"Your cape comes next: this white collar is pinned at the neck and these white cuffs are pinned at the wrists of your *waiste.* You pin on this white veil when you go to chapel. Just like in the Prep School, there's an outfit for every day and one for Sunday—you should never wear your Sunday outfit or your Sunday shoes during the week."

Suzy now informs me that I have exactly fifteen minutes to dress: the first bell for chapel will be ringing soon. With that, she closes the curtain of my cubicle and scurries off.

Used to dressing quickly, I move as fast as possible. I tissue off the last traces of lipstick and makeup and begin to undress. I pile worldly apparel, under and outer, in a neat stack on the bed and begin to dress as a postulant.

In later years friends will share with me the poignancy of this moment for them. Eyes had filled with tears as they glanced at themselves in the mirror one last time, as they removed lipstick and lacy underwear and favorite dresses.

For me, however, there is none of that. Mother has always praised me for not being vain and clothes conscious as are so many girls my age, and though under the surface I care a lot about how I look, I would never admit it even to myself. There had been one strange moment outside Church when a parish woman had told me what a pretty girl I was. Pretty? It was as if the delicious, unfamiliar word floated at me from some other universe.

Such moments had been few and far between, however: deep-down convinced that I am really not very pretty at all, I usually keep my mind on more profound, less depressing matters.

As I remove my worldly clothes there is also the realization again that I am entering the hospital for necessary surgery, that this drab black-and-white garb is but the hospital gown. The surgery, the gown, nothing matters: my eye remains on the future, radiant and bright.

Suzy returns and giggles in spite of herself as she sees me. "Well, Sister, you didn't do too bad: your stocking seams are a little crooked, and your collar's inside out, but that's not too bad for a beginner."

She picks up my stack of worldly clothes and begins to leave with them, and I ask her where they will be stored. Her face darkens just a bit as if I have been impertinent, as if I have asked something I have no business knowing. Her reply is curt: "They're stored in a secret room; only the Mistress of Novices has the key. You won't see them again unless, God forbid, you fail to persevere, in which case you would wear them home again."

Suzy whisks away my worldly clothes without further ado, and I continue to unpack. A moment or two after an electric bell sounds, Suzy reappears and we head down to chapel. She helps me to find my prie-dieu, or church pew, and then hurries off to take her place as prayers begin.

First there's Vespers, the afternoon office. A novice at the back of the chapel rises and intones a Latin chant, and everyone else rises and continues it. One side of the chapel chants a stanza, and then the other side a stanza; sometimes we stand, sometimes we sit, back and forth, up and down. Though understanding few of the words, I am immediately transported by this haunting sea of sound. Every morning for four years, I stood in the cold halls outside Church and listened to the nuns chanting their morning office: I was always mesmerized by the strange almost eerie beauty of this ancient ritual. Now I am on the inside, one with the chanting, one with God: though the Latin is foreign to me, my heart sings.

After Vespers there is Benediction, then rosary, then a half-hour of spiritual reading. Every now and then I pause and ponder. I close my eyes and whisper my love to Jesus in the tabernacle, and my heart is again filled with an overwhelming sense of peace.

The half hour of spiritual reading passes quickly: before I know it there is a rustling in the quiet chapel as a group of novices, servers for the week, leave to "set up." Each server will pull her veil forward, fasten it with a straight pin, and then flip it back over her head so that it will be out of her way when she carries food to the tables. In an elaborate ritual called "pinning up," she will take straight pins from the disk-shaped pincushion that hangs on a black string from the waistband of her petticoat (like one's pocket, one's pincushion can be reached through a slit in the skirt); she will flip back her cape, pinning it to the shoulder on each side; she will gather up the voluminous folds of her habit and tuck and fold and pin, revealing black-stockinged legs under a heavy black petticoat. All this will be done as she hurries, in silence, down the quiet corridors en route to the refectory. There she will put on blue-and-white-striped serving aprons, taking care that the bib is straight-pinned over her bosom. There are to be four layers between skin and world at all times: if one is ever so immodest as to forget to pin up her bib, she invites a harsh rebuke.

Fifteen minutes after the servers have left, the electric bell sounds again. Books are put away, and everyone kneels to say the reunion prayer. Sisters of Blessing throughout the states and in the two foreign countries in which the order has missions join hearts and souls as they renew their sisterhood and their commitment to God's important work. It is a thrilling moment: I feel a sudden surge of esprit de corps, a sudden sense of shared vision and purpose. I look around the chapel at the sixty or so postulants who will share my life these next few years, and already I feel a certain bond.

There is a silent, single-file procession to the refectory: everyone walks slowly with eyes downcast as if still in prayer.

Reaching the refectory, the single-file line continues past head table. Each novice, her hands clasped in front of her, bows a tiny bow to Sister Amadeus, Mistress of Novices, and Sister Carmelita, Mistress of Postulants, and each postulant awkwardly follows suit. Those who enter the refectory late will similarly pass head table and "bow in" before taking their seats. Sometimes, if Sister Amadeus feels that a sister could use a little extra mortification, she will allow her to stand there a moment or two, sweating and blushing, before she nods permission to sit down.

There is some shuffling around as postulants search out the napkin rings that tell them where to sit; then again there is silence.

My hands folded on top of my chair, I steal a glance at the two women who will be in charge of my physical and spiritual life for the next three years: God's whole will in my regard will be revealed through their directives. Both have the lean, ascetic look of exemplary religious; both were chosen for their important positions because of their holiness. Exact and unswerving in their adherence to the order's Holy Rule, both will expect the same exactitude from their charges. Maternal and kind, they will listen with patience and understanding as their daughters confide their inner spiritual struggles.

As I wait for grace to begin, my eyes roam over the refectory. The sixty or seventy postulants are interspersed with forty or so white-veiled novices. Two black-veiled nuns also sit in our midst. It is apparently the responsibility of one of the black-veiled nuns to stare eye-roamers into submission, for she catches my eye and rivets two steely black eyes against mine. The pressure feels almost physical; my shamed eyes drop immediately.

I will later learn that these two nuns, Sister Mary Bede and Sister Hyacinth, are part of the formation team. They will assist Sister Amadeus with the novices, leading walks, censoring mail, and keeping eyes and ears open for infractions of the Holy Rule and other "irregularities." Since their job is the formation of the total person, some of the irregularities they will watch for will be poor grooming and hygiene, lack of etiquette, use of slang, and incorrect grammar or spelling. Like many of my group, I will do my best to stay far away from their ever-watchful eyes and attentive ears. One wise-cracking member of our group will sum up the feelings of many of us: "One of the worst penances I can imagine is having to sit next to Mary Bede (the older of the two) in the refectory. And the *very* worst would be having to sit next to her at a meal when we were allowed to talk!"

Grace is ready to start now, and throughout the refectory, red-faced postulants blow their noses on big handkerchiefs. I want to reach out to them, to comfort them, to assure them that it grows easier as time goes on. My four years of Prep School training will come in handy, I am sure: I am confident that my prior experience will assure me a position of leadership within the group.

After grace, Sister Amadeus taps her bell and says sweetly, "Benedicamus Domino." The response is a subdued, but grateful "Deo Gratias!" Breakfast will always be silent; the privilege of talking at other meals will be awarded by Sister Amadeus as she sees fit. Like the others, I will learn to wait eagerly for a "Benedicamus Domino," which announces that talking will be allowed at the meal.

Six unfamiliar faces—three novices and three postulants—await me at the table, the companions that God has selected for me for the week. I experience again how fortunate I am not to have to make even these smallest decisions, with whom I will sit or to whom I will talk: everything is decided for me by superiors who know God's Will better than I. Other teenagers might have to flounder around, trying this and trying that and embarrassing themselves by all sorts of awkward bumblings and false starts and silly mistakes. I will be spared such growing pains; the most minute details and decisions will be handled for me so that my mind can attend to higher things.

One of the three novices at our table, Sister Raymond Marie, is talking now: "Wasn't the altar beautiful tonight? I hear that Sister Ann Cleophas's father sent money for the flowers." The three other postulants are silent, almost sullen. The other two novices nod politely.

The novice at the head of the table, Sister John Lucille, chubby and cherub-faced, selects a large serving spoon from the silverware laid out in front of her and lifts one egg from a bowl of eggs. She passes the bowl to her right and reaches for another dish.

Meanwhile, two of the postulants have selected dinner rolls and spread them with butter, and Sister Raymond Marie patiently points out that all plates should first be passed to the head of the table. A third postulant cracks her egg against her plate, thinking that it is hard-boiled and stares in dismay as egg yolk comes oozing out. "Here's the way we eat eggs in the novitiate," smiles Sister Raymond Marie, a model of sisterly patience, and she proceeds to demonstrate. She taps her egg delicately with her knife and splits it evenly along some invisible equator. With her spoon she scoops one-half into her bowl and follows with the second half. She salts and peppers and begins to eat, explaining that hard-boiled eggs are handled the same way, except for the fact that they are to be eaten with a fork.

One of the postulants who had taken bread out of turn passes the eggs, without taking any, and again our smiling instructor comes to the rescue: "We're required to take something of everything as a practice of obedience," she whispers.

Meanwhile, the third novice, Sister Martha, smiles a thin, beatific smile and says nothing. Her bony fingers pick at her food as if eating is an unbearable burden, and her face is gaunt. The slack *serre-tête* that hangs at the edge of her face reveals how much weight she has lost. She seems to float in a state of other-world rapture, speaking only when spoken to. When someone *does* address her, she is a model of charity: she gives the person her full attention, smiles and nods, chuckles appreciatively at jokes. Though everyone recognizes her as a saint ("I'm sure she sees visions—did you ever notice how glazed her eyes become when she kneels in front of the tabernacle?"), superiors have recently begun to wring their hands lost as to how to deal with "this fanaticism." Fasting and mortification is one thing, but destroying one's body, the temple of the Holy Ghost, is another. When admonitions and lecturing failed, they made it a point to see that she always sat next to hearty eaters, hoping that she would benefit from their example. Nothing seemed to work, however. (At the end of the year, Sister Martha was to go on to the next stage of her training, and eventually we would hear the rumor that Martha kept losing more and more weight. One day something inside snapped: she started screaming obscenities in the refectory and had to be carried out, strapped to a stretcher. From that point on, her name would never be mentioned again.)

The other two novices continue chatting back and forth. Sister Raymond Marie enthuses over the morning's instructions—"Sister is such a saint. I feel *so* inspired when I listen to her!"—and Sister John Lucille mumbles her agreement as she takes another helping of stewed tomatoes.

I say something to one of the postulants, assuring her that I know how hard it is to become used to all these little customs. She gives me a strange look and says nothing. The other two postulants (one is gagging over her now-cold poached egg) now look at me curiously, and I wonder if I have said something wrong.

Just as a worldly teenager delights in displaying her knowledge of the adult world that she soon will enter, so I pride myself on my knowledge of all the little norms and customs of the adult world that *I* have entered. I feel proud of the fact that I know convent table etiquette, that I know how nuns eat their eggs, and I am confident that everyone will envy my knowledge.

But the looks I receive don't convey envy, and I begin to experience a vague, unsettled feeling in the pit of my stomach as I watch my fellow postulants, sullen and silent.

The servers bring bowls of canned figs for dessert, and they are passed around. The postulant who gagged over her cold poached egg now spoons one fig onto her plate and Sister Raymond Marie once again points out the breach of community etiquette: "We put our dessert in our bowls," she instructs.

Already slightly green from her struggle to down her cold, runny egg, the postulant is now aghast: "But my bowl is smeared with egg!" she protests, not quite believing this is really happening. Sister Raymond Marie smiles patiently and explains that one sometimes needs to put one's own likes and dislikes aside if one is to live in community.

After supper Suzy helps me finish unpacking what I will need for the next few months; then we carry my trunk down to the trunk room on the basement floor. She now completes my tour of the building. On the basement floor an auditorium divides the two wings: novice rec room and study hall are on this side, postulant rec room and study hall are on the other. The two groups will only have contact with each other at mealtime and at occasional joint recreations: most of the time one will stay with one's own band, the group of postulants with whom one entered the community.

Suzy shows me the trunk room where all luggage is stored, the ironing room where we will remove spots and press our skirts and capes every Saturday, and the laundry room where we will pick up our clean clothes after they are laundered. At coming recreations I will sew number tags (my number is #133) on all articles of clothing.

At the end of the hall is our postulant rec room and just around the corner Sister Carmelita's office and our postulant study hall.

Satisfied that I now know my way around, Suzy sends me off to recreation with my sewing box and a stack of shorts that need number tags. A group of postulants are standing around watching a ping-pong game as I enter, and others sit in loose circles around the room. One postulant plays a melancholy song on the piano. Sister Carmelita will eventually call her over and tell her that she should play something bright and cheerful or nothing at all. The postulant will choose to play nothing at all.

As I enter the room, Sister Carmelita is sitting with a group of postulants and darning a stocking as she talks. I have the definite sense that she is somehow carefully monitoring everything that goes on in the room.

When I walk in, she looks up at me and smiles the sweet charitable smile of a good religious at recreation. There is an empty chair by her, and she beckons me to come sit by her.

Despairing at the thought of having to wait still longer before locating Bonnie or Karen (Karen, my old Precious Blood tennis partner, entered the aspirancy in her senior year of high school) or any other aspirancy friends, I clutch my sewing box and my stack of shorts and make my way across the room.

"You're Sister Agnes Anita's niece, aren't you?" Sister Carmelita begins as I sink into the seat next to her. "She's such a good religious. You are certainly blessed to follow in the footsteps of such a holy woman!"

I tell myself that this is beginning to grow a bit old; yet I savor the recognition in spite of myself. "Yes, we're all quite proud of her," I answer, noting the jealous looks of the fawning postulants who surround her.

But my place in the sun will be short-lived. I try to make conversation about the weather: what could be safer? "It's sure getting cold outside, isn't it?" I venture. Without looking up from the stocking she is darning, Sister Carmelita replies stoically, making her point: "I *never* complain about the weather."

Shriveling, I sink back into the chair and fight tears: so much for convent nepotism. The strain of the day is beginning to wear on me, and I turn to the collation tray for consolation. There are creamy dark chocolates and thin-layered chocolate mints, the kind of candy I've only seen in expensive candy stores. It's a far cry from the peanut-butter-and-jelly sandwiches and cheap chocolates of Prep School collations. Since I'm sitting next to Sister Carmelita and her court, I daintily select just one chocolate mint and let it comfort me as it melts ever-so-slowly in my mouth.

Recreation drags on as Sister Carmelita recounts amusing stories from her days as a grade-school teacher, and the sycophants around her titter at all the appropriate moments. Good religious carefully collect such stories, entertaining their sisters with them at recreations.

Eventually Sister Carmelita rings her bell and says "Goodnight, Sisters," and we gather in the chapel for evening office, Compline. Afterward we climb the stairs in silence and begin to prepare for bed.

For the first time I appreciate the novitiate's modernity. Instead of rusty Victorian tubs with lines of girls outside each, there are plenty of nice modern showers: how luxurious to be able to wash my hair in the shower! How luxurious to be able to go to the bathroom in the middle of the night without fearing a midnight swoosh of bats!

I shower and wash my hair, brush my teeth, and wash out my black stockings. The drying rack is already full of stockings. I can see I'd better get my numbers on my things right away! Newspapers catch the drips under the drying racks and I chuckle to see two novices, desperate for news from the outside, down on their knees reading them.

I finish readying everything for the next day, and as the warning bell rings I am turning back my bedspread. The final bell rings, I fall to my knees by the side of the bed for a few quick prayers and then crawl into bed. Postulants are stumbling around in the dark; I can still hear them running into things, giggling, swearing, as I fall off to sleep.

The morning bell rings at 5:15 A.M. and though my stocking seams zigzag up the backs of my legs, I make it to chapel with two minutes to spare. What are those novices doing up there at the front of the chapel, kneeling on the hard tile in front of the crucifix, their arms extended upward in cruciform fashion? I wonder if that is the penance assigned to people who talk about the past or the weather or who don't know how to eat their eggs. I will later learn that this is a voluntary penance, practiced by a pious few who seek a closer identification with their suffering Lord.

I myself will try it a few times, leaving my arms extended above my head so long that they begin to tremble and shake with exhaustion. Usually, however, I will be lucky to make it to chapel by the time the bell rings.

One breathless novice now comes tearing up the aisle at the last minute, her cap on crooked and her *chaplette*, or rosary beads, banging loudly against the prie-dieus as she passes. She slides into her prie-dieu just as the bell rings, and I can hear her breathe a loud sigh of relief, tuning out the snickers of friends all around her. Others who aren't quite so lucky now stand at the back of the chapel, waiting for the end of office. At that point, with faces red, they will walk up the center aisle together and genuflect in front of the altar before taking their seats, thus proclaiming to the whole assembled congregation the identities of those who don't care enough about the Lord to be on time when entering His house.

I open my office book to follow the morning office, lauds, and settle in for the hour and a half of morning prayers that consist of office, meditation, and Mass. I pick up the meditation book that is in my prie-dieu and start to read the section that tells me how to meditate. Within three minutes I am sound asleep. Sure that I will be in some sort of terrible trouble, my prie-dieu partner (the postulant who shares my pew) nudges me awake, for which I am duly grateful and write her a little note telling her so. With that a beautiful relationship is launched. In weeks to come we will write notes whenever things become dull: notes about the fat novice who sits behind us and always sings off-key, notes satirizing some particularly archaic passage in our archaic meditation books. She will let me read her letters from home and I will let her read mine; she will write comforting little notes when I am sad and depressed, and I will do the same for her. There is something so close and intimate about a prie-dieu relationship!

At exactly 7:00 A.M. the bell rings again and we file out of the chapel and down the hall to the refectory. As I stand at my chair waiting for prayers to begin, I can see all the way past the barns and the clumps of autumning trees, all the way to the morning horizon where the sun is one long red streak.

We say grace and take our seats, and a novice at a little reading table adjusts her microphone and begins to read a pious treatise on the suffering of Christ. I am not listening: my eyes are still on the morning sun, rich and red and full of promise.

After breakfast we gather in the postulants' study hall, and there is nervous whispering back and forth as we await Sister Carmelita's entrance. I locate Bonnie and Karen, and we compare notes about our first day. Within minutes a sentry posted at the door hears the sound of approaching beads and signals everyone to take their seats.

Everyone rises as Sister Carmelita enters. There are prayers and then silence as she goes over her notes.

Sister Carmelita looks tiny and frail up there in front of this group of robust young women; yet it will be her job to assess and evaluate each one, to make the crucial decision as to who is "community material" and who is not. Those who are frequently ill or depressed will be encouraged to leave as will those who don't seem sufficiently docile or "formable." Many of the least formable, of course, will leave on their own as will those who miss old boyfriends, who are constantly homesick, or who just don't feel that novitiate life is for them.

Finally Sister Carmelita clears her throat and our first instructions as postulants begin.

"My dear Sisters," she begins solemnly, "welcome to the novitiate. You have answered Christ's call, you have left all things to follow Him, and now your training in the religious life is about to begin. Those who persevere, who prove themselves to be worthy of such an honor, will one day be allowed to take vows of poverty, chastity, and obedience as a Sister of Blessing. Since the virtues of poverty, chastity, and obedience are practically nonexistent in our modern world—people chase after money, give in to their bodily lusts, and stubbornly refuse to bow to natural law and to the laws of the Church—it will at first be difficult for you to put old ways aside and to begin to live in the spirit of the vows. You will need to pray, to do penance, and to struggle with your unruly wills."

Sister Carmelita enumerates some of the little ways that we will be able to practice each vow.

"Poverty: this will be a hard one for those of you who come from homes in which you were handed everything. Here, for example, you won't be as wasteful as you were at home: instead of throwing away articles of clothing when they have holes in them, you'll be expected to darn stockings, to patch underwear. Much of this sewing will be done at recreation, as good religious are never idle even at recreation. Every now and then, I or one of the older sisters who will be sent to teach you proper darning will come around for a 'patch check,' making sure that your darning and patching are properly executed.

"Once a year you'll lay all your clothes out on your bed, and a superior will come around and inspect everything. You will be allowed to discard only items of clothing that have been patched and repatched and still are wearing thin.

"Chastity: you will practice chastity by keeping a close watch on your thoughts and feelings. The devil will try to tempt you with impure thoughts and feelings from time to time, but as long as you are aware of his tricks you will be able to push such thoughts out of your mind. Remember that impure thoughts are venial sins as long as you struggle against them. They become mortal sins only when you allow yourself to *enjoy* them!

"Modesty too is a practice of chastity. You should never pin up your cape without quickly putting on your work apron and pinning the bib over your *waiste*. You should never at any time leave your cubicle without being fully dressed, except at night; then you will wear your nightgown and robe.

"Obedience: there are so many little ways to practice obedience. First there's silence. From the end of recreation at night until the end of breakfast the next morning, there should be no talking for any reason at all. This time is called *Profound Silence.* Profound Silence involves not only stilling one's tongue but also guarding one's eyes: a good religious practices custody of the eyes as a way of shutting out external distractions in order to turn inward. She uses the time to examine faults and failings of the day and to prepare for Jesus's coming in Communion."

Sister Carmelita goes on to say that the bell should be

heard as the voice of God. "If she is mending, a good religious stops in the middle of a stitch at the sound of the bell. If she is playing basketball, she drops the ball immediately. If she is conversing, she stops in the middle of a sentence."

A few giggles, suppressed until now, can no longer be restrained. Sister Carmelita's face darkens a shade, but she presses on.

"Most of you will be starting college courses tomorrow—you will find your schedules in your desks. Many courses will be taught right here in the novitiate, but others will be taught in the college buildings. Some of you will have classes with the college girls. It goes without saying that there will be no intercourse between you, that you will speak to them only when you are spoken to." There are more giggles and a mumbled comment or two, and Sister Carmelita's trained eyes now dart from one face to another as she takes note of the dissidents: they will be called into her office before the day ends. She knows mutiny when she sees it, and she knows that she must take quick action before the mutiny spreads.

But it is too late. The feeling in the room has already shifted: strangers have reached out to each other without talking, their covert looks and smiles melding them into a group. Whether she knows it or not, the fire of rebellion in this year's postulants will not be so easily doused. For it is 1961, and a new rebelliousness is bursting into flame here and there across the globe. Even the cloister will not be entirely safe from its sparks.

It is only at recreation that afternoon that I realize the extent of the rebellion that is brewing.

We are gathered once again in the postulants' rec room: Sister Carmelita hasn't come in yet, and everyone is standing around in little clumps. From the fringes of one of the more vocal clumps, I can make out what is being said.

"How'd you like that breakfast reading? Jesus being crowned with thorns, the blood and sweat running down His face, the gore—I'm supposed to eat my breakfast while listening to *that?*" A burst of laughter.

"I wasn't even listening—Molly here tried to eat her orange with a spoon, the way Sister Mary Holy Novice showed her, and she squirted herself and half the table in the process!" More laughter.

A new voice: "Do you think it's really true that they put saltpeter in the salt?" And everyone laughs again. I ask the postulant next to me what saltpeter is and she says that it's something to dampen your sexual urges. "Would they *really* do that?" I wonder, though I'm unwilling to further reveal my naiveté by asking such a question.

For the next few weeks I watch in childlike amazement the skirmishes taking place on the battlefield around me. The oldest lead the troops. Many have come from "the college" (Saint Raphael's) where they admired their nun teachers; they felt moved to follow in their footsteps but had no idea what would be in store for them once they entered the novitiate. "Why didn't anyone *tell* me?" is the frequently heard complaint.

There are many departures. A postulant who wants to leave telephones her parents and makes arrangements for them to come get her. Some parents who opposed their daughter's entrance into the convent in the first place are delighted. These are the parents at one end of the spectrum.

We frequently hear stories about this type of parent, stories which evoke our sympathy for the daughter: a courageous Juliet, bucking parental pressure, remains true to her Divine Romeo. Such stories circulate not only through the novitiate but through the whole order, and those who have persevered in the face of such parental opposition are community heroines. There's Sister Andrea Marie, for example, whose parents disowned her when she entered the community and have not written since. There's Sister Mark Joseph whose mother died after years of not speaking to her: at her death the family wrote a terse note announcing that her mother had died of heartbreak.

Here in the novitiate stories of parents who try to block their daughters' vocations soon become legends. Some write long doleful letters begging their daughters to come home: "I cry myself to sleep each night, and I worry that your father's heart won't hold out much longer. You are our only child: don't you even care how we feel? If you don't give us grandchildren I'm not sure we'll have a reason to live!"

Most letters of this sort never reach the postulant: Sister Carmelita reads all mail, and anything that might cause turmoil and doubt is thrown in the wastebasket.

There are many jokes about the half-letters we frequently receive: we'll be reading along, then come to the end of a page, and the letter will stop short, midsentence. "Your father's been ill lately; he wanted me to be sure and tell you that . . ." End of page, end of letter. We are never quite sure whether the rest of the letter contained something Sister Carmelita didn't want us to hear or whether she simply became bored with it and tossed the rest in the wastebasket.

Letters from parents at the *other* end of the spectrum always get through: parents who rave on and on about how proud they are of their daughter's lofty vocation, who express shock when other parish girls come home from the convent. "I saw Mary Ellen Martin in Church the other day; she looked so unhappy. What a difficult adjustment it must have been for her, leaving the peace of the convent in order to make a life in this dog-eat-dog jungle out here. I feel so bad for her parents; everyone had such high hopes for her!"

Most parents fall somewhere between the two extremes. My parents' letters, for example, never say that they will be disappointed with me if I leave, but neither do they remind me as they did so frequently in high school letters that I can come home whenever I want. Like many Catholics of the time, my parents have strong feelings about the evils of divorce, considering a divorcee just one notch above a common pros-titute. In my own mind I put ex-nuns in the same general category in some vague way and am sure that my parents do too.

Though it will be a while before I will even allow thoughts of leaving to enter my consciousness, I can picture what others go through when they leave. Their parents welcome them home as cheerfully as possible, trying to hide the disappointment and shame in their eyes. The rumor spreads quickly around the parish and eyes at Sunday Mass are averted. Pious women still come up to their parents after Mass, but the adulation, the awe, are gone. Instead, their voices are full of sympathy as if there has been a death in the family. Though they long to ask questions, they restrain themselves for the sake of the family: surely the family has already suffered enough!

Back home everyone muddles through the best they can. If the family has money, the daughter will go off to pursue a college education; if not, a job must be found for her, and eventually she hopefully will marry. It will not be easy: the parish is tight-knit, and the label *ex-nun* is like an unerasable scarlet letter. Chances are that she won't marry: she'll be the parish old maid for years to come.

It's a dismal scenario, one I'd like to avoid at all costs.

Those who *do* leave must do so in shame and secrecy and in the dark of night. Forbidden to announce their departure even to their closest friends, they spend predeparture hours in the trunk room, secretly packing. Suzy had stressed the importance of never going to the trunk room without permission but as usual had offered no explanation. On a bitter cold night in October, I run out of toothpaste and decide to make a quick stop in the trunk room "just this one time!" Opening the door, I suddenly realize why Suzy had given me such a strange look when she told me about the regulation.

There by the light of one lonely bulb, a postulant packs her trunk. She turns and my heart stops: it's Bonnie! Oh no, it can't be! Four years of sticking it out together and now this!

Bonnie looks up, startled, as if caught in some forbidden rite, some shameful act; then her eyes fill with tears when she recognizes me. Wordless, we rush toward each other and sob in each other's arms until she eventually pulls away and begins to walk me, arm in arm, to the door. Even now, it never occurs to us to rebel, to spurn harsh rules that forbid good friends a proper good-bye. Our good-bye must be short and silent: the pain in our eyes says it all.

That night, after everyone else is asleep, Bonnie's parents drive up to the back door of the novitiate and, turning out their car lights as they have been instructed, begin their lonely wait. Eventually the door opens and Bonnie emerges, and they drive off as quietly as possible. Forced to steal away like criminals, all three will remember the silent shame of that night for a long, long time.

I cry myself to sleep, and the next morning try to tell myself it had all been just a horrible dream. But Bonnie's place in chapel is empty as is her place in refectory, and at the beginning of instructions we hear the solemn, terse announcement: "Sister Bonnie is no longer with us. She didn't persevere."

End of discussion. Without further ado I am to erase from my mind the memory of a friend who was an intimate part of my life, day in and day out, for four years. Close as sisters, we had watched others come and go and had stuck it out together. Our eye always on the goal we had laughed our way through all the petty nonsense along the way. But now she is gone. *Gone!* My heart doesn't want to believe it, and I cry my way through the day.

Sister Carmelita notices my despondency and calls me into her office. Closing the door, she takes her seat behind a plain wooden desk and beckons me to take the straight-back chair at the side of the desk. As I sit down, she folds her hands on top of the desk and begins to speak, her voice maternal and solicitous.

"It's very difficult when friends fail to persevere. Know that Jesus realizes the pain that you're going through; know that He will give you the strength to endure it. Our sweet Lord never gives a cross without also giving the ability to carry it. Try not to indulge in self-pity, to dwell on the past. Sister Bonnie is gone now: you should put all thoughts of her out of your mind, except to pray for her."

As Sister Carmelita talks, helpless tears run down my cheeks, and it's all I can do to hold back the sobs that want to come surging up from my chest. I do my best to listen, to hear her well-meaning words.

"Learning to control one's emotions is difficult sometimes. Smiling sweetly when one is crying on the inside takes diligent practice. . . ."

The bell rings for afternoon prayers: Sister Carmelita stops midsentence and smiles sweetly. It suddenly occurs to me to wonder how often *she* is crying on the inside. I blow my nose on a tear-soaked handkerchief and thank her: I paste an unfelt smile on my lips and assure her that I will do my best to keep it there.

Later in chapel more tears come and, afterward, a few sizzling sparks of a strangely unfamiliar feeling: anger—anger at Bonnie for leaving me after all this time, anger at Sister Carmelita and at the order for depriving us of a proper good-bye!

I will be even more angry when I realize that all communication with Bonnie will be abruptly cut off from this day forward. She will write, but I will never receive her letters; I will write but my letters will never be mailed; and like all other postulants or novices who leave, she will never be allowed to return for a visit.

My anger is tiny, buried under layers of guilt and fear and self-doubt. But it is there, a tiny silent pilot light, waiting.

If parents seem to divide into three groups, postulants do too. At one end of the spectrum are the superpious.

This group always seem to make it down to chapel in the morning in time to say an extra rosary, make the stations of the cross, and kneel arms outstretched before morning prayers. They insist that everyone including their own parents address them as "Sister," and they don't drink from the drinking fountain without first asking permission. Many tend toward various degrees of anorexia nervosa, and many are plagued by severe scruples. They are sometimes called "the statue touchers" as there are places on novitiate statues where the plaster has been worn down from being kissed and touched. The statue of Saint Peter, the community patron saint, receives particular attention: sometimes a heartfelt note is even thrust in his outstretched, plaster hand.

Not only are their own consciences red and raw from the constant scouring, the statue touchers expect a similar exactitude from their sisters and quickly report them when they don't come through. One reports my friend Jean for doing exercises in her cubicle. Associated in community thinking with hedonistic overconcern with one's body, exercises and calisthenics are strictly forbidden. Another reports Laura for reading *How to Teach Yourself Russian* during instructions.

Still another reports Nancy for throwing away her death book. A death book is a meditation book geared toward helping one face the inevitability of death by imagining in vivid detail one's own death. ("Picture your breathing getting raspy . . . your toes getting blue. . . .") We are supposed to meditate on our death books on retreat Sunday each month, but Nancy has other ideas: she throws her death book away and inserts a somewhat livelier book inside its black cover. The ruse works well until one of our well-meaning sisters reports her—for Nancy's own good, of course.

At the other end of the spectrum are the postulants who never let anything as petty as rules and regulations deprive them of a good time.

This group has its own unique relationship with the statues. A lily is missing from Saint Joseph's hand, so a cigarette is promptly substituted. A statue of the Little Flower, roses and all, is missing one morning from its niche, and there are rumors: could it really be true that a midnight delegation carted it out to Saint Pat's Lake and tossed it in? Meanwhile, a rather irreverent band member folds her hands devoutly and climbs into the niche, bestowing solemn blessings on all who pass.

This group makes pacts with college girls to meet them in the campus museum dedicated to Mother Matthew memorabilia. "The Mother Matty Exchange" they call it: at the appointed time, hamburgers, malts, and cigarettes are delivered by their college girlfriends. Then they steal off to feast and smoke behind tombstones in the little community graveyard. The surrealism of the little graveyard scene only adds to the drama, which in turn makes the rebellion all the more delicious.

There is much bragging about the letters from old boyfriends that squeeze past Sister Carmelita's watchful eye ("She just thinks I've got a lot of male cousins. . . ."), about the innocent-looking chocolate balls that clear inspection (the minute one is bitten into, the whole study hall smells like a tavern), about the gin that's smuggled in via shampoo bottles.

The unacknowledged leaders of the rebellion—and of the band as a whole—are Marty and Beth. Marty, a tiny sharp-tongued art major from the college, received her B.A. last June, and Beth, her wise-cracking sidekick also from the college, worked as a secretary for a year before entering.

Nobody messes around with Marty and Beth. A few weeks after we arrive, a fervent, brave soul stands up in a noisy study hall and reminds everyone that study hall is a place of silence. Marty and Beth lead the jeering throng, nicknaming her "the Little Flower," a nickname she will carry through the rest of novitiate. Even the superpious quickly learn to be somewhat discreet about their fervor.

Stories circulate about the latest adventures of Marty and Beth, their latest quips. One time Carmie, a name that Sister Carmelita was christened soon after our arrival, is instructing us on the importance of staying together as a large group when we take our cross-campus walks: just as in the prep school, we take long walks every day, come rain, sleet, or snow. Trying to dramatize the dangers lurking outside the safety of the large group, Carmie says, "Try to picture it: a small group of you are out walking and all of a sudden you realize that a man is following you. What would you do?" From the back of the room comes Beth's quick answer: "I'd say 'Take *me*, take *me!*' " The whole room erupts, and even Carmie smiles in spite of herself.

Another time we have just been introduced to the community custom that involves the bell being rung in the middle of recreation, and volunteers sharing thoughts from their meditation or spiritual reading. The more devout among us even copy out passages from spiritual-reading books and keep them in their sewing boxes. "Please, Sister, may I share?" queries the volunteer when her name is called. One night Beth, having had quite enough of such little customs ("What are they going to spring on us next?" is the frequently heard complaint), raises her hand as if to share, and we all hold our breaths, wondering what she is up to now. The room grows silent as she is called. Her voice drips with piety and deference as she requests: "Please, Sister, may I go home?" This time Carmie doesn't even smile, and if we laugh it's that hysterical, stuffed-inside, gasping kind of laughter that inmates of novitiates quickly learn.

Marty too is responsible for her share of the legends. When she runs out of things to sew at recreation, for example, she does the only sensible thing: she cuts big holes in her vests so she'll have something to sew.

When it comes time for the postulants to plan their first program, a traditional humorous program scheduled for late October, Marty gathers us together for our first band meeting.

A music major from the college is put in charge of music, a drama major in charge of skits, and the rest of us follow along and read and sing our parts.

Many of the songs and skits reflect the struggles of the first few weeks. Sung to "This is the Army":

> This is the convent, little girls.
> No more spike heels and fancy curls.
> You sure were stylish but things have changed
> And your wardrobe is now prearranged.
>
> This is the convent and, you bet,
> You're gonna miss that cigarette,
> Your car and your radio and sleeping late . . .

Then, lest anyone think we're complaining, a happy ending is added:

> But you're still gonna think it is great!

Another song depicts a typical postulant recreation:

> Sew, sew. Sew, sew.
> A-mending we must go
> It's not our fate
> to recreate
> But to
> sew, sew.

From eating oranges with spoons to kneeling to put on stockings, no custom escapes friendly little barbs. For example, our seemingly interminable daily walks inspire a parody of "The Merry Widow Waltz":

> We are walking, we are walking, oh so far.
> When we're talking, we are walking, oh so far.
> Nothing seems to matter when we recreate,
> As long as it's a certainty our walks will terminate.

Marty will leave eventually, but Beth will still be a part of the order twenty years later. When I interview her for my book, I tease her about the fact that no one would have expected her to still be around after most of us, less rebellious, have gone our separate ways. "I don't get it: what's your secret? Twenty years ago, had there been such an award, you certainly would have been voted the postulant least likely to persevere!"

She smiles an old familiar smile, her eyes dancing, and hastens to explain. "Well, Ag-en-ness, remember how if anyone wanted to leave as a postulant, she had to wait in line for a conference with Carmie?" I assure her that I well remember. "Well, remember how long those lines used to be?" I assure her that I remember that too. "Well, every day I stood in line, but every time I would get as far as her office the bell for prayers would ring. I never left because I could never get in to see her!"

We both laugh, and I find myself half believing her.

One of the hottest controversies during our postulant year revolves around the use, or nonuse, of tampons. Tampons are confiscated and replaced with sanitary pads, and such a hew and cry goes up from dedicated tampon users that Sister Carmelita decides to approach Reverend Mother about the possibility of changing community policy in this regard. Mother, in turn, approaches Dr. Winkler, an elderly village doctor who has been the order's expert on medical matters for the past fifty years. Dr. Winkler's studied answer settles the question once and for all: "I can't imagine any reason why a virgin would want to use a tampon!" Reverend Mother repeats his answer word for word to Sister Carmelita, and she repeats it word for word to us. The rebels howl with laughter and indignation, and I do my best to hide my innocence and ignorance: I haven't any earthly idea what using tampons has to do with being a virgin!

Actually I haven't a clue as to how one would even go about using a tampon. A few years later, when tampons finally receive the seal of approval of the Sisters of Blessing, a more-experienced friend will stand outside a bathroom stall and shout instructions as I struggle with layers of clothes and card-

board tubes and a minimal understanding of feminine anatomy. We will both giggle hysterically, but my embarrassment
will be very real.

But such changes will be slow in coming; for now, the
tampon is driven underground and begins to do an active business in the novitiate black market. Carmie's spies, two tight-
lipped novices, are assigned a top-secret employment: they are
to carry out routine inspections of cubicle drawers, making
sure that underwear is folded correctly, that all hair has been
cleaned out of hairbrushes, that toothpaste tubes are capped.
In the process they are also to check for contraband tampons,
frequently hidden at the bottom of feminine-napkin boxes.

(Years later I will learn that we had actually been *lucky* to
be allowed to use feminine napkins: in the old days, they had
used baby diapers, sewing number tags on them and sending
them off to the laundry when they were soiled!)

Mail, both incoming and outgoing, is another source of
controversy. If your family writes and says things that might
upset you or put doubts in your mind, you probably won't get
the letter. If you write and tell them how homesick you are
and how rotten the food is, you'll get the letter back to re-
write. (Actually, food is the one area where few complain: our
first convent meal of runny eggs, stewed tomatoes, and canned
figs was far from typical. A week or so after we arrived, the
novitiate hired a new cook; meals for the most part have been
hearty and delicious. In fact, so many write home about the
good food that Sister Carmelita in one of her rare playful
moods teases that she is starting to find our lengthy meal de-
scriptions rather boring reading.)

One Italian mother, ashamed of her broken English and
poor spelling, stops writing when she discovers that superiors
read our mail. Another mother telephones, full of concern:
she hasn't received Sister Ann's monthly letter; is something
wrong? Embarrassed, Sister Carmelita apologizes profusely:

she had set Sister's letter aside, meaning to point out to her that *fizzle* is spelled with two *z*'s instead of one, but she had become preoccupied with other things and the letter had never gone out.

There is also some protest about how departures are handled, but as usual the protests fall on deaf ears. We are again reminded that no one ever said religious life would be easy.

(Though I didn't know it at the time, the more rebellious in our midst, laughing at rules the rest of us follow so conscientiously, threw "tub parties" for departing friends. After the last bell had rung and everyone was in bed, a little group quietly gathered in one of the tub rooms: should anyone hear the whispering, and come to inspect, those involved could simply lock the door to the tub. The departing member modeled her going-home clothes, and everyone whispered and hugged their best wishes. Sometimes one of the group even managed to get the key to the beverage room and provide refreshments for the party. I would only learn of such parties as I would learn of many of the pranks many years later.)

For now Mary Agnes, the good girl, has become Sister Mary Agnes, the good postulant. If the rebellion I see all around me sometimes strangely attracts and excites me, I remind myself that the risk, were *I* to rebel, would be huge. What if I were to be thrown out? My parents would die of shame. My aunt too: what if it got back to her that I was one of the novitiate troublemakers?

The thought of my aunt sobers me. Back in her day the superior would make you kiss the floor just because your collar was on crooked. But my aunt made it through without complaining, without questioning and objecting to every little thing; who am I to make waves? Sister Carmelita is right: we are simply willful and proud if we think we know how postulants should be trained. The community has been in the business for many years. Who am I to think I know more than they?

Though there are many departures, perhaps none is so dramatic as Sister Rosemary's. Superiors afterward try to hush up the story, but a number of us will never forget the screams in the night.

Sister Rosemary is a saintly type from Kentucky who usually keeps to herself and spends free moments in front of the tabernacle. One night she rises from bed and moves from cubicle to cubicle, waving her rosary beads above her head and emitting wild sounds. Everyone is terrified, but eventually she is restrained by a group of strong novices. A community nurse arrives and gives her a tranquilizer and Rosemary is carried off in the night, never to be seen or heard from again.

The next day at instructions, a pall of terror hangs over the group. Sister Carmelita says only that Sister Rosemary is no longer with us and that she is sick. She invites anyone who may have heard strange sounds the night before to come talk to her.

Many heard strange sounds, but few go to talk to her. By now most of us have become only too adept at hiding our inner turmoil even from ourselves.

Years later I will still be wondering what became of Sister Rosemary: did her psyche heal nicely once she returned to the world, or does she sit even today in the back ward of some state institution? Perhaps I will never know.

At the moment, I am totally committed to confiding my inner workings to no one. Sister Carmelita and Sister Amadeus scare me: I don't want to allow them close enough to see any fatal flaws in my character. Like everyone else, they profess such esteem for my aunt: how could I let them see that I don't always measure up to her illustrious example?

The thought of talking over worries and conflicts with friends never occurs to me: recreations are such out-in-the-open public affairs, and only necessity, charity, and politeness are valid reasons for talking at other times. Even were there an appropriate time and place, however, I would find it hard to put words on all that is beginning to eat at my soul.

There is first of all a growing sense of personal worthlessness, of guilt: there are so many rules, so many regulations. And even if one follows all the rules and regulations, there are a myriad of little religious practices that one should observe if one is *really* to make advancement on the path of perfection. At the end of the day, my mind frantically scurries over the various rules, regulations, customs, and practices: if I have been lazy or lax in any area, I remind myself that I haven't quite made it today. The mighty realization that I didn't quite make it again today gradually begins to weigh heavily on my soul.

Then too, through my four years of high school I was liked and respected; I was a leader. Here I feel as if I am back in eighth grade again, clinging to the edges of a clique I will never be able to penetrate. It is not just the fact that so many of the girls are older, more worldly wise, for girls as young as myself giggle and tell secrets at the very center of the clique. Is it my imagination that the fact that I went to the Prep School has something to do with the social isolation I feel? Is it my imagination that certain postulants begin to befriend me and then, learning my background, back off? Is it my imagination that we candidates subtly avoid each other's company as if somehow ashamed of each other?

I do my best to be friendly and to make my talents known. I let it be known that I'm pretty good at writing skits and parodies and that I can play the piano by ear. But it's as if I'm invisible: others are given the assignments, and I retreat to my anonymous place at the edges of our tiny society. What is wrong?

It is only when I overhear a conversation in the laundry room, one day in late October, that I realize that my suspicions have not been unfounded. I am standing in the ironing room pressing my skirt when I hear them next door. They are plotting mischief of some sort, and they obviously don't know that the door is open or that I am in the next room. "Just don't let any of the candidates know about our plans—you know how they are." Everyone laughs. "I wanted to go to the Prep School when I was in eighth grade, but my eighth-grade nun had the smarts to talk me out of it. She said that I should first have a good time, get some life experience, and *then* decide. I think I may have gotten a little more experience than she had in mind, but I have been grateful to her ever since!" Everyone laughs again.

"I can't imagine *you* going to the Prep School, Polly. They would have thrown you out the first day!" More laughter.

"The thing that gets me most about them is that they're all so naive, so innocent! You can tell how sheltered they've been. Most of them have probably never even been out on a date. Can't you just see them teaching high school someday: how can they possibly teach teenagers when they have never had normal teenage experiences?"

The tears sting my cheeks and roll down on the skirt I am ironing. I have been pressing it so hard that the iron leaves an outline: I have almost burned a hole right through the material. I pull out the plug, and go straight to the chapel where I can cry in peace. So that's it: we candidates *do* carry a stigma!

I sob even more when I think back to how homesick I was when I left home at a mere fourteen, how hard it was on my family. Through four years I had told myself it would all be worth it once I got to the novitiate, but now I think that I probably would have been better off had I gone to a regular high school. I left my family as a child and gave up four years of my life: for what? Besides, the little group in the laundry room had been right: what *would* I do when my students started asking me about my past? All the popular nuns I knew *loved* to entertain their schoolgirl admirers with vivid stories of how many boyfriends they had had before they heard Christ's call. Girls loved that. Maybe nuns were normal human beings after all! But what red-blooded American girl would listen to someone who had never even gone to a prom?

In later years I will talk this all over with others who had been postulants with me at the time. Noncandidates themselves, they agree that the prejudice had indeed been there. One says, "You know, Mary, there *was* a lot of joking around about you candidates and looking back I think a lot of it really stemmed from the fact that many of us didn't feel all that experienced ourselves. Oh, maybe we had had a date or two, but few of us were really all *that* experienced. I really think we were trying to make ourselves feel better when we put you guys down; we were reassuring ourselves that there were actually girls who were even *more* inexperienced and naive than we were."

But such nice analyses and kind assurances are all in the future. For now there is no balm; there is only the hurt, the rejection, and the fragile, spindly legged self-esteem that is slowly beginning to die.

If all is not well on the social front, academically I continue to hold my own.

My desire to be an English major, an English teacher, continues to intensify. Psychology, a bloodless discussion of charts and graphs and studies about rats, is the only class I don't enjoy. I tell myself that if I have anything to do with it I will never again take another psychology course!

Most classes are taught in the novitiate building, but I have two late-afternoon classes in one of the college buildings, Grailey Hall. Grailey is a long walk from the novitiate, but I don't mind: I love the walk, and besides, walking *alone* across campus this way gives me a certain sense of freedom, of independence. I also find it thrilling to have classes in the college buildings, out-of-bounds to me for many years: instead of being tucked away in some back quarters like an unwanted stepsister, I can now claim the whole campus as my own.

It is on these late-afternoon walks across campus that I first fully appreciate the heavy shawl that my aunt sent me. At first I looked wistfully at the various shawls that the other postulants received, all fancy and fringy and feminine looking. Mine in comparison looked like a horse blanket. But on these late-afternoon walks across campus as winter deepens and the temperature dips below zero I am glad to have my horse blanket! A coat would be even better, but it will be a few years before Sisters of Blessing will change their habits enough to make coats practical. For now I supplement the four layers I already wear with a sweater vest and a hug-me-tight, a sweater with oversized, billowy sleeves. Both go under my cape; then I wrap my horse-blanket shawl round and round on top. With boots, gloves, earmuffs, and neck scarf, I am ready to face the elements.

As days pass, I gradually begin to find my niche in the group. Even some of the older postulants start to befriend me. I will remain eternally grateful for their friendship and for forgiving the fact that I was once a creepy little candidate, a fact that I too do my best to forget.

In early November we have our first visiting Sunday. Sister Carmelita reminds us that the day is really more for our families than it is for us, that today is our big test: if we cry, we can be sure we haven't yet released family ties.

She also reminds us that a good religious is on duty twenty-four hours a day, seven days a week. Even while visiting with our families, we should watch for opportunities to help, advise, inspire, edify.

When Visiting Sunday arrives and we are sitting on folding chairs in the auditorium, I remember her injunctions. I ask Pat if he still sometimes thinks of being a priest and suggest that Andi might want to join the sodality at her school. "They have a lot of social activities. It will put you in touch with other teenagers who share your Christian values." I give Mom and Dad a list of books that they might find inspiring, and I present Danny and Cathy with special holy cards: "Use them as bookmarks. They'll remind you that God loves you and that I do too!"

And never once do I cry.

I have always loved the seasons of the Church just as I have loved the seasons of nature, so as Advent wreaths are lit and the campus sits under its first snow, I am filled with joy at the thought of spending this Advent and Christmas here at Saint Raphael's, so close to the heart of the Church.

I pen longing-filled Advent prayers in my journal as my heart begins to prepare for the feast of Christmas.

> O Emmanuel!
> Just when things are bleakest,
> blackest, the sky lets go:
> down sifts the snow
>> lulls,
>> stills,
>> as it sifts,
>> pillows as
>> as it piles deep
>> deep drifts
> where only blackness was.
> The snow lets us know
> without raising its voice
> how little all our bungling matters
> when He comes.

Soon, classes are out. College girls leave for Christmas vacation, and we have our snow-covered woodland home to ourselves. We spend each morning scrubbing and waxing and polishing: even washing windows becomes a part of the pre-Christmas excitement.

Once the cleaning is complete, decorations begin to appear: a huge, to-the-ceiling tree in the auditorium and brightly lit trees in each rec room and study hall. Gaily wrapped packages from home begin to pile up in Carmie's office.

Worn out from the manual work of the morning, we gather every afternoon in the auditorium to work on the Christmas program, traditionally written by the postulants and presented to the entire community on Christmas day. There are skits and songs to write, costumes to design and sew, and props to build. By now I am right there in the thick of things, writing part of the program and providing piano accompaniment. We while away the better part of every afternoon laughing and teasing and joking around as we rehearse. We have to repeat the same song over and over again, but we don't mind: we love these noisy, raucous sessions far from the solemn watchful eyes of our superior.

By Christmas Eve everything is ready. One by one during the day we open our packages from home in Carmie's office. Each fills a small container with goodies from home and then places the rest in a common pool for future collations. Other gifts are carefully surveyed and sorted by Sister Carmelita: we are only allowed to keep practical items, and these must meet the usual community standards. Frivolities of any sort are promptly confiscated. One of our Christmas-program skits will joke about the predictability of convent gifts: "Twelve handkerchiefs, eleven cotton vests, ten tons of fudge—and a boatload of scentless hand cream."

That evening, we go to bed for an hour or two right after supper and then gather for the walk over to the main Church. It is cold and snowy, and the sky is filled with stars. I pull my shawl tight around me and breathe in the night's beauty. Had the first Christmas been a night just like this? Had Mary pulled her shawl close around her as she and Joseph looked for shelter? My meditation for the day had encouraged me to unite with Mary, to share each tiny moment leading up to the Christ Child's birth. "See Mary, riding on a donkey, quiet, uncomplaining. See her sorrow as the innkeeper turns them away: 'There's no room in the inn.'" How often have I been that innkeeper, turning Mary away, finding no room in my heart for her and her Divine Child?

We walk in silence and prayer, and when we eventually come in out of the biting cold, we discover a chapel ablaze with lights and candles and poinsettias. We pray in silence for a while. Soon the first faint sounds of an approaching procession are heard. The hall outside the church is full of nuns carrying lighted candles and singing songs in honor of the Infant Jesus. At the head of the procession Reverend Mother carries a statue of the Infant to be placed in the waiting manger.

There are traditional carols; then at precisely five minutes to midnight as we sit in silence and prayer and the snow falls softly outside, the choir begins "Silent Night," accompanied by organ, harp, and violin. It is a transcendental moment, ethereal in its beauty, and I want it to last forever. Bells announce midnight and all the lights go on at once. The choir bursts into jubilant song as Mass begins.

When Mass is over, we pray and sleep our way through two more low Masses and then head home through the cold night air for hot chocolate and sweet rolls, all still in silence. Then we go back to bed until time for morning prayers and breakfast.

The rest of the day is one big celebration with festive table decorations and lavish meals and unrestrained chatter. Christmas is the one day during the year when we can legally talk all day, and talk we do. It is wonderful to talk! We talk and laugh and sing our way through the day and then present our Christmas program in the evening.

The next day I write my family a lengthy, exuberant letter describing in great detail my first Christmas in the convent.

Soon after Christmas it is time for the first of many solemn ceremonies to mark the break with old identities and the taking on of new ones: reception of black caps. Each of us will be carefully interviewed and assessed by Mother Rosalie, with the help of Sister Carmelita, and those who are felt to be ready for such a step will receive little crescent-shaped caps and new names.

Once Mother Rosalie has placed a black cap on a postulant's head, her head is never again to be uncovered. She will wear the cap during the day, and a little white cotton nightcap at night; when she goes swimming she will put on a swimming cap before emerging from the dressing room. A covered head is a symbol of consecrated virginity.

Similarly, once a postulant receives a new name she is never again to use the name of her birth. She is to make a clean break with her personal history.

A small office is set up for Mother Rosalie, and one by one we are called from chapel to be interviewed. Mother asks about our level of commitment to the community, about our exactitude in keeping profound silence and other rules. Apparently there are some who are especially scrupulous and honest in their answers, because when black-cap day dawns and we are summoned to the motherhouse community room, eleven of our group are told to stay behind. They will receive their caps and names a few days later in a smaller ceremony, but the disgrace of the postponement will follow them the rest of their lives in community: they will always be known as the group who weren't capped with the rest of the band—a considerable stigma.

Those of us who have perhaps been more rule conscious and perhaps less honest kneel one by one in front of Reverend Mother, and she presses the little cap on our heads, pronouncing for the first time the name that we will be called for the rest of our lives in community. We have each submitted three names, and with the help of her council she has made the final choice.

Masculine names and Irish names are especially popular with our band, names that friends in the world are currently giving their baby boys: Sean, Brian, Brendan, Matthew, Andrew. I receive my first choice, Sister Mary de Paul, keeping my own first name and adding that of a favorite saint, Saint Vincent de Paul. Most of the time I will be called simply *De Paul* or any of a number of nicknames. The rule insisting that we address each other as *Sister* and that we never use nicknames will only be observed when superiors are present: the rest of the time we are *Puzzled* or *Rosebud* or *Heloise*—even *Jellybean!*

Days pass and our training intensifies. Instructions now focus more and more on the three vows that will be the basis of our lives as religious.

The vow of chastity is straightforward: we will not marry. Jesus alone will be our lover and spouse. All external temptations to chastity have been by now severed. Letters from old boyfriends are intercepted; worldly magazines, newspapers, and books are banned. Once I am given permission to read C. S. Lewis's *The Four Loves* but only on condition that I skip the chapter on erotic love. Men might be a temptation—any men at all!—but our superiors take pains to see that the only males we encounter are the eccentric elderly priest who says Mass each morning and the ten-year-old acolyte who sleepily follows him around the altar.

The vow of poverty demands that we imitate Jesus, Who embraced poverty by being born in a stable. Gradually we have grown used to the idea that we will never again own money or material possessions, that everything we use right down to the tiniest pin in our pincushion is community property. Since nothing really belongs to us, we have a responsibility to use community property carefully and sparingly and to economize as much as possible. Water should be turned off while we are brushing our teeth; showers should be quick. If we sometimes waver, we remind ourselves of Christ's warning about the danger of riches: that it would be easier for a camel to pass through the eye of a needle than it would be for a rich man to earn heaven. We want, above all, to merit heaven.

Obedience is practiced by observing all the rules, customs, and practices of the order and by making the will of superiors our own. Asking permission is another practice of obedience: we are encouraged to bring our own wills under subjection by asking permission to do anything that diverts from our lockstep routine. If a superior isn't available and there is a pressing need—for example, if we need to go to the second floor to get a clean handkerchief or to change feminine napkins—we are permitted to assume a permission, but even these assumed permissions are to be carefully listed and reported to Sister Carmelita once a week.

Some moan that soon we'll have to ask permission to inhale, but most of us take it all in stride: if this is how we are to become the tough, disciplined army needed by the Church, we will conform.

It is summer 1962. We have been in the convent almost a year now, and the most-vocal dissenters have left. Our ranks are now down to forty-two. Day in and day out we have been instructed, shaped, and molded—and labeled as willful and proud if we have resisted any part of the molding. Few areas of our personalities have been left untouched.

An ex-nun friend looking back on this period of our training will put it this way: "It was as if they were baking a cake. At first we were all batter and no form, but then, before we knew it, we were cake—*their* cake."

Another will put it this way: "At first we asked questions, all sorts of questions, but when we never got any answers, we stopped asking. It was like we got to a point of no return. At the beginning we still had some sense of ourselves, some objectivity; then we just kind of went along with this, went along with that, until eventually we just 'went along.' "

As our first year in the convent draws to a close, we are like Alice stumbling through a topsy-turvy wonderland. We have stumbled along, stumbled along, until the topsy-turvy world of the convent has begun to look rather normal.

CANONICAL NOVICE (1962–1963)

It is August 6 1962 and our last recreation as postulants has begun. In just forty-five minutes, Sister Carmelita will ring her little bell, say "Good night, Sisters" with special solemnity, and our eight-day retreat in preparation for reception will begin.

Usually there is a rather frantic tone to the chatter and laughter throughout the room as we desperately try to cram into our recreation period all the talking we've been saving up during the day, but tonight there is almost a frenzied feeling. Soon the bell will ring and we will enter eight days of total silence, of total custody of the eyes. The next time we will talk to each other, will look at each other, we will be novices.

During canonical year, the year of strictest training mandated by canon law (Church law), any last contact with the world we may have had as postulants will be cut off. We will take no regular college courses, will receive no visitors. Though we will still be allowed to write our usual restrained letters to our families, taking care never to express feelings or to reveal any secret community customs, we will receive letters from them only on Christmas. Severed from all outside distractions, we will pursue closeness with God and spiritual perfection.

"Well, girls, it won't be long now. Soon we'll all be good little novices, gliding silently down the corridors, smiling at each other's guardian angels," Sister Joan Peter snickers as she stitches one more patch on a vest that must have been patched five times.

The six of us who sit around her look over our shoulders

to be sure Carmie isn't within earshot, then giggle nervously. Sister Mary Aquinas looks up from the stocking she is darning: "I never got the reasoning behind that. Why do they tell us to smile at each other's guardian angels instead of at each other?" She asks it innocently, really wanting to know.

Joanie smiles, as if talking to a child. "Because we're not supposed to *like* each other, remember? We're supposed to love each other with impersonal love. You know, feelingless love, like God loves." She ties a knot in her thread, clips it sharply with her scissors, and then continues. "Besides, do they ever explain anything? Like the bit about staying close to the wall when you walk down a corridor: what's that all about? Or the rule about only talking in doorways: are they afraid of earthquakes or something?"

One postulant excuses herself and moves to another group. I tell myself that she has more nerve than I: I know I'm guilty of bad example by sitting here listening to such irreverent talk, but I can't bring myself to risk Joanie's biting scorn. Besides, a part of me thinks Joanie's funny, and I can't resist giggling when she talks like this.

Eventually, however, I take myself in hand and wander to another part of the recreation room where a group of postulants is singing. One postulant had brought her ukelele to the novitiate and, somewhat surprisingly, had been allowed to keep it in the recreation room. She taught a couple of us to play so that at practically every recreation someone plays the uke and a little group sings. Increasingly in recent months I have chosen to sing rather than to converse, heading straight for the music the minute I enter the rec room. Forbidden to share feelings with family and frightened to share them with superiors, I have now begun to take the further step of withdrawing even from friends, not wanting anyone to see the miserable, self-centered, worthless person I now know myself to be. A year of searching my conscience for faults and failings, of resolving to be better the next day, and of never quite making it is beginning to bear fruit.

Only in song can I express all that is pent up within me. Forbidden to indulge in self-pity, to think about the past, we pour hearts and souls into songs such as "Sentimental Journey," "Jamaica Farewell," and "The Sloop *John B*," singing plaintive lyrics about stealing away, going home, and taking to the sea.

As the end of recreation nears and everyone races around the room exchanging last minute words and hugs before retreat starts, I clasp hands and eyes with a friend or two, wishing them a good retreat, and then return to my music. Sister Carmelita rises to ring the bell as we finish the last lines of "The Sloop *John B*": "I wanna go home, I wanna go home, this is the worst trip, I've ever been on. . . ."

"Come and rest awhile, my child, away from the noise and the tumult of the world. Alone together, let us talk over the needs of your soul, the aspirations of your heart. . . ."

As we have been taught to do, when inspired or moved by a passage in a meditation book, I close my eyes and let Jesus's words sink into every corner of my being. This is the *real* meditation, we are told—these wordless moments when even mental activity stops and there is nothing to do but bask in Jesus's love.

We have finished night prayers and Compline and are sitting in chapel, waiting for our retreat master to arrive. Steps are heard behind the altar; then a hulking blonde priest, handsome and thirtyish, emerges from the sacristy, genuflects in front of the tabernacle, and takes his place at the podium. He introduces himself as Father Bob. Then to relax the group he tells a joke about two good little nuns who appear before Saint Peter.

Launching into his discourse, Father Bob speaks with unabated exuberance of the nuptials to come, making numerous vague references to "blushing virgins with garlands in their hair." Sometimes his farm-boy background breaks through as he rhapsodizes: "What a glorious scene: great big bosomed

Mother Church calling you, her pets, to her side!" The imagery is embarrassing, but most of us are so overjoyed at having contact with a real live man—a rather young one at that!—that we're willing to overlook any faults.

In the coming days Father Bob presents spiritual discourses twice a day, and the rest of the time is spent praying, taking silent walks, organizing retreat notes, and preparing for this next big step. Every afternoon from one to three, we take a siesta, as retreat is to be a time of physical rejuvenation as well as spiritual. Siesta, like all other parts of the retreat program, is mandatory; we are to stay in bed the whole time.

Father is available to counsel with and give spiritual direction to anyone who wishes. Many take advantage of the opportunity, forming long, silent lines outside his office. What a luxury to be able to pour one's heart out to a man, to sit in a room and experience his maleness so near, to bring one's petty feminine turmoils and conflicts to him for advice! Being a man, he will be able to counsel, to advise with great wisdom and objectivity, will be able to offer guidance in a way that no mere woman can.

I too would like to talk to him, but I wouldn't know where to begin. Besides, the thought of revealing my foibles and failings to this perfect blonde god is just too humiliating; as always, I decide to keep my thoughts to myself.

Sister Carmelita has stressed that reception is a big step, that each of us should think long and hard before taking such a step. Do I really have a vocation? Am I really ready to make the total commitment that religious life requires? I want to look at such questions objectively, so I press myself to try to picture myself in some other life-style, but my imagination doesn't even provide me with the building blocks for such fantasies. Try as I may, I have put doubts and questions aside for so long that I can't even picture myself taking a different path. Others, maybe, but not me.

Confident that I have now prayed and pondered and chosen freely, I look ahead to what the future has in store for me. On Sunday I will dress as a bride of Christ and receive the habit of a Sister of Blessing. With that, canonical year (1962–1963) will begin. Next will come scholastic year, when we resume college classes. At the end of scholastic year, our novitiate training as well as two years of college will be finished. In the old days sisters would be sent out to teach at this point, returning to the motherhouse in ensuing summers to pursue their remaining college classes.

Now, however, there is an additional training program beyond the novitiate: called the juniorate, this two-year program prepares young sisters for mission and allows them to complete their college courses before being sent out to teach.

We will renew vows after a year in the juniorate, promising to be poor, chaste, and obedient for another year, and then at the end of both our college courses and our juniorate training (summer 1966), we will take three-year vows and be sent on mission. Most will be sent to teach in the grade schools and high schools that the order services throughout the country, perhaps one or two will work as housekeepers, cooks, nurses, or foreign missionaries.

At the end of three years on mission, we will go through a final training called *tertianship*. We will make a thirty-day retreat and then take perpetual vows, binding ourselves to the congregation for the rest of our lives.

The training will be long and arduous, but I know that ultimately it will pay off: I will leave Saint Raphael's well steeped in spirituality and well prepared for God's important work in the world.

I think about tomorrow's ceremony. For so long we have looked forward to this special day: even back in high school we sang dreamy songs about the nuptials to come.

Bride of Christ. In my early years of high school, the image had been appealing in some vague way: Jesus would be the bridegroom and I would be the bride. As I became older, however, I began to see the image as sentimental and maudlin, so I laugh with the others when, the day before reception, small pieces of stationery are placed on the front desk in front of study hall: we are to write little love notes to Jesus and stick them in our bras on reception-day morning!

Before we went on retreat, the prevalent topic of conversation at every recreation had been our bridal dresses. Though most of us feel a little silly about the whole nuptial imagery, after a year of unrelenting black serge we can hardly resist the opportunity to dress up in frilly white.

Ann Robert will wear her mother's wedding dress, a family treasure. Martha Mary's mother sent a creamy *peau-de-chine* dress, cut in a contemporary style. Those who have no family heirloom dresses and who want to spare their families the expense select dresses from the community storeroom, a collection of bridal gowns worn by young nuns down through the years. My own mother gave her wedding dress to my aunt to wear on her reception day twenty years before, and the dress had subsequently become a part of the community collection. As I try on dress after dress, I fantasize that I will find my mother's dress.

I never find her dress, of course: too many years have passed. But I do find her spirit here, and I experience again how intertwined our lives are—Mother, my aunt, me—how interwoven with the life of this community.

I eventually choose an old-fashioned gown of smooth off-white silk with pearl buttons down the back and a veil to match. Mother sends sheer nylons, lacy underwear, and the white "spikes" I have requested. After a year of wearing "sensible" granny shoes, I can hardly walk in the spike heels, so I practice walking around and around my tiny cubicle each evening before the lights go out.

Finally, everything is in readiness.

Reception day, August 15 1962, dawns, and as usual we rise at 5:15 in order to perform our spiritual exercises. Breakfast follows; then we cross the street to the motherhouse where we will dress for the ceremony.

At 8:00 A.M. it is already hot and humid, but a slight breeze ripples my hair. Tears fill my eyes as I realize that this is the last time I will ever feel the sun on my head, the wind in my hair: soon my hair will be cut and my head will be covered, never to be uncovered again. A slight tremor of rebellion races through my body, but within seconds it too surrenders.

I look around at my fellow band members: pin curls peep out beneath black caps; I try to picture what they will look like in veils.

Arriving at the motherhouse, we enter the room set aside for us and hurriedly begin to dress. I know that my family must have arrived by now; I can picture them being ushered into the Church, all dressed up in their best clothes. They'll sit in the section set aside for families and crane their necks to catch a first glimpse of us as we come down the aisle. I can picture how proud they'll be of me.

I give my hair one last swish of hair spray and take a quick look at myself in the mirror. Just a quick look, though: it would be a sacrilege to care too much how I look on such a profoundly religious day.

An older nun helps me to adjust my veil; then everyone lines up two by two in the hall. Church bells chime, announcing that the ceremony is about to begin.

As I take my place in the procession, I am suddenly aware of the beauty of my sisters bedecked in resplendent white all around me. No one speaks or catches another's eye, but there is a certain poignancy, a certain sense of the morning's solemnity that passes from one to the other. I sense my friend Donna's presence as she takes her place beside me, and without lifting my eyes I reach out and take her hand.

Donna's hand feels clammy as she squeezes mine tight, and some unrealness breaks around me as we stand there clasping hands. For the first time I hear the click of my high heels on the polished wood floor, feel the day's moist heat on my brow. This isn't a dream after all; this is really happening here and now, the day we have anticipated for so long.

The procession starts, and as we move silently toward the Church I am filled with a deep peace beyond words. Tears stream down my face, and I feel a oneness with God that I have never known. Bells ring jubilantly; a summer bird outside the window chirps excitedly. Here and there, older nuns line the sides of the halls as we pass, their radiant smiles adding to the excitement. As I near the Church, a hand reaches out to me and I look up to see my aunt, her own eyes filled with tears. We hug quickly, and she whispers that I look beautiful. I am filled with joy when I realize that after this day we will no longer be aunt and niece: we will be sisters.

The procession enters the back of the Church and then stops. After just a few minutes, at exactly 9:00 A.M. as church-bells proclaim the hour, the organ booms triumphantly and we process solemnly down the center aisle. Flashbulbs pop and mothers weep, just as at any wedding, and the altar is a mass of flowers and flaming candles.

Still basking in the rush of joy that had broken forth in me, I go through all the motions expected of me, walking down the aisle, taking my place in a ribboned pew.

Once there, I let go into the stillness within myself, consecrating myself to my God and whatever work He will ask of me in His world. I know deep inside that this is what the essence of the day is all about, that everything that follows will simply be form. I somehow sense that the form could change radically without the essence ever really being tampered with.

The postulants in front of me now rise, and I know that this is my cue to rise and start moving toward the altar where the bishop has completed the blessing of the habits. My euphoria has transported me nicely up to this point, but as I gather my voluminous skirt and step out of my pew, a certain chilly numbness begins to spread inch by inch through my body and my psyche. Despite the nuptial imagery, this is not a wedding like any other, full of orange blossoms and honeymoon dreams. I am going to join my crucified bridegroom: like Him, I too must die. On His altar I will lay the life I might have lived, the children I might have had. Merciful numbness moves in to deaden the pain. I will do it, then, without thinking, in one fell swoop: I will bow to the scissors that will hack away my long hair, the Rule that will hack away all that is individual, selfish, spontaneous. Before I have a chance to hesitate, I place one white-satined foot into the aisle, then another, and numbly follow where they lead.

The organ plays softly as each bride steps to the altar and receives a small bundle containing the various pieces that make up the holy habit. Then we file silently out of Church and gather in the community library.

Each postulant has a *sponsor*, a nun who was especially instrumental in her entrance into the community, and our sponsors now help us dress in the habit for the first time. My sponsor is, of course, my aunt. She finds me quickly and, without a word, takes me to the corner of the room where four novices have been assigned to cut hair. Some postulants cry softly as they wait their turn, watching in dismay as huge chunks of hair are chopped off and thrown to the floor. I am stoic as the scissors whack away at my hair with no attention to evenness or style, but when I reach back and feel how jagged it is, how ugly it must look, panic suddenly shoots through the numbness. But there is no time for such thoughts: my aunt hurriedly shows me how to put on my *serre-tête*.

She shows me how to put my face through the circle of white cotton, how to then wrap the linen around my neck, and how to pin it at the back with straight pins. Like the Amish, we use straight pins on our clothes instead of the newer, more-modern safety pins. Two straight pins secure the linen bands at the back of the neck; then the top part is gathered and straight-pinned at the back of the head. The trick is to make it taut but not too tight; if it isn't tight enough, stray strands of hair will peek out where the *serre-tête* rims the face; if it is too tight, it will cut into the skin under the chin. Mine hurts so badly that I beg my aunt to loosen it, but when she does, hunks of hair emerge around my face. We finally compromise, pulling it tight enough that I will be presentable, but not so tight that I won't be able to make it through the day. My aunt whispers that I should take it to the sewing room the next day so that it can be adjusted.

I now slip off my finery and begin to put on my waiting habit. By now I am fairly adept at putting on the first layers. Over the cotton underwear I put a new knee-length black cotton slip and a new black *waiste*. Next come tight-fitting sleeves that are held up at the elbows by black garters. Over these I put heavy serge sleeves that snap onto the *waiste*. When I go to Communion, these outer sleeves will be unfolded so that they touch my wrists: when I scrub floors, they will be folded back two times.

I pick up my habit skirt, kiss it as I have been instructed, and slip it on over my head. I now feel not only ugly (my chopped-off hair) and sore (the *serre-tête* digging into my chin), I also feel as if I weigh 200 pounds. To make matters worse, a starched white collar is now fastened around my neck, and a starched white cap is pinned over my ears. Another layer is added to my head, a white cotton veil, and before long I notice that I am finding it increasingly difficult to hear what my aunt is saying. I try moving my cap off my ears, but when I do, the whole thing is thrown askew. Telling myself that it is just a matter of adapting to all this, I pull the cap back over my ears so that it is straight again and resolve to grin and bear it through the day.

There is a solemn hush in the Church as we file back in: we had departed as radiant brides and now return dressed in the sober garb of a nun. I am sure there isn't a dry eye in the Church: no one could help but be moved by this sacrificial immolation of young lives.

Our part of the ceremony is now over, and the focus

turns to the other groups involved in the day's ritual. Novices who have completed both their canonical and scholastic year, the two years of novitiate training, now come to the front of the Church and take solemn vows of poverty, chastity, and obedience for the first time. Although they are encouraged to take their vows as if they are taking them forever, they are only ecclesiastically binding for one year, at which time they can be renewed for another year.

Next, those up for renewal step forward and take vows: two groups take one-year vows (scholastic novices and first-year junior sisters); one group take three-year vows (second-year junior sisters).

The last group, the tertians, now come forward to take perpetual vows. Unlike temporary vows, perpetual vows can be released only by means of a special dispensation from the pope. It is considered a profound tragedy when someone under final vows leaves the community, and it happens very rarely.

There is an eerie stillness in the Church as this group comes forward. The bishop asks, "My dear Sisters, what do you ask?" and standing in a half-circle in front of the altar, they respond in unison: "I ask to be permitted to take perpetual vows of poverty, chastity, and obedience as a Sister of Blessing." There are more questions, more answers; then the Church becomes like a tomb as young voices in unison pronounce the brave words that will bind them to their vows forever:

Until the word *forever* is spoken, there is still a chance to back out, to change their minds, but with the saying of the word aloud the die is cast: *forever*.

Once the word is pronounced, the tension in the Church turns to relief and jubilation: a joyful Mass of celebration follows. After Mass I quickly find my family and we head for the benches out under the trees, seeking refuge from the 92-degree heat. There are hugs and kisses and much exclaiming about how wonderful I look. Mom, Dad, the kids, Grandma, aunts, uncles, cousins—everyone is proud of me and they all turn out to tell me so.

The celebration rages on around me, but I am preoccupied with one thing: making it through the day. My *serre-tête* digs into my neck every time I talk; my cap stabs at my ears. In the steamy August heat, my habit is a heavy woolen blanket. I only want the day to end so I can peel off all these horrible, oppressive layers.

But I can speak of this to no one, of course. I must smile and look angelic and pretend that this is the happiest day of my life. Mother shoots me an appraising glance that tells me she suspects my secret misery, but nothing is said.

An uncle asks if the habit isn't hot, but my cousin, Sister Donald, hastens to explain that the habit is so heavy that it actually shuts out a lot of the heat. For the sake of the seculars, I smile and say nothing, but inside I ask myself if she and I are wearing the same habit.

As I look around at my brothers and sisters, I realize again the chasm that has grown between us. Forbidden to share my feelings with them, I take refuge in small talk—how they are doing in school, how the wrestling meets are going. Heartsick for the old closeness, I yet struggle to love them impersonally as God loves. Mom and Dad too—I hear the hollow formality in my voice as I speak to them as if I were no longer flesh of their flesh, and I long to rush headlong across the chasm and be simply their little girl once more, not this cold, defleshed statue. But Jesus's words ring in my mind: "Unless a man leaves father and mother, he can never be worthy of me." "Help me, Jesus," I pray silently. "Help me put all other loves behind me so that I can love but You alone."

Noon bells ring, and we head into the novitiate for lunch. Other postulants' families protest, as usual, the rule about our not being able to eat with them—"That's the silliest thing I've ever heard; here, at least take a handful of potato chips!"—but conditioned by many years of visiting nuns, my family rises immediately at the sound of the bell as if they too hear it as God's voice. "You better hurry: we don't want you to be late," says Dad as they gather their things and head off to get picnic baskets.

Inside it is celebration time as we gather for a festive noon meal. Even Sister Carmelita smiles: her work with us is now finished; she has formed us as well as she could. She will now turn us over to be further trained by the Mistress of Novices, Sister Amadeus.

There is much excited chatter throughout the room as everyone checks out each other's new garb, but by now I am in too much pain to participate. I take the two tablespoons of everything that is required of me, but every time I chew, I feel the *serre-tête* digging a deeper hole under my chin.

After lunch, my family and I small-talk away another hour or two and then I open presents: the usual handker-chiefs, hand lotion, and chocolate-covered cherries. Dad mis-chievously steals a few pictures of Sister Agnes Anita, Sister Donald, and myself—as long as we blushingly protest and re-frain from posing, it's OK—and I make a few last attempts to talk to my brothers and sisters. Andi sits beside me, sullen and silent, waiting for the day to end. She remembers the days when we used to play with Eddie Fisher/Debbie Reynolds paper dolls, dressing them in tux and bridal gown and process-ing them down my chenille bedspread. Who would have guessed it would come to this? Now the nuns at her school ask when she's going to follow in her sister Mary's footsteps. Are they crazy?

There are other things I'd like to share with my family too, the good things. I'd like to tell them about all the funny little things that happen each day. I'd like to tell them about the time the refectory reader read *chocolate mouse* instead of *chocolate mousse*, about the time I came sailing into refectory late and genuflected to Sister Amadeus instead of bowing. Everybody had laughed hysterically that day, Sister Amadeus included. When it was obvious that we weren't going to be able to pull ourselves together no matter how much we tried, she eventually rang her bell and let us talk for the rest of the meal.

Then there had been the time that we had just been introduced to another practice of poverty. Since nothing we used throughout the day belonged to us, be it a straight pin or a bottle of shampoo, we were to make reparation every time we carelessly broke something that belonged to the community. Each morning before breakfast started, those who had been so careless the day before were to kneel in the aisle in front of Sister Amadeus's table, each holding a piece of the article she had broken. After grace before meals, each would confess her transgression aloud—"My dear sisters, I humbly ask your pardon for breaking a dish"—then bow down and kiss the floor. Two days after we were taught this little practice, a broken toilet pulled away from its plaster bearings just as one of our band members went to sit on it, and she obediently knelt in front of Sister Amadeus with a piece of the plaster, confessing that she had broken a toilet. Wildfire laughter raced through the refectory that day too, but if Sister Amadeus laughed this time, she hid it behind tight, prim lips.

How could I tell these stories without revealing secret community customs? And besides, in retrospect, the little things that threw us into hysterics day after day now seemed so trivial, hardly funny. Surely if I told my family some of the crazy little things that set off a delicious chain reaction of belly-deep mirth in chapel or in the refectory, they'd smile at me politely and wonder what postulant year had done to my mind.

I longed to tell them how good it felt to laugh like that, and I longed to tell them other little things too. I longed to tell them how warm and cozy I felt when my prie-dieu partner sat down next to me in chapel, her arm brushing mine as we wrote funny little notes to each other. I longed to tell them how my spirits soared when my teachers wrote a big red *excel-*

lent at the top of a paper, and about the rare, still moments of union with God when nothing else seemed to matter. But how do you put all of that into words—especially to seculars, who would never understand such things?

At the end of the day, I stand in my cubicle and begin to undress. There is a prayer to be said as each part of my habit is removed: I taped a copy of the prayers to the inside of my cabinet door and I read them now as I remove and kiss each sacred piece, taking care never to let any part of the conse-crated cloth touch the floor. A strip of black tape has been sewn along the bottom edge of the habit skirt so that the holy habit itself will never touch the floor.

Once my cap and *serre-tête* are off, the pain over my ears and under my chin stops as if shut off by a switch. I lay out my clothes on my cabinet shelves, careful to place them in precise order of dressing for the next morning. Is it really possible to make my bed, wash my face, go to the bathroom, brush my teeth, put my stockings on kneeling down, swaddle myself in my multiple layers, properly position and pin all that needs to be positioned and pinned—and still make it down to the chapel in a half-hour? How do the novices do it?

Feeling suddenly naked and light in my nightgown and robe, I cover my chopped-off hair with my nightcap and set off to wash.

When the warning bell rings at 9:55 P.M., I turn back my bedspread and fall to my knees by the side of my bed. I cover my crucifix with kisses, telling Jesus how happy I am to at last be His very own: "Take me, sweet Lord, I am yours."

When the final bell rings, I climb into my narrow little bed, pull the sheet up around me, and fall to sleep clutching my crucifix. The fact that someone might find this a rather strange way to spend one's honeymoon night is a thought that never occurs to me.

The next day my *serre-tête* is adjusted and the open sore on my neck begins to heal. Like many of my band members, I will walk around for a few days with a piece of gauze under my chin, protecting my skin from the offending rub of the linen. My cap is also adjusted so that it no longer jabs into my ears: sounds of life around me remain somewhat muted, but at least the pain is gone. And the heat: the fact that the chapel is one of the few air-conditioned rooms in the building spurs a sudden rash of prayerfulness in many of us soon after reception.

Canonical year now begins: all contact with the outside world comes to a sudden halt. The only classes we will take will be theology, ethics, and community history, and all three will be taught in the novitiate building. We will only leave the building to go on our daily walk, to the gym, to the main Church, or to a cleaning assignment in another building. Mornings will be devoted to domestic work, which unlike intellectual work leaves our minds free for prayer; afternoons are set aside for instructions, religious studies, and prayer. Talking will be allowed just twice a day, at our two recreations, and the rest of the day will be spent in silent, prayerful contemplation.

I look forward to the year and the peace it promises. No tests, no hurried schedule of classes and activities. I will have time to reflect, time to pray; perhaps I will be able to find at long last the closeness with God that I crave; perhaps I will be able at long last to bring my unruly ego and emotions under control.

At first, canonical year is all that I have dreamed: with head and body hidden, covered, I begin to follow the path that leads inside.

I soon discover that whoever designed our religious habit, heavy and shroudlike, calculated well the ability of one's apparel to affect how one sees the world. A thick, blanketing dullness now hangs between me and the riotous stimuli of the external world: a certain black-and-white flatness now separates me from all that is colorful, sharp, bright.

Paradoxically, the habit also seems to bring a certain

lightness, a certain disassociation with the sediment of here-and-now so that I can fly with the angels. I feel in a way graceful and queenlike, now that I have mastered the art of lifting my long skirt to climb the stairs. I feel that I have left behind my plain old earthly self in order to keep company with royalty, saints, and mystics. Admittedly, I am only a neophyte in their midst, but my quaint other-world garb nonetheless marks me as one of their own.

Determined not to become so focused inward that I lose sight of the big world out there, the world that I will one day help to save, I go to the library and check out a book entitled *How to Prove the Existence of God*. I know that in just a few short years I will be out there in the thick of things: it would behoove me now, while I still have the time and the leisure, to bone up on a few essential skills. Surely, being able to prove the existence of God is one of the most essential. Who knows: maybe my beliefs will one day be challenged by a pagan professor on a pagan college campus. We are always warned to be careful of this type. Will I be prepared? Will I be ready to stand up for my faith? Will I be able to whisk out, at the first sign of attack, arguments and proofs that will leave him defenseless? No, it is obvious that I have a lot of good solid work to do before I will be ready for such a confrontation. I will start by memorizing these proofs of God's existence: I will copy them, one a day, and carry them around in my pocket, glancing at them, rolling them around in my mind at every opportunity. By the end of canonical year, I will have them memorized and be well armed for mission. I chuckle to myself, my cleverness and foresight making me feel just a bit superior.

It doesn't take me long to discover that cleverness and foresight are quite low on the list of qualities expected of a canonical novice. At the top of the list, I soon discover, are such things as eagerness to follow orders, ability to apply an even coat of wax, and willingness to work beyond the point of exhaustion.

My first employment takes me to the motherhouse building, Athanasius Hall, where I work four hours each morning under the direction of Sister Ann Irene, the housekeeper-in-chief. A slow-moving, portly woman, she does her best to teach us some of the housekeeping skills our mothers so sadly neglected to teach us. "Didn't you ever scrub a floor before, Miss Priss? You've gotta get down on your hands and knees and use some elbow grease. You all act like you had servants at home or something. . . ." Then she goes off on a tirade about how, just because we are receiving college educations, we shouldn't think we are better than everyone else. "I could have gone to school—it's not like I'm dumb or something—but Mother needed me here." A sweet, docile smile crosses her lips, and she reaches down and fingers her *chaplette.* "Mother: she's such a kind, holy soul. It's a privilege to clean her room, to wax her floors. Just last week she stopped to thank me for doing such a good job. That's Mother for you, so gracious, so thoughtful." Leaving me to meditate on Mother's many virtues and to compare my own mediocrity against them, Sister Ann Irene lumbers off, confident that she has contributed something significant to my training.

When I work in the infirmary it's much the same: Sister Arthur, the nurse in charge of the floor, loudly bemoans the fact that girls joining convents today don't seem to have any practical skills at all. "I had a novice in here last month," she raves as she shows me how to set up trays for lunch. "I told her to cook some macaroni and d'you know what she did? She poured the macaroni in the pan and turned on the stove without even adding any water!" Sister Arthur doubles up with laughter—it's one of her favorite stories. "Back in my day we didn't have all the advantages you girls have—it took me thirteen summers just to get my B.A.! But at least we had some common sense. I wish I could say the same for today's novices. You've all got your heads in the clouds!"

I finger the proofs of God's existence that I carry in my pocket like a secret stash and resolve that Sister Arthur, like Sister Ann Irene, will never know.

Sometimes when Sister Arthur isn't watching, I slow down the speed of my dust mop and chat with the infirmary residents, most of whom are older sisters suffering from a variety of ailments. I love listening to their reminiscences of their teaching days.

I especially enjoy the accounts of Sister Helen Clarita, a legend in the order because of her extraordinary success as a boys' teacher. There had been a time when the order had refused to teach in any schools where there were boys as it was felt that the teaching of the male of the species required a particular skill, a particular unflinching ability as a disciplinarian, a skill and ability that not all possessed. Sister Helen Clarita, however, had taught boys year after year, ruling her classroom with an iron fist that even the most intransigent did not defy. Yet her students had loved her—she had always been fair, always straight shooting—and after more than fifty years of teaching, they still flocked to see her.

Rocking in her wooden rocker as I scrub the tiles of her bathroom, Sister Helen Clarita tells me the story of two old students who recently visited: "Herbert and Joseph: I remember them well—I had them in second grade. Joseph was a rather quiet boy, but that Herbert was a terror." Sister Helen Clarita smiles at the memory; then her bony fingers push a lock of gray hair back into her night cap. "Recently they came to see me—it must have been fifty years." She pulls a handkerchief out of the pocket of her robe, coughs up some phlegm, and then continues. "Both must be in their fifties now. Joseph was as shy and polite as always, but that Herbert was his old scoundrel self. He told me he still had the marks from where I used to hit him with the ruler! Can you imagine?" Sister Helen Clarita cackles at the memory, and since I have moved on to clean the toilet, she scoots her rocker a little closer to the bathroom so that I can hear every word. "Do you know what I told him? I told him I was too easy on him: as mischievous as he was, I really should have cracked him harder!" She cackles again, and I laugh appreciatively.

As I move on to scour the tub, she lapses into a reflective silence. Eventually she asks me to hand her a glass of water, and when I do, she sticks her finger into it and then pulls it out slowly. Thinking that her sharp mind is beginning to go at last, I am dismayed. More serious than I've ever seen her, she says, "There, Sister, you see the effect my finger has on the water? That's about the effect a teacher, even a very good one, has on the lives of her pupils."

She says it without a trace of bitterness or self-pity, this woman who has been an extraordinarily successful teacher for over fifty years; yet I am aghast. "But Sister," I protest passionately, "you've touched so many lives, brought so many to Christ: how can you say you haven't had an effect?"

Sister Helen Clarita merely smiles indulgently and tells me that I will understand some day. Thanking me for listening to her "prattle," she pads off to say her rosary, leaving me to clean her tub and ponder her words.

My mind fights desperately: but it *is* possible to change the world—my generation will do it! War, poverty, ignorance, all of it—we'll turn it all around! Why else would I be here, buried under all these clothes, scrubbing an old woman's bathtub? I only stay because I know that this is all just an arduous training for the day when we will change the world.

Yet as I move on to scrub another bathroom, I find that I can't put her strangely haunting words out of my mind. What could Sister Helen Clarita have meant? I must remember to ask her more about this.

I enjoy working in the infirmary, and I especially enjoy taking night duty. When a novice is assigned night duty, she sleeps in the afternoon in preparation and then reports to the infirmary at about 10 P.M. The nurses brief her on the particular needs of each patient and explain who is to get what medication at what time. Sister Alphonsus needs to be turned at 11 P.M., and be sure to watch for Sister Ann Louise who might soil her sheets. Sister Margaret Robert might not want to take her medication, but you just have to be firm with her. And don't pay any attention to Sister Roch who might come to her barred window on the locked unit and call out that she is being raped. But you really should watch for Sister Winifred who loves to strip off all her clothes and parade down the hall in the middle of the night. If there are any serious problems, call the nurses immediately.

I enjoy night duty, enjoy taking care of these oldest members of our convent family: they are my sisters, and I consider it a privilege to be able to make their last days as comfortable as possible.

I also like the way night duty seems to jolt me out of the deadly sameness of my daily routine. Two novices are always assigned to take night duty together. Sitting at the little nurses' station on second floor, we drink black coffee to keep ourselves awake, read spiritual books, and rediscover the amazing reality that the world does indeed continue to exist after the 10 P.M. bell. Then in the morning when the nurses come on duty, we crawl into bed and sleep for the rest of the day. It seems a trivial thing, but this break with lockstep routine somehow frees my spirit, somehow reminds me that there *is* life outside cramped convent parameters of space and time. My stomach always seems to relax its almost-constant clench every time I crawl into bed after a night of infirmary duty, and I always lie there trying to figure out why.

Everyone's experience of night duty isn't so pleasant, however. One morning I am sweeping out the furnace room in the novitiate basement, and I am suddenly startled to hear a familiar voice. I turn to see my friend Liz, pale and trembling and near to tears.

"Liz, what's the matter?" I ask. In the five years that we've been friends, I have never seen her so upset.

"Oh, Maggie, I just came from night duty. All night long I had to sit with Sister Agnes Rose—they didn't expect her to make it through the night. The nurse said I should sit there and watch her: if she made any strange noises like she was dying, I was to call the nurse. I've never been around dying people before: I don't know what dying *sounds* like!

"It was so eerie sitting there all night in the semidark and stench of the room, waiting for her to die. Her face was gray, her breathing was raspy: every now and then she'd make a sound and I would panic, trying to decide if I should go get the nurse. What if I didn't call the nurse on time and she died without Extreme Unction?"

I can understand the sense of responsibility Liz must have felt. Here was a nun who had dedicated her whole life to God; yet her fate for all eternity depended on the state of her soul at the moment of death—and the state of her soul depended on Liz getting the priest there in time for a last confession! Who knows the thoughts in another's heart? Despite her many years of selfless service and sacrifice, Sister Agnes Rose could damn herself for all eternity by just one moment of despair, one moment of cursing God. In the next moment she could, of course, set the score straight by making an act of perfect contrition, but her contribution would have to be just that: perfect. She would have to be sorry for her sins because she had offended God: if any fear of hell crept in to contaminate her motive, the act of contrition would not work. Only by confessing one's sins at the moment of death and receiving the priest's absolution—only then can one be assured a life of eternal happiness.

Sister Agnes Rose lingered until the next morning, dying an hour after Liz had gone off duty, but it would be a while before Liz would shake the memory of that frightening night.

Unlike Liz who will always carry the memory of that night in her soul, I am working in the infirmary the morning Sister Helen Clarita dies, and I am left with quite a different memory.

Kneeling at the door of Sister Helen Clarita's room, I watch as physical family and spiritual family gently merge at her bedside, whispering their last good-byes. Soon the word will go out to all the Herberts and Josephs of her fifty years of teaching, and they will fill the church to overflowing at her funeral.

At one point she opens her eyes just a crack and sees me kneeling by the door; then she beckons me to her side. A bony hand clasps mine one last time as a twitch of pain moves through her body. She opens her eyes and looks directly into mine. I am startled by the look of tranquillity and peace I see there, and I bend close to hear her whispered legacy. "About the water, Sister: we can never change the world; we can only change ourselves." Touched beyond words, I kiss her forehead and whisper that I will always remember.

A few moments later I am again kneeling outside the door when the room is suddenly filled with a strange silence. Morning sun streams in at the window, and through swimming eyes I stare at a half-filled water glass that sits on Sister Helen Clarita's night table.

In her graciousness my sister has taught me this one last lesson: that the surrender of death holds no terror for one who has been surrendering—changing herself, not the world—all her life.

When I work in the infirmary, all the little dramas of infirmary life pull me out of myself. There is human contact, human interaction: in reaching out and soothing another by my touch and by my words, I too am soothed.

Once my stint in the infirmary is over, however, I am again left to face myself, my faults, and my failings, and as the year wears on, a strangely absorbing self-consciousness and self-scrutiny begins to preoccupy me, extending tentacles into the furthest reaches of my soul.

It comes on gradually at first, this unnamed fear. I first become aware of it when I raise my hand to give an answer in theology class and all of a sudden am overcome with fear. My hands tremble, my voice shakes. Desperate, I try to pull myself together, but the more I try, the more nervous I become. Eventually I stop raising my hand and begin making sure that I am ill every time I am scheduled for an oral report. Grades that have always been high begin to dip drastically.

Things grow worse. I am scheduled for portress duty one week, and for the whole week I live in fear of the phone ringing. When canonical novices begin to be assigned as refectory readers, I scan the assignment list each week, terrified of seeing my name. I am always relieved when one after another band member is called upon to read, but never me, and yet the glaring omission only serves to confirm my fears that there really *is* something wrong with me, that others see it too!

A quick-spreading cancer, the fear grows by leaps and bounds. I become obsessed with the fear that I will be appointed hebdomedaria. As "heb," it would be my responsibility to intone each section of the office, and the thought of my trembling voice floating through the quiet chapel fills me with humiliation and terror. Again, others are appointed heb, but never me: I am sure that everyone around me knows of my strange cancer.

I now feel so desperate that I am sure I will explode if I don't talk to someone. Maybe I will talk to Sister Amadeus— she seems kind and gentle enough, if austere. But if she learns of my strange problem, she may send me home. That is her role: to watch each one of us carefully, to weed out those unsuited for the rigors of religious life. She told my friend Liz that if she didn't stop looking so discouraged and glum she was going to have to send *her* home. What if she said the same thing to me?

The thought of being sent home sends me into sudden panic. My roots, my identity are all here. What would I do out there? Who would I be? Always threatening, the world outside convent walls now seems distant, unreal, and I can't even fantasize a life for myself there.

No, I can't talk to Sister Amadeus. I will just have to pull myself together, gain control of myself. I will pray and sacrifice and ask for God's light. Maybe if I say an extra rosary each day and give up desserts . . .

Everyone sits silently, waiting for instructions to begin. I slip into the back of the auditorium and take my seat, breathing a sigh of relief that Sister Amadeus isn't here yet. I am still pinned up, so I take the pins out one by one and stick them in my pincushion. Someone gave me some new pins and I admire them now as they circle the perimeter of my pincushion: each has a bright speck of color at its head. I traded two blue for two red just yesterday, and they shine up at me now like tiny rubies. I like the way they look when I am pinned up, a tiny jewel at each shoulder.

Suddenly remembering, I shoot a glance across the room to see if Liz is in her seat. My heart sinks: her seat is empty. Would she really leave without giving me a clue? But then she has been so depressed lately, biting her nails constantly and losing so much weight.

It also seems as if Liz has been getting into a lot of trouble: just the other day Sister Amadeus called her into her office and reprimanded her for reading a *Newsweek* she had found in the trash. Liz is intelligent, and the lack of intellectual stimulation has really been getting to her. "I feel like my brain is atrophying," she moaned when Sister Amadeus chastised her about the *Newsweek,* but Sister Amadeus simply reprimanded her further for her insolence and her intellectual pride.

I hear a rustling in the back of the room: it's Liz! Oh thank you, Jesus, thank you, thank you!

Soon Sister Amadeus enters: instructions are about to begin.

Everyone rises and recites the usual prayers. Afterward most of the group sit down, but about ten novices remain standing. I am tormented by my usual dilemma: should I stand up too? Feeling my knees get wobbly, I push myself onto my feet and wait my turn.

"My dear Sisters, I humbly ask your forgiveness for talking when it wasn't really necessary." The first novice's face flushes deep red and the voice stammers. Embarrassed for her, I try not to hear the awkward stammering. Then, kneeling down, she kisses the floor.

"My dear Sisters, I humbly ask your pardon for showing my feelings.

"My dear Sisters, I humbly ask your pardon for being moody.

"My dear Sisters, I humbly ask your pardon for having a particular friend."

Deathlike silence fills the room as one after another confesses her failings to the group and then kisses the floor. Everyone's voice seems so strange, disembodied.

My heart pounds as I wait my turn. I'm determined to do it this time without my voice trembling. Be cool, be casual. Are you going to become all nervous and embarrass yourself again? I rehearse my lines over and over and over. Oh no, just one left to go. Should I start when she goes down to kiss the floor or when she stands up? Or maybe right in the middle. What did the others do? Oh panic! Keep your voice steady, don't let it shake, don't let it shake. This is crazy, this is insane, it doesn't matter, nobody cares. (Don't let it shake, don't let it shake, don't let it shake.)

I'm the only one left—hurry, get it out before you make a fool of yourself. "My d-d-dear Sisters, I h-h-humbly ask your forgiveness for being m-m-moody a-a-and depressed." My voice creeps out weak and tremulous, and my hands won't stop shaking. Cowering with embarrassment, I kneel to kiss the floor and wish that I could stay down there so that no one can see my face.

It is the same thing, morning after morning. We are encouraged to confess our faults and failings to the group and, determined to make spiritual advancement, I press myself to take my place among the penitents. Determined to put an end to my nervousness, I press myself to pull myself together. I'm not sure whether or not I am making spiritual progress, but I *am* sure that I am making no progress at all in pulling myself together.

For many years I have worn the cloak of superficial good-ness, not wanting people to see the essential fallenness that rotted somewhere at my core, but canonical year brings me face to face with myself and all my shortcomings. Jesus and the saints are always out there in front of me, light years ahead of me. I am continually out of breath and discouraged in my efforts to catch up.

Not only do we have the laws of God and the laws of the Church to follow now; we also have our Holy Rule as set down by Mother Matthew. Now that we are canonicals, each of us has a copy of the Holy Rule; by reading it we can learn how a Sister of Blessing is supposed to live each day, what kind of attitudes she should have, and how she should behave in various situations. No room is left for confusion about how to advance on the path of perfection: it is all covered in that one little book.

Nightly examinations of conscience and weekly confes-sions will not suffice now that the pursuit of perfection has grown more intense: through the course of the year we are gradually introduced to more elaborate methods of self-exam-ination. At the end of each day we draw up recreation lists, naming all the people we recreated with during the day. Then once a week we turn our lists in to Sister Amadeus so that she can keep a better eye on our friendship patterns. If a list shows that we have recreated with the same person a number of times in one week, we are sure to be called into her office where she will again lecture us on the importance of keeping our friendships general.

We are also to fill our silence slips, little slips of paper where we note how many times we violated silence on each particular day. These too are turned into Sister Amadeus at the end of the week.

Each of us is given a set of examen beads (also called perfection beads), a tiny strand of beads to be worn under one's cape. Examen beads move up and down and are used to tally transgressions against whatever virtue one is working on at the moment. If one is working to develop charity, for example, she pulls down a bead every time she has an uncharitable thought. Then at the end of the day, the beads are counted and the number is recorded in a little black book called an examen book.

Just trying to keep all these lists, slips, beads, and books straight seems a futile task: how can I begin to set things straight in my chaotic, fault-ridden soul?

Along with the more sophisticated methods of tallying our faults, we have also been introduced to new practices of penance, new ways of bringing our stubborn wills into subjection. The doors are closed discreetly and the drapes are shut: the very dust in the air stands still as the mistress of novices lowers her voice and introduces us to yet another means of self-discipline.

Many of the penances have to do with food, as eating is the only "pure" pleasure allowed behind convent walls. The point is frequently made at instructions sessions: good religious never pursue pleasure for the sake of pleasure, never slip into worldly hedonism. Every action should have as its goal the worship and service of God: if pleasure results, so be it, but pleasure should never be the end.

We should read and study in order to prepare ourselves to be teachers and never for the sheer joy of reading. The fact that our courses of study are assigned, that no electives are allowed, underscores this attitude. We should approach recreations and visiting days as opportunities to enlighten and entertain others rather than ourselves. We should feed and exercise our bodies in order to keep them in good working order, *not* for enjoyment.

It is at this point, however, that there begins to be some confusion: surely indulgence in chocolate fudge cannot be rationalized as building strong bodies and increasing gray matter. Though superiors never in any of their talks connect chocolate fudge and hedonism, everyone knows that only the act of eating such goodies comes dangerously close to being pleasure for the sake of pleasure. Because it can so easily be used for one's own pleasure instead of for some higher purpose, food will be the object of many of our practices of penance.

Like all Catholics we don't eat meat on Friday, and in the novitiate we don't eat at *all* on Good Friday. It is also a community practice of poverty never to eat meat and butter at the same meal. The more pious forgo dessert and/or collation from time to time, and as canonicals we are introduced to two new practices of discipline: taking a meal kneeling and taking a meal standing.

In order to take a meal kneeling, a novice sets plate and silver on her chair during a silent meal and presses her knees into the hard terrazzo floor as she eats. To take a meal standing, she stands against the wall until the others are through eating and then takes her meal at second table. Reminiscing about these practices, one ex-nun friend will grin: "I *loved* taking a meal standing: I got to eat more that way, since they brought all the leftover food to second table!"

We can also do penance by watching for every daily opportunity to mortify our senses, to impose some small suffering on ourselves. Examen beads are also helpful in keeping track of these little mortifications. If I bite my tongue when I start to say something that isn't really necessary, I reach under my cape and pull down a bead. If I pass up the candy tray when it comes around, I pull down a bead. If I really want to move quickly in the way of perfection I sit next to a superior or a bore (not mutually exclusive) at recreation and pull down a bead. (It's a little hard on the ego when someone sits down next to you, and you see her reach under her cape for a bead!

We're pretty careful about keeping our beads hidden, how-ever: if we flaunt our holiness we'll commit the sin of pride and lose all the benefits of the penance.)

There is much joking around about all this at first. Joanie, for example, has been told to kiss the floor so many times that we fear for the state of her lips. "Joanie, you'd better shape up before you wear out your lips on the floor."

As usual, however, Joanie has the last laugh. "You think I'd kiss the floor? Kiss some cow shit that somebody dragged in on her shoes from a walk to the barns? Forget it, girls—I kiss my hand every time I go down!"

With such joking around, we stave off the panic that is always there just an arm's length away: "What are they going to spring on us next, whips and chains?" We all laugh and take big gulps of happy camaraderie, the only oxygen we have left. But it is going fast.

Even those of us who took it all in stride at the beginning began to bristle more and more as time went on. Eventually it was as if we came together in some unspoken commitment: we would not let "them" get to us; we would hang onto our sanity.

Now, however, one by one we break ranks and go to join "the enemy." At recreation each evening, there is less joking around about "what they're going to spring on us next"; at instructions each morning there are more who stand to con-fess their faults and kiss the floor in self-reproach.

I reflect on all this one steel-gray winter morning as I stare out refectory windows at the all-encrusting snow. Spring is a word I have long ago forgotten—is there really spring under all that frozen earth?

It comes on me gradually: it feels murky and sordid and scary. I am *sure* I can't talk about *this* with anyone.

I feel myself pulled by some magnetic force to want to spend as much time as I can with one other sister. In my sleeping hours I dream about her: I see us walking hand in hand through life together, hugging each other in the rain, forming a safe little world together, and keeping all the others out. In my waking hours I try to set it up so that I am around her anywhere she goes. If she signs up for gym, *I* sign up for gym; if she goes to pray in the chapel, *I* go to pray in the chapel. I don't need to talk to her to be near her: just being in the same room with her is exciting enough.

For a time she seems to know what is happening, to play along with the game. I am her special friend. She comes and sits by me at recreation (I am so nervous and trembly I can hardly talk!); she shows up in the laundry room when I am there folding my clothes. We never talk about it, never touch—but we both know the magnetism is there.

And then she moves on to someone else, just like that. I am despondent. Through my pain I watch the whole scene, see the other sister become equally stirred before she too is left behind. I don't know what this is all about, but I vaguely sense that it has to do with all those sober warnings we always receive about the danger of particular friendships. I try talking about it in confession, but the priest just laughs and says there is nothing wrong with friendship: I shouldn't let some crotchety old nuns put funny ideas in my head.

But I know he's wrong. I have friends, lots of them, but this is different. The feeling is different. It is strong and powerful and totally new. I am frightened.

A few weeks later I have my answer. My friend now has a new companion and this time the alliance sticks. My friend, the older of the two, is somewhat boylike in appearance and the way she carries herself. The other novice is pretty and young—almost frail looking. Totally indifferent to all the regulations about spending too much time with one other person, the two become inseparable. It is obvious that this isn't just friendship; there is a certain way they look at each other when they are together. I have never even heard the word *lesbian* before, but I begin to hear it whispered around as time after time we see them sneak up to the second floor together.

I am shocked, as more sophisticated friends explain to me what is going on. *Sex* is a word that isn't in my daily vocabulary or consciousness; if it were, it would be driven out *fast* as soon as it cropped up. Dirty thoughts are just venial sins, but I know that they can quickly become mortal sins if one lets herself—God forbid—enjoy them. Thoughts of normal, natural sex as God preordained it for the procreation of children: these are certainly bad enough since we are committed to chastity. But *that* kind of sex, as described by my worldly mentors? The thought is literally unthinkable, and I am sure that the act must rank with the worst of mortal sins.

I am disgusted and at the same time frightened. Within a week or two both novices are asked to leave, but I am left with my feelings. Do I too have such abnormal tendencies? The thought of how the older novice stirred something inside me terrifies me. Thank God I didn't let anyone know about those feelings. No one ever will. I resolve that I will never let *anyone* stir me that deeply again.

It is a bitter-cold morning in early February and the campus lies buried under heavy snow. For the past few days our walks have been short: even the heaviest shawls provide little protection against the biting Illinois winds.

When I arrive at instructions, I discover that the windows are covered with dark paper, that the chairs are lined up in rows facing each other, monastic style. The whispered word goes around that we are about to experience our first chapter of faults.

Word had leaked out about chapter of faults while we were still postulants: one postulant discovered a copy of the community's Holy Rule left in a prie-dieu, and she plied Sister Carmelita with questions about chapter of faults. Sister Carmelita had been shaken: there were certain things that we were not to learn about too soon, and chapter of faults was one of them. She promptly confiscated the Rule book and made a note to see that the novice who had been so careless as to leave it there was properly reprimanded.

Then with the coming of canonical year, we ourselves received copies of the Holy Rule. But though it mentions chapter of faults, we have never yet experienced that particular spiritual practice, and our curiosity and apprehension are at a peak.

I take my seat this morning and through force of habit look over to see if Liz is here. Some near-numb place in my heart flinches as I again realize that it is all over now: Liz left last week. Her family had heard through college-student friends how much weight she had lost, how emaciated she looked, and they had insisted that she come home for tests. Just being home again had broken the spell, according to Liz: though she still believed in a lot of the ideals of religious life, she just couldn't put herself through the struggle anymore. I was grateful to her for defying Sister Amadeus's solemn warnings, for letting me cry in her arms like a baby when we said good-bye.

I look around the room, assuring myself that other friends are still here. Ellen is missing, but I know she's always late; Anita has infirmary duty.

As I look around the room I suddenly become aware of how depleted our ranks have become. From a boisterous, ebullient sixty-five, we are down to a rather whipped-looking, tense, and tamed twenty-seven. I think of some of the ones who have left—how much fun they had been, how alive! A part of me died with each departure. Then I do the only thing I know to do when I struggle with such feelings: with all my might I push them aside and say a fervent prayer for perseverance.

Chapter of faults is starting now, and Sister Amadeus in a particularly solemn voice is giving directions. We are to keep our eyes closed throughout the sessions, and, row by row, each of us is to stand and announce her failings and shortcomings of the past month.

Already my hands are clammy: now there is no escape; everyone has to participate. The dimmed lights, the papers on the windows, the secrecy—I know I am letting my imagination get the best of me, but I can't stop the images that run through my head. I fantasize Sister Amadeus grimly flagellating certain holy novices; I picture others receiving the stigmata from the Lord Himself, mysterious bloody wounds in their hands, gory reminders of their crucified Lord's suffering.

Something suddenly snaps inside me. What on earth is wrong with me? Am I going crazy or something? Daring to open my eyes just a crack I look around the room at my fellow band members and suddenly realize that they too are caught in the craziness. Anna Louise is now down to 90 pounds, and her face is all dry and shriveled. Philip Marie picks at her fingers until they are raw, and Carrie and Roberta Louise haven't had their periods for over a year. There is some strange, contagious disease that has spread through our group, striking first one, then another. People who were fun loving and carefree are now tense and compulsive. People who were spontaneous and witty now weigh every stilted word with precision—necessity? charity? politeness? People who were poised and self-confident are now racked with self-consciousness. People who had been alive and vibrant now walk around like zombies.

Expressions of anger and hurt and discouragement have not been tolerated, so we have learned to shut down on negative feelings. Expressions of friendship and affection have been discouraged, so we have learned to shut down on positive feelings. Many of us have learned to shut down on *all* feelings. Alive, happy girls have been transformed into sexless, emotionless robots—surely this isn't what holiness is all about! Didn't I read somewhere that *holiness* really means *wholeness*? I know that I don't feel very whole!

I'm not sure yet what I am going to do with my new realization, but it feels good to at least be able to wrap some words around what has happened. It feels like this very naming process might be the first tiny step out of this nameless quagmire. Maybe spring will come after all.

Spring comes, then summer—one of the hottest and stickiest in Illinois history. My skirt is an oven around my legs; my *serre-tête* is constantly soaked with sweat.

When the college girls depart for summer vacation, we are assigned to clean their buildings, scrubbing, waxing, and polishing until everything is ready for the nuns who will occupy the buildings during the summer. In the afternoons we work in the cannery or in the laundry. In the cannery we sit in rows on hard wooden benches, peeling tomatoes in silence. Sometimes someone reads to us from a spiritual book. The tomatoes itch my hands as I peel; their pungent odor stings my nostrils as they cook. The laundry is the hottest: we sit for hours over the hot mangles (big institutional irons) running damp handkerchiefs and *serre-têtes* through the steaming-hot rollers until they are dry and neatly pressed.

I tell myself that if this is the dark night of the soul that the great mystics talked about, the dawn had better come fast. I am sure I can't hold on much longer.

The more I hold on and hold in, the more my stomach tightens, and eventually the pain is so bad that I know I can no longer put off saying something to Sister Amadeus. If she feels that my symptoms are serious enough, I will be allowed to talk to a community nurse who will in turn decide whether or not I should see a doctor.

Eventually I am sent to a doctor in town. Tests are ordered, and it is determined that I too, like a number of my fellow band members, have an ulcer. Like them, I will carry a bottle of ulcer-relief medicine with me wherever I go—is it my imagination that every other locker in the locker room contains a bottle of ulcer-relief medicine?

The novice who shares my locker now walks with a cane.

In a rare defiant mood one day, I decide to violate silence and ask her what happened. She tells me that she has always had trouble with foot perspiration, that she told Sister Amadeus this and asked permission to let her parents send her another pair of shoes so that she could alternate pairs each day. Sister Amadeus talked it over with Reverend Mother and Mother let her know in no uncertain terms that such "irregularities" should not be tolerated, that the novice should not be treated as a "special case." The order needed strong, healthy women, not whiners who asked for special dispensations all the time. Finally, the novice developed such a severe case of bursitis that Sister Amadeus had no choice but to send her to the doctor; and when the doctor bellowed that, community practice or no, this novice needed to have two pairs of everyday shoes, Mother had no choice but to concede. Since it was so close to August and to profession of vows, she was sent over to Lingerie in the motherhouse, and here she selected a pair of shoes from those that had belonged to sisters who had departed or died. (After vows, young sisters who need new shoes, bras, or girdles will select them from this collection.) Though ill fitting and ugly, at least they are dry, and as she hobbles around on her cane, her feet are slowly beginning to heal.

For the first time I am filled with indignation and scorn at this and other atrocities, and I say so aloud. Encouraged by this unexpected show of rebellion, the other novice contributes a few angry comments of her own to my diatribe, and a sister who in the past had been content to smile at my guardian angel as she passed me in the hall each day suddenly becomes a soulmate, a fellow rebel.

When I mention my ulcer to a couple of my friends, they are solicitous. "Oh no, Maggie—maybe they won't let you take vows. You know how they are about admitting people who might be medical liabilities!"

I smile the thinnest of rueful smiles, and for the first time I hear myself say that I could think of worse fates—namely, going on like this.

24 §෴

SCHOLASTIC NOVICE (1963–1964)

In August, though no ceremonies other than the issuance of new *serre-têtes* mark the transition, canonical year ends: we take off our work aprons, brush our habits and shine our shoes, for soon we will be returning to school, most of us as college sophomores.

The past couple of months in the novitiate have been months of radical change. Just when it seemed that the tension had reached an absolute peak, Sister Carmelita and Sister Amadeus were suddenly transferred and new superiors appeared on the scene, superiors who would make a major difference in our lives. Vatican II, opened the previous fall by Pope John, was beginning to make its effects felt within the novitiate: winds of change had been blowing through the church, and now even the windows of the novitiate were suddenly blown open. The fresh air was bracing, invigorating, and we breathed deeply, savoring its promise of broadened horizons.

The council's agenda as laid down by Pope John was renewal and updating of the church (*aggiornamento*) and movement toward unity of all Christians. Key concepts were collegial authority (authority of the group), the primacy of person (as opposed to the primacy of institution or structure), the imperative of conscience (individual freedom and responsibility), and the universality of divine truth (formerly thought a Catholic monopoly). The transformation of religious life from a highly structured, tightly regimented monarchical mode of life to one of participatory democracy had begun.

Our new superiors are open, enthusiastic women who

have just come from college campuses where their own vision of the church and of religious life were greatly changed and opened up. Long lines begin to form outside their offices as our guilts and fears and morbid self-analyses come out of hiding. How freeing it is to talk about things that have been locked up inside for so long! Untiring angels of mercy, they sit in their offices for hours at a time as we drag our maimed psyches to them—and slowly we begin to heal.

A tightly wound ball of confusion and self-reproach, I find it hard at first to talk about all that I have kept inside for so long: scruples, fears, guilt. But Sister Kathleen, who functions both as superior/counselor and theology teacher, is so gentle and compassionate that it's not long before it all comes tumbling out. I get up the nerve to talk to her about friendships. Her eyes twinkle as she tells me about some of her own experiences in this area: "You know, when I was first sent out on mission, I missed my friends so much that when summer rolled around and we were all due back at Saint Raphael's, I wrote to my home superior, the counselor assigned to me, asking if I might be able to have a room near a couple of my friends! How naive I was! Mother made a special visit to our convent in Chicago and interrogated me and everyone around me about my friendship patterns: did I have 'certain abnormal leanings'?"

Sister Kathleen's flashing eyes suddenly sadden: "Of course everyone gave good reports, everyone, that is, except one middle-aged nun who had at the beginning cultivated my friendship and then turned on me with a viciousness that shocked and sickened me. I didn't know what was going on; I only knew that she had at first wanted to be with me all the time, had wanted to be my mentor—she encouraged me to come talk to her when I was upset, and she was surly and sullen if I spent recreation time with someone else. When I eventually saw what was happening and stopped hanging around with her, she spread rumors about me—she probably even wrote home to Mother, putting doubts in her mind."

Sister Kathleen leans against the back of her straight-backed wooden chair and with one finger pushes a wandering lock of black hair back under her *serre-tête*. "She was a sick one, and there *are* sick ones out there, make no mistake—'the couples,' we call them. They go around like Siamese twins, never out of each other's sight, jealous of any friendships that might endanger the twosome. Sometimes there's a history of becoming involved and then moving on, dropping people without any warning, leaving a trail of broken hearts: that kind of a thing can definitely play havoc with a community. But that's not friendship; that's something different, and you'll recognize it when you see it.

"But friendship—there's been too much paranoia about down-to-earth, honest friendship. People have been afraid to admit their fondness for each other for fear of being reported. Thank God the community's moving away from that kind of thinking. Thank God it's starting to encourage good, strong, nourishing friendships—with men and women both!"

Sister Kathleen's words are so comforting that I get up nerve to press one step further. I tell her about the boyish postulant who left, about the wildly overwhelming feelings I had had for her. Surely those tortured, chaotic feelings had not been the feelings of normal friendship—had I too, at least briefly, been "sick" in that way?

There, the words are out! I am afraid of what Sister Kathleen will think of me, but I just can't carry such a secret in the pit of my stomach any longer.

Looking up, I am surprised to see that she still has the same all-accepting smile on her face, the same twinkle in her eye. "That kind of thing happens all the time, though few talk about it. It's certainly nothing to worry about. Look at it this way: you're locked up with a bunch of women day in and day out without any contact with men. Before you know it, you're having some stirrings toward someone of the same sex. It doesn't say anything at all about your basic sexual orientation—in fact, some would say you're a lot healthier if you *do* have some of these stirrings in a situation like this. At least you're feeling *something*, instead of letting your feelings dry up inside you!"

A slim, sleek white dove releases itself from my heart, heading straight for the sky. I feel so clear, so free!

I hug Sister Kathleen and thank her for all that she is doing for me, for all of us. She presses my hand and tells me to hang in there, that better times are coming.

In the past, conferences with one's superior were private, secretive affairs with doors and drapes closed; now we begin to speak to each other about our various conflicts and about the advice our new superiors have given.

Jeanie admits that she only stayed because she didn't want to disappoint her widowed mother, a devout Catholic: she is advised to leave at once and will be given help in breaking the news to her mother.

Mary Rose confides that she still thinks of her old boyfriend night and day and of the babies they would have together: only a fear of God's wrath over a spurned vocation has kept her in. She too has now been advised to leave: "God is obviously calling you to serve Him as a wife and mother, an honorable vocation in itself. Happiness is one of the surest signs that one has found one's true calling!"

Linda seeks help for a case of scruples so severe that no external assurance of God's forgiveness can touch it. Her soul is ragged and raw from the constant scourgings: both confessors and superiors plead for self-acceptance, self-love, but she knows that that is only because they don't *really* know how bad she is, how lazy and selfish. She is sent into town for weekly psychotherapy and eventually leaves.

Among those who remain, signs of healing are everywhere. Half-finished bottles of ulcer medicine fill the trash cans, along with perfection beads and silence slips and old prayer books that advocate self-reproach. We begin to boycott the musty old spiritual-reading books available in the library, to pass around among ourselves the latest works by the new liberal theologians, Rahner and Kung and Moultmann. The fact that their thinking has not yet been approved by the church—that it is in fact held to be rather suspect—makes their books all the more exciting. In the same way we begin to savor the religious thinking of great Protestant and Jewish thinkers, Tillich and Niebuhr and Bonhoeffer and Buber. Through reading their works, I begin to realize for the first time that one does not necessarily have to be celibate or even Catholic in order to put religion at the center of one's life.

Father Gunther, the priest sent to say Mass for us each morning and to provide spiritual direction, doesn't agree with a lot of the new thinking to which we are exposed: one morning another novice and I launch a debate with him over the issue of the superiority of celibacy over other states of life. "Our parents weren't celibate, and a lot of them were more deeply spiritual than a lot of the nuns and priests I've met!" I challenge, a rather cocky affront from one who just a few short months ago was afraid to open her mouth in public.

This type of talk worries Father Gunther, a lanky fatherly type with slicked-back gray hair. He thinks of us as daughters, as virginal in mind as we are in body, so he takes it upon himself to try to preserve our intellectual innocence. "You don't need to read that stuff," he admonishes when he sees someone carrying Chardin's latest work. "Just say your prayers and meditate on Our Lady—she'll teach you all that you need to know. The good sisters who taught me in school didn't strive to be theological scholars; they left all that to the priests. They concentrated on being good teachers, on saying their prayers and keeping their Holy Rule. That's all you need to do if you want to be a good nun.

"If you insist on dabbling in theology, at least stay with the tried and true! All these young upstarts! Nobody knows yet whether or not they're going to get the pope's approval. Some of them are pretty far out. I'm sure it'll be just a matter of time before the pope silences them. If you stick to Saint

Thomas's *Summa,* on the other hand, you can't go wrong: there you've got a summary of all theological truth as recognized by the Church, everything you need to learn."

I detest Father Gunther, his intellectual myopia, his condescending paternalism. I confess my sins to him in weekly confession as he is the only one who has the power to absolve me of my sins, but I do not confide in him, nor do I seek his spiritual direction. For the first time I look to women as my mentors, my guides.

And so we continue to let our heads and hearts enter doors that up to now have been locked to us. Cardinal Suenen's ground-breaking book *The Nun in the World* is read in the refectory each morning: hearing his ideas about how nuns should not be so cloistered excites and liberates us, and we hang on every bold word. We begin to see the Church as an instrument for the humanization and divinization of people, not as a Swiss guard; we begin to see the world as the vineyard where we will labor, not as a treacherous wasteland full of land mines.

We learn that if we want to love and serve God and His people, we have to first learn to love and serve ourselves.

We learn that we needn't be afraid to love each other, to let our friendships nourish us.

We learn that if we keep our feelings bottled up inside, we will soon fall ill and be of no use to anyone.

We learn that the theologians are now talking more about the resurrection of Jesus; that to only identify with His crucifixion, to concentrate on renunciation and penance and to forget Christian joy is to cling to a warped perspective on Jesus.

We learn that being a nun doesn't require a denial that we are women first.

As the knots in our stomachs and our psyches slowly unravel, summer at Saint Raphael's becomes a time of joy. At noon recreation we play our guitars and ukeleles under the shady trees and sing out any lingering tightness in our souls:

the joy of expanded vistas, of bright futures emerges thick and lusty in our songs. In the evenings as the red yolk of sun cracks and runs along the horizon, we laugh and sing our way to the strawberry fields, where we harvest the summer's plumpest offerings. Sweat-dripping woolen clothing, the torrid heat—none of it matters to me now as coolness spreads through my soul: I am becoming free.

Now that we are scholastics, most of our time is devoted to our college courses. In the past, college majors had been assigned according to community need, but greater emphasis is now being given to individual leanings and proclivities. I ask to be allowed to major in English and minor in French, and I have no problem receiving program approval by the community's director of education. Like the rest of my band members, I will also take education courses to prepare me for teaching and enough theology courses to constitute a second minor.

Two other band members also opt for English, and the three of us settle down to life as English majors. Every day we leave the novitiate, pulling our shawls tight against the bracing bite of fall, and make our way across campus to the college buildings where we attend class with the college students. At the end of the day we wend our way back through the day's new fall of leaves to the pristine stillness of prayer and the warm comfort of community. I have never been happier.

The changes that were set in motion the summer before continue to expand their effect into all the hidden recesses of convent life and routine. Older practices drop away; more contact with the outside world is allowed. After a year of not seeing our families (mine had come to Saint Raphael's to visit my aunt in early summer, and when they passed us on a walk, I had only been permitted to wave), we are again allowed regular visits. Though we are still not supposed to converse freely with the college students with whom we have class, they are allowed to visit us at certain set times. I strike up a friendship with a wildly creative art student named Lori, and we make all kinds of intricate arrangements to meet and talk before class, during class, after class, whenever. She will go off to Switzerland to study for a year; then when she returns we will pick up the thread of a friendship that will last for many years.

1963—we feel ourselves a part of some monumental change sweeping the Church. We are "The New Breed": we will sweep away cobwebs, will restore the Church and our community to pristine vigor. We will not be fearful to change what needs to be changed, to press our Church to be at the cutting edge of society. Wordsworth's words seem to be written just for us: "Great was it that dawn be alive—but to be young was very heaven!"

In November 1963 we receive word that President Kennedy has been shot. I am listening to a lecture on Jacques Maritain's philosophy, when a messenger suddenly appears at the door, goes to the front of the room, and whispers something to the teacher. The teacher, pale and shaken, tells us the tragic news and leads us as we drop to our knees and together say a rosary aloud for the repose of his soul.

Kennedy entered the White House as the first Catholic President the same year our group entered the convent, 1961: a new era for the Church in the United States began at that time, inspiring pride and euphoria in the hearts of Catholics throughout the land. Now he is dead: a pall hangs over all.

In the novitiate a huge TV suddenly appears out of nowhere (the first TV we have seen since entering); it is set up in the auditorium and left on throughout the coverage of the funeral. We rush back from classes and employments in order to join those already clumped in front of the TV, eyes glued to the screen. Just as we take care never to leave Jesus unattended when the Blessed Sacrament is exposed on the altar, it seems that there is always a group in front of the TV keeping silent vigil. It is our ritual, our liturgy, the only way we know to pay our last respects to our slain hero.

When summer comes again, we take first vows. Although the words are traditional, the newer theology gives them a different context. We now see them as the means of freeing our lives so that we can better serve the world.

Poverty means that we won't have to concern ourselves with money, that we will live simply in identification with the world's poor. Obedience means going where we are needed. Chastity means freeing ourselves from the drain on time and energy that marriage and child-bearing involves.

We see all three vows as an opportunity to travel lightly, unencumbered by material possessions and unruly wills and family ties. Through them we will enhance rather than inhibit our freedom.

And so it is with great joy and eagerness that I stand before the bishop on August 15, 1964 and join my sisters in pronouncing the vows that will bind me to be obedient, chaste, and poor for one year. I remove the white veil of a novice and at last put on the black veil and *chaplette* of a full-fledged Sister of Blessing.

25 §

JUNIOR SISTER (1964–1966)

For the last two years of formation, we move across the street to the juniorate, situated in a back wing of Athanasius Hall, the central motherhouse building. Here, as junior sisters, we finish our college courses, complete our training as teachers, and prepare for mission.

Convinced that it's time we take our focus off ourselves,

our superiors, Sister Laurena and Sister Alicia, take small
groups of us on Saturday afternoon visits to Washburn, a
depressed area a few miles from campus. Women of height-
ened social conscience, they are adamant in the warnings they
issue before we set out each Saturday. "Look, these people are
doing *you* a favor in allowing you to come visit them. They
don't need you to pity them or give them advice. The experience is more for you, to jolt you out of yourselves and your
petty preoccupations: they will be your teachers. Remember,
you're not there to talk religion, to convert: you're simply
there to listen, to be a friend. And if somewhere along the line
you discover how you might make a contribution to these
people's lives, that will be wonderful." With that, those of us
who accompany them for the afternoon lift our voluminous
skirts and climb into the waiting taxi, and fifteen minutes later
we step out into the dust and stench of Washburn.

Our superiors' attempts to draw our attention away from
ourselves are eminently successful, at least as far as I am concerned. I discover a world where families of nine huddle in
one-room shacks, where a retarded boy is kept chained in a
back yard, where an old woman pulls a wagon full of firewood
through a snowstorm. The old woman introduces herself as
"Granny," and we promise we'll come visit her the next time
we're in Washburn. We offer to pull the wagon for her but
she won't let us. (Word will circulate, one day soon after
Christmas, that Granny has been found dead in her shack,
frozen to death, and bitter questions will tear at my mind.
What are we—a bunch of Girl Scouts carrying fruit baskets to
Washburn while an old woman freezes to death? Surely there's
more that we can do for Washburn. It is 1964, and, like many
of my contemporaries across the country, I want desperately to
"get involved.")

Summer comes, and Sister Alicia receives Poverty Program funds to set up a neighborhood youth program in Washburn. I immediately volunteer, and am delighted when I am

selected to work on the project, along with a young priest in the area who is skilled in community organization. Washburn and our program there soon become a central part of my life. At the end of summer, we again take one-year vows, this time in a quiet ceremony in our juniorate chapel. My inner peace continues to grow, thanks to the warm concern and counseling skills of both Sister Laurena and Sister Alicia.

When I'm not working in Washburn, I am busy with my studies. My mind continues to journey far beyond its former narrow confines. I read all the existentialist philosophy I can get my hands on; at night by a flashlight, I read novels and poetry. I read each new issue of *The New Yorker* and *Harper's* and *The Atlantic Monthly* as soon as they come out, devouring them with the insatiable appetite of one just coming off a steady diet of *The Catholic Digest*, *The Sacred Heart Messenger*, and *Our Sunday Visitor*.

Writing becomes a passionate interest and I soon apprentice myself to a creative writing teacher named Mr. Peletier, submitting some of my secret treasures to his ruthless scrutiny. One of the things that fascinates me the most about Mr. Peletier is the fact that he doesn't seem to have the kind of fawning admiration for nuns that lay people back home always seemed to have. In fact he seems, sometimes, to merely tolerate them, observing them coolly from behind his pipe, smiling at their piety. I like it that he doesn't lump us all together—the nuns—but deals with each of us as individual persons. I especially like it that he seems to have a certain liking for me. I am head over heels in love with Mr. Peletier, the first nonrelative, noncleric male who has come into my life—but I have to admit that I am head over heels in love with every other male I meet too!

It is through my contact with Mr. Peletier that I begin to understand that a person can be a dedicated teacher without being a priest or a nun. Except for a handful of college students who did their practice teaching in the aspirancy, my teachers have always been nuns. Now I am all of a sudden confronted with a man who has a wife and kids and yet is as committed as any priest or nun I have ever known. In spite of myself, I begin to picture Mr. Peletier holding his wife at the end of a long day or wrestling affectionately with his tiny children, and I begin to wish in my heart of hearts that such a life had been my destiny. I lie in my narrow convent bed with the sheets pulled tight and uniform at the corners and try to picture what it would have been like.

Back in high school I had had similar thoughts about the lives of the college girls. Whenever we went to the auditorium for a program of some sort, I always made sure that I sat in the front row of the balcony, where I could watch the college girls milling around down below. I loved to watch them, these distant goddesses; I loved to see their fashionable high heels and their angora sweaters; I loved to smell their expensive perfumes. Recipients of some charmed destiny, they took their good fortune for granted, not knowing that I watched and dreamed.

But now as then, I don't really dare to imagine myself in such a charmed scenario someday. Rather, I simply try to imagine how my life *could* have been if God's Will for me had been different. For I remind myself that Mr. Peletier is probably an exception, one of those outstanding lay people who are always winning lay-person-of-the-year awards. I realize that I am *not* so outstanding, that without the community to support me and to kind of nudge me along I would undoubtedly wander away from God and spiritual discipline. Convinced by years of training that I am selfish and hedonistic and "fallen" at my core, I remind myself that I can't rely on any kind of inner control to keep me pointed in the right direction: others might be able to live in the midst of the world and still walk with God, still be moved to serve humankind, but I am sure *I* wouldn't be that strong. No, I need external control, vows and rules, the support of community, and I am fortunate to have found it all within the arms of this congregation.

Taking myself in hand, I remind myself what a waste of time it is to daydream about a vocation to which one has not been called, and so I turn my mind to other things.

The haunting sound of the toll pierces the afternoon. It is now February, and I am hurrying back to the juniorate, rubbing my numb fingers together inside my mittens. It has been a long day of classes, and I am tired.

Again the toll sounds. I know it must be for Sister Agnes Marie: she wasn't expected to make it through the day. I make the sign of the cross and pray for the repose of her soul.

It really *does* seem to be true what they say about nuns dying in threes. First there was Sister Florence Ann two days ago, then Sister Leonard, and now Sister Agnes Marie has also been called to receive her last reward.

What a darling old lady she had been! During canonical year I always loved to clean her room in the infirmary and listen to her stories culled from over fifty years in community.

But she is gone now; tears come to my eyes as I picture her tiny, frail body being wheeled to the embalming room in the infirmary. I had always hated cleaning that room, had always hated getting my broom and dust rags out of the same closet where they stored the embalming supplies.

An older sister passes me on the path and asks if I know who is being tolled. I tell her I am sure it is for Sister Agnes Marie. She makes the sign of the cross and murmurs something I can't hear. Then she reaches down and, picking up her *chaplette*, kisses the crucifix. When she eventually goes on her way I notice that her step is a little slower along the path.

I know that we will be having funeral practice when I reach home, and I try to figure out when I will have time to study for my philosophy test. Since the funeral will be tomorrow morning there will be no time then. I decide that I'll just have to obtain permission to stay up late tonight.

For three days now Sister Florence Ann's body, dressed in Sunday habit, has lain in state in the motherhouse parlor, the cold fingers touching the *chaplette* she touched with reverence so often in her lifetime. It has been my week to lock up, to check windows and doors and to turn out lights. Each evening I have pulled the shades in the musty-smelling parlor, taking care not to go too close to the coffin in the corner where a familiar starched cap juts up above the casket's edge.

There will be the funeral Mass and burial in the little community cemetery, and then Sister Florence Ann's relatives will return to the parlor where two junior sisters will serve them breakfast before running off to their first classes.

"*Dies irie, dies illa . . . :*" Oh day of wrath, oh mournful day. The traditional funeral chant fills the halls as, bearing lighted candles, we follow the pallbearers carrying Sister Florence Ann's casket from the parlor to the church.

Mass is starting now: relatives and a handful of old students sit in a little clump at the front of church, and we, her sisters, sit in back. The requiem Mass seems to drone on forever, begging God to have mercy on the deceased. The Latin rites are full of references to sin and hell and damnation, and I can't help thinking that this is a strange way to bury a woman who spent her whole life dying to herself in order that she might one day receive her eternal reward.

And yet there is also a simple austere beauty to it all. After Mass, we relight our candles and form a procession out of the church, through the still-dark halls, and out to the little community cemetery just as the sun is rising.

Standing at graveside I am struck by the black-and-white simplicity of the scene, the starkness of its message. "*Quod non est aeternun, non est*"—What is not eternal, is not. My cold, chapped fingers rub each familiar bead at my side and try to rub the message into my brain: "*Quod non est aeternun. . . .*"

In May of 1966 we receive our first mission assignments. In the old days no one knew where she was going on mission until August 15. After reception and profession ceremonies in the Church, friends and relatives went outside while the professed Sisters received their assignments—their "obediences"—for the following year. Though Reverend Mother and her council, drawing on their grace of office (the special grace God gives superiors), had decided where to send each sister many months before, individuals only received word of their assignments the day before they were to depart.

An older sister described to me what it had been like: "At the end of the ceremonies, all lay people and novices left, and the sisters remained. The bishop entered the sanctuary: we all knelt as he began to read alphabetically the list of missions with the superior's name first, then everyone else from oldest to youngest. He slurred names so badly—said 'Mary' instead of 'Marie' and so on—that you weren't always sure who he called. You had to listen for the name of the place, the city, the superior, and *your* name. There was much excitement and many tears. You knelt until you heard your name called; sometimes lots of people would still be kneeling at the end because they didn't hear their name or because the bishop had mispronounced it or omitted it altogether!

"Then later that day after your guests had left, you'd finally meet your new superior and race around to say good-bye to all your friends. The next morning you'd wake up, pick up your bags, and go where you were sent."

Today things are different: obediences are given out in late May so that the sisters have ample time to plan ahead for the coming year.

As our first obedience day dawns, nervousness and excitement hang in the air. One might be sent to teach grade school or high school, to a rich parish or a poor one. The superior may be understanding and supportive, or she could rule the house (and you) with an iron hand. If you teach in a parish grade school (most high schools are free of parish ties), the pastor may be a benevolent father or an eccentric tyrant; whether you teach grade school or high school, the sisters in the house may be fun and young-at-heart or a bunch of frustrated sour old ladies. Most important of all, you may be sent to a location within a few minutes of where your family lives (though such a situation is avoided by our superiors as much as possible), or you may be sent thousands of miles away and not see them for years. A lot hangs in the balance on obedience day.

We kneel in the chapel and say morning prayers; then there is a chasmlike silence as everyone sits back in her priedieu and opens the little white envelope that contains her destiny for the following year.

My fingers tremble as I tear open the envelope: already there are gasps of surprise, moans, and sighs of relief all around me. My eyes focus on the type, and a moment later my brain takes in what the words are telling me: God's will is that I teach seventh and eighth grades at Our Lady of Perpetual Help Grade School, Cincinnati.

Relieved beyond words, I kiss my crucifix and thank God for His abundant mercy. For one thing I am happy to be starting out in grade school. Like many of my friends, I have always ridiculed the community custom that often sends a neophyte teacher to teach elementary school even if she has been trained to teach high school. Different explanations of rationale circulate: some say the purpose is to teach us humility, as if teaching first grade is somehow lower in status than teaching high school. Others say teaching grade school is a good preparation for teaching high school, as if the two are not largely separate skills.

And yet, though I would never admit it to my fellow scoffers, I am secretly relieved to be starting out by working with younger kids: the thought of trying to control a classroom full of high school kids totally terrifies me. Gruesome stories have circulated throughout the community about nuns who lost control of their classrooms because they weren't strict enough. Master teachers in the community always stress that a new teacher shouldn't smile for six months, and though I don't consider myself much of a smiler by nature, I remain nevertheless doubtful that I could sustain a six-month-long frown.

So despite my big talk, I am happy to be starting out in grade school. And Cincinnati is near enough so that my family can visit frequently: I could have been sent to the east coast, the South, or even California! My delight is compounded when I hear that O.L.P.H has a reputation as one of the "better" houses, that the nuns there are jovial and friendly, a happy little family, community at its best.

June brings graduation; my family again takes its places in Maria Chapel, the scene of my high school graduation, reception into the order, first profession, and now my graduation from college. Nun students are today mixed in with lay students: we wear the graduation gowns over our habits and, along with the rest of the graduates, process to the front of the Church to receive our diplomas. Though our families attend, there will be little celebration surrounding academic graduation: spiritual graduations such as the ceremonies surrounding profession of vows are given more significance in our world. At the end of the summer I will be sent on mission after renewing vows for three years, and the next time we will gather here will be three years from now when I will pronounce my final vows. There is no doubt in my mind that I will be standing here at the altar three years from now, pronouncing with the rest of the group vows that will bind me to this community forever.

As I process up the aisle I smile at my family, sprawled out the whole length of one pew. It's strange: in my heart I have never really felt that I have "left" them, not in any real way. I carried them in my heart, I was one with them, we were family. But gradually there came the realization that they had in a way, left *me*. It was as if I had lined them all up the day I left and then told them not to move while I went off to prepare for my life's work. Somehow I had always thought they'd be right there in that same pose when I returned.

But they *did* move, of course; they went right on without me. Now I wonder if I will ever be a real part of their lives again.

I remember some of the letters I received over the past five years. The kids' letters all assured me that they were studying their catechism extra hard for Our Lady, that they were praying for me, and that they hoped I would pray for them now that I was becoming a sister of God. *A sister of God:* they used the expression often, underscoring their realization that I would never again be *their* sister, not in any real way. Now I belonged only to God.

Mom sent chatty, happy news of the family and neighborhood, and Dad sent jokes—tasteful ones, of course. One time a letter from Dad fell out of a book, and since the only identification was the salutation "Dear Toots," it was hung on the bulletin board until someone might claim it. Years later nuns would still come up to him telling him how much they had enjoyed that "Dear Toots" letter. Dad was delighted, of course, and I was too: it made me proud and happy to have everyone know that I was "Toots" to somebody!

How safe I have been on my little altar, an icon surrounded by flowers and candles and reverence! And yet it is beginning to dawn on me what a price I have paid for my perfumed existence: I am beginning to realize how hard it is to become close to an icon. Respect was enough for a while, but now I long for closeness: I had it once, and I want it again. Soon I will be going on mission: that will be returning to the world in a way. Hopefully I will find my way back to the family I have lost.

The bishop is now handing out diplomas and once again I climb the marble steps that lead to a whole new chapter of my life.

Once the college students have departed, big buses start to roll up the boulevard, bearing smiling nuns who are happy to be home for the summer. They have taken down their bulletin boards, cleaned their classrooms, and watched their students graduate or move to the next grade. Now it is time to spend time with old friends, to rest and relax before fall again summons them to the Lord's vineyard.

Summer life is slow and easy. Those who wish take up residence in alcoves set up on the screened-in porch. On summer nights we sit on our windowsills, basking in the magic of the moon and the stars and the cool night breeze.

By day there is plenty of time for long walks to the lake and picnics in the orchard, time to rekindle old friendships and to make new ones. The campus brims with workshops and concerts and celebrations of every kind; the esprit de corps is contagious. Many an afternoon we gather in the college auditorium and hold enthusiastic community meetings, locking our arms and singing proud songs about our community, 1800 strong.

Most of our meetings focus on renewal. The last session of Vatican II ended in December and it is now official: all religious congregations are to hold special general chapters where the specifics of community renewal and reform will be legislated. We have never been told much about the administrative structure of the community: we only know that God's Will comes to us through our superior, who in turn hears God's Will through the Mother General. Sister Alicia now gives us a minicourse on how the structure works.

She explains that a general chapter is held by the congregation every six years for the purpose of electing a new superior general and council and to legislate changes; the council is the group of six nuns—also called home superiors—who assist the superior general in her administration of the congregation. The work of the chapter is performed by Sister delegates, elected by the rank and file. I will later learn that the whole process in the past was anything but democratic: no nominations were made, no campaigning permitted. Even discussion of candidates was forbidden with the result that most of the same delegates were elected year after year.

The general chapter met recently and elected a new superior general, Mother Mary Paul, as well as a new council. My aunt, Sister Agnes Anita, is one of the new councilors, so she will reside at the motherhouse—now when I'm ready to go on mission! The special council mandated by Vatican II will meet at the end of 1968 and be a sort of miniature Vatican II for our community: it will, in fact, be so important that it will be preceded by a period of intense study, discussion, and experimentation throughout the community. Though in the past grass-roots input into general chapters has been extremely limited, the special chapter will be different: there is even a possibility that the junior professed (those who haven't yet taken final vows) may be permitted to send their own delegates.

Sister Alicia stresses that nothing integral to the community's specific identity and traditions will be sacrificed: it is simply a matter of renewal from within, of returning to the real essence of what the community was all about in the first place.

I listen with excitement, somehow grasping that there are implications to all this that go beyond my present understanding. I only know that life has never seemed so new, so fraught with wonderful possibilities, and that I am ever so lucky to be a part of it all.

I have the opportunity over the summer to take many a long walk with my aunt, and for the first time we really get to know each other. During my nine years at the Heights, we have written to each other on holidays and feast days or when a sister from her house would visit the motherhouse and act as mail bearer: frequent correspondence through the mail is discouraged, as it violates poverty. Occasionally my aunt herself would visit the motherhouse on business; we would visit then, and she would frequently come to novitiate and juniorate rec-reations when she came home for the summer.

But there had always been a certain distance between us, possibly because I still placed her on such a pedestal and possibly because she didn't want to do or say anything to affect my "formation." She remained the aunt and I the niece.

Now that I am a full-fledged member of the community, we relax with each other; we laugh and chat like sisters and take turns telling funny stories from our respective novitiate days. "You knew what I was in for; why didn't you warn me?" I protest, knowing full well that community policy forbade her to share such secrets with the uninitiated.

As we talk I discover that my aunt is an open, progressive woman—a woman who has sometimes suffered in community precisely because of those traits. She has been a woman ahead of her time, but it seems that her time has come at last: a number of sisters tell me that they see her election to the council as a hopeful sign that the progressives are beginning to win the day.

I also have occasion over the summer to visit with my cousin, Sister Donald, who sometimes comes to our juniorate recreations. Though there's still a certain fondness between us, it's increasingly obvious that the two of us are by now headed in opposite directions. Sister Donald laments many of the community's changes and exhorts me to remain faithful to community practices, especially devotion to Our Lady. She gives me a new rosary as a profession gift and encourages me to say an extra rosary each day for the congregation that "radi-cals within" will not be allowed to substitute "atheistic secular humanism" for "strict observance of the Holy Rule." When I finally share with her a few of my own views, the visits abruptly stop. I will not hear from her again, but I will eventu-ally hear from the family that she left the order to join a stricter, more-contemplative order.

On August 15 1966 I pronounce three-year vows with the rest of my band in our tiny juniorate chapel. Formation is now over: I have been instructed and trained for five years, and my mission is to begin at last.

IV ❧

MISSIONARY (FALL 1966–SUMMER 1968)

*The nuns at St. Bastion school had one goal in life: to get out of it
and into Heaven. When they first became nuns, they took three vows
that were designed to accomplish this goal: the vows of Poverty,
Chastity, and Obedience.*

*The first vow was easy enough to keep, not only for the nuns but
for anyone in St. Bastion Parish. And considering what most of the
nuns looked like, Chastity offered no formidable challenge either.
The vow of Obedience simply meant that the nuns had to worship
the ground the priests walked on, which the nuns did with absolute
relish.*

—The Last Catholic in America *by*
John Powers

26

OUR LADY OF PERPETUAL HELP
GRADE SCHOOL, CINCINNATI
(1966–1967)

"Cheer, cheer, for old Notre Dame. . . ." We are barreling down the interstate and Sisters Jean Louise, Martin, and Alma Mary are singing their hearts out. Mr. Hickey, one of the parishioners from Our Lady of Perpetual Help Parish, Cincinnati, is at the wheel and he is singing too. The fighting Irish have just made another touchdown, and loyal Catholics throughout the land are ecstatic. It's half time, so Mr. Hickey turns down the radio just a bit and tells Sister Jean Louise to fetch the box of homemade cookies in the glove compartment: "A little surprise for the good sisters from Mrs. Hickey," he smiles, schoolboylike.

Wedged in the back seat, I watch the cars whizzing by, fascinated: it has been five years since I have been more than a few miles from Saint Raphael's. Our training is over and I am at last going on mission; the exhilaration of it all is overwhelming.

The chatter goes on around me, and I toss in a word or two now and then to make it clear that I am not unfriendly or aloof. So far the conversation has revolved around football scores, lesson plans, and Mr. Hickey's ailing mother ("I'm depending on you sisters to pray her back to health: your prayers are worth more than mine are").

After the game is over, Sister Jean Louise, the oldest of our group (Sister Daniel Ann, our superior and principal, has gone ahead to handle school and house business), suggests that since we aren't going to be back in time for afternoon prayers, we may as well make them up now. She reaches into her satchel and takes out her office book, and everyone follows suit. Soon the car is quiet as each sister silently recites her office.

I take my office book out of a black vinyl portfolio, a graduation present, and hasten to join the others in "making up" prayers. It is a new and foreign concept to me, this making up of prayers: for nine years, day in and day out, there has never been anything so important that it would warrant any of us absenting ourselves from community prayers. On mission things will be different: the focus will no longer be on the pursuit of perfection, but on apostolate—sharing with others what we already have. According to Catholic theology, nuns live in a "state of perfection," even though individually they may not yet be perfect. After years of struggling toward goodness, it is a heady, wonderful feeling. Nothing to do now but recite my prescribed prayers, keep the Rule, and I will be OK at last.

When our prayers are finished, Mr. Hickey suggests that we stop for hamburgers, and everyone applauds. I sit quietly—stunned. Hamburgers at a fast-food place: this really *is* being back in the world again!

Mr. Hickey goes inside to place our order while we wait in the car and then a few minutes later reappears and delivers each nun's request, right down to the last onion ring. But he has forgotten pickles for Sister Alma Mary: curling her lips into a pout, she complains that she can't imagine eating a hamburger without pickles. So Mr. Hickey goes back in to get the pickles.

When we have all been served, Mr. Hickey eats his hamburger at a table inside: aware of convent rules against eating in front of seculars, he makes sure we have plenty of time to finish before he returns to the car. "Isn't he a thoughtful gentleman?" coos Sister Jean Louise, and Sister Alma Mary and Sister Martin cluck agreement.

Hamburgers finished, we napkin away remaining traces of mustard and catsup, and Mr. Hickey returns to collect the trash. Then we're off: he has promised Sister Daniel Ann that he'll have us back to the convent before dark. "She'll have my head if I don't," he chuckles, his fondness for her apparent. I haven't met Sister Daniel Ann yet, but I have heard only good things.

The hamburgers have hit the spot: I feel content and chatty. I start a conversation with Mr. Hickey, asking him about his children, what grades they're in, and so forth. Then I ask him what he thinks about all the changes taking place in the Church. Flattered by my display of interest, he responds at length; excited at the thought of having a real conversation with a lay person—a man, at that!—I expand on a few of my own most treasured ideas.

Immediately I feel the daggers flying at me from three sets of eyes. What have I done? And then I remember: I have violated religious decorum: I have not kept a proper distance in dealing with a secular. Some friendly chatter is allowed, of course, in the name of Christian charity, some lightweight bantering back and forth perhaps about football scores. And it is certainly permissible, even admirable, to listen sympathetically, to offer words of inspiration, promises of prayers: that is what the laity expects from their Sisters. But beyond that, one should tread with caution. One should be especially careful not to share controversial opinions too casually lest the lay person become confused and think these opinions represent those of the community as a whole.

Embarrassed and resentful, I settle back against my seat and fight the rage that wants to break through. Once I am quiet, the other nuns again smile sweetly and draw me into the conversation, making it clear that they are willing to be patient with a faux pas here and there. It's my first time on mission, and I have a lot to learn; stern yet solicitous older sisters, they will patiently supervise my efforts and applaud my progress.

We arrive in Cincinnati just as the sun is starting to go down. We pull up in front of an ordinary-looking suburban house on the other side of a church parking lot, and a friendly looking nun who appears to be in her early thirties comes rushing out to greet us.

First she hugs the other three nuns, telling them how happy she is to have them back for another year; then she turns to me, introducing herself as Sister Daniel Ann, and hugs me too. She shoos us all aside, reminding us that the others are awaiting our arrival.

I pick up my suitcases—the same one I entered the convent with five years ago—and walk up the sidewalk. Once inside, I see that the interior of the house has been remodeled to make it more suitable for convent living. There is a small entrance hall and parlor in front for receiving seculars; then on the other side of big sliding doors that close off the cloistered area, a large central community room. Off to one side is a small chapel just large enough for eleven nuns, and off to the other side is the kitchen and dining room.

Sister Daniel Ann leads me down a long hall, and when she stops in front of my room, I am incredulous. The bed is covered with a brightly colored spread, and there are flowered curtains at the windows. There is a light over the bed so that I can read in bed and a private bathroom. After nine years of white curtains and spreads and communal bathroom facilities, I feel luxuriously rich and worldly. This is a part of mission life that I hadn't anticipated!

When I have washed my face and put on a clean *serre-tête*, I hear a knock at the door. It is Sister Richard Ann, the other eighth-grade teacher: I had met her only briefly at Saint Raphael's the previous summer. She had told me a bit about the class I would be having for homeroom ("Not a bad bunch, but they'll take advantage of you if you let them!") and had shared bits of gossip about each sister in the house. "I'm sure we'll be the best of friends," she had whispered conspiratorially, and I had muttered a vague "I'm sure."

Now she sweeps me into her arms and welcomes me, and as I resmooth my habit skirt and adjust my cap, she again does her best to demonstrate how valuable she will be to me this coming year. "We'd better get moving," she whispers. "Daniel Ann is a real fanatic about everyone showing up at recreation time." The slack folds of her face crease into a you-know-how-superiors-are look, and I thank her for the tip.

In the community room Sister Daniel Ann introduces me to the sisters I haven't met yet. There are eleven of us in all, including two retired sisters who help out around the house and school. Everyone is seated around a long table: one sister is knitting a shawl, another is making flash cards for her classroom, and the sister sacristan (the sister in charge of the church altar) is arranging a huge vase of gladiolus for the altar. I pull up a chair next to Sister Martin and offer to help her with her flash cards. Sister Daniel Ann beams, and I know that I have made at least one right move; hopefully if I make enough of them I'll be able to redeem my faux pas in the car.

As I watch the two youngest, however, I'm not so sure I'll be able to keep up with them. They really have it down, all the things the youngest on mission are supposed to do to endear themselves to their elders. Young Sister Lawrence is talking to old Sister Clare Robert about their proposed trip to Sister Clare Robert's doctor the next day: she tells her they'll have to leave by half past ten in order to allow themselves enough time. Next she asks Sister Daniel Ann if she wants her to pick up groceries on the way back.

Sister Roberta, the other young nun, sits at Sister Daniel Ann's right hand and seems ready to fulfill her superior's slightest whim. When Sister Daniel Ann's needle runs out of thread, she quickly rethreads it for her; when Sister Daniel Ann mentions that we might as well sample some of the goodies Mrs. Eck brought, Sister Roberta is immediately on her feet and en route to the kitchen.

Though the competition is awesome, I resolve to do my best. The sisters here are congenial enough: I will win their acceptance and will experience the kind of supportive community that religious life is supposed to be about. I take a magic marker out of my portfolio and attack the flash cards as if my life depended on it—knowing that, in a way, it does.

My first morning on mission is a morning of natural rising, one of those glorious experiments being tried throughout the community, in which we are allowed to stay in bed as long as we wish. Morning prayers can be made up during the day, and each picks up her own breakfast.

I dress and wander out to the kitchen. There are muffins in the bun warmer and the coffee pot is perking away. I find a skillet, fry myself a couple of eggs, and sit down to savor my first morning back in the world. It is an exquisite feeling.

Sister Daniel Ann comes in while I am eating and tells me that the pastor is going to come over in a few minutes. He is eager to welcome everyone back and to meet his newest sister.

We all gather in the community room, and an hour later, in strides Father Myers. A short stocky man, he walks with the gait of a general inspecting his troops. His gray hair is slicked back neatly, and his cassock is precisely pressed. A strong smell of after-shave lotion thickens the air as he crosses the room. Everyone rises to greet him.

I am shocked when I realize that he let himself in without knocking or ringing the doorbell, but then I remember that the pastor is, in effect, the convent's landlord and has a right to show up whenever he pleases. Father Myers settles his body into a large easy chair and gestures to Sister Roberta to bring in from the entrance hall the "little surprise" he has brought for the sisters. Sister Roberta scurries out and returns with a gallon of ice cream and a package of cones. Everyone oohs and aahs.

I notice that Sister Roberta, young and pretty, sits at the opposite end of the room, her blue eyes downcast. She laughs at his jokes as politely as the others, but she seems careful to avoid his frequent glances in her direction. But the more she pretends not to notice, the more he stares.

He now begins to expound on his hopes for the coming school year.

"I know I can count on all of you to make this the best year in the school's history. Our reading scores were a little bit down last year, but I know we can get them up if we all put our heads to it. Little Sister Daniel Ann, here, has a lot to learn about being a school principal, but let's not be too hard on her since last year was just her first year." He gives Sister Daniel Ann a fatherly wink.

Sister Daniel Ann blushes furiously and opens her mouth to say something, but then seems to decide against it.

"I'll be coming around to all of your classrooms as soon as school starts, talking to the students about the building fund. What better way to get to the parents than through the children? I hope to instill some parish pride in them, and it will be your job to nurture that pride. The people of Saint Susannah's went all out in building their new church, importing marble from Italy and putting in only the finest statues: surely we won't let them show us up; surely we can count on our people to be just as generous, just as dedicated. It will be your job to inspire that dedication."

Exhausted from his display of pastorly zeal, Father Myers sinks back into his chair. He gratefully accepts the glass of beer that is offered him and downs it quickly. (According to Sister Richard Ann, beer and wine are always kept on hand in the convent in case Father Myers or his assistant or some other priest stops in. We nuns have to be content with ice cream.)

Finishing his beer, Father rises with the hurried air of a very important man who has just remembered an appointment. Slipping to her knees, Sister Daniel Ann asks sweetly, "May we have your blessing, Father?" and the rest of us follow suit. *"In nomine patris . . ."*—a hand raises in blessing, a solemn voice booms.

Sister Alma Mary holds the door for him, bowing slightly as he passes, and with one last parting glance at Sister Roberta he is gone. The minute he is out the door all hell breaks loose:

I watch in amazement as anger and outrage replace sugary smiles. There are complaints about the fact that the good father feels he can barge into the convent any time he feels like it: "What if we're sitting here in our night caps when he barges in?" protests one, and everyone shivers at the thought. Most of the protest, however, has to do with the way he insists on humiliating poor Sister Daniel Ann—last year he even put her down in front of a secular!

Sister Daniel Ann makes a few weak attempts to remind everyone that after all he is a priest of God, a man of the cloth; we should try to overlook his frailties and remember his holy calling. Besides, we have to do our best to try to get along with him: it's *his* parish, *his* school. Then too, he's almost seventy now—surely it won't be long before the bishop removes him.

"But Sister, he shouldn't be allowed to treat *you* like that," Sister Lawrence wails, despondent at the lack of respect shown to her revered superior.

"It would take more than that to get me down," Sister Daniel Ann assures her with a big sunshiny smile, pulling herself together for the edification of the group. "Now let's talk about something more pleasant. Roberta, why don't you bring your guitar out here and play us a few songs?"

That night after prayers, Sister Richard Ann, like a playground whisperer of dirty secrets, decides to further my education. "Did you see the way that man leered at Sister Roberta? It's been going on for some time now. Watch him at Communion some time: it's disgusting. Whenever he gets to poor Roberta and places the host on her tongue, he draws the whole thing out as long as he can. First he puts his face up close to hers with that lewd smirk on his face, and he keeps it there until she blushes deep red. Then he presses the host down on her tongue, hard, leaving his fingers on it extra long, brushing her lips with his hand. It's terrible to say, but it's almost like he gets his kicks that way. I heard Roberta tell someone that most mornings she comes out of chapel and wants to vomit. We've all encouraged her to speak to Reverend Mother, but I guess she's just too embarrassed: how do you tell a Mother General something like that?"

Sister Richard Ann goes on to explain that even if Roberta *did* tell Mother, there would be little that Mother could do other than remove her. But Roberta doesn't *want* to leave: she loves the school and the sisters with whom she lives. Of course, Mother could make a complaint to the bishop, and maybe if enough complaints come in Father Myers might have his hand slapped by the bishop. "If he was a young priest just out of the seminary," Sister Richard Ann explains, "it might be different. But he's been around for a long time; he's much valued in the diocese because of his administrative and financial skills."

As I prepare for bed, I find myself still thinking about my conversation with Sister Richard Ann and about the cross that Sister Roberta must bear in silence. This must be one of the situations our superiors had in mind when they devoted so much of our juniorate training to preparing us for mission. And now Roberta is having her first opportunity to show what kind of mettle she is made of. So far, by not complaining, she is passing the test.

As I fall off to sleep, I find myself wondering what kind of crosses will be in store for *me* this year, and I ask myself if I will be able to suffer in silence as valiantly as Sister Roberta.

At first I am content. We attend Sunday Mass in the parish Church, lining up in the rows along the front, and as we emerge from Church, clutching our shawls around us for the brief walk to the convent, parishioners move out of the way, cuffing their children if they don't immediately stop talking and greet us reverently as we pass. "G'morning, Sister. Lovely day, isn't it? Johnny, stand up straight and say good morning to the good sister." Floating through the crowd like royalty, bestowing smiles on all, how could I doubt my indisputable basic goodness under such circumstances? To the parishioners we are angels, untouched by human frailty, human emotions, and I am quite happy to begin to see myself the same way.

In the classroom too, things are fine. I did my practice teaching while still in the juniorate, teaching English literature to fourteen senior candidates, but I had remained unsure of how I would fare in a regular classroom. After a week or two at O.L.P.H., however, I discover that I can truly hold my own. I go through all the phases a neophyte teacher typically goes through, of course—I relax a bit too much, then overreact and tighten up a bit too much—but ultimately I strike a happy if somewhat precarious balance between strictness and lenience.

In the convent too I feel that I am doing quite well. I am doing my best to fit in and to show community spirit; for the most part I feel that I am succeeding.

I am not at all prepared for my first conference with Sister Daniel Ann.

She has tried to say it as gently as possible, but still I am devastated. We are sitting in her bedroom with the door closed, and I can't hold back the sobs that are now wracking my body.

A month has passed since my arrival, and she thinks there's something I should know. It seems the others have been complaining about me. For one thing, they don't like it that I don't show more community spirit. It's true that a lot of recreations are optional now, but most of the nuns still prefer to gather in the community room whenever they have some free time, and it really doesn't look good when I hole myself up in my room and read instead. Maybe I should give it some serious thought: my apostolate is to teach seventh and eighth grade—how is reading all that philosophical stuff going to make me a better teacher? And why else would one read? Some of the best seventh- and eighth-grade teachers in the community are real community women, practical and full of common sense: if *they* don't need to fill their heads with a lot of useless knowledge, why should I?

Which leads to the next area of complaint: the last time I was in charge of breakfast I forgot to plug in the coffee pot and I burned the oatmeal. It seems that my head is always somewhere else. And one sister complained that she couldn't sleep because I always took a shower at night.

"But why didn't they tell me?" I wail, by now hysterical. "They didn't have to come to you. I know I'm forgetful sometimes; I'm trying to work on that. And the shower: I had no idea it bothered anybody."

Sister Daniel Ann calmly points out that it's her role to act as mediator, that if one sister has complaints against another it is appropriate that she tell the superior instead of talking to the other sister directly. "It is my job to see that nothing disturbs the peace of the house. If two sisters try to talk about something like this directly, there are sure to be harsh words and hurt feelings. That's where the superior comes in: she can talk to each of the parties coolly and objectively and avoid potential clashes."

"But I want to know who complained, who's unhappy with me. They all smile at me and act so sweet. I'm afraid if you don't tell me, I'll suspect them all and become completely paranoid. If I could just talk to my detractors head-on, it would feel so much better!"

Sister Daniel Ann shifts in her chair, and I notice that her hands, folded quietly in her lap, are trembling. It occurs to me that she is again just doing as she is told, playing the role expected of her as my superior—and enjoying this role no more than she enjoys her other role as Father Myers' docile little principal. The Good Lord surely tries one sometimes!

But by the grace of her office, her voice is steady, and she reminds me that *who* complained is of no consequence: what matters is that I receive the criticism gratefully and act on it. "Believe me," she says soothingly, "the sisters have your good at heart. You're still young in religious life: they share with me the task of your continued formation."

You can't live under the rule of superiors for nine years

without recognizing a useless battle when you see one. I thank her for her suggestions and return to my room, where I sit at my desk for a long time, staring at the blotter.

I think of our superiors' warnings about how hard it might be sometimes, and I think of my friends scattered in parishes throughout the country. I wish that I could talk to them, that I could have them here to comfort me. I wonder if they're having their own hard times adjusting to mission life.

Remembering Saint Raphael's and nine years of knowing who my friends were, I blink back a new deluge of tears, take out my journal, and again pour out feelings that have nowhere else to go.

Not knowing who my detractors are, I find myself wondering constantly. I try to remind myself that many of the smiles and offers of friendship are undoubtedly genuine, but I can't seem to conquer the new sense of mistrust that now hangs at the edge of all my interactions with my sisters. An unfamiliar loneliness begins to creep through every corner of my being.

One of my band members, Sister Ann Paul—"Annie"— lives at the other Sister of Blessing convent in town, and every now and then the two houses get together and we have a chance to talk a bit. Talking on the phone, of course, is not permitted, nor are social visits to see one another, so these quite public moments in the community room are the only contact we have with each other. On these occasions, of course, we must not arouse suspicions that we are particular friends, so we are careful to keep most of our conversation general and public. At one point, however, we share a private word or two when her witch-eyed superior is engaged elsewhere, and I learn enough to know that Annie is miserable. Before she can tell me more, however, the witch lady turns and fixes a chilling stare, and we both lapse into silence.

The next time the two houses get together, Annie is gone,

and nobody will tell me what happened. One more friendship plucked suddenly from my life, and once again, the silence.

In late fall I have an opportunity to visit another band member. Sister Richard Ann, in many letters back and forth to the motherhouse, has been trying for some time to get permission for us to go to Peoria for a special workshop for junior-high school teachers. Eventually permission is forthcoming, and Sister Daniel Ann is instructed to hire the necessary lay teachers to cover for us the days that we're out.

When we arrive in Peoria after a long bus ride, my father picks us up and drives us to the convent where we will be staying during the workshop. It is the first time I have seen my father since I left St. Raphael's: he now has a few more gray hairs, and a few new jokes, and he is ever so proud, after all his years of chauffeuring nuns, to have a daughter who numbers herself among those august, revered creatures. I am not allowed to visit my family home, of course—we are only permitted to go home for the death of a parent—but Dad drives us past the house, and I see that everything is just as I left it five years ago. The trees are taller and the two-story house wears a new coat of paint, barnlike red, but everything else is the same. I glance up at the window of my old bedroom and wonder whose bedroom it is now. Dad drives us to the convent where we unpack and have supper; then the family comes to visit, lining themselves up on spindly legged, needlepointed chairs in the prim convent parlor. The conversation is equally prim: I am at a loss as to how to begin to be a part of them again.

The next day before the conference begins, Mother gives me a ride to Sacred Heart Convent to visit my friend Emily. Sister Richard Ann goes along as the ever necessary nun-companion and agrees to read in the parlor while I visit with Emily.

I have heard rumors that Emily is faring the worst of us

all, but I'm not too sure what the problem is. Once I set foot in her convent, however, I know that there's something strange about the house: fear hangs in the air, as real and tangible as the musty-smelling drapes that shroud the windows.

"What on earth is wrong with this house, Emily?" I demand, gripping her by the shoulders. "I get cold chills here. Something is very, very wrong."

Always pale and thin, Emily now looks haggard, almost haunted. She nervously picks at the skin around her fingernails as she whispers: "Don't talk so loud, Mar; someone is always listening. I don't know—sometimes I think there's something wrong, but sometimes I think it's just me. . . . I try my best, I really do!" One thin tear now squeezes out of dazed eyes as we step outside the kitchen door, seeking privacy. A November wind whips at our habit skirts, and we tuck chapped hands under our capes.

"I do everything they expect the youngest in the house to do: I sit next to the older nuns at recreation and ask about their rheumatism; I do all sorts of extra housekeeping jobs around the house; I know it's hard for Sister Helen Jean to do her employment with her bad knee and all, so I usually do it for her—I do everything I can to get them to accept me, just like they taught us in the juniorate, but it's no use."

More tears stream down Emily's face now, but the icy wind stops them halfway, stinging and chapping. I ache to put my arms around her and comfort her, but I spot a night-capped nun watching us from behind the curtains of a second-floor bedroom. I move closer instead, my arm pressed against hers, and we stand there shivering together on the convent back porch.

"I heard them the other day," she goes on, blowing her nose and dabbing at her face with her handkerchief. "I left the dishes in the sink while I went down to the basement to check on the laundry. When they discovered the half-finished dishes, two of them started mocking me, not knowing I overheard. 'Would you get a load of her!' one said, and the other said 'If *that's* how they trained them, we'll have to retrain her!' Then they both laughed.

"And that wasn't the only time," Emily goes on, rubbing her hands together under her cape to thaw them. "It seems like they're always mocking my enthusiasm or something. Sometimes they even repeat my words, mimicking me. I signed up to teach CCD (Confraternity of Christian Doctrine, religion class for Catholic children in public schools) on Saturday morning, and one of them snickered to the other, 'Isn't she the holy martyr?' "

"Have you written to your home superior, Emmie? That's what home superiors are for: they're supposed to be your advocate at the motherhouse in case any problems arise on mission. Surely she would do something about the situation— transfer you or something. You really look terrible, so thin and pale: this *can't* be what God wants!"

"I *have* written to her a number of times, but I've never received a response. I don't know what to do. My confessor keeps assuring me that it's not all in my mind, that others have spoken to him too. He says if things don't improve, he's going to speak to the bishop himself. Still, I can't help it. I keep thinking it's me. You know how they always stressed in the juniorate that we should see problems as challenges and opportunities: I keep reading my juniorate notes over and over, trying to figure out what I could do different."

Emily shows me her bedroom, a tiny sun porch that two other sisters have to cross in order to get to the lavatory. Then we hug quickly and say goodbye.

Emily and I eventually lose touch and see each other again only after both of us have left the convent. At that time very little will be discussed about the details of either leaving, Emily's or mine; we will attempt rather to put the past behind us as quickly as possible, to get on with our new lives without looking back. Only at the reunion fifteen years later will I learn what happened to Emily after our conversation that November day.

It seems Emily kept struggling along, trying to see problems as opportunities, saying her prayers, and doing her best to forgive her detractors. Frail anyway, she developed an ulcer and had to go on a bland diet. "Well, would you look at this: she's so special she even gets special food now!" jibed one of the sharp-tongued ladies of the house, and Emily felt her stomach tighten even more.

Things became worse. She vomited in front of her class a couple of times, but still she managed to drag herself to school day after day. By the time Christmas vacation rolled around, she was *really* ill and told the superior she was going to have to go to bed.

It was unheard of—the youngest in the house staying in bed during Christmas house cleaning. Who would do all the cleaning and decorating? "You're just trying to get out of work," snapped the superior and refused to allow food to be brought to Emily's room. Too weak to protest, Emily lay in bed and tried to figure out what to do. Her home Superior, Sister Theophane, still hadn't answered any of her letters— could the superior possibly be intercepting them?

One of the other nuns in the house, though too frightened to call a doctor, began sneaking Emily food, but Emily continued to weaken. One day soon after Christmas she crawled on hands and knees into the superior's room and told her she knew she was going to die if something wasn't done. Suddenly alarmed, the superior *did* call a doctor at last, and it didn't take him long to diagnose pneumonia.

Emily eventually recuperated, and in the meantime she received word that Sister Theophane would finally see her. One of the parishioners drove Emily to Saint Raphael's for her conference; the superior and one of her cronies sat on either side of her in the back seat. Not a word was said during the whole trip.

Once there, the superior and her sidekick accompanied Emily into the conference, sitting on either side. Emily told her story to Sister Theophane: the other nuns' constant ridicule, her own pneumonia, the superior's unwillingness to let food be brought to her. Sister Theophane turned to the superior, who smiled ever so patiently as she explained: "Sister, she had a *cold;* she was just pampering herself. Many of the sisters in the house are old and unable to handle a lot of the household chores. I depend on the younger ones to help out, to be generous with their time and energy. Sister Emily tends to be rather selfish and self-indulgent, complaining and whimpering every time she's the least bit ill. Ask Sister Thomas Rose, here—she's well aware of the problem as are most of the sisters, though they've been angels of patience."

Without waiting to be asked, Sister Thomas Rose nodded her agreement and hastened to add: "Sister, I can assure you that there's never been a superior as motherly and kind as our dear superior. She treats each of us as if we were her own children. Like any mother, she sometimes has to be firm, and though she's been truly an inspiration to all of us because of her patience with Sister Emily, in the end she had no choice but to put her foot down."

Sister Theophane listened carefully to all three and then instructed Sister Emily to go back to her convent and obey her superior. "No one ever said religious life was going to be easy," she said as she closed the case.

The worst part of the day came when Emily had to ride back to Peoria again between the superior and her buddy: they could not contain their laughter. For Emily the turning point came when she sat there between those two nuns and some voice deep inside, some quiet, clear, and *very sure* voice said suddenly: "Emily, are you crazy? An ulcer, pneumonia, and now this? What are you waiting for? Get the hell out of here!"

From that point on, according to Emily, everything changed. She called Sister Theophane as soon as she got back to Peoria and told her it was all over: she wanted a dispensa-

tion from her vows. Sister Theophane tried to talk her into a
leave of absence so that she would have time to think things
over. A dispensation was very final: she would be severed from
the community forever. "That's exactly what I want: to be
severed from all this *forever*," Emily shrieked into the phone,
surprising even herself.

Once Emily made her decision, she experienced a new
freedom, almost a recklessness. The plan was for her to go
home to Saint Raphael's for a week in the infirmary so that
she might get her strength back before leaving. So Emily began
to pack her things, and one morning when she was getting her
trunk from the convent basement, an incident happened that
brutally shattered any lingering schoolgirl ideas about convent
life.

As she was dragging her trunk across the basement floor
one morning, the janitor, a fiftyish foul-smelling man with a
lewd grin, appeared out of nowhere and offered to help her
with her trunk. Emily had never liked the man. Though she
had always tried not to think too much about it, she had
sometimes wondered about the relationship between him and
the superior: the two seemed inseparable. Joe was always
around the convent fixing something-or-other that was broken, and whenever the superior needed a ride somewhere Joe
was always called. Without ever giving an explanation to anyone, she never bothered to take a sister companion when she
went somewhere with Joe. You could hear the two of them
giggling outside the car as they prepared to run errands on a
Saturday morning. It amazed Emily to see how coy and flir-
tatious her superior was around Joe: though she tried not to
think too much about the resemblance, her superior on these
occasions sometimes reminded her of her own giggly boy-crazy
fourteen-year-old sister. "Judge not, lest thou be judged," she
had heard over and over, and she did her best.

Despite her suspicions and fear, Emily couldn't resist
Joe's offer to help with her trunk; otherwise she would have to
drag a heavy trunk up two flights of stairs alone. Together they

pushed and pulled the thing until they reached Emily's tiny room. She thanked Joe and turned to resume her packing; then he closed the door of her room, pulled her to him, and pressed his moist lips to hers. "We're going to miss you, honey," he whispered as his boozy breath choked her and his hands began to move under her cape. "Don't be frightened: there's nothing wrong with a little human affection. . . ."

Somehow Emily struggled out of his grasp and down the stairs. She ran as fast as she could across the parking lot to the school, up two flights of stairs to the superior's classroom (the superior had an eighth-grade homeroom as well as being principal of the school). Without stopping to catch her breath, she banged loudly on the classroom door, and when the superior came to the door, purpling with rage when she saw who it was, Emily closed the classroom door behind her and said slowly, determinedly, between clenched teeth: "I want you to call the motherhouse and tell them I've leaving tomorrow instead of Friday: I'm not willing to live in this sick house *one more solitary day.*" Emily spat the words out one by one.

The purple in the superior's face darkened another shade and she started to speak, but Emily cut her off. "And if you don't call, I'll call myself. And somewhere in the conversation with mother, I'll give her a little piece of information which may interest her: I'll just happen to mention the various rumors circulating about you and Joe. . . ."

Emily didn't need to say any more. The purple drained out of the superior's face, leaving it white and corpselike. "I'll call right after school," she whispered, her voice trembling.

That night after recreation, all the Sisters in the house lined up to tell Emily good-bye. The tornado of change sweeping through the Church had touched down even here: a departing Sister was allowed a proper good-bye, formal and impersonal, of course, but at least a good-bye. "I cried when I saw them there, all lined up," Emily remembers. "I felt so sorry for them. I felt I was somehow betraying them by leaving them behind. I was glad to be leaving the ones who made it so hard on me, but there were a few others who had befriended me. Angela Mary, for example—she's the one who brought me food when I was ill, though she knew she could get into a lot of trouble for it. Then there was Sister Agatha Martin. She had told me that all her life she'd wanted to be one of the order's missionaries, but the community insisted that she go into teaching. She taught for twenty years, day in and day out, hating every minute of it until she had a nervous breakdown. She was sent home to Saint Raphael's for a rest, then put on tranquilizers and, sent right back into the classroom. The kids called her 'Old Sourpuss,' threw tomatoes at her classroom windows, and did their level best to make life miserable for her. She popped her pills every morning, clinging to the conviction that this was just the dark night of the soul that the mystics talked about. A dark night of the soul that lasts for twenty years? I wept when I said good-bye to Old Sourpuss.

"And there were others—sweet, holy women who always tried to encourage me, to defend me when the others jibed and criticized. I hated saying good-bye to them too."

Emily goes on to describe how she took a bus to St. Raphael's at the crack of dawn and was put in a secret room in the infirmary for a week. "Nobody was allowed to come visit me—none of my friends even knew I was there."

"Didn't you even tell anyone about Joe?" I ask. "To tell you the truth, Mary, I was so confused and mixed-up, so full of self-doubt, that I somehow blamed myself. I told myself I should never have let him carry my trunk up: after all, didn't the Rule say we should never be alone with a man, be he father, brother, friend, or foe? Also," she giggles here, "I was pinned up and didn't have my work apron on, and you know how they drummed it into us that it was disgraceful to run around so unclothed!"

We both laugh at the image of a woman with cotton drawers, undershirt, garter belt, stockings, heavy cotton skirt, long-sleeved blouse, pinned-back cape, and overskirt thinking of herself as unclothed.

At the end of the week, Emily was secretly escorted to one of the parlors at the crack of dawn while everyone else was in chapel. "They brought me the dress I had worn to enter the convent. Can you imagine making your grand debut into the world in a pink chiffon dress that you wore for your high school graduation?" We both double up with laughter at the image, and she goes on to describe how she shivered in that cold parlor as she took off each piece of habit, how they loaned her a coat and gave her $50 to help her get started in the world.

An old pain creases her eyes as she reflects: "A childhood of wanting to be a nun, nine years of training to be one, years upon years of looking at the world from one deeply rooted perspective. Then one day—*whack!*—all of a sudden the roots of a lifetime are lopped off, and I have to start all over again."

As if she has been watching a sad movie that has suddenly become too much for her, Emily tosses her head determinedly and pastes on an unconvincing smile. "But why go back through all that, Mary; why open old wounds? It's over and done with; it's in the past." I mumble something about how I think it's important to go back and integrate old parts of ourselves that we threw away or that we *thought* we threw away, but it's no use: the interview is over, the subject is closed. Reaching into her purse, she asks if she has shown me pictures of her children: Johnny's now in fifth grade and doing so well, and Sarah took her first step last week. . . .

I meet a number of sisters from various communities at the Peoria workshop and garner many practical insights about classroom discipline and motivation. The enthusiasm and dedication of so many teaching nuns inspires me and makes me proud to number myself in their midst.

Because of my conversation with Emily, I return to Cincinnati with new eyes. Everyone was right: I *do* live in one of the better houses. I resolve to jump into community life with both feet and give it all I've got. No more holing up in my room with a book: when I've got an unexpected free moment I'll make a batch of cookies for the sisters or volunteer to make table favors for a coming feast. I'll offer to do Sister Clare Robert's pressing—her arthritis is so bad—and I'll be available to drive anyone who needs a ride somewhere.

It is the first year that Sisters of Blessing are allowed to drive cars: the cap has been adapted so that it allows adequate peripheral vision, and sisters everywhere are beginning to drive. Huge amounts of community money are put out for insurance, driver training, and drivers' licenses, and many parishes buy shiny new cars for their sisters. At first there are reports of numerous accidents. The week before we arrived in Cincinnati, a Sister of Blessing was killed in a car that she was driving, and one of the Sisters in our house was one of the passengers. Shaken, Sister Daniel Ann insists that anyone in her house who wants to drive must first go through extensive training.

Though I drove around our quiet neighborhood and briefly on family vacations, when I was in high school, I have many doubts about my skill and appreciate the opportunity for the training. Once the lessons are over, I long to practice to build up my self-confidence, but as I am never allowed "out on the streets" without a sister companion, the only practice I get is when I drive the older sisters on their errands. They try to be patient but they are nervous, their false teeth clacking, their bony fingers pointing out pedestrians, traffic lights, and other cars.

So grinning and bearing their nervousness, their clacking false teeth, and their constantly pointing bony fingers, I do my best to endear myself to the older sisters by driving them around. For the sake of the others, I study football scores, crocheting, and housekeeping and bone up on the latest findings related to lesson plans and discipline. For the sake of both, I do my best to forget that I ever loved Faulkner, Hemingway, and existentialist philosophy.

But it's no use: I am increasingly bored and miserable in

the role I must play, increasingly full of doubts. "Is *this* what it was all about?" I ask myself as I sit on my purple-flowered spread and watch evening fall over the asphalt playground. "I gave up my family and marriage and a normal life for *this?*" Somehow I had been able to keep going through all the years of training by picturing starving babies and bloated-bellied men that I would one day—in some vague way—help. That had made it all worthwhile.

But now the reality of it—the purple-flowered spread, the asphalt, the nuns gathering in the community room to correct spelling papers and chat about the events of the day—begins to grow.

It's not the kids; they're wonderful—young and spontaneous and full of life. Just being around them makes me feel young myself. What *isn't* so great is the role I must play and the incredibly demanding schedule I must follow.

I start out in the morning supervising an eighth-grade homeroom, making sure that everyone is there and that they have sold enough raffle tickets or chocolates or whatever else we happen to be selling to raise money for the building fund. Then the classes start, one after another with only a three-minute break in between. I teach French and English and religion and music, first to the seventh graders, then to the eighth graders. At noon I walk over to the convent for lunch and then come back to continue the dizzying schedule until the final bell rings at three, leaving me exhausted and drained. There is no time to talk to students between classes, no time for the human contact I crave.

Eventually I start hanging around for a while after school, and a lot of the kids stay around to talk. They seem grateful to have someone listen to them, to treat them as individuals. I begin to relax around them too: one day they even get me on a skateboard, and I go sailing across the parking lot, veil flying in the wind! To my amazement, letting down my guard a bit after school doesn't seem to have the dire effects my mentors had predicted: in fact, when I let slip a tiny glimpse of the humanness that throbs somewhere under all those clothes, my students seem to have the opposite reaction. They are more cooperative, less hostile, and sometimes they even open their ears a fraction when I speak to them about religion! I feel that I have made a wonderful discovery, and I am eager to share it with my sisters.

But back in the convent the whisperings have increased. "What's she trying to do: win a popularity contest?" and "Why doesn't she come back to the convent at the end of the day, like the rest of us? What's she trying to prove? Doesn't she know the kids won't have any respect for her if she lets them get too close?"

One day I overhear someone calling me a "teenage nun" and "immature," and the self-doubts start again. Maybe they're right: maybe there really *is* something wrong with me since I seem to prefer the company of thirteen- and fourteen-year-olds to that of my sisters.

So once again I try to cram myself into the role expected of me. I herd my students to Mass and hover over them to be sure that no one talks. In religion class I try to find some enthusiasm for Catholic doctrine that is as dull and lifeless to me as it is to my students. I toe the line of an inhuman schedule. But the dam has already cracked, and it will be just a matter of time before it tumbles altogether, releasing an overwhelming surge of anger and rebellion that can no longer be contained.

It starts to overflow one day when I receive a letter from my sister Andi. Her letter holds the usual account of parties and dates and college football games, and the contrast between her life and my own is just too much for me.

I long to write to her, to pour out my heart as she has done to me so many times in the past, but a sense of loyalty to the community restrains me. From the very beginning of our training it has been impressed upon us that we should never let outsiders see the tears and bitterness that often hide behind the beatific, smiling countenances we show the world.

Just when I am ready to explode with it all, a person walks into my life who knows a lot about life and love and shaky dams. His name is Tim, and he will make all the difference in the world.

"A couple of old bitches around here probably think we're having an affair," he laughs, taking a deep drag on his cigarette. We are sitting in the tiny convent parlor with both doors closed. I tell him about the passage in our Rule forbidding us to ever be alone in a room with a man, and we both laugh. "See, that's what I told you: repress anything and you'll become obsessed with it. Ordinary people out there take sex for granted as a part of life, but nuns and priests are so afraid of their sexuality that they're absolutely driven by it."

Tim is a Jesuit who gives weekend retreats for nuns. During the week he goes to various convents to hear confession and to be available as spiritual director/counselor to anyone who may wish to talk to him. I assure him that the time of his coming could not have been more propitious in terms of my life, that I need very badly to talk to someone about all that has been stored up within me for so long.

Tim also shares with me about his own life. He tells me about a woman with whom he is in love, a nun of a different order, and about his struggles to remain celibate. "I've gotten in touch with some pretty powerful human feelings: I never want to shut down on those feelings again. Yet I'm committed to celibacy, and I want to find a way to express those feelings within the framework of that commitment."

I am amazed at how comfortable I am talking to Tim: I feel that I can truly tell him anything. Tim helps me to continue the process that I had started during the later years of my training, the process of getting to know my deepest self, of discovering what was available to me, the amazing breadth of my options. Every time we talk I am invigorated and excited—and scared. Where will this all lead?

———————

Tim is not the only one who senses my growing restlessness. Sister Daniel Ann, one morning in February, asks if I
might be interested in joining her in a new project: a parishioner who is a social worker in the inner city told her about a
new program where they need volunteers in an adult reading
program. "Adults right here in our own country who can't
read—can you imagine that? Mrs. Delaney says most of them
are blacks whose children are learning to read in school: it's
very painful and embarrassing for them when their children
can read and they can't.

"It's a new program, sponsored by the Saint Vincent de
Paul Society. I've always had the feeling you were much happier when you were working with the poor than you are now
with these middle-class kids: your face always seems to light
up when you talk about your program in Washburn. So I
thought you might be interested in this project. Maybe we can
see who else is interested and start going on Sunday afternoons. . . ."

I am touched by her concern for me and enthusiastic
about the project. One other sister, Sister Victor Marie, is
interested, and soon we are driving the convent station wagon
into the inner city each Sunday.

I soon begin to live for Sunday afternoon. A black man
with gray-flecked hair breaks down in tears one afternoon, a
few weeks after I have started working with him. "You know,
I was always so ashamed of the fact that I couldn't read. My
kids would want me to read to them the way other kids' parents did, but I'd always tell them it was too much of a strain
on my eyes. Eventually they found out, of course, and when
they did, they tried to hide their shame. But I could see it in
their eyes. Now I'm actually learning to read after all these
years: I don't think I've ever been so happy!"

A young mother with six children under eight years of
age leaves the children with their father every Sunday afternoon and comes to tutoring. "It's hard for me to believe," she
marvels. "All my life I thought I was dumb, that I'd never

learn to read. So I dropped out of school and had a bunch of kids, and now I find out I can read after all! It's just too amazing. Once I'm good enough, I'm going to get a library card and take some books out so that I can read to my little ones!"

Sunday afternoon makes my week. I feel needed, useful, and that I'm at last living out the dreams that inspired me through my years of training. On the way back in the car each Sunday, Sister Daniel Ann, Sister Victor Marie, and I share accomplishments and excitement, and I discover a feeling of community that I don't have back at the house.

Through the tutoring I begin to know Sister Victor Marie a little better, and she frequently tells me stories about what it was like to be a Sister of Blessing in the 1940s and 1950s. Sometimes I am not quite prepared for what I find out.

One afternoon for example, Sister Clare Robert, one of the retired sisters, receives an urgent phone call. When she doesn't hear my rap on her door, I suspect that she might have her hearing aid turned off, so I shove her door open just a crack.

She *must* have it off, for she doesn't even hear me when I push the door open. I stand there for a moment, stunned by what I am seeing, and then close the door gently.

Shaken, I go to Sister Daniel Ann's room to tell her about the phone call, then count the doors down to Sister Victor Marie's room. From the neck down, Sister Victor Marie is in full habit when she answers the door, but she wears her nightcap instead of *serre-tête*, cap, and veil. After school we frequently strip off our head coverings as eagerly as fat ladies strip off binding girdles; we replace them with the loose-fitting nightcap, our casual attire. Within a year, things will have changed so radically that we'll be allowed to watch TV in the community room without nightcaps, but for now the stern ruling about always having our heads covered is in full force.

I tell Sister Victor Marie that I need to talk to her, and

she quickly invites me in, motioning me to sit on the edge of the bed.

"What on earth is wrong?" she queries. "You look like you just saw a ghost."

"No, something much worse," I moan, still not wanting to believe it. "I pushed open Sister Clare Robert's door to give her a phone message. Her drapes were pulled, her light out. At first I thought she might be napping, but then I saw her. Victor, what on earth was that woman doing? She was kneeling in front of her crucifix with her robe and nightcap on, and she was—well, she—I mean, she seemed to be beating herself with something. Is there something they never told me, Victor? Something I might have missed when they told us about chapter of faults, meals kneeling, and examen beads?"

Sister Victor Marie now enjoys a good laugh at my hysteria. "I never dreamed they never told you guys! Back in the old days some of the sisters used a discipline. Nobody had to; it was a totally optional practice of penance. A few of the older sisters still use a discipline today. There are no sharp edges or points; it's simply a cloth cord, knotted in a few places. One simply takes it in her right hand and whips herself over the left shoulder, in identification with the beating that Christ endured at the hands of the soldiers. I don't really know, but I don't think anybody ever hits herself really hard. It's more a symbolic thing."

"But why do it in the first place?" I protest. "That's the sickest thing I've ever heard."

"Now, now, my dear," she smiles, as she removes her nightcap and pulls on a fresh *serre-tête*, "things were different in the old days. People looked at things differently."

I ask Sister Victor Marie to take a walk with me, and soon we are crossing the playground and heading down one of the streets of the surrounding neighborhood.

We stop to chat a moment with a group of children riding bikes in a quiet cul-de-sac; then we continue on, walking briskly and pulling our shawls tight around us. Soon we pick up the thread of conversation about convent life in the old days.

"I bet you guys never even got black marks when you were in the novitiate," Victor says.

"Black marks? What in God's name are black marks, Victor?"

"Well, in my day . . ." My friend goes on to tell me how black marks were given out for any so-called irregularities: a lid left off toothpaste, running up stairs, having more than five needles in one's pin cushion. Senior novices were assigned as checkers: it was their responsibility to go through the younger novices' personal belongings and check that everything was in order. Then once a month they had to stand up in front of the group and give their reports: "Sister Barbara had spots on her habit skirt; Sister Ann didn't clean the hair out of her hairbrush. . . ."

"The worst part was that those silly black marks determined our college hygiene grade, the grade that went on our transcript. A friend of mine received permission to go on to graduate school, but before she could be accepted she had to write back to Saint Raphael's and have her hygiene grade changed on her transcript."

"And I thought *we* had it bad!" I exclaim.

"Actually, you had it quite easy, being able to finish your education before going out on mission and all. That was the hardest part for me. We went out on mission after just two years of college. They gave us education courses, but they were all theory, nothing practical: no methods courses. Then they sent us out to teach. Every summer we'd come back to Saint Raphael's and work on our degree a little bit more. The head of the Education Department, Sister Frances Martha, made out everyone's schedule and never bothered to stick too closely to courses that were required for the degree. For some reason known only to her, it seemed she was always assigning me German and psychology courses, helpful neither in the classroom nor toward a degree. It took me eight summers to finally get my B.S.!"

Victor and I puff our way up a small hill—the puffing partly due to the German chocolate cake Mrs. Smith brought for the sisters after school and numerous other such gooey treats ingested frequently during the past few months, and partly to the yards of heavy, thick serge we drag with us everywhere we go.

Once we recover from the hill, I tell my friend that I haven't quite recovered from the sight of Sister Clare Robert kneeling there in front of her crucifix, hitting herself with a discipline. "*You* never did that, Victor, did you?" I demand, almost afraid to hear her answer.

"Hardly," she laughs. "Community life was always hard enough for me just by itself; I didn't need to invent some external means of beating myself up." She is quiet for a moment and then goes on, a sadness I've never seen shadowing her usually jovial face.

"My family was always close—a hard-working German farm family. We didn't have much money, but we had a lot of love. When I first went away to the convent, the annual family vacation consisted of packing eight kids into a car and coming to visit me. It was a long ride from Pennsylvania to Illinois: they had to start in the wee hours of morning in order to make it by the opening of visiting hours. That's why I always resented it so much when the bell sometimes rang right in the middle of our visit and we had to go inside for a half-hour chapter of faults. Can you imagine? We weren't allowed to tell our parents why we were going, of course. I can remember how uncomfortable I always felt when I came back out and they'd see my pale face and ask questions, and I wouldn't be able to answer them. That made me sadder than anything, I think, the chasm that began to grow between myself and my parents."

Sadness shifts to anger as Victor continues. A gloved

thumb rubs one *chaplette* bead after another in controlled fury. "I'll never forget what happened one year: they set out as usual in the black of morning, but halfway to Illinois, something went wrong with the car. Dad eventually fixed it, but by the time they arrived it was quarter to five, and visiting hours had just ended. They told our superior their story, but they weren't allowed to see me, not even for a moment. They had to load their eight kids back into the car and begin the long trip back home."

By now Victor is kicking every stone in sight, and tears of fury are running down her face. "You know, my mother died the following year: that visit would have been my last chance to see her. By the time I got word, she was dead."

Stunned and speechless, I take Victor's hand and we walk in silence for a moment or two. Eventually she smiles sheepishly.

"I've cried about that so many times that I'm surprised I still have tears left to cry. In a way, I guess, it was probably best that Mother died suddenly: it spared my making the tortured decision that so many of my friends had to make. You know: the rule about going home specified that you could go home just one time, at a parent's death. If a parent was on the deathbed, you had to make a choice: you could go home to be with them before they died, but if they lingered for a while and you had to return to your duties, you couldn't then go home later for the funeral. It was only one time, the dying or the funeral. I have friends who are *still* tortured and guilt-ridden because they aren't sure they made the right choice."

"Victor," I begin, putting one word in front of the other, determined to get out of the morass of doubt and confusion in which I've been trapped lately, a morass only further thickened by what my friend has shared with me. "How did you stand it? I mean sometimes I feel *I* can't stand it, that surely God doesn't want me to be this miserable. And I haven't even gone through *half* of what you've gone through!"

Now the tables are turned. Back to her old hearty self

again, Sister Victor Marie stops for a moment and tightens her shawl around her. She again clasps it with her left hand and with the other hand takes *my* hand.

We start off again as she begins to share with me her secrets for survival in the convent, and something in her tone, her buxom, hearty self-confidence and contentment, staves off the panic I was starting to feel.

"You just take things too seriously, Mary de Paul. I know it's hard on you—the first year on mission is always hard. Back in my day, they didn't even let us have visits from our families our first year on mission since they were so afraid we'd run off with them at the first opportunity, even though we were still under vows. I guess before they made the rule, somebody actually did that. Anyway, the first year is always hard. In *my* first year on mission, the seventh-grade teacher fell ill in the middle of the year and they sent a replacement who was seventy, looked eighty, and had had at least four heart attacks. Needless to say, she wasn't able to control her new class, a rowdy, rambunctious group, and it was decided that I should trade classes with her since I had a group that was more docile. If they were docile, it was because I had struggled for six months to make them that way! My principal/superior saw the unfairness of the situation and wrote home to Mother begging her to reconsider. 'She's young and flexible; she can handle it,' Mother wrote back, and the next day the older sister appeared before my startled youngsters, and I walked into the seventh-grade lions' den. And how do you think I survived a situation like that? I cried a lot at first; then I laughed. Next I threw myself into my work, and eventually I forgot the whole thing."

Sister Victor Marie again laughs her deep hearty laugh, and I try to join in, but I am too busy comparing myself with her, wishing I could be like her. Why can't *I* have such a perspective? Why can't I just laugh it all off?

By the time we arrive back at the convent, it's almost time for afternoon prayers. We cross the playground and come across a group of Victor Marie's sixth-grade boys playing basketball. She chats with them for a few moments—their fondness for her is apparent—then takes the ball and executes a perfect hook shot. They applaud and whistle, and she lifts her hands above her head in the gesture of a champion. We head back to the convent as the sun is going down, and I realize again how happy Sister Victor Marie is. I resolve to be happy too.

"How could you do that?" she shrieks, not even caring that we are in the sacristy behind the church, laying out the vestments for the next day's Mass. "You should know better: if you make him angry, Sister's the one who'll suffer, not *you*."

I am yelling too: "If she lets him push her around like that, that's her problem, but I'm not going to let him do it to me anymore. I'm sick of the way everyone kisses up to him and then tears him to pieces once he's gone. We're not children: we don't have to let him treat us like that."

It had started earlier that morning when some of the kids in my class approached Father Myers about the possibility of having a guitar Mass for graduation. I knew that he went into a rage whenever anyone even mentioned some of the liturgical innovations with which other parishes were experimenting, but I thought I may as well let them ask him. The little band of envoys came back pale and shaken, and I knew I would be hearing from the good father soon. I just didn't know how soon. Within five minutes he was at my classroom door, bellowing.

"Sister, I'd like to see you at once."

"Father, I'd be happy to talk to you, but I'm right in the middle of giving a test. If you could wait just a moment . . ."

"I said *at once!*" he screamed, looking alarmingly precoronary.

"I'd be glad to talk to you, Father, but you'll have to wait just a moment," I repeated sweetly. By now he was sputtering, and I was enjoying the deliciousness of my defiance. How many times had he come stalking into my classroom without a moment's warning? How many times had he interrupted an exam or a heated discussion, without even bothering to knock or announce himself? Yes, my defiance had been ripening for some time, and it now tasted oh so sweet.

With that he went storming down the hall and into Sister Daniel Ann's office. "You're going to have to do something with that young one: I'm tired of her attitude. What's the matter with you? Don't you have any control over your house? They never should have made you a superior if you can't do better than that! And as far as what you're doing as principal, it's about time. . . ." On and on he fumed, stopping only long enough to take a breath before hurling another accusation. I heard it all from my classroom and as usual heard only an intermittent "Yes, Father" from Sister Daniel Ann.

The fact that Father Myers would take it out on Sister Daniel Ann was a fact that had kept me docile for a long time: as my superior, she was my sole representative to officials outside the house, whether they be physicians, janitors, the pastor, or the superior general. After all, she *had* been good to me. She had understood my restlessness to work where the needs of people seemed more critical than they did in this comfortable suburban parish and had always been kind and supportive when I approached her about problems in my classroom. Even when she had told me of the other sisters' criticisms, it had obviously pained her to do so.

But the way she let Father Myers talk to her was something I could no longer stomach. I finally decided that she could do what she wanted: *I* was no longer going to tolerate his condescension and rudeness. If my decision put her in a bad position, causing him to vent his wrath on *her*, I was sorry, but I could no longer let that stand in my way.

A couple of the nuns smile indulgently when they hear the story, a couple even cheer me on (in private, of course), but a vocal few feel that Sister Daniel Ann's cross will be all the heavier because of my indiscretion. Sister Richard Ann, who from the very beginning had taken pains to let me know her lack of esteem for our superior, marches at the forefront of the angry throng, lamenting how poor Sister Daniel Ann will have to suffer now. Sister Richard Ann has been increasingly cool toward me for the last couple of months, and when I talk to Victor about it she says she probably feels betrayed by my popularity with the seventh and eighth graders and by my friendship with Victor.

Amazingly, Sister Daniel Ann doesn't even mention the incident: in fact, she almost seems friendlier. Could it be that she too has had just about enough?

In May I open my little white envelope and discover that I am being transferred to Josephina School for Girls in a wealthy suburb of Chicago. My year of learning humility and basic teaching skills is over: according to the supposed scenario, I should now start to teach high-school English and/or French.

I soon learn, however, that I won't be teaching English this year either. A few days after I receive my obedience, I receive a phone call from Sister Laurena, a superior from juniorate days who will be my new principal/superior. She tells me that she wants me to assist her in setting up a new Religion Department at Josephina and that she's made arrangements for me, another sister, and herself to attend a special workshop for religion teachers in Boston this summer. "We want to implement a process-oriented, discussion-group approach in Josephina's Religion Department next September, and the workshop will teach us how to do that. The old way clearly isn't working: it's time to try something new."

Though somewhat disappointed at the thought of not teaching English (will I never again have an excuse to read James Joyce?), I am excited at the prospect of working with students in a less-formal situation. Forty students lined up in rows in nailed down desks, stuffy religion books that do nothing at all to stimulate a hunger for God—I always knew there had to be a better way!

27

SUMMER (1967)

At the end of the school year, we clean our house and class-rooms and prepare to go on a week's vacation. I am scheduled to go to the workshop after that.

Vacation: it is the first year that the word has been heard behind convent walls. Until now, most sisters have spent their summers at Saint Raphael's taking classes. This year, however, a new experiment is being launched: each sister will be allowed to spend a week at a nearby vacation spot, resting and recu-perating. The expense for the community will be minimal: as usual, the good laity have come forward to help, offering sum-mer cottages near rivers and lakes.

Sister Daniel Ann has arranged for the sisters in our house to stay at a cottage on a lake in Indiana. I hear through the convent grapevine that a group of my buddies will be vacationing at a cottage on another side of the same lake, and since I won't be returning to O.L.P.H. next year anyway, Sis-ter Daniel Ann approves my request to stay with my friends.

A parishioner drives us to the lake and drops me off at my friends' cottage before taking the rest of the sisters to the other side of the lake. My friends watch from behind the cur-tains, and once the car has pulled away, they come out to greet me. I gasp in surprise: their heads are bare, and they wear baggy Bermudas and sleeveless blouses. How comical they look: hair matted against their heads by years of *serre-tête* pres-sure, shaggy uneven haircuts, wire-rim granny glasses (plastic frames aren't allowed) hooked over ears that don't seem to know what to do with their new freedom. How comical, and yet how wildly unfettered and free!

My friends take me in and offer to mix me a drink from the cottage-owner's supply: "He told us to drink all we want!" Desperately searching my mind for names of drinks that I've read about in books, I eventually ask for a bacardi. I don't know what that is, but I remember Dad offering someone a bacardi the last time I was home. When my parents drink at all, they usually drink beer or a little whiskey, nothing fancy.

When they say they don't have any bacardi, I say, "Anything, then," and my friend brings me a gin and tonic, which I think tastes bitter though I don't say so. Everyone is smoking cigarettes, and when someone offers me one, I ask: "Does anyone have any Winstons?" At least in cigarettes I have some worldly knowledge.

When I'm shown to the box of assorted Bermudas and blouses ("Melva's sister gathered them for us—wasn't she a doll?") I fold my hands in mock timidity and query: "Are you sure this is what Reverend Mother had in mind?" Everyone laughs, and I'm the only one who knows that I'm actually half-serious. It's obvious that she didn't have this in mind at all, and I'm not sure what will happen if word of our rebellious little group gets back to her. I notice, however, that I care a lot less than I would have a year ago or even six months ago: in fact, as the drink begins to take effect, I find that I hardly care at all. What a wonderful cottage! What a wonderful group of friends! "Could I have another one of those tonic things?"

Relaxed and blissful, I chatter with my friends in front of the fire until late in the night and then eventually fall asleep in a big chair.

The next morning we put on skirts and blouses and go into the nearby village for early Mass. "No one will recognize us this way—we don't want any stories going around."

And so we set off, nine ladies of assorted ages and girth in ill-fitting skirts and blouses and chopped-off hair. No one recognizes us, but then we don't exactly blend right in either, a fact that occurs to none of us, so blissful are we in our new unfettered state.

After Mass we come back to the cottage for breakfast and a day of sitting in the sun, boating, and playing tennis on a nearby court. In the afternoon we chant our office together and have a prayer service where we read passages from the Bible and sing some of the latest liturgical songs: "God Is Love," "Sons of God," and so on. We feel ever so wicked to be neglecting our rosary and substituting, instead, some of the songs from the unofficial top ten of liberal Catholicism.

At the end of the week, we put on our habits and prepare to return to our convents. As I wrap the white linen tightly around my neck and fasten each heavy black layer around my body, I for the first time question my sanity right out loud. The hot sticky cloth on my poor sunburned body seems somehow symbolic of convent life itself: chafing and constricting, oppressive to body and spirit.

When I arrive in Boston for the religious-education workshop, I watch in sullen silence the nuns pouring out of various cars. I feel strangely alienated as if I no longer have a place in their midst.

Watching them, their long black habit skirts dragging in the dust, I think back on the week at the lake and how young I had suddenly felt. It had been almost impossible to feel young at O.L.P.H. where sixtyish parish women cooed over me, treating me like a revered elder and plying me with the same rich goodies they took to great aunts who were ill. "Enjoy yourself, Sister. How nice not to have to worry about your figure!" It was hard to feel lighthearted and young when I wore shoes so old-fashioned that even Grandma wouldn't be caught dead in them and clothes so heavy and cumbersome that I was no longer sure I had a body under it all.

But the summer had changed all that: the feel of the warm sun on my bare arms is with me still, stirring some part of me that will no longer be silenced. There is much that is beginning to stir within me, but I as yet have no words for it.

To my amazement, I soon discover numerous kindred

spirits under the old-fashioned garb, young sisters from all over the country who are experiencing the same sort of restlessness in their communities as I am experiencing in mine. One in particular, Sister Margaret Marie (eventually "Peggy") will become a lifelong friend: we will write long letters back and forth through the conflicted yet splendid months to come, as our personal evolutions as well as those of our respective communities take amazingly similar paths.

At the workshop we are introduced to some of the newer approaches to religious education, and various textbook representatives are there to show their wares. At the end of our workshop each day, Sister Margaret Marie and I and a small group of friends meet for pizza and soft drinks in the student cafeteria. I have been allotted a small amount of money for the summer and am amazed to discover that I still know how to count change! We share laughs and frustrations and hatch many a brave new idea for bringing reform to our various communities. "The New Breed" has become a common expression used to describe the group of young Catholic liberals who are pushing for change in the Church, and we pride ourselves on being in its vanguard.

Sharing the vanguard with us are absurdly handsome young priests and seminarians who sit on the other side of the cafeteria, smiling and nodding to us as they pass, their long hair creeping defiantly over their crisp Roman collars, making a statement of its own. How we wish we had a few of *them* in our nun-filled workshop! Though we rarely speak, we know we are all on the same team.

We see them again at a Pete Seeger concert, and then one night in the cafeteria they come over and share their beers with us and teach us a rolicking song poking fun at Gomer de Pauw, the head of the Catholic Traditionalist Movement. I think that my heart will burst with joy.

When the workshop is over, I catch a plane to Cincinnati, armed with a whole new absorbing reason for staying a nun. United with my brothers and sisters throughout the country, I will help to bring change to my own community and to the Church as a whole. The song says it, and we feel the truth of it in our bones: "The times, they are a changin'. . . ."

28 §⌇

JOSEPHINA SCHOOL FOR GIRLS, CHICAGO (1967–1968)

After a week in Cincinnati to pack my things and say my good-byes, I go to Chicago to begin my first year of teaching high school. I immediately love the big old building in which I will live: it houses an exclusive Catholic girls' school, Josephina School for Girls, as well as the thirty or so nuns who teach, cook, and run the school.

Formerly a boarding school, Josephina sprawls out over four spacious floors. On the first floor there are formal parlors, an elegant lobby with a soaring ceiling (site of the traditional Christmas tree), library, offices, and chapel. Most classrooms are on the second floor; included is the tiny yearbook room where I will hold sway as yearbook moderator, directed at practically every turn by a lovable but meddling retired sister who was in charge of the yearbook for twenty years before our respective obediences directed her to retire, which she did with reluctance, and me to take her place, which I did with equal reluctance. Nuns' bedrooms and a large recreation room are on the fourth floor. Of course, Josephina girls are strictly forbidden to travel the stairs that lead to this floor. Kitchen, nuns' refectory, and lay-teachers' dining room are all on the basement floor.

I am enchanted with the elegant old building—its soaring

ceilings make my spirits soar—and even more excited when I discover that the campus also includes a gym and a swimming pool. One of the things I found most difficult when I first went to Cincinnati was the lack of opportunity for exercise. At Saint Raphael's daily walks had been *de rigueur*, and we had gone to the gym or pool at least once a week. In the winter we had taken to the hills with sleds and toboggans at the first snowfall. In Cincinnati our usual exercise consisted of walking across the playground from convent to school and sometimes taking an occasional stroll through the surrounding suburbs. We had no access to a pool or a gym, and exercises performed in the privacy of one's room were frowned upon as hedonistic and vain.

Now pool and gym are there for me to use whenever I wish, and beautiful Lake Michigan is only a hearty walk away. That was the other thing that was difficult in Cincinnati: the tract homes and minilawns of the suburb surrounding our convent had been a far cry from the trees and gulleys and ravines that had been my lush stomping grounds for nine spoiled years at Saint Raphael's. I desperately missed Saint Raphael's vast uncaged beauty. Now tree-lined avenues and awesome Lake Michigan, all power and fury, beckon: I feel that I can breathe again.

Within the convent too, all signs point to better days ahead. Sister Laurena, who I have by now grown to love and revere, has made some far-reaching changes in the Religion Department, and I am eager to be a teacher in her new program. I will also teach two French classes and run a homeroom, besides acting as moderator of the yearbook.

Convinced that the old indoctrination method of teaching religion hasn't worked, Sister Laurena has studied the newer catechetical theories and has been impressed in particular by the work of Brother Gabriel Moran. According to Moran, teaching religion isn't so much a matter of imparting information as it is of clearing any obstacles that might be in the way of the students' tuning in to the spirit of God that is already within them; the best way to clear obstacles is to allow students to talk, to ventilate, to begin to discover their own answers inside—the God inside. Moran doesn't go in much for ready-made, spoon-fed answers or for a prepackaged, predigested God.

Boldly deciding to restructure the entire Religion Department, Sister Laurena has had special rooms built, just big enough for small-group discussions: students who desire a less-traditional religion class are allowed to sign up for small-group discussions in these rooms.

I facilitate three group discussions each day, learning a great deal as we go along about the dynamics of group process. As time passes, I become more and more willing to set pre-planned subject matter aside and go wherever the students' real concerns lead. I begin to notice the natural healing, the deepening, that happens when people speak candidly to one another and listen carefully without judging, and I become more and more convinced that when you help people wake up to themselves, you help put them in touch with the God within.

Not everyone agrees, of course. The traditionalists in our midst accuse us of substituting secular humanism for Church doctrine, and some parents become irate because we don't spend our religion classes telling their kids that they'll go to hell if they don't go to Sunday Mass. They tell us outright that they have given up on getting their kids to be good Catholics and that the only reason they are willing to put out so much money to send their kids to Catholic schools is so that we nuns will knock some sense into them. "What good is letting them express their *own* opinions? What's important is that they hear the pope's opinions!"

Though I know that I will never go back to dogma-oriented religion classes ("conversion by concussion," someone calls it), I feel a certain compassion for these parents who remember with nostalgia how nice the family used to look at

Mass each Sunday, all lined up there in the row together in their Sunday best. Now their kids won't even go to Mass, despite (because of?) the fact that they have heard "the pope's opinions" ad nauseum through the last eight years of Catholic education. Their parents miss the obvious fact that that kind of teaching had failed miserably and now, in their panic and confusion, they expect us to provide more of the same. Although they would never admit it, I know that they feel like failures as Catholic parents, that all their sacrifices to give their children a Catholic education have been in vain.

One of the hottest controversies in most communities at this time has to do with the religious habit. Some communities have already changed theirs, usually shortening the skirt and getting rid of tight headbindings. Some have gone so far as to get rid of the veil altogether: we are admonished to pray for this group!

The very first day that I arrived at Josephina, I was warned that modification of the habit was simply not an acceptable topic of conversation here, and that was that. The warning had come not from Sister Laurena, of course, but from a spokeswoman for the little group of conservatives who had dominated the convent and school for years.

And yet renewal and change are in the air, and within a few months word comes down from the motherhouse that the community is going to initiate a period of experimenting with a modified habit. No decision as to future policy is being made; before such a decision can be made, it is necessary to go through a period of experimentation.

With that decree the cold war becomes hot, and clear battle lines are drawn. Conservatives refuse to relinquish an inch of wool, and progressives look forward to shedding as many inches as possible. *Serre-têtes* are the first to go, along with the traditional cap and veil. Instead we wear a cap and short veil that leave a patch of hair showing in front, and for the first week the students won't look at us directly for fear they will be struck dead because they have looked at a nun's hair!

Guidelines that come down regarding the habit itself specify that it has to be loose fitting and either black or blue. The skirt has to come to well beneath the knee, an awkward midcalf length that in this era of minis and miniminis looks incredibly dowdy and awkward. Because there is no standardization yet, everyone's home-sewn attempt at modernization comes out a bit different, and we look like such a motley crew these first few months that if it weren't for the fact that the sore under my chin is beginning to heal, I might be tempted to join the conservatives.

Gradually, however, some of the more glaring problems of aesthetics are ironed out and a certain standardization is introduced until there is basically one traditional habit and one modified habit—and a community split right down the middle.

Nineteen hundred sixty-eight, the year of unrest and riots and revolutions all across the planet, is waiting in the wings to be born. Inside me too is something waiting to be born, though I am too afraid, too unsure of myself as yet to give it a name. In my tortured ambivalence I sometimes catch an electrifying glimpse of the inner freedom that comes when you dare to follow your heart, but usually I shut down on such "upstart thoughts" rather quickly. And yet I have an exciting sense as the new year draws near that my inner restlessness and rumblings will soon be coming to a head.

Our cigarettes are like tiny beacons in the blackness of night. We take one last drag and then toss them into the lake, starting the three-block trek back home.

We have been walking down to the lake like this for the past few weeks, sneaking away after night prayers. Mary Lucia is in charge of locking up, so getting in and out of the big old building is no problem. And getting cigarettes is no problem: Lucia seems to have a consistent source.

By the end of the day we need to get out of the place, and it feels good just to walk and talk. Sometimes Ann Janet or someone else from our little group goes along. We form our own convent underground, stealing into each other's rooms late at night to chat and laugh and to give each other enough support to make it through just one more day.

"They're dedicated to form, I tell you!" Lucia is ranting and raving in her usual style, her black boots kicking their way through the snow. We both have on heavy black coats, which are allowed now, and though we look more hideous than ever (whoever designed them was careful to make them as unfeminine and stodgy looking as possible) we are warm. "That's all they care about. The essence was forgotten long ago. No wonder they make such a big deal about the Holy Rule: that's all they've got left. They're just a bunch of dried-up old ladies."

I listen in silence, knowing that Lucia has just about had it. Like me, she knocks herself out trying to fit into the mold expected of her. For the sake of community, she drives the old nuns around; when Vietnam or civil rights comes up at the dinner table, she bites her lip so hard that it bleeds. But it doesn't matter: she walks into the recreation room and all of a sudden there's silence. She washes out a pair of nylons in the bathroom and hears them whispering about her on the other side of the room. Nothing she does is right: her skirt is too short, and too much of her hair shows. But worst of all, instead of teaching the girls the good solid Catholic doctrine they need, she fills their heads with that secular humanism fluff—if she fills their heads at all. Most of the time she lets *them* talk: what good is *that* supposed to do?

Lucia goes on to tell me that she has been reading Moultmann's *The Revolution of Hope*, which describes people who want to control life because of its uncontrollable spontaneity. "They would rather kill it than expose themselves to it and merge in the world around them," she says, quoting the book. "Does that sound familiar?"

When I reach home, I think about our conversation and about some of the feelings I have been having lately. I have been becoming more and more aware of the deadness I see all around me—the deadness of tired, tense bodies clinging to a ritual, of people who patch up all life's cracks so nothing new can sink in. I see their intensity and I see their seriousness; I see their compulsive concern for the slightest deviation from the Holy Rule. And what is most frightening, I see the hugeness and monstrosity of their commitment to suffering. I write in my journal:

February 12 1968

> I hate this sugary show of community
> with old encrusted resentments
> festering underneath.
>
> I hate the way they package life
> and label it
> and file it in some dark drawer
> unlived.
>
> Worst of all I fear I might end up like them,
> building an existence around my trivias,
> my silent, secret martyrdoms. . . .

When we complain about the old die-hards who rule convent and school at Josephina, we are not necessarily referring to women who are chronologically old. Most of the nuns who are chronologically old are angels, and we love doting on them like revered ancients of a very large clan. "Old die-hards" on the other hand (sometimes called "the birds" in community parlance) are disgruntled souls whose spirits seem to have died somewhere along the way: they bring shadows wherever they land, giving all nuns a bad name.

Sister Gertrude Anthony, for example, is a veritable cesspool of bitterness. She gossips continually and nastily and complains about the "nigger girls" who never should have been admitted to our formerly all-white school. Attending a convention in Peoria, she runs into my aunt, Sister Agnes Anita, who is there on community business, and later that evening she telephones my mother and asks if she has seen her sister lately. "If not, you're in for a shock," she warns. "She looks terrible!" With that she hangs up, leaving my mother to wonder if her sister has contracted some dread disease. Talking to her later that evening my mother discovers the source of the problem: Sister Agnes Anita now wears a modified habit, a rather svelte version of which the older sister apparently doesn't approve.

And then there's Sister Alphonsus Beatrice (a few nuns take religious names combining the names of their parents, no matter how cacophonic the combination). Sister Alphonsus Beatrice is an example of what we call "the spoiled nuns." From a wealthy family she can never quite bring herself to use clothes and supplies from the community cupboard: instead she insists that relatives send her expensive fountain pens and underwear and other luxuries from all the best shops. She is especially proud of her collection of expensive corsets which she hoards in boxes in her closet. She is never home: faithful students from past years take her to restaurants they can't afford, and her family sends money for a trip at least once a year. It is widely recognized that her life-style makes a joke of the vow of poverty, but no one knows quite what to do with her. (Once a sister has taken final vows, she can only be expelled from the community if there is grave and serious cause.)

"The birds" cause problems for Sister Laurena too: they ridicule and sabotage her earnest efforts to instill a spirit of community in the house and write long vitriolic letters home to the motherhouse, complaining about her "incompetent" administration of house and school. Understanding all too well the frustration and restlessness of the youngest members of her house, Sister Laurena pretends not to notice when rooms are empty after night prayers or when habits smell of smoke.

Sister Laurena shares her frustrations with me, and I share mine with her, and she does her best to remind me that better days are coming. "You young people are the hope of the community: you can't give up on us now!" It will be a reason for staying that, interwoven with all the others, will keep me "in" for many months yet: how could I possibly "give up on" women like Sister Laurena, my aunt Sister Agnes Anita, and all the other Sisters of Blessing whom I have come to love?

In the spring of 1968 Martin Luther King is shot and Chicago becomes a powder keg. Rioting, looting, and fires overtake the inner city, and the sisters from our largest inner-city school come to the suburbs to stay with us. I chafe at the feeling of being, as it were, encapsulated, cut off from the history being made outside convent walls.

I am disillusioned and angry, but for now disillusionment and anger only inspire me to stay and try to change things. I am full of revolutionary fervor: the struggle itself gives intense meaning and purpose to my life. The possibility that change might take longer than I am willing to wait is a possibility that only rumbles around at some preverbal level.

But as time goes by, more and more people who care about me are starting to push me toward verbalizing that possibility. Tim is one of those people. Since coming to Josephina I have kept in close contact with him. We write back and forth, and whenever he is in the area he comes by to see me. I continue to use him as a sounding board as I sort things out. I now write to him, putting into words some of my growing impatience:

April 1968

I still have this ideal of total commitment. It seems that religious life is the only workable framework for what I mean. Communities as they are presently set up may not be able to make the radical adjustments necessary if this potential is to be utilized. Yet I see people with tremendous vision moving into positions of power in our community. The question is: will they be able to make that vision concrete despite the tradition and red tape and canonical status (this above all) that are ours? Everything hinges on this. I am so damn sick of words and committees and discussions—I want to see if all this big talk really means anything.

I also tell him about my plans for the fall. Vatican II has had its effects, and much of the old idea of obedience is crumbling around us: instead of just handing over their lives to their superiors, nuns are now starting to take responsibility for their own lives, to make their feelings and wishes known if they feel drawn toward a particular apostolate. The principal focus of my community will continue to be on education, but the council has urged nuns to also consider other apostolates that might more directly address the world's needs. The new word is *diversify*.

I tell Tim that I hope to be a part of a remarkable experiment going on in the heart of the ghetto: The Ecumenical Institute. The people involved in this experimental community come from a variety of religious backgrounds, professions, and racial groups: there are couples-with-children, singles, and a handful of priests and nuns. All maintain their own lifestyles and private lives; yet they have meals together, share child care, and contribute a certain amount of their earnings to the community. All are intensely committed to being a strong, unified force for constructive action in the inner city.

I meet some of the institute's leaders, and they impress me as strong, savvy community-organization types. Interested in going through their training program and becoming a part of their group, I make the necessary contacts and inquiries. Reverend Mother gives her tentative approval, pending permission from Cardinal Cody, and Sister Laurena hires a lay-teacher to replace me the following year.

Tim doesn't approve of my plan. He feels that I am stalling for time instead of really looking straight-on at some of the deeper issues. I write back:

May 2 1968

Maybe it's an evasion of the real issue; I don't know. I understand your objection that something like this is kind of a halfway deal. But it *is* a step somewhere. Unless I would get a dispensation from vows or something right away (and I'm not ready for that), I would be back here next year selling raffle tickets at homeroom and stumbling over a whole convent life-style I have grown to detest.

Tim writes back immediately. I pick up my mail from my box after lunch and save his letter until I will have a quiet moment. When the bell rings for last period, I take my place in front of the large study hall. As study-hall proctor I am supposed to sit at the big desk at front of the room and correct papers or prepare lesson plans while I keep the room under control. It is my nunly duty to keep a check on any whispering or giggling that might crop up in the room and to intercept the travels of any notes. The students are the animals, restless in their cages, and I am the zookeeper. I am 25—not much older than they—but the fact is a bloodless statistic.

It is one of those blossomy, balmy days of early spring when everyone has spring fever and sits there waiting for the last bell of the day to ring. I don't correct papers and I don't prepare lesson plans; I am riveted by one line in Tim's letter, staring up at me in all its black-and-white starkness: *"I know you'll leave eventually."*

He's sure I'll leave eventually: it's something I've never really faced as a genuine possibility for *me*. Others maybe, but not for me. It would be too radical a break with my personal history, too sharp a turning away from everything I have always known to be my destiny. Who would I be without that destiny shaping my life?

Someone giggles in the back of the classroom, and without even thinking about it I look up and put on the stern look I have been trained in for so long. I don't feel stern, but I have mastered the look. As I do so, it suddenly strikes me that I am not much older than these girls whom I am supposed to supervise; yet their futures are bursting with possibilities and options, while I at 25 have my life all sewed up tight with no room for dreams or fantasies that don't fit. Yet here is the bold and daring prophecy of a trusted friend, that eventually I will break through all that and follow a dream that I have never even allowed myself to dream.

"I'm convinced you'll leave eventually." The words are terrifying, yet somehow exciting.

A few days after receiving Tim's letter, I go to see one of the Theater of the Absurd plays, *Waiting for Godot.* The fact that the play is in French probably has something to do with its impact on me. If it were in English I would probably go through my typical English-major number, preoccupying myself with all the little symbolisms, ironies, and turns of speech. But my French isn't good enough to allow me to keep up with the speed of the dialogue, so instead of attending to all the little details and getting the *meaning* of the play, I experience the *play* itself.

En attendant, en attendant, en attendant Godot. Waiting, waiting, waiting for Godot.

I suddenly understand that I am doing just that: waiting futilely for some signal, some answer outside myself. I suddenly understand that it is all up to me, that decision is everything.

When the play is over, I walk out into the lobby feeling suddenly freed. There is immense relief: the feeling that I can now go wherever life leads me, making my own choices, deciding my own path.

It is an incredible experience, and I do my best to put it into words when I write to Tim.

Went to see *En Attendant Godot* last night. I love modern theater because it captures so much of what I feel. *En attendant*—waiting, waiting, for what? Whose decision? Why put it off? I feel I've really moved into some further state. I once heard that when you're thinking of leaving you should put the thought out of your mind for one month while you live the life you're leading now to the hilt. Then when that month is over you do the opposite—pray, ponder, weigh pros and cons.

The people I know who have done it have stayed. I can see why. I don't know that much about psychology but it seems to me your way of looking at things is much colored by previous decisions. For instance, if I assume I am staying, I look at everything that happens to me as a rationalization for what I have chosen. Am I making sense? Last night during the play, though, I think I came to a new point: I faced the fact that there is a high probability that I *will* leave, and all of a sudden I found myself looking at religious life as an outsider, objectively. It knocked down the majority of reasons that have kept me in. I won't go into all this. One huge block, though, is still the idea of commitment. . . .

I go on to list all the reservations that will keep me in for a few months more. But I have made the plunge, have experienced my freedom to *choose* rather than to follow blindly some preordained destiny. Life will never again be the same.

Her voice is firm. "Cardinal Cody says no, and I absolutely won't go over his head."

My hand is shaking as I hold the telephone receiver. It is the first time I have ever talked directly with the new Superior General, Mother Mary Paul: in the past all communications with higher superiors had been handled through my local superior. It also is the first time in seven years that I have made a long-distance phone call: we rarely use the telephone, and long-distance calls are even rarer. But there are urgent decisions that need to be made, and my superior has suggested that I call Mother Mary Paul at once.

So the whole occasion seems rather monumental as if I am calling China or something, and for a minute I have a hard time processing what she is telling me. Then it hits me, and my heart sinks.

"But I thought everything had been approved. I already told the people at the Ecumenical Institute that I'd be coming."

"I know. I thought so too, but the cardinal says no, and that's that."

She says it with such vehemence that I have the impression she expects me to argue with her. That surprises me. I am angry, but it never would have occurred to me to ask her to go against the cardinal or even to ask for an explanation: meek, unquestioning obedience is a hard habit to break after so many years.

Hardly stopping to catch my breath, I go right on to my next question. I want permission to stay in Chicago for the summer: a nun in our community has received a poverty-program federal grant to set up a summer program for kids in the inner city, and I want to join her. I know that the rest of my band will be coming home for the summer, that this is the summer for preparation for final vows, but I really feel I want to work in the Chicago program.

There is a long silence at the other end of the line. Then, "If Saint Raphael's doesn't mean that much to you, that should tell you something. I think you'd better come home and decide. . . ." Decide? I am shocked. Now another person in my life is speaking about the possibility of my leaving. "Decide? Yes, I guess maybe I'd better. But I really don't want to come home this summer, Mother. I really feel that this is where I should be, working in this program."

I can't believe what I am saying. After years of asking permission and doing exactly as I was told, I am unequivocally stating my own feelings and preferences—in effect, my plans. I know that Mother Mary Paul won't forbid me to stay in Chicago, but I also know that she isn't very pleased with the idea, and I realize as I hang up the phone that my decision to go ahead with my summer plans, despite her feelings, marks a definite turning point in my attitude toward obedience.

I think about what she said about my not wanting to come home: I suspect that she is right. The fact that Saint Raphael's is the last place in the world I want to be makes me realize how completely alienated I have become. Until recently, I would have jumped at the opportunity to go back and spend a summer with my friends, just as in the old days before we had all gone our separate ways. But not this summer: I am restless and tired of being where the action isn't.

But what about the fall? Josephina already has a lay teacher hired to take my place. I suddenly realize that I have nowhere to go come September. Reverend Mother hasn't suggested any alternative.

I don't have much time to consider my various options, for Sister Laurena soon approaches me and tells me that the archdiocese is looking for teachers who might be interested in a new fellowship program they have just set up. The diocese will provide full scholarships to nuns and priests who want to go away to receive graduate training in religious education and then would be willing to come back to the Chicago area after their graduate work to help train area teachers and pastors in some of the newer, more progressive methods of teaching religion.

At this point I am interested in *anything* that will get me out of what I am doing and give me some breathing space. I apply for the fellowship and am delighted when I am selected as one of the recipients. I feel sure that the community is delighted too: I will be out of their hair for a year, and in the event that I *do* remain in the community, they will have avoided the costly expense of my graduate education and will be able to reap some of the benefits.

The archdiocesan committee allows me to select what university I will attend. Aware that Fordham University has an excellent Religious Education Department, and eager to spend a year in New York, I decide to pursue a master's degree in religious education at Fordham. Somewhere deep down I know even now that the training the city has in store for me goes far beyond the university campus, although I'm not exactly sure what shape that training will take. But the decision is made, and like most of the heart decisions of my life, I will never regret it.

We sit at an old oak table in Marci's kitchen, and polish off the last of the chili. I finish my beer and give a few scraps of bread to her dog Reuben who has been waiting eagerly. Marci's boyfriend, Todd, wanders into the living room and puts on a Bob Dylan record. Kicking off his shoes, he lights up a joint and plops down on one of the cushions on the floor while I help Marci clean up the dishes.

"Todd always teases me about what a pair we make," she laughs. "Me the SDSer, and you the radical nun. What a duo!"

"It's all your fault, Marci. If you hadn't come along to teach English at Josephina, I never would have been corrupted. I'm not even supposed to have seculars for friends, but you—you're not only a secular, you're a non-Catholic. No wonder our friendship is causing a stir around old Josephina."

"You didn't mention that I also belong to a pinko organization and live with a man and smoke marijuana, let alone that I belong to an encounter group. What's a good little nun doing hanging around with a lady like me?"

"The truth is that I've taken you on as a challenge. You're my latest apostolate: I'm out to convert you away from your wicked ways."

"Good luck," she laughs, and I laugh too. I like Marci. We always have a good time together, and I feel really comfortable in her presence. We first started talking to each other when we both showed up at school one day reading *Summerhill*. We hit it off immediately and started getting together to talk between classes. We enjoyed each other's company so much that we even started having lunch together, a decision that caused a fairly major uproar since nuns weren't supposed to eat with the lay teachers. Oblivious to the icy stares all around us, we'd cross the Mason-Dixon line that separated the two dining rooms: either she would come eat with the nuns, or I would go eat with the lay teachers. The lay teachers and some of the nuns got a big kick out of the whole thing, while the old guard fumed.

Eventually I started sneaking out of the convent, whipping off my cap and veil the minute I was in Marci's car. One day we campaigned for McCarthy, carrying placards and passing out fliers as he arrived at the Chicago airport. Another time I attended a party at her apartment, where she introduced me to her SDS friends as "my friend, the radical nun."

Today we took part in a demonstration. The Democratic convention is now just days away and the demonstrations are intensifying: when the young people of Chicago poured into the streets of Chicago today, we were right there with them, walking in a ragged group behind Rennie Davis.

Finishing the dishes, I say good-bye to Marci and Todd and head back to Josephina, arriving just in time to catch the evening news with the other nuns. As we watch the TV coverage of the day's demonstration, the conservatives tsk-tsking the demonstrators and cheering Mayor Daly's hard-line handling of the situation, I take a rebellious delight in the fact that, unbeknownst to them, one of their members had been right there in the streets with the demonstrators.

29 ❧

EARLY SUMMER (1968)

Like a wife determined to give a dying marriage one last try, I will during the next few months make herculean efforts to put all thoughts of leaving out of my head and live to the fullest the life to which I have vowed myself.

The summer program I work in is one of the federally funded programs that sprang up throughout Chicago's ghetto areas after the riots. We provide remedial classes for school-age youngsters, as well as a wide variety of field trips and activities. We teach classes in black literature and culture, using Baldwin and Gregory and Malcolm X and the rest.

We open the convent doors at nine in the morning and close them again at three in the afternoon. I gradually come to realize how little I know about the conditions in which my students live: forbidden to wander far beyond convent walls, we are like queens, each day opening the doors of our castle just long enough to mete out our works of charity, like crumbs to the starving masses. Then at the end of the day the draw-bridge goes up again and the shades go down.

As the summer wears on, I, like a number of the others, begin to chafe at such a role and become involved with other organizations, groups, and individuals working in the area. Sometimes we attend neighborhood meetings that last long after convent doors are closed for the day.

There are a few icy stares when we miss community prayers or recreation, but nothing is said. In midsummer, how-ever, the new superior of the province (the order has recently been divided into four geographical provinces, each headed by a superior called a provincial) comes for visitation, an official visit, and I am one of the sisters called in and interrogated about my "irregularities."

"There's speculation, Sister, that when you aren't back in the convent in time for prayers, you're dating men. Is there any truth to that? And what about the recreations you've missed: don't you young people have any concern for the older sisters who are left with no one to talk to? When was the last time you sat down and played a game of bridge with them? It's all well and good to concern yourself with the poor and the needy, but your sisters have needs, too: they are your first obligation!"

The part about my dating men almost makes me laugh out loud: me in my dowdy calf-length skirt, my ever-crooked cap and miniveil pushed back to free a clump of hair! And as far as the needs of the older sisters are concerned, I have done my best to be kind and thoughtful to them, to attend commu-nity recreation whenever possible. Whenever I *have* stretched the rules and seemingly disregarded convent walls and sched-ules, I have done it in the sincere conviction that I could thus better serve the people with whom I worked.

I explain this to the Provincial as calmly as possible, convinced that I can make her understand. But she remains suspicious—I can see it in her eyes—and I leave our little session sad and disillusioned. Had I been chastised the previous summer, when word got back to the Motherhouse about our week of drinking and smoking in the sun, I might have understood. But *now*, when I feel more committed than I have ever felt, a representative of the community that is supposed to support me in my commitment arrives on the scene and, instead of supporting and encouraging me, interrogates me. Is *this* what community life is all about? Is it for *this* that I sacrificed husband and children and a life of my own shaping?

Others confide that they have been similarly interrogated, and gradually we form a little subculture of our own within the larger community. Each night we gather on the roof, after the others have gone to bed, and smoke and drink beer and talk about how things will be once "our side" gets into power within the community. We want the community to survive, to be relevant to the world's needs, to be at the cutting edge of history rather than an anachronism. There is a revolutionary tone to our talks, a shared idealism that makes staying in and fighting a shining and noble cause.

Little do I know, on these balmy nights of summer, as we look out on the lights of the city and plot our little revolution, that by the time the next summer arrives I will have lost interest in the fight, breaking all ties with the community that has been my home, my family, my very world, for eleven years of my life.

V &

BACK TO THE WORLD (AUGUST 1968–DECEMBER 1968)

How I envied my father the clarity of his enemies, even as I watched the peace marches on television, looking for Liz and her babies in the crowd.

I was the only one who understood Liz's jokes about the peace movement: nuns in Ship 'n' Shore blouses who made her want to join the Green Berets just to be on the opposite side; priests with no sense of irony losing their virginity in their forties; concerned laity, all overweight or underweight, with bad taste in shoes and bad complexions. And, of course, Eugene McCarthy was the man every Catholic girl had dreamed of marrying, as Dan Berrigan was the priest we yearned to seduce.

—Final Payments by
Mary Gordon

LATE SUMMER (1968)

We are sitting in a pizza place having pizza and beer: Ron, Sarah, Bill, and I. Ron and Bill are both diocesan priests; Sarah and I are both nuns.

It is suddenly the thing to do in the nun-priest world: after years of being told that anything but the most superficial contact with members of the opposite sex is fraught with danger and temptation, we are encouraged to develop good healthy relationships with each other.

At Sarah's invitation, Ron reaches over and picks all the anchovies off her pizza, transferring them carefully to his piece. I see Sarah flush as he brushes her arm, and a patch of red creeps up from under Ron's Roman collar. Feeling the electricity all the way across the table, I enjoy a sudden pleasurable rush that has become increasingly familiar to me these past few days.

Then there's Bill: all he has to do is *look* at me and I feel a rush. Actually, I feel rather foolish. I made a resolution that I wasn't going to act like a lot of the new-breed nuns and priests I see all around me: they always seem so awkward and giggly when they are around each other. I read somewhere that being mature means being able to be involved in the world without losing one's balance, and I want above all to be mature. But it seems as if I have been suddenly plunged into a kind of late-blooming adolescence; I'm not used to feeling so out of control, although I have to admit that I like what I'm feeling!

Bill takes another bite of pizza and continues his critique

of the religious-education workshop we are all attending in Atlanta. (Sister Laurena received permission for all the Josephina religion teachers to attend.) "This college-and-banner business is getting to me," he moans. "They're just trying to pour the same old wine into new skins. The kids are smarter than that: they see right through that stuff. The new religion books coming out are all the same: there's a lot of groovy stuff at the beginning of each chapter; then once they've got them hooked, they hit them with the same old doctrinal stuff, most of which has absolutely no relevance to their lives."

A trace of anger flickers over Bill's youthful, handsome face. I picture him in front of the classroom in his Irish knit sweater: I know he must be popular with the kids. I am proud of him, proud to be a part of a Church that includes men like him. And because of our shared commitment to the Church and to celibacy, we have a very special relationship as brother and sister. Bill seems to enjoy my company too. We met the opening day of the workshop and have sought each other out for lunch and heated discussions ever since. He seems to like a lot of my ideas, and when he tells me I'm the sharpest-looking nun he's ever seen, I think my heart will never stop singing.

When I say my prayers, I pray for grace never to do anything to endanger Bill's commitment to celibacy: I would never forgive myself if I did anything to draw his focus away from his important work. Although a man, he is also a priest, and there is surely no sin so base as seducing, or even being attractive to, a priest. Catholic tradition from the time of the Fathers of the Church had always seen woman as the source of man's problems—Eve enticing Adam to taste the forbidden apple—and as a Catholic woman I carry that image of myself and of all women in my very bones. As a nun I had set myself off from all of that, disconnecting myself from the rest of women, denouncing the part of me that caused men problems—my femininity. I had covered my body in thicknesses of wool and linen, making it clear that I didn't want to have anything to do with that side of myself. Now, however, those days are gone. We show our hair and we show our waistlines; instead of long habits that drag in the dust, we wear almost feminine-looking skirts that end somewhere around our knees. It is too confusing. On the one hand I am loving the experience of feeling feminine again, the experience of feeling attracted and attractive. On the other hand I know that sexy is bad, that for a nun it is even worse, that for a nun in the company of a priest—well it is almost unmentionable. So as a result I usually brave superiors' screeches and hem my skirt to just above my knee in keeping with the other hemlines of the day, but then when I sit down I often take futile little tugs at it now and then as if to cover my knees. "At least I'm trying to be modest," say the little tugs.

I watch Sarah, trying to imagine what it would be like to dress in lay clothes as she does. Her community just recently shed the habit altogether, and slower-moving communities like my own are aghast. Even I am not sure I would want to go *that* far: I think we should retain at least some symbol to distinguish us as nuns—a cross around the neck, maybe. I still feel that witness is important, that a person can have his mind raised to more transcendent things just by looking at a nun. And since nuns and priests are out there in the streets now, taking part in demonstrations and peace marches, it seems even more important that they be visibly a part of the Church, to demonstrate the Church's willingness to be involved in political and social matters.

Finishing our pizza, we divide up the bill. I reach into the small change purse I now carry and pay my share. It feels so strange to be handling money again after years of being told that "a Sister with a penny isn't worth a penny." Clothes and other necessities are still provided by the community, but since I have to eat many meals out while at the workshop, I have been given a small allotment to cover expenses. I know that I should leave some sort of a tip, but I have no idea how much. I watch furtively as Ron lays a few coins by his plate and carefully count out enough to match what he has put down.

We go back to our workshop, and when it is over for the day, we go our separate ways, Sarah and I to the convent where we are staying, Ron and Bill to their rectory on the other side of town. A week later when the workshop is over, Bill and I say good-bye, locking eyes and hands for the briefest moment. I go back to the convent, shut the door, and cry.

31 §❧

SAINT ALBAN'S CONVENT, THE BRONX

Sister Pascal meets me at the door, her long traditional habit flowing around her. "Welcome to Saint Alban's," she says. "Mother Mary Paul wrote and made the necessary arrangements, and I'm sure you'll be quite happy here."

The silence inside the convent is tomblike, familiar. With just a glance at Jim, who now blows me a kiss and drives off, and another glance at my short skirt, she picks up one of my suitcases and we begin the climb to the fourth floor where all the boarders have their rooms. I thank God and all His saints that I will just be renting a room here and won't be under Sister Pascal's jurisdiction: her pursed lips and a certain sour look tell me all I need to know about the kind of a superior she must be.

As we climb the stairs, I think about the idyllic day I've just spent. Jim, the brother of one of my friends, is a Christian

Brother who teaches in one of his community's high schools here in New York. When his sister told him that I was coming and that I didn't know anyone here, he volunteered to meet me at La Guardia.

It was a beautiful fall morning, and since there was no particular time I had to check in at Saint Alban's, Jim decided to take me on a whirlwind tour of the city. We ended up spending the whole day together, poking through the Village, having *dim sem* in Chinatown, and by the time I arrived at the convent I was exhausted. Jim promised to show me some more of his favorite places around the city at a more leisurely pace the following weekend.

Sister Pascal stops at the second floor and points out the chapel which she says I am free to visit at any time; and here is the refectory where meals are served three times a day; and down at the end of the hall is the recreation room where her sisters have recreation each evening, after their day of teaching in the parish school. I notice that she emphasizes that the recreation room is for *her* Sisters, for which I also thank God and His saints. I have had enough mandatory joy, enough straining to have a good time just because a bell says it's now time to have a good time.

The four other boarders are all in their rooms studying, and she introduces them to me one by one. There's Sister Margaret Mary, Sister Elaine, Sister Peter Marie, and Sister Michael, each from a different order and each studying in a different department at Fordham. They are all young and dressed in modernized habits, and I know immediately that we are going to get along quite well.

When we reach my room, I thank Sister Pascal and plop down on the bed. There is a letter from Bill waiting for me on the night stand and I tear it open.

Dear Mary,

Hope this finds you well and settled into life in the Big Apple. A few months down the road your mother superior may have second thoughts about letting you wander off to the big city. You know what they say: "How're ya gonna keep them down on the farm, now that they've seen New York?"

Since I've been back in Boston I've had a lot of time to do some thinking, and I've come to realize what a valuable experience it was for me to get to know you this summer. Ron, Sarah, you, I—didn't we have a great time? You know, the short time we spent together (you and I) made me realize something that I have evidently been trying not to admit: all the while I've been telling my students to be true to themselves, to be really human, I have been rejecting my own (maybe suppressed is the better term) awareness of myself as a man.

I am truly grateful to you for bringing me to this awareness. It's a strange awakening!

I wish our respective apostolates didn't take us so far away from each other, you in New York, me in Boston. Maybe it's better that way, though: I have a feeling we'll have a better chance of keeping our friendship on a celibate track precisely because of the geographical distance. Also, that way I won't have to take so many cold showers!

I look forward to expanding our friendship via the mail, and to supporting each other in our respective commitments to Christ and His world.

Love,
Bill

P.S. Don't let them crush your spirit. You're beautiful!

One of my students had given me a small transistor radio as a going-away gift, and I now turn it on. It might have been an expensive tape deck, so great is my bliss at hearing worldly music again. I hold it up to my ear and begin to doze off. "If it takes forever, I will wait for you; for a thousand summers, I will wait for you. . . ." The melody lulls me off to sleep, to a land where very uncelibate dreams refuse to play by the rules.

I wake up the next morning, still fully dressed, and discover that I am too late for breakfast. As a matter of fact, it is almost time for lunch! It's exhilarating to realize that there is no bell to answer, no schedule to follow, no superior watching my every move.

Taking myself by the scruff of the neck, I sternly remind

myself that I will have to be careful: it would be altogether too easy to become an undisciplined slob now that I have no one monitoring my behavior, too easy to forget about Christ now that I have no definite times set aside for prayer. It will be up to me to keep myself on the right track, to be sure that I allot time every day for prayer and reflection so that I preserve the spirit of my vows. I kneel on the floor and ask God for the guidance I will need during the coming days: I can't depend on *myself*, that's for sure. Temptations will be rampant in my new life, and I know that without God's help I will never be able to withstand them.

I shower and dress and then head down to lunch just in time to meet up with the other boarders. They are a friendly, chatty group, and we all sit at a table in one corner of the refectory. The Saint Alban's nuns, a few of them quite young, smile politely, but it's obvious that they aren't to have much to do with the boarders: undoubtedly Sister Pascal doesn't want her nuns corrupted by too much contact with us. Just the fact that we wear short skirts and show our hair makes it obvious that we come from communities that have carried this whole renewal business a bit too far.

After lunch Peter Marie says she has to go to the library, and I decide to go with her so I can learn my way to Fordham. Stepping out of the convent is like stepping onto a different planet. There is a burned-out building across the street and next to it a huge tenement stretching into the sky. Sirens wail and dogs howl and black children play tag in filth-littered streets.

Carefully sidestepping a pile of dog droppings, we start the three-block trek to the campus. "I'd never attempt this walk if I weren't wearing a habit," she smiles. It's an argument one often hears in favor of keeping some kind of religious garb: because of their habits nuns can walk unscathed through even the roughest areas. "Even at that, I'm sure that knowing a little karate wouldn't hurt around here," I laugh, and she laughs too, agreeing.

When we reach Fordham, I find my way to the religious-education department and sign up for my classes. Afterward I walk back to the house and, not having anything better to do, wander in the neighborhood for a while. As I walk, it suddenly hits me that I am now totally alone, hanging, as it were, in midspace far both from my family and from the community that has for so long been my home. The loneliness that overwhelms me is like nothing I have ever experienced.

My classes at Fordham are interesting enough, but I have had enough of theory. I want to try some of it out, want to see how it holds up out there in the world. It isn't long before the real educational process of the year begins. After school each day, I go out and walk in the neighborhood. One of the new friends I make is Dora, a black welfare mother who lives in a tenement building near the convent. At the end of the school day I often climb the six flights of stairs to her apartment, and we sit and talk until it's time to fix supper. Through her, my eyes are opened to what it is like to be a welfare mother in a big-city ghetto. She tells me about the pushers and pimps who live in her building, about the absentee fathers who visit their women once a month on "mother's day"—the day the welfare checks come. She shows me the flimsy lock on her door and the marks where the door has been pried open by robbers so many times. She is afraid for her safety and her child's safety when she stays in the apartment; she is afraid of being robbed of her meager belongings when she ventures out.

The building is full of rats and cockroaches, and there is a huge hole in one of the stairs between the fourth and fifth floors. Tenants have made numerous complaints to the superintendent, but nothing has been done. I pass the hole every day as I climb the six flights of stairs to Dora's apartment, and I am always afraid a child will fall through and be killed before anything will be done. To my horror, that's exactly what eventually happens: one day when I go to see Dora, there are men repairing the hole, and, shaken, she informs me that a child fell through and was killed that very day.

Most of the people there live lives of quiet desperation, surviving from day to day in lives as windowless as their tenement, and most have despaired of ever escaping either hellhole. Dora often tells me of her many futile attempts to rent a place in a better building and of always being turned down because she is on welfare.

And a few doors away, nuns play Irish records in a tidy recreation room while the world burns around them. I am sure of it now: such convents are useless anachronisms sitting right in the middle of the ghetto, and my former decision to associate myself with such structures is a useless anachronism sitting right in the middle of my life.

Just when I start to become quite cynical about the freeing qualities of a celibate life, I meet someone who makes me have second thoughts. His name is Paul, and he is the assistant pastor of a nearby parish. Paul makes a big impression on me because of his obvious commitment to the people in the area: it is clear that his concerns go far beyond filling the collection basket and building bigger Church structures. Paul's people are all the neighborhood people, not just the Catholics, and he is a savvy community organizer. It's said that Paul knows everything that goes on in the neighborhood. Like many of the priests and nuns I know who are most powerful and most effective, he is the object of frequent investigation and censor at the archdiocesan level.

Paul and I become friends, and he introduces me to various organizations and individuals working together to solve some of the neighborhood's more glaring problems. One day he introduces me to some of the people who are involved with Phoenix House, a program that uses trained ex-addicts in the treatment of drug addicts. Mayor Lindsay, impressed with the Phoenix track record in the treatment of hard-core addicts, brought Phoenix concepts and personnel into the city drug-addiction program, and a whole network of community outreach programs began to spring up throughout the city. Programs were set up not only for the addicts themselves but for pre-addicts, for relatives of addicts, and for parents concerned about the narcotics traffic in their kids' schools.

People interested in working with any of these programs are screened and trained by means of a weekend group session, similar to the confrontive group sessions that take place in Phoenix houses, the therapeutic communities for addicts. Curious, I sign up for one of the weekends, having little idea what is in store for me. Had I known, I probably never would have gone, thus missing what was to be one of the most intensely painful, yet transformational weekends of my life.

32 §≈·

DECISION

My travel alarm goes off at 6:30, and afraid of oversleeping, I rise immediately. I take a shower and put on my best black knit suit and a bright print blouse I bought the day before. I brush my hair (I now wear my veil only to Church) and put on some lipstick. The lady in the store told me that the pink, glossy kind is what everyone is wearing these days. I roll the waistband of my skirt an extra turn to bring my skirt above my knees.

I am determined to experience this weekend without the protection of the habit. My world has always been peopled with women who, though we might differ on specifics, pretty much shared my values and convictions. There have been a sprinkling of male and female secular friends these last couple of years, but even in those situations the fact that I was a nun still set me apart. Even my most worldly friend Marci never let me forget my role as "my friend, the radical nun." There was a certain safety in all of that, and I am now determined to take one cautious step outside of that safety, to test the waters.

I feel so pretty, so worldly as I walk the six blocks to the Third Avenue elevated: I feel for once that I fit comfortably into the world around me. For years "the world" has been held up to me as the root of all that is evil and base: in the world people run after money, lust after sex and power. But like a teenager ignoring her mother's most solemn warnings, I am falling in love with the very world about which I have been so often warned. I toss my veilless head, liking the feel of the wind in my hair.

I board the el and ride for a while; then I change to a subway. Eventually I arrive at my destination: a seedy back room in Manhattan. I take a pocket watch out of my small black vinyl purse and check the time: ten minutes to nine.

The exhilaration drains out of me suddenly as I enter the room. There is one other woman dressed like me, but she looks as if she's probably in her late fifties. The people who are *my* age all wear jeans and turtlenecks, work shirts and old corduroys. A couple of the girls wear miniskirts and sweaters. They all look comfortable and casual, at peace with their world.

I suddenly realize how stuck between the two worlds I am, with feet planted firmly in neither. One foot tentatively tests the here-and-now while the other is sucked down by the quicksand of the past. No wonder I feel so off-balance, so ungrounded.

Feeling awkward and out of place, I sit down on the folding chair next to the older lady. I am determined not to look nunny, so I cross my legs and resist the impulse to pull my skirt down over my knees.

No one talks: we just sit there, all thirteen of us (eight men and five women), waiting. I am dying to know if the others are as much in the dark as I am: I feel as if my lungs are going to burst with anticipation and dread.

At exactly 9 A.M., a muscular, rather fierce-looking man walks into the room and introduces himself as Pancho. He has each of us go around the circle and introduce ourselves, and without further ado the session begins.

Pancho says we'll start by each giving a fifteen-minute autobiography of ourselves. His intense-looking eyes circle the group for volunteers, and I make sure I am blowing my nose when he comes to me.

Chet, a black man who looks like he is in his mid-twenties, volunteers to go first. He seems so cool and at ease as he talks that I feel he must have been through this type of thing before.

The autobiographies go on and on. Each person tells his or her life story, and Pancho or one of the others from the group hits them with questions.

Pancho: "You talk about your father's death like it was something you saw on TV. How the fuck did you *feel* about it?"

Rona: "You smooth over everything with laughter, but I get the feeling there's a lot of hurt down there, that you really feel pretty shitty about yourself."

Art: "I sense that you really get off on being a god-damned martyr. What kind of payoff do you get from that, anyway?"

I am in shock: I have never heard people talk like that to each other. I watch in horror as one after another group member is confronted: what kind of a sadistic sideshow *is* this?

I am especially distressed by their vulgar language. It's crude and disgusting, and I am determined not to be brought down to their level. I pull my skirt down as far over my knees as I can and cross my arms. I tell myself that the world in which I live is totally different from theirs: they obviously won't be able to understand things having to do with religion and spirituality and dedication, things so important to me. I know I'll have to hang on for dear life to my values and beliefs.

But as the day wears on, I begin to become confused: there is a ring of truth to everything that Pancho says, and he really *does* seem to have an uncanny insight into people. Not only that, it is also becoming more and more obvious that he isn't acting out of any kind of viciousness or desire to hurt people; in fact, he really seems to genuinely care about the people in the group.

When it's my turn to get feedback, Pancho turns to me: "Mary, you've got it wired that we're going to try to talk you out of being a nun, and that it's your God-given duty to resist. What I want you to see is that we're not going to try to talk you out of anything: we'll accept and support you any way you decide to go. But your presence in this group indicates that you're interested in feedback, in my letting you know what I really hear you saying so that you can begin to know yourself a little better and make your decisions out of that self-knowledge.

"And so if I call the score exactly as I see it, I have to tell you that, from everything you've said in here, I get the distinct impression that you're afraid you can't make it out there in the world on your own, without the identity that membership in your community affords. You'd be out there just as *you,* with no big noble cause to make you feel OK about yourself. How could you survive without the Church's good-house-keeping-seal-of-approval?

"You entered for a lot of reasons, good and bad. But if I'm reading you right, you've changed a lot inside your gut since then. You're a butterfly who's outgrown your cocoon, and you're afraid to fly away. That cocoon is all you've ever known. You're staying now for one reason and one reason only: fear of trying your own wings."

The tears are brimming but I hold them back. "Don't give in, don't give in," counsels my mind, fighting for its life.

"I also see, Mary, that part of what keeps you hung up is your not wanting to feel wrong about your past. After all, if you left, wouldn't that be admitting to yourself and to the world that you have been wrong, that a whole big chunk of your life had been wrong? And most people would do *anything* to avoid ever being wrong.

"I don't think anyone in this group would like to push you one way or the other. What we *would* like to do is to get you to look at all your options. You never really did that before: if doubts came up for you, you quickly put them out of your mind as the work of the devil. Can't you see what a number you've done on yourself by buying into all that? Can't you see how terrified of your own freedom you are?"

Genuine concern, almost tenderness, is written all over Pancho's face, and his voice is gentle. Somehow it's the gentleness that touches me at last, finally shattering the broken record in my head that tells me to hang on, to resist.

And so I let go. The tears come, and I cry harder than I've ever cried in my life, letting up all the pain that has been shoved down for so long. I talk and cry my way through another two hours, the rest of the group sitting there in that tight little circle, willing to sit there as long as it takes. They seem to me a group of seasoned, wizened midwives; I am beginning to trust them.

But the trust is not quite total, and I leave the group that evening, shaken to my boots but not yet ready to surrender. I will think about what has happened and fathom its implications. But I will do it on my own: I want to be sure I'm not being pushed into anything.

I get a ride back to the Bronx with one of the other people in the group, and when I get home I call my friend Paul. Would he like to go out for a hamburger?

Paul says he'll pick me up in fifteen minutes, so I wash my face and stretch out on the bed for a few minutes. I am still pretty much in a state of shock, and I know I can depend on Paul to help me sort it out. If there is anyone who's a committed celibate, it's Paul. I know he can help me look at everything the group said to me from a religious perspective. We celibates have to help each other at times like this, and I have never been so much in need of help.

At the restaurant, we order hamburgers and beer, and I tell Paul about my group experience. I tell him that I think I might be on the verge of leaving, but I'm not sure. I want to surround myself for a while with people like myself, people who share my values and convictions. I need someone to pull me back in line, to reconvince me of all that I will be walking out on if I do decide to leave.

Paul is quiet, letting me talk. When there are no more words, I sit there crying softly, and he reaches across the table and laces his fingers through mine.

"Mary, I don't know how to tell you this, but I'm afraid you're talking to the wrong person if you're looking for someone to sing the glories of celibacy. I would have told you where I was on this before, but there was never the opportunity.

"The truth is that I've been in a relationship with a woman for about a year now, and I love her very much. My whole life is different since she came into my life: I've discovered a whole range of feelings I never knew I had. No one will ever again be able to convince me that human relationships on any level, including the sexual level, get in the way of one's ability to serve the world. My experience has been exactly the opposite: because of Sue's love and support, I have more energy than I've ever had. Because I've been fulfilled, I've had more to give to others. Funny that the Catholic Church hasn't wakened up to the reality of how that works."

Paul's face darkens. "I'm afraid I've become rather cynical about the Church. Like most priests, I'd like to marry and still be able to continue my ministry, but I'm afraid it won't come to that in my lifetime. The Church changes, but it changes slowly. The problem is that I have only one lifetime. I can just picture myself sitting in a wheelchair at 95 in some dismal retirement home for priests, hearing the news that the pope has just made celibacy optional for priests. No, thanks—I'm not going to wait until it's too late. I think I deserve to have it all and to have it now. And if that means Sue and I have to sneak around for a while, that's the way it will have to be. Sue understands that too. And maybe, if enough of us priests keep making our voices heard on this issue, Rome will listen. After all, we diocesan priests don't take the three vows the way order priests do: canonically, celibacy is not integral to our way of life. As we always like to point out, the first pope, Saint Peter, had a mother-in-law, so there's a pretty good chance he had a wife too."

Paul suddenly remembers me and asks how I'm doing. He pours me another glass of beer. I am staring up at him wide-eyed, my tears gone. I am overwhelmed by this totally unexpected confession, flattered by his willingness to confide in me. All thoughts of my own confusion have disappeared.

"But Paul, what will you do if the Church stands fast on its position about married priests? What will you and Sue do then? You can't keep living this way forever."

A shadow falls over Paul's face. "If that's what it comes to, then I'll have no choice but to leave, as many of my friends have already done. The thing is, I know how convenient it is for the Church to repress sexuality: there's no more powerful way to control people. Sexuality is life force, energy: control that and you've got them by the balls."

We both laugh at the image, me in spite of myself. "So much for my propping up your old decisions, Mary. You've got to sweat this one out for yourself, as we all have to do. I want you to know, though, that I'll support you whichever way you decide to go. If you do decide to call it quits, I've got this buddy over on Long Island. . . ."

I laugh and tell him I'll get back to him on that.

I go back to the group the next day, feeling a lot lighter about everything. Now that my defenses are down, I feel close to everyone in the group and, amazingly, for the first time in

my life, unafraid. I have made a crucial decision to stop trip-
ping myself up in lies, and with that decision has come peace.
There are no tears left, no deep dark secrets to be pushed back
into the abyss over and over again. I will face my future head-
on.

The next day I go out and buy a bright red dress with
some of my book money. And the day after that I hail my first
cab and attend a party given by one of my new friends from
the weekend.

By the end of the week, I am writing to Tim:

October 14 1968
Typing the date on this seems almost dramatic to me, because I am
sure I will look back to this date in my life as a turning point. I have
reached very deeply into myself, in a blend of peace and agony, and
have come forth ready to take definite steps.
    The first thing I am sure of is that everything in my life is saying
that who-I-am-becoming would be best expressed in marriage, not
celibacy. Different things have pushed me to this conclusion. Some
of these things were there for a long time, but only in the last two
hours of peace have they come to the surface. One of my problems in
the past has been that I wasn't able to let go of the idea that religious
life was really God's will for me, and that opposite ideas were nothing but temptations. For a long time I have verbally denied this
conception of God's will, but its roots went deep in me. In the last
couple of hours, however, as I prayed before my crucifix and read my
Bible, old arguments melted away with such ease that I can attribute
their being brought to the surface and dispelled as the action of
nothing but the Spirit.
    Secondly, I am ready to take definite steps. I am now living in a
convent, but in early November I am going to move into an apartment with two other sisters who are in a transition stage. The time
before Christmas will be short, so my life-style will be basically the
same, except for the casualness of apartment living. I have already
gotten rid of the veil, but the suits I am now wearing should do until
after Christmas when I hope to begin to purchase a regular wardrobe. I don't intend to say anything about this first shift to anyone
except you. . . .

I also tell Tim that, after much thought and prayer, I have
decided to follow through on my plans to go to the commu-

nity-wide meeting coming up in January. This is the general chapter that we have all been planning for so long, and I have been elected to represent the junior professed from our province. The word that I was elected to attend this important meeting came, ironically enough, the day after my Phoenix experience, and I was at first not sure I should attend, given my present precarious commitment to the community. Finally, I decided to go, feeling that I could represent the young sisters who had elected me as well as anyone could. They elected me because they knew where I stood on various issues and that I would work for the changes that we all saw as essential. Nothing has changed in all that. I know what they want said at the chapter, and I will say it. I know what they want accomplished, and I will do my best to accomplish it.

Besides, as I take great pains to point out to Tim, it isn't as though I've decided to leave for good, I have just decided to take a leave of absence. I see a leave as a breathing space, a neutral time: there will be no commitment to stay, no commitment to leave.

Within a few days Tim writes back, and our correspondence over the next few weeks allows me further to clarify things. He also reminds me that *our* relationship, his and mine, will be radically altered if I decide to leave. "I know that I need the friendship of celibate women if I am to continue to aspire to celibacy. I must be candid: if you leave, the level of communication between us will probably not continue. . . ."

I am pained by Tim's words, but I know that he's right: our friendship is held together by common bonds that will no longer be there if I take another path, as it is now increasingly evident that I will. It is the last time that I will hear from Tim: we will meet briefly one last time when he visits New York, then we will lose contact.

Tim is the only one who knows how close I am to leaving. Because I still want to be allowed to represent the younger sisters of the chapter, and (as I so frequently remind myself) since I haven't actually decided to *leave* but only to *allow* myself that option, I decide not to say anything to anyone else until things are more definite. The chapter itself will provide me with a perfect opportunity to finalize my decision one way or another: I will rub minds with some of the most powerful women of the community: if there's still anything in the community for me, it will surely call to me through my contact with these sisters.

Knowing none of this but undoubtedly suspecting, both Mother Mary Paul and Sister Laurena come to New York in late October. They visit with me and with Sister Kathleen, my beloved counselor and mentor from novitiate days who is also studying at Fordham and living in a residence for sisters a few miles away. When we talk I can see the compassion in their eyes, their concern, and though I love them for it I know that it is not time yet to share with them all that is in my heart.

With Sister Kathleen too I have become increasingly distant. Before the group experience I confided in her just as in the novitiate, but now I am polite but evasive. It's almost as if I'm afraid that if I'm around her too much a sense of guilt for "abandoning ship" will begin to set in. When I'm clear and objective about it I realize that Sister Kathleen, like Mother Mary Paul and Sister Laurena, only want me to decide what's best for me. It's just that I remember so vividly Sister Kathleen's theology classes where she talked about the "Anowim" in the Old Testament, the "remnant" of God's people who always remained faithful to Him no matter how many others fell away. She had talked of the "Anowim" with great fervor, and I had resolved to always be a part of that faithful remnant. Now I am on the verge of leaving. I can't help feeling that she will be disappointed with me. And God? Does He really understand that I'm not leaving Him, that I will always be a part of the faithful "Anowim," that I will never cease to seek His face?

33

MOVING OUT

On November 4 1968 I move out of the convent. My belongings are meager: one suitcase full of clothes plus assorted books and school supplies. I will live with two other nuns who are also students in the religious-education department and in a transitional, vaguely defined stage of their lives, with one foot still in their respective communities and one foot very definitely out.

We share a rather strange living arrangement. The house we live in is owned by a family who lives downstairs and rents out the upstairs floor. My friends Donna and Alice rent one bedroom, I rent another, and a priest also a student at Fordham rents a third. The four of us share a small living room, an even smaller kitchen, and a tiny bathroom with leaky pipes.

Moving in, I take on not only a new living arrangement but a whole new circle of friends. The four of us have meals together and take turns doing the cooking, shopping, and cleaning. Joe, the priest, introduces us to some of his priest friends, also studying at Fordham, and before long we have a tight-knit little group of friends. We go out to dinner or to a pub; we go out dancing or come back to the house and roll up the living-room rug and dance there.

It is all happening too fast for me: my world is spinning dizzily, ready to go careening off its solid orbit at any moment. And yet I am becoming addicted to the spinning itself. As long as I let myself spin with it, I can forget the panic I feel when I realize that a whole lifetime of meanings and life definitions are crumbling beneath my feet.

I am not alone in all of this: long-repressed sexuality is beginning to seep out uncontrollably all over the place. No wonder mother generals and father generals lose sleep over the young nuns and priests they send away to study, knowing that the risks of a lost vocation are high! And it isn't just with *our* group: flirtations and romances and secret affairs are cropping up everywhere. In classes and at department parties the electricity of emerging sexuality seems to bounce off the very walls. Smoldering looks, covert touches, suggestive conversations ripe with double meanings—a lot is churning right beneath the surface, ready to break forth at any moment.

In our little group most of the sexuality stays right there, just beneath the surface. There is a lot of harmless flirting and joking around: "Did you hear that the pope came out with a new ruling that nuns and priests can now sleep together? Just as long as they don't get into the habit." Only one in our group, David, is more serious: he and Aleta, a divorcee with two children, have been seeing each other for the past year. She followed him from Detroit to New York when his diocese sent him here to study a year ago; he keeps telling her he's going to make the break and leave one of these days, and she keeps hanging in there, wanting to believe him.

Another couple in our midst, a priest and a nun, are also in love but are committed to staying within the bounds of celibacy. Everyone talks about them, half-admiring, half-wondering why they don't go ahead and leave: they walk around like two open wounds, trying to be strong. But the theologians are always there to inspire them with some new rationale for the necessity and beauty of celibacy: celibacy is for the apostolate, celibacy is for the kingdom, celibacy is for witness. Our long-suffering friends eventually *do* leave, announcing their departure with their own addition to the litany: "Celibacy is for the birds."

For most of us our little group provides a sense of belonging at a very uprooted time in our lives, a taste of worldliness when our feelings toward the world are still somewhat ambivalent. Within the safety of the group we can experiment without the fear of making fools of ourselves in the larger, more sophisticated world. We are neophytes and we know it, and we encourage and applaud each other as we take our first awkward, toddling steps into the realm of adult male-female relationships.

At Thanksgiving I attend a preliminary chapter workshop in Washington, D.C. I room with my aunt and realize that the time has come for me to break the news to her. She had been the original inspiration in my wanting to be a nun in the first place, and through the years she has been a source of consistent support and encouragement. We cry and hug each other for a long time when I tell her, both of us knowing that our relationship as sisters will now be radically altered. And yet I can tell she is happy that I have made a decision that brings me so much peace and contentment.

Next I call my sister Andi, who is living in Washington, D.C. I have never shared with her any of my doubts about religious life, and so my decision comes as a shock to her. For almost as long as she and the rest of my brothers and sisters can remember, Mary has been a nun or training to be one, and it will take some doing for that image to get turned around.

The days pass quickly now, and before long I am on my way home for Christmas. It is a cold, snowy day, and as I fly across country high above the clouds, my spirit flies too. The future seems to stretch before me like the panorama of sky outside the airplane window. I am no longer afraid of the days ahead; in fact, I look forward to the future with childlike excitement and anticipation. I am gradually growing used to the experience of freedom.

As Christmas nears, nothing can bring me down. I am so ecstatically happy that I keep asking myself why I lied to myself for so long. I talk to my parents the first night I am home, and the next day I write in my journal:

December 1968
Last Christmas I was a china angel
safe on a shelf.
This Christmas I am spirit-clay me.
On this feast of a God who
came down to earth
I think I heard Jesus say
welcome!

Talked to Mom and Dad last night on the edge of their bed. The love is definitely there, and they do their best to support me in this radical turnabout from all they know to be me. But though the words are never said, I can sense their confusion, their disappointment, and I fall all over myself trying to help them understand what has happened, and why, and how content I am in my decision. . . .

As the days wear on, everyone begins to realize how happy I am, and they share in my happiness. I take great pains to point out to everyone who will listen that I'm not going back to anything—it's not like I tried something and failed and am coming home now, my tail between my legs. The title *ex-nun* still holds negative connotations for me, and I am defensive. According to my mental pictures, an ex-nun leaves the convent and lives with her parents for a while as she begins the process of "recovery." Like a retarded child recently released from the back wards of some state institution, she is taught and cared for by solicitous family members who worry and fret and feel the burden, though they would never admit it. They advise her on worldly matters and maybe help her financially; they cross their fingers and make novenas to Our Lady, hoping against hope that she will have a boyfriend or two.

It's a scenario I hope to avoid at all costs: I know I have much to learn, but like a mother dog who creeps away to bear her babies alone, I will seek the anonymous big city as a place to do my learning. For now I am home for awhile to be with people I love, to water my roots, and to be nurtured by their caring. Then I will be off again to begin my new life in the world.

34 ❦

CHAPTER; LEAVE OF ABSENCE

After Christmas I attend the chapter meetings. I fight with everything in me for the changes that I feel will benefit the community, and try to keep myself open to anything that might make me want to be a part of all this again.

But though I do my best to represent the people who have elected me, I notice a certain detachment in myself as I take part in the various meetings. It's ironic: such an opportunity to help shape the community's future would have excited me in the past when I had been filled with such enthusiasm for community change. Now that I am on my way out, I am rubbing elbows with some of the most powerful decision makers in the community. There is a certain poignant sadness when I think back to how much such an opportunity would have meant to me just a few short months ago.

I am probably able to make a contribution to the chapter precisely because of this detachment. I no longer have to phrase my words very carefully for fear of being branded as a radical: because I no longer have anything at stake, I can speak my mind freely, with complete frankness. It makes me feel good to involve myself so totally at the chapter meetings: it gives me a sense of truly making a contribution to this community of people who have been so much a part of my life, for better and for worse, for so many years.

There are many heated discussions at the chapter meetings, but one of the most heated has to do with the habit. Vatican II asked religious orders to update their habits in the spirit of renewal and in faithfulness to the original aims of each congregation's foundress, but it left the specifics to the individual congregation. Conservatives argue that the habit surrounds its wearer with an aura of mystery and reverence, lifting the minds of onlookers to high things. Then there's the matter of protection: according to the conservatives, everyone knows nuns can walk unscathed through back streets that no ordinary woman would dare enter. The arguments go on and on, pointing to the probable loss of esprit de corps if the habit is discarded, the loss of modesty, and the expense of keeping up with ever-changing fashion. Stories of dramatic airport and train-station conversions are also brought forward ("He never would have poured out his heart that way if he hadn't known I was a nun"), along with passionate arguments for preserving the same habit Mother Matthew wore.

Progressives reply that Mother Matthew wore clothes not much removed from the common dress of the day. Surely she didn't intend that her followers wear medieval garb that would separate them so blatantly from the people they serve! Such garb symbolizes isolation and withdrawal, whereas Vatican II laid stress on involvement in the world. Then too, a voluminous habit is impractical and inconvenient, denying a nun comfort and mobility. Worst of all, the moment one puts on a habit, she loses something of her individuality and takes on a corporate personality. As Erving Goffman made clear in *Asylums* (most of us in the progressive camp have read *Asylums* and found Goffman's analysis of "total institutions" frighteningly accurate), enforced uniformity of clothing is one of the means that "total institutions" use to nullify individuality and implement totalitarianism.

The battle rages on, with much more than hemlines at stake. Eventually the progressives win the day: it is decided that those who wish may discard their habits and begin wearing lay clothes. The clothes are to be modest in decorum, and the wearer is to display some kind of insignia identifying her as a Sister of Blessing.

The authority structure of the congregation will no longer be monarchical, with superiors issuing orders and subjects cheerfully obeying them to the letter. Superiors will be replaced by community representatives who, instead of interpreting the Will of God for individual sisters, will simply function as administrative links between the local house and the larger community. More contact with families will be permitted, including overnight visits home, and out-of-convent living situations will be permitted in some circumstances.

There are other changes, many of them significantly altering the future of life as a Sister of Blessing. Some modifications would bring outright schism to the community if adopted today, so they are put on the back burner for future chapters to discuss and eventually legislate.

I am pleased with the changes that the chapter legislates and am almost surprised that they don't inspire the slightest inclination in me to stay and experience postchapter life. Through it all, any lingering doubts have vanished, and by the end of the last session I am completely sure of my plans. I will speak to Reverend Mother as soon as chapter is over—I will make arrangements to sign papers severing me from the community.

I whisper my plan to an older sister friend, a woman I love and admire, and she confides: "I would leave, too, if I were your age," which saddens me terribly.

One of the reasons I had wanted to come to chapter was so that I might completely immerse myself in the life of the order one last time before leaving and live for a few intense days at its heart. Having done just that, having experienced the rhythms and pulse of the community more totally than ever before, I am overwhelmed with respect and tenderness for women who for the rest of my life will remain in a deeply personal way my sisters.

The day after chapter ends—two days after my twenty-sixth birthday—my aunt is a silent, solemn witness as I sit in Mother Mary Paul's office and sign leave of absence papers. My three-year vows will expire in August, so getting a dispensation from the bishop—a time-consuming, tedious procedure—

is unnecessary; a simple leave of absence will free me to live in the world until my vows expire.

And that's it: no secret, silent ritual of packing one's suitcase in a dark convent basement, no sneaking away in the black of the night. Today things are "civilized," businesslike: one simply signs her name to a paper and it is all over. Elaborate ceremony and ritual had surrounded all the other transition points of my life, but for this most significant "crossing over" there is only a bare wooden table, a formal document, a pen.

From the minute I sign the papers severing me from the order, I will never once question whether I have made the right decision. One part of my life is over and another is ready to start: it's as simple as that. Yet later that evening as I sit down to write in my journal, the reality of it all hits me, and I experience a sudden, drastic aloneness like nothing I have ever known.

I write:

January 12 1969
My God, my God—why have you forsaken me? Never in my twenty-six years have I felt so lost, so alone. I poured every last drop of blood into the chapter meetings, and now all of a sudden, it's over, all of it, a whole lifetime of it, and the reality of what I've done is beginning to hit me. . . .

Calm returns the next day, and I write:

January 13 1969
I feel a deep calm, like after the storm. No longer now can I find ready-made meaning in some "cause" handed to me. I have to *create* meaning: I now see that choice, decision is everything. . . .

Stripped of ready-made meaning and ready now to take my life in my own hands, I say my good-byes and board the plane for New York.

VI ဢ
WORLDLING

If I were a tree or a plant, I would feel the soft warm influence of the earth—but since I am a woman, do not be astonished by my joy.

—Chinese Proverb

STARTING OVER

At first very little is different—at least externally—when I return to New York. I still live in the same place and hang out with the same group of friends. For the most part I even wear the same clothes, having very little money to invest in a new wardrobe.

Eventually my mother sends me an electric blanket and my sister sends me a "care" package, including a coat that will help me make it through the bitter New York winter. As I go through the clothes, trying on each item, I feel very rich and worldly. Gradually, I throw out all my black, nunny clothes: it will be at least ten years before I can bring myself to wear black again.

I have no cash reserve, no insurance, no car—only one box of hand-me-down clothes. I am still receiving a monthly allotment from the Chicago archdiocese, but that just covers room, board, and school expenses. Usually the community gives a departing member a small sum of money to help her get started in the world, but because of my scholarship the order feels (and I agree) that I am adequately covered.

It feels good to be on my own at last. I learn to do all the little everyday things that most people take for granted: I shop for groceries, cook dinner in our little kitchen, do my laundry at the neighborhood laundromat, and experience a kind of simple, quiet pleasure from doing these everyday tasks that I haven't done for years. It's as though in doing all the homemaking kinds of things that my mother did, and her mother before her, I am reestablishing my identification with that chain of women.

Though by worldly standards I am financially in pretty dire straits, nothing can mar my happiness. My parents offer to help me, but I am determined to make it on my own.

One of the things that makes leaving so easy for me is the fact that, in a lot of ways, I simply left one community for another—for two others, in fact, for when I return to New York I burrow down deep into the love and nurturance of two different groups, my group of nun and priest friends (most of them in the process of becoming ex-nuns and ex-priests themselves) and my group of friends connected with the Phoenix program.

With both groups I feel safe and secure at a time when I am extremely vulnerable. With my ex-nun and ex-priest friends, I know I can be myself in all my awkwardness and self-consciousness: we have similar pasts and similar hang-ups because of our pasts, so there is nothing to hide. With my Phoenix friends I know I couldn't hide even if I wanted to: they are street-smart and tough, and they can see right through me. They take me under wing and do their best to make my emergence into the world as safe and painless as possible.

And so, like a young animal who wanders away from her jungle home and is raised by animals of a whole different species, I let my worldly friends mother and father me along during the first few months. Because of the cultural environment in which they "bring me up," my emergence into social adulthood is totally different from that experienced by my friends in Peoria. My surrogate mothers and fathers are white, black, and brown; they're Jewish and Catholic and agnostic. Many of them received their educations on the streets of New York.

Maria, in particular, takes it upon herself to oversee my emergence into worldliness. A strikingly attractive Puerto Rican woman who somehow manages to raise four delightful teenagers as a single parent and make a name for herself as a tough, uncompromising community organizer in the local community, Maria takes me on as her fifth child. She teaches me how to dance, how to put on makeup, how to buy clothes

(I don't even know what size I wear), and tells me all there is to know about contraceptives.

The day I go to open my first checking account at the bank, I first stand near the window for a while, listening in as one after another person opens a new account. After years of having all my material needs handled for me without lifting a finger, my financial concerns are now mine to handle and I quickly have to learn what it means to balance a checkbook, make a deposit, and establish a budget.

After setting up my first checking account, I set out for the beauty shop. Maria had told me that while one doesn't make an appointment at the bank, one very definitely makes an appointment at the beauty shop, so I found a place in the yellow pages and set up the appointment. It is a clean-cold snowy day, and I don't mind walking the ten blocks. Every now and then I check my new watch (an ex-student had sent the watch as a coming-out gift): I want to be sure I'm on time.

Arriving at the beauty shop ten minutes early, I sit in the waiting room until my name is called. I washed my hair twice this morning in preparation. Maria hadn't told me to, but I am sure that the beauty parlor operator won't be very happy if she has to cut dirty hair. I glance at myself in the pocket mirror I carry in my purse: I have been letting my hair grow out ever since I got rid of the veil, and I made a secret vow to never wear it short again. Short hair had made me feel boyish, neutered. Now that it is long and thick I feel feminine, almost (dare I think it?) sexy.

Maria, however, has persuaded me that I should at least have it styled, even if I want it long: the way I am wearing it isn't very fashionable. Maria knows about such things and I don't so I have no choice but to listen to her, just as I had listened to her when she told me to wear more eye shadow and perfume.

I watch, wide-eyed, the various rituals of setting, drying, spraying, teasing. As a teenager I had laboriously set my hair in pin curls each night, but styles are totally different now. Here is another whole skill I will have to master—will I ever catch up with the contemporary world? I feel like Rip Van Winkle, rubbing his eyes after a long, long sleep, waking up to a world totally different from anything he had ever known.

Soon a woman comes forward and introduces herself as Betty. She looks me over as she chews a big wad of gum, and her eyes keep coming back to my hair. She doesn't seem too crazy about what she sees. I squirm uncomfortably.

Betty leads me past a row of ladies sitting under driers and proceeds to wash my hair for the third time today. It's a strange feeling: I haven't had someone wash my hair since my mother washed it at the bathroom sink when I was a child.

I keep trying to be helpful, anticipating how Betty wants me to hold my head, moving this way or that in response to her slightest touch. Betty keeps telling me to just sit back and relax.

As she washes, Betty asks me how I want it styled. She names a number of different current styles and asks me what I think of them. I tell her they're all great styles, but I'm sure she knows a lot more about hair than I do, so I will leave it up to her expertise to decide which style will look best on me. I think that sounds like a pretty intelligent answer, one that will hide my ignorance and at the same time, flatter Betty's ego. In all those years of relating to women, I have learned a *few* things that will help me out here in the world!

Apparently it's a good answer because Betty seems to warm to me. "Y'now, hon," she says, lowering her voice almost to a whisper, "I hate to be blunt, but your hair sure needs conditioning. It looks like it hasn't had a conditioner in years."

Seven, to be exact, I think to myself. I murmur apologetically as if I've somehow offended her personally. "I'm sorry. I'll have to do something about that."

I am embarrassed, and I ask myself if Betty *suspects*. I am *always* wondering if people suspect, wondering if a certain residue nunniness of which I'm not even aware makes me stick out like a sore thumb.

Patting my hair dry, Betty sets to work with comb and scissors, talking the whole time to the beauty operator next to her. Every now and then she stops and takes a drag on her cigarette and a sip of her soft drink. I am glad that she's talking to the other operator instead of to me because my mind is already absorbed with another dilemma. I have forgotten to ask Maria if one tips a beauty operator and, if so, how much. It's fairly obvious that one does: I watch carefully as each customer pays her bill and then slips something in the beauty operator's pocket. But how much? If only I could take some-one aside and ask her. But it's too late for that, so I decide that I will slip fifty cents into Betty's pocket and then walk out quickly without waiting to see her reaction. Is fifty cents too little: cheap? Is it too much: ostentatious? Walking out and never returning is the only way—I just hope I never run into her on the street.

Betty adds one last flourish of spray and then gives me a hand mirror so I can look at the back. I want to praise her for her work but don't want her to think I'm vain, so I say it looks pretty and that she's done a good job, but I make sure to emphasize the part about her doing a good job rather than the part about it looking pretty.

Only when I have gotten through that dilemma do I have a chance to really take a look at my new hairdo, and when I *do,* I realize that it looks nice, but it doesn't look like *me.* Of course I realize I have no idea what hairstyle *does* look like me, just as I have no idea what clothes or apartment or life-style looks like me, but I tell myself that maybe that's the first step—realizing what is *not* me.

But now, another dilemma that I haven't anticipated. Betty is saying that I really should buy this type of shampoo and this type of conditioner and this type of cream rinse and this type of hair spray if I want my hair to look right. I panic: should I ask her how much they cost, or would that be cheap?

Will she be insulted if I don't just trust her judgment? Panicing, I say, yes, yes, I'll go with whatever you suggest; you're the expert. Then I draw in my breath as she tells me the total: I realize I just spent my grocery money for a week. My hands shaking, I write my first check in my new checkbook and then flip to the check register as Maria has taught me and carefully record it there. I keep trying to think fast as I write. Maybe I can still back out. Maybe I can tell her I forgot I still had all these supplies at home. Maybe I can tell her I forget my account was overdrawn. Maybe I can tell her—horrors!—the truth. No, no time to back out now. Surely she'd be angry, and besides, maybe that's just the price you have to pay if you want your hair to look nice! No, I'll pay the bill.

Trying to act normal, I hand her the check. Thanking her again for the wonderful job she has done, I pick up the sack of supplies and walk out of the shop, completely forgetting the tip!

It is late afternoon, and the snow is beginning to fall more heavily. As I wait for the Jerome Avenue bus, I suddenly remember about the tip, and I can't help laughing right out loud. A couple of people passing by look at me rather strangely, but I don't care. I love these moments when the humor of it all bursts right through.

I look forward to being home and having a drink with Donna, Alice, and Joe before dinner. Joe is cooking tonight, so I know I can expect his one specialty, spaghetti. It looks as if it's going to be blizzardy: maybe instead of going out we can have the gang over and make some popcorn. And Mom sent a new cookie recipe I've been wanting to try.

I light up a cigarette and inhale slowly, savoring the waning day. There's a toast that Donna, Alice, and I always use when we're down, and I think of it now. "Here's to us. We may not know where we're going, but we're damn glad we know where we're *not.*" How true, how true, I think; I'm happy to be alive and charting my own course. Life is indeed good.

36 ✑
SPRING (1969–1970)

In the spring I get a job as a substitute teacher in a South Bronx blackboard jungle. The teacher whom I replace had a nervous breakdown, a piece of information that no one bothered to share with me when I interviewed for the job, and neither did anyone tell me that though I could teach English, French, and music, I would be assigned to teach Spanish, hygiene, and art.

But the course description doesn't matter much anyway in this school where knifings and shootings are part of everyday life. My main job will be to keep them from killing each other and, hopefully, me! I have never seen anything like this in my life: windows have been shot out, every other adult is an undercover police officer, and packs of kids run wild in the school corridors.

And in the midst of it all, the principal walks around in suit and tie, smiling like some schizophrenic who is totally out of touch with what is going on around him. I can never quite figure out what he does with his time besides walking around and smiling benignly at the chaos. For that, it is rumored, he is paid a rather sizable paycheck every two weeks.

But I need the money, so I stick it out for three weeks until a full-time teacher is found. I congratulate myself that I have been able to keep myself afloat financially as long as I have, given the fact that I have never had a modicum of training in such matters. Not only have I never had to handle money; I also have never had to interview for a job or to write up a resume. Suddenly on my own, I have had to learn and learn fast.

After that, I sell encyclopedias. I last exactly two days: the sales trainer tells us to try to get women to sign on the dotted line without first consulting their husbands—"You can talk women into *anything* if you tell 'em it's for the good of their kids"—and I tell him thanks, but no thanks. Next I fill in as a secretary in Fordham's Sociology Department (me, the fragile hot-house flower: my high-school hot house would never have dreamed of offering anything as commercial as typing or shorthand).

At one point I even try out for a job as a piano player in a beer-and-peanuts sing-along place. My audition involves playing along with the group on Friday night when the place is packed, and thanks to both my ability to play by ear and the fact that I have sense enough to down a pitcher of beer before going on stage, I am offered the job. I'm actually tempted to take it, but eventually decide that the Friday/Saturday night commitments cut into my social life too much.

Since January I have also become more and more involved with the Phoenix program and have gone through various Phoenix training groups. Working in conjunction with a Spanish-speaking black psychologist in some of the ghetto schools, I run "rap" groups where parents (mostly Puerto Rican) and teachers (mostly black) air their conflicts.

In the spring I am offered a full-time community organization position with the Phoenix program. By now my love affair with New York is in full bloom and I would give anything to stay, but I have commitments back in Chicago. The terms of my contract with the archdiocese specify that in return for my fellowship covering my graduate work I will teach in a Chicago Catholic high school for three years and serve as a consultant to the archdiocesan Religion Teachers Association, the group responsible for training local religion teachers and pastors in some of the newer religious-education theory and practice. It will be very hard for me to leave New York and the friends and work that I love, but it never occurs to me that I have other options. Years later I will look back and wonder why I didn't offer to pay the money back over a period of time: others had received fellowships and were now returning as consultants, so there was no real pressing need for my services. But years of conscientious, literal, and unquestioning adherence to commitments have left their effects.

Resigned to returning to Chicago, I write to a number of different high schools and amaze myself by easily landing a job. Not only that, my salary for the year will be $7,000. After years of working for nothing, the figure seems ridiculously astronomical. What will I do with all that money? Will it change me? Am I now on my way to becoming selfish and bored and unhappy, like most rich people? Am I abandoning my linkage with all the poor people of the world? How can it be right that I have so much and they have so little? I accept the job but with some very definite misgivings, and I promise myself that I will never become so rich that I forget the true values of life.

37 ❧
SUMMER

Lori is curled up on the sofa sketching her cat. I am sitting at the kitchen table typing a paper for class. I take a sip of diet cola, and turn up the radio. They're playing "Hey, Jude" and I think of Mark. I wonder how he's doing, how his test went, if he's thinking of me. "The minute you let her into your heart, then you can start to make it better, better, be-e-tter." At the sound of my voice the cat howls.

I empty my ashtray which is now quite full and check our

African violet to see if she's dry. In the process I chip the polish on one of my nails and do a quick repair job. It is only June 2 and New York is already simmering: I roll up my jeans and admire my tan calves, wondering if I can talk Mark into going water skiing next weekend.

I love living with Lori. Arriving in May to start graduate work at Fordham (I had written her about the program), she rented a one-bedroom apartment in an older building near the school and offered me the couch until it would be time for me to return to Chicago. After my cramped little room, connected by a narrow hallway to other peoples' cramped little rooms, the place seems airy and spacious and will be the scene of many happy summer memories.

My friendship with Lori goes back many years: back to the time when nun students were first being allowed to speak to secular college students, Lori and I found every excuse to get together. After she graduated we wrote back and forth for a while; then, to my joy, she entered our community. I was on mission at the time; she only stayed a few months. She visited me in Cincinnati and again in Chicago: we were so close that at one time there were even whisperings that we had one of "those" kinds of relationship.

Now here she is in New York, studying in the same department as I am, and we are roommates. In the old days she would show me her paintings, I would read her my poems, and we would discuss French literature and philosophy. Now we still exchange paintings and poetry, but we talk mostly about ourselves and our relationships, especially our relationships with men. And now and then we talk about the old days and how things used to be.

I put the cover on my typewriter, pour Lori a gin and tonic, and carry it in to her.

"So where do you want to go for your birthday dinner, old buddy?" I ask. "I promised Jeff I'd take good care of you while he's out of town."

"To tell you the truth," she says, her eyes never leaving

the sketch pad, "if birthdays don't stop sneaking up on me this way, I'm afraid I might decide to go back to celebrating my feast day instead. Could I persuade you to postpone the celebration till the feast of Saint Teresa?"

I laugh, remembering the convent custom. "Those days seem so long ago. Remember how we used to have secret little birthday parties for each other and exchange medals and relics and spiritual bouquets?"

"And gold-edged holy cards with sweet-faced Madonnas on them," Lori adds. "I'll never forget how furious my mother was when she discovered that they didn't let me have the cards and presents she sent me. I thought she'd never get over it."

Lori now puts away her sketch pad and stretches out on the sofa. She lights up a cigarette and takes a sip of the gin and tonic. I sit cross-legged on the floor.

"Because my aunt had already paved the way in our family," I explain, "my parents took most stuff like that in stride. What I found hard, though, was the way I got so cut off from my family. The kids would write about how they were studying their catechism or praying hard to Our Lady: I am only now getting bits and pieces of what was *really* going on with them all those years, and I can assure you it didn't have much to do with studying catechism or praying to Our Lady."

"I know what you're talking about," says Lori, warming to the topic. "They didn't even tell me when my sister got a divorce or my brother was picked up for shoplifting. It kind of reminds me of the alumnae magazine I receive from the college: every issue is full of accounts of how Susie Smith drives her seven beautiful children to the parish school each day, how Mary Jones teaches Sunday-school classes and Nellie Nice is chairman of the parish liturgy committee. Needless to say, there's never anything about all the alums who are divorced, have bratty kids, or got pregnant before they were married."

"Or the ones who are living with their boyfriends, have drinking problems, or got married out of the Church," I add, mentally tallying the ones I know in each category.

Lori goes on: "My heart goes out to every woman out there who thinks she's the only one with a messed-up life, the only one who didn't wind up with things going exactly the way the books said they should go, the only one who let the good nuns and dear old alma mater down. I wish I could bring them all together in one room and let them tell the truth to each other, drop all the facades: there'd be so much relief in that room that it would practically blow the roof right off!"

She becomes pensive: "You know, I become really embarrassed when I think of what pompous asses we were taught to be, always looking for ways to inspire people, always looking for ways to help them. How did our families put up with that for so long? It must have been great fun for our parents, with years of experience under their belts, to be the recipients of so much unasked-for inspiration and help. Looking back, I think they probably humored us with the same ambivalent feelings with which they had humored so many nuns in the past. On the one hand, there had to be a certain reverence because, after all, nuns had a higher calling. But on the other hand, they sure were naive about a lot of things!"

"I know," I agree, "and sometimes now it's hard to get everyone to let go of those old pictures of me. Just last week when my sister was in town, I realized again what a shock it is for all of them, how hard it is for them to get used to the change. We were sitting in a bar and, as usual, Andi was telling me about her love life. Suddenly stepping out of long-established character, I started telling her about mine. Of course she knew on an objective level that I no longer crocheted shawls in my free time, but it was like the reality of it all had never really hit her. Right there in that goddamn bar she broke into sobs, trying the whole time to assure me that she knew it was silly, but she just wasn't used to thinking of me in that way, out here in the world just like her."

I look at my watch. "I hate to end this seminar, but the mundane world calls—I'm starved! So where will it be?

Jeff gave me the sheckels to do your birthday in style, so just name it."

Lori puts out her cigarette and thinks for a minute. "I've been wanting to try the Village Green—why don't we go there? I can be ready in fifteen."

We both dress and I call for reservations. Within a half-hour we are in a cab en route to the restaurant.

"How fun!" Lori exclaims: "A night out with the girls. It's been a long time. I'm surprised Mark let you off tonight."

"Look who's talking. The only reason I get to see you tonight is because Jeff's out of town!"

"You know it really is crazy how that kind of thing gets started, how you start spending all your time with one person. And neither one of us even wants to get all that involved at this point in our lives. I have to admit that I sometimes miss the friendships with women that I had in the convent: you're my closest friend, and you and I even have trouble finding time to get together. I hope that that's one of the things that starts to balance out after I go through this little phase of ODing on men."

"I know what you mean about ODing. And it's not just men. We couldn't drink in the convent, so I drink like a fish. We couldn't smoke, so I smoke over a pack a day. Our lives were routined and regimented down to the last detail: my life is so free-flowing, so unscheduled now, that it's hard to get anything done. I know deep down that someday the pendulum will swing back to the center, but for now it's anything goes. Sometimes my life looks like I live by only one rule: 'Nothing in moderation!' "

Lori looks out at the lights as we cross the George Washington Bridge. I know she loves New York as I do, that, like me, she sees the city as one great big celebration honoring her coming out. We sit in silence for a moment or two, taking it all in.

My mind has swum to shore and is basking in the here-

and-now, but when she suddenly chuckles to herself, I realize she is still out there, swimming around in the memories.

"Do you remember how you used to always fall asleep at meditation? Laura Patrice was your prie-dieu partner, so it was her responsibility to nudge you every time you fell asleep. At that point you were to stand up, and the change of position plus the humiliation were supposed to wake you up. Every morning we'd watch you: about ten minutes into meditation you'd fall sound asleep, and faithful Laura would do her duty. You'd stand up, and in five minutes more you'd be asleep on your feet. You'd sway so much that we were convinced you were going to fall right into the aisle some morning. We took bets on it. You must have had some amazing inner radar going on; although you'd tilt woozily from side to side, you never quite managed to fall."

Choking with laughter, Lori can hardly get the words out: "I just remembered something even funnier. Remember the time in the conserve? A visiting orchestra was doing a masterful job on Beethoven's Fifth, but, as usual, you were dozing off. Some good soul next to you, sure that you wouldn't want to miss anymore of the orchestra's marvelous performance, poked you in the ribs and you sprang to your feet. For a minute I thought the orchestra was going to have to stop playing until the audience pulled itself together. Even Amadeus had big tears rolling down her cheeks!"

By now Lori and I are laughing so hard we can hardly breathe.

"You know," Lori confides, drying her eyes, "we had some pretty good times, when you think about it. I don't think laughter has ever been as delicious as it was back then, especially when we'd get started in the chapel. Remember how it would only take some dumb little thing to get us started. We'd read something especially preposterous in one of those ancient meditation books, we'd show it to our prie-dieu partner, and before long the prie-dieu would vibrate with all the laughter we were trying so hard to stifle. The more we tried, the more the prie-dieu would rock."

"Laughter, for sure," I agree, "and music." Music was another way we'd get out all that was pent up in us all day. We were always singing: we literally sang our hearts out! Music too was delicious!

"And nature. I don't think I'll ever feel as close to nature as I felt back then: a snowfall, daffodils in the spring, the summer stars. We were God's innocent children, and the world of nature was our home."

As the taxi nears the restaurant, I take out my billfold and get my money ready. Knowing that once inside, our conversation will turn to other matters, to the details of our here-and-now lives, I take one last lingering look: friendship, laughter, music, daffodils—not a bad life when you think about it.

Then I carefully fold up each memory and tuck it away into my heart for safe keeping.

> *Tous les livres a peine lûs,*
> *ces amis a peine aimés,*
> *ces villes a peine visitées,*
> *ces femmes a peine prises. . . .*

"And what is *that* supposed to mean?" I demand, pointing to the French passage tacked on Mark's bulletin board.

"You can read French as well as I can," Mark laughs, pulling me down to the couch and kissing me.

Teasing, I pull away. " 'All these books never read, these friends never loved, these cities never visited, these women never made love to. . . .' You ex-priests are all the same: always trying to make up for lost time. What am I doing getting involved with the likes of you?"

Trying to look hurt, Mark lights a cigarette. "Look who's talking, sweetie. You ex-nuns have a reputation for being a bunch of nymphos: 'So many men, so little time!'—right?"

I throw a pillow at him, and we both laugh. Then he gets up and pours us each a glass of wine.

Mark is wonderful. We have been going out for the past two months, and we can't seem to get enough of each other's company. But each of us knows, and lets the other know quite clearly, that the other isn't *the* one. We know we are still both adolescents when it comes to matters of the heart, that we're not even open to discovering *the* one just yet. We have miles to go and promises to keep—promises to ourselves: promises to keep things nice and slow and easy, and, most important, free. Now that it's August, we will spend another week together en route to a friend's wedding in South Dakota; then Mark will drop me off in Chicago and head on up to Montreal where he has landed a university position.

I have come over to help him with his packing, but a superserious discussion is beckoning. We always tease each other about our superserious discussions, but we seem thoroughly addicted to them nonetheless.

Mark starts. "Do you know that when I was in the seminary we had this ritual where we all went to a lake outside of town. We each had to tie a necktie around a rock and throw it far into the lake, symbolizing the death of our masculinity. Eunuchs, goddamned eunuchs, that's what they were trying to turn us into." An old anger emerges and edges Mark's voice, making him look older than his twenty-seven years. I hold him close, wishing desperately that I could caress away the years and the pain.

I take another sip of my wine. "You know, Mark, the antibody conditioning was so total that sometimes I'm surprised that those of us who went through it are doing as well as we are. Like you, I know that some psychological fallout will be there for me to deal with for the rest of my life, but I've talked to so many ex-nuns and ex-priests and they all seem to agree that loving and expressing that love physically seemed to come so naturally once they left. It was as if a whole side of them was just put on hold for a while while they developed other sides, and when it came time to free that side there were no really big problems or traumas involved, other than the awkwardness that inexperience breeds."

Mark thinks for a minute, then says, "You're right, for sure. In fact I can't help thinking that in a lot of ways we're probably better off than a lot of our Catholic and ex-Catholic friends when it comes to sexuality. So many of them on the surface appear liberated and nonhung-up, but when you scratch beneath the surface they admit to guilts and conflicts that go back to something some nun said when they were in the sixth grade!"

"I know," I laugh. "The fact that I *myself* was once one of those stern-looking disembodied creatures has done a lot to defuse the whole mystique for me! It's as if I let the monster, the institutional church, eat me up, and living within its belly I saw it from the inside in a way that few people have had an opportunity to see it. That experience totally changed me, smashing the control that the institutional church had over my mind and my psyche."

"I had the same experience," Mark agrees. "I had as friends people who held high positions in their communities and their dioceses, and that experience did a lot to bring crashing down around me all my old pictures. And studying current theology gave me an opportunity to turn over within myself, in a critical light, some of the Church's teachings and taboos. So many of my Catholic and ex-Catholic friends never really had that opportunity: like most of us they sat through eight long years of parochial-school education, their young minds soaking up everything the nuns had to say as well as all the subliminal messages that floated intangibly in the Catholic air. From there, they either drifted away from the Church or moved gradually into the roles expected of them as respectable parishioners. Many of them never had the same opportunity I did to go back and critically examine a lot of the old teachings and taboos rumbling around on some preconscious level. Some of my ex-Catholic friends, though virulently non-

Catholic, still baptize their babies just in case! They confide that although they have broken off all contact with the Church of their childhood, they can't get rid of the nagging voice in the back of their minds that says: 'But what if they're right?' "

It is now dusk, and the day is cooling off a bit. I can hear mothers calling to their children in the street below. I can smell the jasmine blooming outside Mark's window. I nestle close, feeling content.

"Mark, if the pope came out and said that priests could now get married, would you want to become active in the ministry again?" I have always wanted to ask him this, and I now decide to take advantage of his mellow mood.

His handsome face becomes pensive. "I used to have a lot of mixed feelings about that, Mary, but now I'm clear. The thing is, I've become so disillusioned with the Church. I suppose I'll always be deeply religious, but when it comes to choosing one particular religious expression or body of beliefs as my own, I'm not sure that's something I want to do at this particular point in my life. Someone said that we're born spiritual and we become religious, and I think that's true. I know that I, for one, don't want to hitch my cart to the pope anymore: I want to open myself to the truth wherever I may find it, and less and less frequently am I finding it within the institution of the Roman Catholic Church. Take the birth-control thing: there's nothing that makes me sadder. Practically every priest I know, when you get him in private, says that the birth-control ruling is outdated, that it should be changed. He may even practice birth control himself! But because of his official connection with the official Church, he'd never get up in the pulpit and tell people that. He'd lose his job. That kind of thing is just intolerable to me, and I never again want to be put in that position of having to be a hypocrite.

"I often think about how everyone praises Mother Teresa of India as such a saint, and I do too. But it burns me to think that for every poor soul she ministers to in the streets of Calcutta, a hundred more are being born into the same desperate conditions. And the Church to which she belongs contributes to that vicious cycle by not being willing to change its policy, by not being willing to encourage people to plan their families responsibly. The Church carries a lot of weight in the world—it's incredibly sad to think of all the good it could do, especially in the third-world countries, by throwing some of that weight where it could do the most good."

Mark had been a missionary in Columbia, so I realize that he knows what he's talking about. It's sad to see his dedication, his genuine concern for the world, and to know that the Church has pushed away one more person who could have made a real difference. And in another way it's *not* sad: the Church is just a vehicle, and I now know that there are other vehicles out there. I believe in Mark enough to know that he will find another vehicle for all the love he has to give the world.

I kiss him and tell him so and remind him that we'd better get to the packing. He kisses me and tells me that the packing can wait until morning.

I tell him I can see his point.

Mark and I attend our friend's wedding in mid-August; then he takes me to Marci's house in Chicago. Here I will stay until I find myself an apartment and am situated. We say good-bye, promising to meet later in the winter for some skiing: Mark is an expert skier, and he has promised me some lessons.

An old numbness, cultivated through many years of agonizing good-byes, comes up to shield me as Mark's car pulls away. I walk through the next few days zombielike. What *is* this? Hadn't we prepared ourselves so carefully for this breaking away? Don't we both know it's really best? Don't we both know that adolescent relationships rarely make it? We both have so much growing up to do that it would be a disaster to take our liaison very seriously. . . . The brave words all sound so hollow now that he is really gone.

I start praying for early snow.

I miss Mark and I miss Lori and I miss all that I have grown to know and love about New York. Is my life always going to be this way, one good-bye after another?

38 ᣥ

CHICAGO

Although I will be teaching in a western suburb and will have to take a long bus ride to and from work each day, I want to live in Hyde Park, the area right around the University of Chicago. Everyone tells me I'm crazy: it's almost impossible to find an apartment there, and the area is growing increasingly unsafe. Yet there is something I love about it, and I decide not to let all the reasonable objections get in my way. Maybe because I am still so unrealistic about worldly things at this period in my life, I don't really worry much about, or feel much limited by, people's ideas of what is sensible, reasonable, or possible, and, amazingly, I seem to get pretty much what I want.

I soon find a little Hyde Park efficiency apartment with a big old murphy bed that drops down in the middle of the one room, and I couldn't be happier. Hyde Park is to me a little island of New York, and I love it. I love walking to the little deli down the street for Saturday morning lox and bagels, love mingling with people of all races and nationalities when I shop at the local stores. The University of Chicago is brimming with intellectual opportunities, and I am determined to avail myself of as many as I can. And yet it will be a difficult year for me, more difficult than I ever could have imagined.

Saint Gertrude's High School is just a few white neighborhoods west of Ashland Avenue, which is presently the Mason-Dixon line of southwest Chicago, the great divide between black and white territory. The local branches of the KKK and the American Nazi party are both within walking distance, and many of our students belong to both. Two black families attempt to move into the area during the time that I am teaching there, and both are greeted with rocks through their front windows and crosses on their lawns.

Convinced that it would be a travesty to teach conventional religion courses under such circumstances, I teach a junior/senior course called Christian Social Problems in which we have a number of lively discussions. By now I know that lecturing and moralizing only exacerbate the problems; that exchange experiences, films, and sessions in which students can ventilate their hostilities and fears in a nonjudgmental atmosphere do the most toward alleviating racial tensions.

I am quite happy with the way most of the kids respond to these process classes. I learn that a lot of them, deep down, feel guilt about the whole racial situation, confiding: "Our parents tell the nuns they're sending us here to get a Catholic education, but we know the truth: they send us here to keep us away from the niggers."

I take the bus to work each day, riding it for an hour through the all-black area and into the all-white, and in the afternoon I ride it back home again. It's dusk by the time I reach home each day, and I know that it's not very safe to walk back to the apartment at that hour of day, but I also know that I don't have much choice if I want to stay in Hyde Park. I haven't yet saved up enough money to buy a car.

I find it hard to talk to the small group of Catholic-school teachers I work with: their lives are so different from mine, and I have no idea what to talk to them about. Most of them live right there on the southwest side of Chicago where they have lived for years. Desperate for friendship, I long to become a part of their tight-knit little group, but I have no idea how to break in.

The lack of community in my life kicks me in the stomach as winter nears. In New York my life had brimmed with the laughter and good times of two circles of friends, but here my aloneness is overwhelming. If it weren't for the love and support of three dear friends who live near me—all of them ex-nuns, Liz, Emily, and Peggy—the year would be unbearable. The four of us are like abandoned waifs in a strange city, sharing meals and confiding in each other and helping each other make it from one day to the next.

Just when I am sure I can't take riding the bus to work another day (the weather is now subzero, and I'm sure I'll freeze to death one morning while standing at the bus stop at 7 A.M.), I am able to put together enough money to make a down payment on a car. If I had been in New York, my friends would have steered me through this first major financial transaction, but as it is, my ex-nun friends are as inexperienced as I am when it comes to such matters. So I telephone my Dad in Peoria, and he guides me through this and other first business transactions.

This is one advantage of being in Chicago: I am near enough to be able to go home every now and then. When I *do* go home we have big family discussions around the kitchen table late into the night, as I try to reestablish my place in the family. Before I entered the convent, I was very much the big sister to younger family members, holding the oldest's special position in the family structure. Once I went away, Andi quickly moved up to take my place. Years later we would still be laughing about how, when she was eighteen and I was twenty-one, she had a copy of my birth certificate made and used it to get into bars. The symbolism is apt: in many ways she "became" me, stepping into my shoes once I left for the convent.

I soon come face to face with the reality that you can't *really* go home again: too many things have changed, within them and within me. As Pat will put it, years later: "It was as if your leaving left a gaping wound. At first we felt the pain; then slowly the wound began to heal. By the time you came back there was only scar tissue—layers of it." Both Dan and Cathy will express similar feelings when, years later, we will still be trying to relate through the scar tissue. Dan, for example, after a trip to California with his wife and children, will write: "You asked about the wall that has grown up between us, and I've given it a lot of thought. I recall vividly the pain I felt when you went into the convent: I felt lonely and abandoned and angry with you for leaving. From that point on, I think I blocked any further emotional involvement with you: you died and I grieved—never to grieve again."

Winter comes and goes, and I make my first pilgrimage back to Saint Raphael's in early summer. Though nothing of convent life retains any lingering attraction for me, the primitive beauty of the place still draws me, and the ghosts of old memories beckon.

The college students have left for vacation, and the big buses full of returning nuns haven't yet started pulling up the boulevard, so the place is almost deserted. I don't contact anyone, don't let anyone know I'm here: I just wander over the grounds touching base with old haunts and old forgotten parts of myself, cementing a link with the past that is as solid as the trees are tall.

I write in my journal:

June 1970

Such voluptuous beauty almost suffocates:
crickets, and wildflowers, and
trees possessed by some restless spirit.

I am back home—home in a different way,
but home.
I have come to water my roots where all is still.
Cows graze still and trees sway still
and saints pray still. . . .

I fly back to New York for the summer to complete my graduate work (I receive my M.A. in July); then at the end of the summer I fly to California for a two-week vacation with my sister Andi. Now and then she explodes with frustration and embarrassment when I miss social cues that a normal person my age would pick up, but for the most part she does her best to be patient with me. In San Diego we visit a cousin who is getting a Ph.D. in human behavior, an interdisciplinary degree, at a place called United States International University. I am intrigued when he tells me about some of the courses in psychology, sociology, and anthropology he's taking, and I go out to the campus with him one day to sit in on a couple of his courses.

One of the courses I sit in on is a course taught by the world-famous psychotherapist, Victor Frankl, survivor of Hitler's concentration camps and author of *Man's Search for Meaning*. I am impressed by Dr. Frankl, and I am also impressed by a handsome young Chinese-American student who, in my estimation, says some pretty brilliant things during the discussion part of the class.

Afterward there is a picnic around the pool campus in honor of Dr. Frankl, who is returning to Vienna, and I am breathless with excitement when the handsome young student comes over to our little group and introduces himself to me. I am even more excited when he asks me to go to a movie with him the following evening.

We go out every evening after that until it is time for me to return to Chicago. When I *do* return to Chicago, he flies out to see me at the end of September and sends me a ticket to come see him in October. We both go into debt trying to pay our telephone bills. He keeps talking to me about moving to

San Diego at the end of the semester, and the thought becomes increasingly more enticing. I am beginning to face the
reality of what is happening to me as far as El is concerned,
and I want to be near him. Also I have looked into the possibility of obtaining student loans, and it looks as if I will be
able to enter USIU in the spring. It is all too good to be true.

Yet I have so many considerations about settling in California: California people are shallow, superficial, antiintellec-
tual; I tell myself they buy plastic Christmas trees and worship
their bodies, that all they ever want to do in life is walk on the
beach. A lot of my thinking comes from my father: when I was
a child, our family camped its way across the country, and
California was the only place he refused to visit. He said that
California was the land of weirdos, that people who couldn't
make it anywhere else went there. So I think about all that
and about how I would miss the seedier side of life in Chicago
and New York. Then in late November an incident happens
that convinces me that I wouldn't miss that side at all.

It is an eerily still November evening, and I have had to
stay late at school for a meeting. My car has been broken into
and vandalized twice during the past month, so on my return I
park as close to my apartment building as possible, directly
under a street lamp. I have moved into a larger apartment with
my friend Liz, and I know that she'll be waiting up for me. I
look around carefully before getting out of the car, then lock
my car doors, and quickly walk the short distance to my apartment building. I have my keys ready, and I carry a small container of mace.

At the front of our building there is an outer door, then a
small vestibule just large enough for two or three people to
stand in, and then the inner door. As I push open the outer
door, a man comes up behind me from out of the shadows
and, overwhelming me, pushes me to the floor of the vestibule, closing the door behind us so that we can't be seen
from the street. He starts tearing my clothes off, and the more

I scream the more he pounds my head against the tile floor. My screams apparently frighten him because he jumps up and tells me not to move: he'll kill me if I get up. He bolts out the door and I manage to get my key in the door and close it behind me, dragging myself up the stairs to our apartment.

I pound on the door with the last of my energy, and when Liz comes to the door and sees my clothes all torn and the blood running down my face, she screams and pulls me inside. Her boyfriend calls the police, and when they arrive they ask me endless questions and fill out countless reports, then take me to the emergency room for stitches in my head. All the way to the hospital, I keep wondering what I have done. I'd been taught that things like this don't just *happen*, that women bring rape upon themselves. Had I walked seductively? Was it my clothes?

At any rate the incident wipes out any lingering romantic ideas about big-city life, and I begin to make arrangements for my departure. I notify the administration at Saint Gertrude's that they should start looking for a new teacher: I will be leaving at the end of the semester. I work out an agreement with the archdiocese whereby, instead of continuing as a consultant for the next year and a half as originally agreed upon, I will write a series of articles for their religious-education publication. I help Liz round up a new roommate.

Christmas vacation arrives, and El flies to Peoria to meet my family and to spend the holiday with them. A psychology teacher in a San Diego college, he has three weeks before he has to be back at school. My family seems to like him, and if there is any reservation in the beginning, it has to do not with the fact that he is Chinese, but that he is Protestant!

The day after Christmas, El and I drive back to Chicago and load all my earthly belongings (which aren't many) into my little Cortina and then drive off into the sunset.

VII
FULL CIRCLE

We shall not cease from exploration
And the end of all our exploring
Will be to arrive where we started
And know the place for the first time.

"Little Gidding," Four Quartets *by*
T. S. Eliot

39 §🙽
SAN DIEGO (1971-1981)

It is September 21, 1981, and I am flying back to the midwest
to attend our twenty-year convent reunion. It was just about
now, twenty years ago, that I received the wildly exciting news
that our entrance into the novitiate would be postponed a
week so that extra beds could be brought in to accommodate
our record crowd of entrants. It was an unexpected reprieve:
one more week to live it up before giving it up, one more
week to experience the world before leaving it forever. I was
eighteen.

I think of the years that have come and gone since then:
five years of formation, then two years on mission, then
1968—the year when all my bedrock foundations began to
crumble. There was the year of almost dizzying sudden freedom in New York when I seemed hell-bent on making up for
lost time, then a year and a half of trying desperately to get the
pendulum to swing more toward center.

By the time I came to San Diego in 1971, the pendulum
was beginning to swing less wildly, and I was becoming ready
to settle down. I think back over the ten years that have
passed since then.

In the spring of 1971, my first spring in San Diego, I
started work on a Ph.D. in human behavior at United States
International University, and I signed a contract to work full
time at a local Catholic high school in the fall. They wanted
me to work in a new program they were setting up, a religious-

counseling program similar to the one I had worked in at Josephina. Since it was a Catholic school, every student was required to take religion, but more and more students were beginning to rebel against the requirement. Some of the students bound by the religion-class requirement weren't even Catholic: a number of them had been expelled from public schools, and their desperate parents had sent them here in hopes that the nuns and priests could shape them up. My religious-counseling groups would be mine to handle as I saw fit: we would have no books, no particular subject matter to cover—it would be my job to keep the "trouble makers" out of everybody's hair so that the other religion teachers could teach the "good" kids, the kids who really wanted to learn about their Faith. Masochism was a hard habit to break after so many years, so I signed on.

Meanwhile, my relationship with El flourished: we became engaged in May and then toók off to Europe for the summer. Just as I was drawn to expand my narrowly western/ Aristotelian/Roman Catholic perspective by exploring the spiritual and philosophical wealth of the East, so El had for a long time been fascinated by Catholic Ireland, its people and its lore. He had traveled there many times and longed to show me all his secret spots. We would explore the west coast of Ireland, Galway, and the Aran Islands; we would track down the roots of my family, the Gilligans.

I came away from Ireland with a new respect for my Irish heritage, for the people of Ireland. I respected their stubbornness, their feistiness, their ability to persevere and to survive.

In a back room in Dublin we had watched old men play their fiddles and sing their songs of nationalism, their eyes filled with some strange mix of melancholy and defiance. It was the same look I had always seen in my father's eyes when he sang the verse in "Galway Bay" that recalled the oppression by the English: "For the English came and tried to teach us their way; they scorned us just for being what we are. But they might as well go chasing after moonbeams, or light a penny candle from a star." It was the only song I ever heard him sing, and he sang it with such feeling that I could picture his father singing it for him—and his father before him—passing from generation to generation a smoldering fury that could never be extinguished or forgotten. It was the son's duty to the father to remember, to carry in his bones the old memory and never to let it dim. It was the least he could do in respect for the brave men who had gone before.

Looking back, I was now able to put together one more piece of the puzzle: my fascination with the supernatural, my early piety, my desire to be a nun—it all made sense within the context of the Irish experience.

For Irish blood flowed in me too and with it, far beneath the surface, old memories that had nothing to do with my everyday life. I was the daughter of my people, and if they fought and suffered, I too should fight and suffer: anything else would have been a betrayal of those who went before.

And what better way to fight and suffer than to immolate one's youthful life for a great cause? And what greater cause than the promulgation and spread of one's ancestral Faith?

An ancient faith, an ancient cause: one more child of the Irish had taken up the fight—and the cross.

Back in San Diego, I continued graduate work and facilitated twenty group sessions a week at the high school. The schedule was harrowing—I would have a roomful of juniors and seniors for fifty minutes; then they would leave and a whole new group would come in—but I was happy to at least be finding my niche. Despite the fact that the administration seemed to regard my classes as a sort of dumping ground for those who couldn't/wouldn't make it in more academic courses, many of the students who took my class were bright, inquisitive types who had had it with pat answers. I delighted in leading them to the place where all their own unique answers lay: in their own hearts.

At the end of 1971, I married El in the tiny Peoria chapel

where my mother had been wed, and her mother before her. We sang Catholic hymns and Presbyterian hymns and had readings from the *I Ching*; I wore a Claddaugh ring, a traditional ring of Western Ireland, as an engagement ring, and El now placed next to it a gold ring bearing the Chinese characters for love and double happiness.

We bought a house in the spring and then put it up for rent for the summer: we were eager to spend another three months traipsing around Europe. At one point in our exploration of rugged Normandy, something kept pulling at me to visit Chantille-sûr-Longe, the birthplace of the Sisters of Blessing. In no particular hurry to go anywhere else, El agreed, and so we set off through the countryside of Normandy in search of the tiny village I had so often heard about in community history classes.

It seemed that no one *else* had heard of it, however: it took us a whole afternoon of asking directions and poring over the fine print of maps before we finally pulled into Chantille. It was raining when we arrived: we sat in the little convent parlor with nuns who still wore habits that collected balls of dust from the floor. I explained what we were doing there in the best French I could muster: I told them that I had once been a Sister of Blessing, that I had always heard of Chantille's beauty. I didn't tell them the part about feeling that Mother Matthew somehow still belonged to me, the part about wanting to experience again an old connectedness with the community and its original vision and impetus. It would have been hard enough to put English words on such feelings: how could I begin to explain them in French?

The French Sisters were quite cordial and after chatting for a few moments told me that I was in for a wonderful surprise. Two American Sisters were spending the summer with them: wasn't that a happy coincidence? They knew they'd be delighted to see me.

Soon they were back with the American nuns, and there was sudden silence in the room. There at the door stood Sister

Gertrude Anthony and Sister Alphonsus Beatrice, leaders of the old guard during my years at Josephina. El and the French nuns looked on, puzzled, while the three of us exchanged a few polite words; than I said that I had promised El we'd only stay a few minutes, and they said that vespers would be starting soon.

Back in the car, the tears came. It had been a romantic gesture, like going back to visit an old lover in a moment of nostalgia, but I had hopelessly romanticized the old lover, forgetting wrinkles and warts. The nuns at Chantille had been friendly and warm, and the beauty of the place, even in the rain, had been haunting. But the sight of nuns who had hoarded corsets and gossiped nastily about Josephina's "nigger girls" had jolted me back into a reality I would have preferred to forget at that nostalgic moment.

It was raining lightly as we headed back to Paris, and the windshield wipers beat a sloshing, comforting rhythm in the night. I lay my head on El's lap and fell asleep and dreamed of beautiful statues that fell from their pedestals and lay in a thousand pieces on the floor.

Soon after starting graduate school I had switched from the human behavior program to the more demanding professional psychology program, and my studies began to occupy more and more of my time. In the spring of 1974 I gave notice that I wouldn't be returning to Heart of Jesus High School in the fall: it would be the first time in twenty-five years that I would be neither student nor teacher in a Catholic institution! I made arrangements to begin my predoctoral internship, working both in a program for post-hospital schizophrenics and as a counselor in a crisis center.

Meanwhile, soon after deciding not to return to Heart of Jesus in the fall, I found out that I was pregnant. We had been trying for a number of months, so we were ecstatic.

Aran Joseph Wong was born in January 1975, and his coming made all the difference in my life. As I held my infant son close to my heart, I thought of the passage from Genesis that I had long ago copied into my spiritual notebook in tiny, tight script, almost afraid to see what I had written: "Give me children or I shall die." Feeling his tiny heart beat next to mine and bending to kiss each tiny finger as he nursed, I thought of the Genesis passage and realized how it had sorely understated the depths of my longing. I was filled with joy, contentment, satisfaction: there were no words to describe the experience.

When I wasn't mothering (and sometimes even when I was), I continued my studies and my internship. I now had a few more courses to take and a dissertation to complete: El was completing his Ph.D. in psychology at the same time, so we took turns carrying Aran in a backpack as we typed. Finally in the summer of 1976 we both completed our doctorates.

Hardly taking time to catch my breath, I went on to do a 1500-hour postdoctoral internship at a hospital and from there became a consultant, first for a community mental health program and next for a school district. Meanwhile, I studied for the state licensing exams which, if passed, would license me as a clinical psychologist and allow me to open a private practice.

At the end of 1978 I passed both sets of exams, written and oral; at the beginning of 1979 I opened an office and hung my shingle. The long haul was over: my new career was launched at last.

I had just begun to become familiar with the administrative and financial aspects of running a private practice when I again felt the familiar nausea of early pregnancy. If I hadn't gotten such a late start in both areas of my life—in birthing both a family and the career of my dreams—I might have gone about both tasks at a much more leisurely pace. As it was, I was thirty-six, and time seemed very truly of the essence.

Raam Darian Wong was born February 19 1980 as lightning flashed and thunder split the sky. He came before we could even leave the house for the hospital and spent his first night nestled close to Mom, Dad, and his proud brother. Eleven years of sleeping alone in cold-sheeted narrow beds: three men shared my bed and my love now—the revenge was ever so sweet.

40 &

REUNION (1981)

I think back on all this as the plane touches down, the sudden shock of the wheels on the ground jarring me back into the here-and-now.

Mom and Dad will be at the airport as usual, hugging and crying and hugging some more, making this homecoming like all others down through the years a grand celebration.

Tears come to my eyes when I think of them: how they've changed and grown right along with their kids. "We didn't really have any choice," they always say when we compliment them about that: "It was either change or be left behind!" I think of Virginia Woolf's declaration that she didn't believe in aging but only in forever altering, her aspect to the sun.

Mom and Dad greet me with the expected fanfare, and we head off to get my luggage, only to discover that it's been lost by the airlines. I am left with only the clothes on my back: jeans, T-shirt, Berkenstock sandals—not the best combination for a cool, crisp Illinois day. Later, my youngest sister, Cathy, goes shopping with me for clothes for the reunion; giggly, we select a couple of slinky dresses and ask the salesperson if she thinks they're appropriate for a reunion of ex-nuns.

While in Peoria, I hear that Ted, an old friend from Fordham, is in town visiting his ailing mother: I call him and,
delighted to hear from me, he suggests that we get together for
dinner. He picks me up the next evening, and we quickly fill
each other in on current news. He is still "in"—a Jesuit priest—
and works as a community organizer in Boston. I tease him
that I never would have expected him to still be in the priesthood, these many years later. Handsome and ruggedly charming, he has been chased by many a woman, and no one would
have dreamed he would persevere in the celibate life.

Over wine, we fill each other in on the happenings of the
eleven years since we have seen each other, and once the wine
begins to take effect, he makes a surprising confession. He
starts by telling me all about his work with Dignity, the organization for gay Catholics. He tells me what a huge load of
guilt and conflict gay Catholics carry: the Church's theological
position is that it's not a sin to *be* a homosexual, but that it *is* a
sin to be *actively* homosexual.

He goes on and on about his work with Dignity, about
the plight of the homosexual in the Church, and once I've had
enough wine I ask the obvious question: "Ted, are you trying
to tell me something?"

Grinning, he explains quite matter-of-factly: "Back when
I knew you, I was still confused about my sexuality: I had my
suspicions, but I desperately wanted to convince myself that
my basic orientation was heterosexual. Only years of therapy
have brought me to the point where I am finally comfortable
with the truth, where I have finally accepted myself as I am.
That's why I'm so interested in working with other gay Catholics: I can understand their agony."

Shocked, but trying not to show it, I try to joke around:
"Well at least we were right about one thing: that, one way or
another, you wouldn't stay celibate for very long!"

Ted smiles but hastens to correct me.

"Notice how you presume I'm active sexually: you
wouldn't presume that if my orientation were *hetero*sexual! I'm

vowed to celibacy: I'm homosexual in orientation, but I don't act it out physically any more than a heterosexual celibate acts it out physically."

He goes on to tell me about the brothers, priests, and nuns he knows who are homosexual. "You know how it was in the old days: everything was so repressed. A lot of priests, brothers, and nuns during the past twenty years, however, have gone through the same kind of awakening and self-discovery that you who have left have experienced, and, in the process, some of them have discovered that they are homosexual."

I tell Ted that it's my impression that, as far as nuns are concerned, few communities are willing to talk openly about the issue of homosexuality in their midst, and he agrees.

"But when you think of it, can you blame them? They'd be opening a bag of worms. Here's Sister Susan, a marvelous fifth-grade teacher, a committed member of the community: everyone suspects, has always suspected, but what would be served, given the present climate in this country, were she to come out of the closet? Once the word got around—despite her twenty-five years as extraordinary teacher, law-abiding citizen, and respectable member of the community—there would be loud protests about how she would be a bad influence on the children, about how young girls are not safe with her. When are people going to stop confusing homosexuals with child molesters? When are they going to realize that most child molesters are *heterosexual?*

"And it's not just the lay people: back in the convent, the great majority of nuns are heterosexual and rather proud of the fact. For years they've struggled with image problems, trying to make it clear to the world that if they opt for celibacy, it's not because they're abnormal or perverted. Within such a context, it's difficult for lesbian nuns to talk openly about feelings that, if word ever leaked out, would reflect poorly on the community, tarnishing the long-fought-for image of normal womanliness."

I toy with my dinner, reflecting. Everyone had always asked me about the incidence of homosexuality in the convent, and I had always given the standard answer that ex-nuns usually give: that there really had been very little, at least that I was aware of, that those who had demonstrated such tendencies had promptly been asked to leave. As I became more sophisticated in such matters, however, and as I talked to others, I began to look back on people and situations with more comprehension, and more pieces of the puzzle had begun to fall together.

Now Ted has given me even more pieces of the puzzle and has inspired a deep compassion. How many sisters live the conflicted, secretive life Ted describes, often burying their secret so deeply that even *they* don't know?

I will probably never know for the emotion surrounding the whole issue, both inside and outside the convent, remains intense, and lesbian sisters, as long as the intensity persists, will undoubtedly continue to be very, very discreet.

On Friday afternoon three fellow band members (two in, one out) come to pick me up at the house: they come in for a bowl of Mom's homemade soup, and my parents are unsure who's a nun and who's not. They know they can't go by the clothes these days—some nuns even wear jeans, and that pack of cigarettes could belong to either a nun or an ex-nun. In the end they give up and call everyone "Sister," which thoroughly delights my friend Carie, mother of four.

As we get ready to leave, I hug and kiss Mom, Dad, and Cathy and tease that I am leaving for the convent. We all laugh, but a chill goes through me when I think of the other leave-taking twenty years ago. As if reading my mind, Mom says, "I'll never forget what Dad said that day as we got ready to drive you to the convent: 'She'll never come home again 'til one of us dies.'" Everyone shivers, remembering, and Dad hurries to change the subject.

The trip to Saint Raphael's is full of excited chatter as

Sister Marcia gives us the latest update on who is coming. Sister Elizabeth wrote to say that she regrets that she won't be able to make it: she is now provincial superior of the eastern province and she's scheduled to visit one of the houses in the province that weekend. But Marcia *was* able to get Mary Alice's address—she's flying in from Las Vegas—and Anna had written at the last minute to say that she'd be flying in from Alabama. One piece of sad news: Phyllis, my first prie-dieu partner in the novitiate, had been one of the first to send in her reservation ("I wouldn't miss it for the world!" she had enthused on the registration form), but her husband called last week to say that she had been killed in an auto accident. As far as Marcia knows, she is the first of our band to die.

After stopping at a liquor store in Avington where we stock up on supplies for a long merry weekend, we drive the remaining few miles to Saint Raphael's, finally pulling into the gates around 8 P.M. As we pull into the parking lot of the campus guest residence where we have rented rooms, we can hear happy chatter coming from inside. I leave my suitcase in the car and race inside. And so the party begins.

Emily and Liz and a little group of us go out to dinner at a restaurant not far from Saint Raphael's, and when we return we find that more people have arrived. I am especially excited to hear that all ten of us from the Prep School will be here: for us, it's also a high school reunion. Liz, Karen, and Bonnie are the only ones I've kept in touch with over the years—it will be good to see the other eight again. Has it really been twenty-four years since we were homesick little kids, crying ourselves to sleep in our white-curtained alcoves? Though I haven't seen some of them in almost two decades, the boarding-school experience had forged a certain closeness, a closeness that I have carried in my heart all these years. How happy I am to see each of them again!

Everyone congregates the first night in the big living room, and it's 2 or 3 A.M. before the last of us wanders off to bed. Twenty years is a long time: there's so much to catch up on. Baby pictures and reminiscences make the rounds, and I stay glued to my chair, afraid that I will miss something.

The next day we take a memory tour of the novitiate and the juniorate. Though we keep everything light and gay and swap funny reminiscences as we go along, I notice a certain hollowness to a lot of the laughter. "This part is really hard for me," one woman whispers: "Walking through these halls brings it all back." Another confides: "I know I have to do it—go back to the scene of my pain like Sybil did as a way of becoming free."

We spend the rest of the afternoon walking around campus—the place is even more beautiful than I had remembered—then we come back and dress for a catered dinner with wine and candlelight. As we are having a glass of wine before dinner, Carie (one of the friends I had lost touch with over the years) leads me to a quiet corner and tells me that she has just come back from visiting with Mother Mary Rosalie in the infirmary. "I couldn't believe it, Mar: though she's ninety-something now, and recovering from a near-fatal heart attack, she recognized me right away and thanked me for coming to see her. Then she broke down and cried and said she knew she had handled my case wrong, that she hoped I would forgive her. . . ." Carie's big blue eyes brim with tears.

Though I always loved Carie and grieved when she eventually left, I was never too sure of the details of her "case." Forbidden to speak openly of such things, we had only whispered rumors to rely on. Even now, I know not to ask too many questions: Carie's pain, like the pain of so many others, remains raw these many years later.

After dinner everyone sits around the living room again, drinking beer and swapping reminiscences until late in the night. Most of the reminiscences are funny: someone remembers, for example, the postulant-mistress's favorite answer to any expression of concern.

Postulant: "Sister, I haven't had my period in ten months."

Sister Carmelita: "That's normal."

Postulant: "Sister, the postulant next to me has been sobbing herself to sleep for two weeks."

Sister Carmelita: "That's normal."

One day a postulant told Carmie that she was having a hard time seeing: it was obvious that she was going to have to make an appointment with an eye doctor. Carmie had pronounced her usual "It's normal," and the postulant walked out of the office, lifting her arms to the heavens in thanksgiving: "I'm saved! I can see!" she testified: "Carmie says I can see!"

There is some concern about what I will put in my book. At one point someone mentions the custom of kneeling on your hands as a penance, and when I express surprise (I must have been mercifully asleep when this custom was introduced!) someone pleads: "Don't put *that* custom in your book, Mary—they'll think we're kooky!" Someone else retorts, "They're going to think we're kooky anyway!" and everyone laughs, agreeing.

Many of the stories put together pieces of old puzzles for me, for example the stories of friends who had left quite suddenly, never to be heard from again. I learn that Joan was asked to leave because she looked so unhappy all the time ("I was shocked—I didn't want to leave!"), that Marilyn on the other hand often talked in her conferences about how unhappy she was, only to be reminded over and over again that God would give her the grace to do even the impossible. Eventually she had tired of doing the impossible, no matter *how* much grace God was willing to send!

The next morning we all attend Mass together in Maria Chapel: our old choir director scurries around, making sure we all have song books, making sure we all sing, just as in the old days. The Mass is attended mainly by the older sisters: apparently Sister Marcia had sensed that we all seemed hell-bent on nostalgia this weekend and therefore made arrangements for us to attend this Mass rather than a more-contemporary service attended by some of the younger sisters on campus.

My stomach growls from lack of breakfast, and my knees hurt from all the kneeling. I ask myself where I used to put my long legs when I sat down: was the prie-dieu always so cramped? How come I never noticed any of this before—did I even *have* a body back then?

I also notice that I suddenly *see* all the fineries of marble and wood and polished brass that were always there for my beholding but never noticed. I guess I had no time for such visual pleasures in the old days when I was always looking within to see if any new faults or failings had sprouted in the dark recesses of my soul!

Around us, nuns sing up-to-date liturgical songs that, while theologically correct, sound ever so thin and colorless. I think of how we all worked for liturgical reform, counting the days until Latin would be a thing of the past and sentimental ditties like "Panis Angelicus" and "O Lord I Am Not Worthy" would be heard no more. Now I watch the bent-over little old nun next to me, her arthritic hands twisting around the songbook as she struggles to read the words of these new-fangled songs, and wish with everything in me that someone would give her back her "Ave Maria" and her "Tis the Month of Our Mother." Remembering my days in the choir, I wish with everything in me that I could hear again a Latin Mass impeccably sung, or crystal-clear Gregorian chant. Did I ever think I'd be so nostalgic?

After breakfast I spend some time by myself, breathing in the beauty of the place: I don't know when I will be back, so I will fill my heart and lungs with the brimming, outrageous loveliness of Saint Raphael's in early fall. Some of the women at the reunion have talked about their feeling of alienation when they come here, their feeling of not belonging: it's hard for me to understand such feelings—Saint Raphael's is my childhood home; my roots go as deep as those of some of the trees. Who could possibly take that from me?

Before packing to leave, I decide to go up to the fourth floor of the infirmary to visit Mother Mary Rosalie. She is sitting up in a chair reading as I come in: though she doesn't recognize me at first, her eyes fill with tears when I tell her who I am, and bony white hands reach out to clasp mine. Unlike a few of the older sisters who still wear the entire traditional habit, she wears the modified habit: her skirt is calf-length, and locks of gray hair peel out at the front of her veil.

As I sit down on a bright-colored vinyl chair next to her night table, she tells me how grateful she is that I've come to see her. After asking all about my family and my present work and listening with genuine interest, she shows me a list of all those who were in the congregation during her term as superior general and tells me how she goes down the names each day, praying for each. "I'm amazed at your memory, Mother: how do you do it?" I ask. "I just don't let you know all the things I *forget*," she smiles mischievously.

We talk about our reunion: who was there, who couldn't make it, and her eyes again fill with sadness, remembering. "I think your group and the other groups who entered in the early sixties suffered the most from all the turmoil of the time, all the confusion. We just didn't know what to do with you. We knew we wanted you to be as happy in the community as we had always been, but we didn't really understand your generation, didn't really understand how to deal with you. I, for one, know I made a lot of mistakes. . . ."

Her voice trails off to some far edge of regret, and I murmur something about how we *all* made mistakes, how we must forgive ourselves, be gentle on ourselves.

But her confession has touched something, healed something deep inside, and my voice as I tell her I have to leave is choked with emotion.

Some are driving; some are catching flights: there's a lot of last-minute scurrying around as everyone prepares to leave.

We laugh and hug and cry our good-byes, promising to all meet again at Saint Raphael's in five years, and I look around and realize how proud I am of each of us. One is a prosperous owner of clothing stores; one a mechanic who also buys and sells antiques. One is an attorney; one a social worker; one will soon join her husband on a business venture in Saudi Arabia; one runs a referral service for musicians. Some are business executives, some teachers, some full-time wives and mothers. Two of the nuns are principals, one is completing work on her Ph.D., one runs a summer camp. . . .

Remembering a bygone time when we tried to fit ourselves into a common mold, tried to eradicate individual differences in the name of community, I rejoice for each and every one of us.

41 §

LAST THOUGHTS

Do I have any regrets about my years in the convent? It's a question I'm frequently asked. I have no regrets. The convent experience left its effects, not all of them positive—there has been much to work out and work through—yet from my present perspective, the good far outweighed the bad, laying a bedrock foundation for the rest of my life. For that I will always be grateful.

Early in life I learned the joy of silence and solitude, learned to leave the whirlwind of activity all around me and find again the silence within. . . .

I learned to open myself to the experience of the God

within, learned the contentment of living in harmony with
nature, its rhythms and seasons. . . .

I learned the incredible nurturance of friendships wi'
women, the incredible and largely unleashed power
women. . . .

I learned a deep compassion for the plight of fell⟨ ⟩⟨hu⟩-
man beings less fortunate than I; I forged a life commi' ⟨⟩t to
do my part toward a better world.

By going away from the world for a while an⟨d ⟩⟨⟩n coming back, I learned a child's wide-eyed apprec' ⟨⟩n of the
world's smallest pleasures. In years to come ⟨ ⟩n I would
begin to succumb to apathy and cynicism, I v ⟨⟩d think back
to how I felt those first few weeks after le⟨ ⟩g the convent,
and I would again be an innocent child, s⟨ ⟩ng it all.

Somewhat paradoxically, going awa⟨ ⟩⟨⟩ a time also gave
me an opportunity to observe the wo⟨ ⟩rom a distance: because of that perspective, I would never again love the world
uncritically. The experience of walking so out of step with the
rest of the culture had emboldened me: I would never again
feel compelled to accept values and conventions just because
they were the values and conventions of the prevailing culture.
In that way the convent experience somehow freed me to be
my own person.

Similarly, because of the years I spent as a celibate forced
up against my own radical aloneness, I would find myself
somewhat less prone to delude myself with woman's favorite
delusion: that she needs a man to complete her circle, that a
man *can* complete her circle, that if her circle isn't complete
it's either because she doesn't have a man or because the man
she *does* have doesn't measure up. I learned early in life
(though I too would find it easy to forget) that "souls are not
saved in pairs."

Like the hero of Jean Anouilh's *Becket*, I now believe in a
very different God than the one in Whom I used to believe: I
now believe that God is "the God of the rich man and the

happy man too." In the old days I thought I had to sacrifice, to "suffer with the suffering," but I now see that those who contribute most are those who first know how to love and nurture themselves. Unlike those of us who clenched our teeth and doled out the thin blue milk of sacrifice ("object of so much vapid self-congratulation"), they give from the abundance of lives fully lived. They have tasted the good life and are pressed, spontaneously, to let the good times roll for everyone. ("In power and in luxury and even in the pleasures of the flesh, I shall not cease to speak to You, I feel this now. . . .")

Like Becket, and along with many sisters both in and out, I have left "this convent" where so many precautions hew God round. I have gone back to my place in the world so that I may do what I believe is my life's work. For the rest, God's will be done!